# Balancing Head and Heart in Seventeenth Century Puritanism

## Stephen Charnock's Doctrine of the Knowledge of God

T0385270

STUDIES IN CHRISTIAN HISTORY AND THOUGHT

STUDIES IN CHRISTIAN HISTORY AND THOUGHT

# Balancing Head and Heart in Seventeenth Century Puritanism

## Stephen Charnock's Doctrine of the Knowledge of God

Larry Siekawitch

Foreword by Densil Morgan

First published 2012 by Paternoster

Paternoster is an imprint of Authentic Media
52 Presley Way, Crownhill, Milton Keynes, MK8 0ES

www.authenticmedia.co.uk
Authentic Media is a Division of Koorong UK, a company limited by guarantee
(registered charity no. 270162)

1615 14 13 12 11 10 7 6 5 4 3 2 1

British Library Cataloguing in Publication Data
A catalogue record for this book is available from the British Library

ISBN 978–1–84227–670-9

Typeset by the Author
Printed and bound in Great Britain
for Paternoster

## STUDIES IN CHRISTIAN HISTORY AND THOUGHT

# Series Preface

This series complements the specialist series of *Studies in Evangelical History and Thought* and *Studies in Baptist History and Thought* for which Paternoster is becoming increasingly well known by offering works that cover the wider field of Christian history and thought. It encompasses accounts of Christian witness at various periods, studies of individual Christians and movements, and works which concern the relations of church and society through history, and the history of Christian thought.

The series includes monographs, revised dissertations and theses, and collections of papers by individuals and groups. As well as 'free standing' volumes, works on particular running themes are being commissioned; authors will be engaged for these from around the world and from a variety of Christian traditions.

A high academic standard combined with lively writing will commend the volumes in this series both to scholars and to a wider readership.

# Series Editors

Alan P.F. Sell, Visiting Professor at Acadia University Divinity College, Nova Scotia, Canada

David Bebbington, Professor of History, University of Stirling, Stirling, Scotland, UK

Clyde Binfield, Professor Emeritus in History, University of Sheffield, UK

Gerald Bray, Anglican Professor of Divinity, Beeson Divinity School, Samford University, Birmingham, Alabama, USA

Grayson Carter, Associate Professor of Church History, Fuller Theological Seminary SW, Phoenix, Arizona, USA

*To my wife Elizabeth*

# Contents

# Foreword

Those of us who know Stephen Charnock by name will connect him with the doctrine of God's attributes. Even for those conversant with theology, this subject may seem somewhat recondite and divorced from the reality of Christian discipleship or the challenges of the everyday world. In this fine study, Larry Siekawitch has not only brought Charnock to life but has shown him to be a creative theologian whose balanced view of head and heart has much to commend it to the contemporary church. As a 'latitude puritan', Charnock was careful not to overemphasize the intellect at the expense of the affections, or to allow the objectivity of revelation to eclipse the obedient response of faith. This is a book to enlighten the mind as well as to warm the heart. It is also a first class contribution to our knowledge and understanding of the seventeenth century mind.

D. Densil Morgan D Phil DD
Professor of Theology
Bangor University
Wales

# Acknowledgements

First of all I would like to acknowledge Dr. Frank James III, Provost of Gordon Conwell Seminary, previous president of Reformed Theological Seminary, Orlando. His help in preparing me for the rigor of Ph.D. work was invaluable.

Second I want to recognize Dr. Densil Morgan. He went above and beyond the call of duty in offering help and guidance in my dissertation. He is an excellent supervisor, but he also became a friend.

Finally and most importantly I want to thank my wife, Elizabeth. She encouraged me to pursue my Th.M. degree after my M.Div. was complete and then persuaded me to go on to my Ph.D. She sacrificially gave so I could put in the time and effort needed to complete this work. She is always available for me to bounce off ideas and give good, critical advice. Without her support I could not have finished this degree.

Larry Siekawitch
*University of Wales, Bangor*
*January 2010*

# INTRODUCTION

## *1. Charnock on Head and Heart*

The intent of this study is to explore Stephen Charnock's doctrine of the knowledge of God to discover his contributions to the restoration English puritan understanding of a balance of head and heart. This balance may be the crucial link to the original reformers and the puritans. Charnock paved a distinctive trail in the midst of diverse paths the restoration puritans were taking, but he also maintained certain characteristics, which were common to the puritan way.

Most agree that the puritans were not identical of the reformers and that their theology was not static, but there are great disagreements concerning the amount of change, the causes of change, and the desirability of the change between the two groups. Were the puritans dry, speculative and scholastic thinkers, were they on the cutting edge of theological progress, or were they in fact somewhere in between? Were the puritans a monolithic group at the time of the restoration of the monarchy or were there variations in their writing and their thought? There is a dearth of studies in post-restoration diversity among the puritans. Charnock himself, though very influential at his time, has been almost completely neglected in the journals and dissertations of recent times. By considering Charnock's doctrine of the knowledge of God we may be able to contribute to the debate on Calvin versus the Calvinists as well as gain from an understanding of the unique contours of his thought.

We will explore the basic traits of English puritanism, characteristics which puritans believed were in harmony with the belief of the Protestant reformers and true to the verities of the orthodox biblical faith. What was essential to them was a right balance between heart and mind. While taking into consideration the diversity of puritanism, there seems, indeed, to have been an element of continuity between their movement and that of the original reformers. What was the crucial link that spanned over 150 years? Were it to be the gospel, the definition would be so broad as not to do justice to the uniqueness of puritanism. Were it to be some particular doctrine such as predestination, then it would include at least the early Anglicans and most of the continental post-reformation reformers as well. If it were to be any specific form of ecclesiology, then we take away large sections of those normally considered puritans, because at the time of the Westminster Assembly there were four ecclesiastical proponents among puritans, Erastian, Presbyterian, Congregational and moderate Episcopalian. Could, therefore, the crucial link between the puritans and the original reformers be an attempt to balance a religion of the heart and of the head?

2 *Balancing Head and Heart*

The restoration puritans splintered into several subgroups with different understandings of ecclesiology, unity and importance of specific doctrines. One peculiar group had been influenced by the Cambridge Platonists and the School of Saumur and elevated both the mind and the heart in a practical expression of puritan Christianity. This small group consisted of pastor-theologians, much like the original reformers, who advocated a practical theology and eschewed the extreme polemic which was common among some other puritans of that time. They promoted both tolerance and an irenic attitude throughout Protestant Christianity in England. They espoused in general a Reformed theology, but toned down some of the more divisive elements of that theology. Neither did they resist the move toward rationalism, but adapted it to what they believed to be scriptural use. This elevation of reason is seen especially in their natural theology but is tempered by their doctrine of the knowledge of God.

In an unpublished article, 'Natural Theology Among the Dissenters: Richard Baxter and His Circle,' Dewey Wallace describes a group he calls *Latitudinarian Calvinists*.[1] He includes Richard Baxter, John Howe and William Bates in this group. Wallace describes this group as moderately predestinarian having a 'dislike for controversy' as well as a 'preference for the practical deeds of religion over theological niceties' although 'this did not seem to preclude involvement in controversy.'[2] Charnock appears to fit into this category perfectly.

In this study we want to look at Charnock's balance of mind and heart especially as seen in his doctrine of the knowledge of God. What was Charnock's opinion concerning the question, "How much influence does the finite nature of humanity as well as the sinful nature since the Fall have on limiting human understanding of God?" Did Charnock divorce the mind from the heart in his description of the knowledge of God? What were Charnock's thoughts and practices concerning speculation? Did his union of mind and heart lead to introspection?

Specific questions that need to be addressed are: 1) How did the reformers and post-reformers' focus on doctrine affect their ecumenism? The early reformers appeared to have a collegiality that accepted minor differences in doctrine, methodology and focus as seen especially in the Consensus Tigurinus; was this true of their puritan successors as well? 2) How important was natural theology to Charnock's system? The reformers never rejected natural theology as such, but it was always held in check to varying degrees. Was its use broadened in the later part of the seventeenth century? 3) Did Charnock's doctrine of the knowledge of God include an experiential side? Most of the reformers and post-reformers gave lip service to the two parts of

---

[1] Dewey Wallace, Jr., 'Natural Theology Among the Dissenters: Richard Baxter and His Circle' presented at the Annual Meeting of the American Society of Church History December 27-30, 1992.
[2] Ibid., 4.

the knowledge of God, but was there a thorough evaluation of the place of experience in knowing God? Did Charnock follow or deviate from the reformers in this? 4) Did Charnock have a concept of the importance of the experience of delighting in God? Was this enjoyment purely cerebral or did it possess experiential and mystical elements as well? 5) Was the concept of mystery only used when things could not be explained, or was it developed as an element of worship?

Several ranges will be evaluated by comparing Charnock and the reformers:

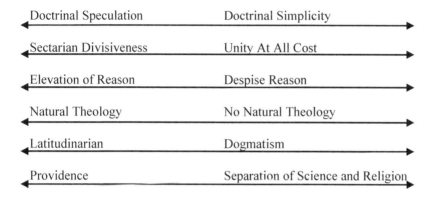

| Doctrinal Speculation | Doctrinal Simplicity |
| Sectarian Divisiveness | Unity At All Cost |
| Elevation of Reason | Despise Reason |
| Natural Theology | No Natural Theology |
| Latitudinarian | Dogmatism |
| Providence | Separation of Science and Religion |

Was there a major shift from the balance of head and heart to an intellectual and sterile faith even perhaps leading to significant doctrinal changes? Or were there simply different nuances depending on the situation of the puritan reformers? Were the restoration puritans able to maintain a balance of head and heart, what George Gillespie called 'a sound head and a sound heart,'[3] and if so how did they do it? Was the balance of the head and heart the crucial link between the original reformers and the restoration puritans? A review of Charnock's doctrine of the knowledge of God may be helpful in answering these questions.[4]

A study of Charnock's doctrine of the knowledge of God reveals several important insights of relevance to our study. A measure of both continuity and discontinuity is seen between the latitude puritans, the original reformers and the post-reformers. All three groups had an amount of continuity in seeing the

---

[3] George Gillespie, *The Works of Mr. George Gillespie* (Edinburgh: Robert Ogle and Olives and Boyd, 1846), 2:62.

[4] For Stephen Charnock's writings we will use the following editions: *The Complete Works of Stephen Charnock* Vol. 1 and Vol. 5 (Edinburgh: James Nichol in 1866; reprint Lafayette, IN: Sovereign Grace Publishers, 2001). *The Works of Stephen Charnock* Vol. 3 and Vol. 4 (Edinburgh: James Nichol in 1865; reprint Carlisle, PA: The Banner of Truth Trust, 1986). *Discourses Upon the Existence and Attributes of God* (New York: Robert Carter and Brothers, 1853; reprint Grand Rapids: Baker Book House, 1979). All references to specific volumes will be to these publications.

knowledge of God as involving more than the mind or understanding, but varied greatly in their emphases. First we will need to take a look at the historical background and influences on Stephen Charnock. Next, by looking at Charnock's holistic approach to the knowledge of God and comparing it with the other groups we will discover the nuances of focus, especially the use of the affections in this doctrine. In chapter three we will observe Charnock's use of natural theology and compare it with others in the reformation tradition to see if varying degrees of focus on the mind may elevate or devalue its importance. In chapter four the importance of special revelation will be examined, seeing that both ends of the spectrum of the reformation – the radical puritans and the more rationalist minded Anglicans and Genevans may have neglected scripture without necessarily holding to an unorthodox position concerning the reformation plank of *sola scriptura*. Finally in chapter five the unity/truth dichotomy will be scrutinized, especially as polemics, unity, doctrine and fundamental articles pertain to the latitude puritan pursuit of a balance of head and heart.

## 2. *Puritanism: The Matter of Definition*

Definitions of groups or movements in history are difficult to decide upon, especially before the onset of denominations with their clear boundaries. The term *Anglican* can be used for all who were in the Church of England or for those who were satisfied with the status quo in the Church of England. In this study we will be using it in the narrower sense for sake of comparison. The term *puritan* is fraught with even more difficulties. No matter how one defines puritanism most agree that there was a conflict between Elizabeth and then the Jacobean monarchs with a group that saw the Church of England as only "halfly reformed." This conflict created two groups; Patrick Collinson elaborates: "A relationship of dynamic and mutual antagonism existed in principle between two well-defined and sharply differentiated kinds of people, the most telling index of which was the abusive language of identification which they employed against each other." [5] At different times between Elizabeth's reign and the Civil War many became separatists and others heretics, but a large minority stayed with the established church to reform it from within. Why did they choose to stay, yet remain so discontented with the status quo? Several reasons can be forwarded.

First, England's reformation was different from that of the Continent in that reform in Switzerland and Germany began as a popular religious and spiritual movement, but England's reform started as an action of the state for quasi-political reasons. Henry VIII, though Catholic in doctrine, took the advice of

---

[5] Patrick Collinson, *The Birthpangs of Protestant England* (New York: St. Martin's Press, 1988), 143.

Thomas Cromwell and severed the link with Rome claiming himself to be the head of the Church of England; this act would eventually lead to the establishment of Protestantism in England but it also guaranteed the politicization of the church.

When Henry died his weakly son Edward became king. With Edward's approval Archbishop Cranmer moved the church toward a moderately Lutheran understanding with his 42 Articles and Book of Prayer.[6] Cranmer was the real architect of reform and though influenced by Bucer and Vermigli toward the Reformed view, he never threw away his earlier Lutheran convictions, at least as far as the issue of *adiaphora* was concerned. There was also an attempt to influence as many bishops as possible with the reformation and so concessions were made, which also ensured division.[7] Cranmer's gradual change as compared with John Knox in Scotland was due to his fear of Anabaptism; he even tried to link Knox's ideas with those of the Anabaptists.[8] The comparative tardiness of reformation, coupled with an indecision between Reformed and Lutheran practice ensured what would appear later to the puritans to be a compromise. Unfortunately for Protestantism Edward died in 1553 reigning only six years and leaving the kingdom to his sister Mary. We can only speculate whether further reform would have taken place if he had lived longer.

Mary very quickly returned England to Rome, executing many including Cranmer, Latimer, Ridley, Hooper and Bradford, and causing many others to flee for their lives to the continent. She died in 1558 and was succeeded by her sister Elizabeth. Elizabeth, the *politique extraordinaire*, oversaw a religious settlement, a compromise with Geneva and Rome embracing Calvinist doctrine (The 39 Articles of Religion) with Catholic ceremony (a revised Prayer Book); she would reign for 45 years. Elizabeth fought the Catholics and the new group called 'puritans' throughout her reign. Two parliamentary acts in particular ensured controversy: The Act of Supremacy which declared her to be supreme governor of the Church of England, and the Act of Uniformity, which demanded all in her realm to worship in accordance with the Book of Common Prayer. The Act of Supremacy originated with Henry VIII declaring him to be the supreme head of the church. John Albro in his "Life of Thomas Shepherd" gives a puritan perspective on the political nature of this act:

---

[6] It is probably true that even in the 42 Articles there was a move toward Reformed theology and away from Lutheranism by its architect, Thomas Cranmer, but it is sufficiently vague and the Book of Common Prayer is much more Lutheran in its acceptance of *adiaphora*. See Philip Benedict, *Christ's Churches Purely Reformed* (New Haven: Yale University Press, 2002), 235-7.

[7] The issue of kneeling at communion is a case in point which was added to the 1552 prayer book, appearing to be a concession made for all the things taken away. "A short but fierce debate among the clergy" ensued. Jennifer Loach, *Edward VI* (New Haven: Yale University Press, 1999), 123.

[8] Ibid.

This Act was the Commencement of what has been called the "Reformation" in England. But it was not such an act as the state of the church demanded. It was conceived in sin, and brought forth in iniquity.... It made no change in doctrine, nor breathed any new life into the dead formalities of the old religion. It simply transferred the church, like a flock of sheep, from a rapacious pope to a brutal and licentious king; and gave to a civil, instead of an ecclesiastical tyrant, the sole power of reforming abuses, heresies, and errors, without the slightest regard to the rights of conscience, or the laws of Jesus Christ.[9]

The indication Albro made is that such a "reformation" could hardly be expected to bring about real reform, thus demanding further reform away from the Act of Supremacy.

The reformation on the continent was brought about relatively quickly and with religious intent for the most part by Luther and Zwingli after the preparatory work of the Waldensians, Hussites and the more radical Roman Catholic orders in previous centuries; the subjects of these areas seemed legitimately to embrace the new evangelical doctrines and practices. In England the effect of going back and forth from Catholic to Protestant to Catholic back to Protestant seemed to ensure indifferent rather than zealous subjects. Philip Benedict states: "Those deeply committed to either Catholic orthodoxy or some brand of Protestantism both formed a minority of the population. In between stood a broad middle group willing to adjust its practice in whatever direction the ruling powers deemed appropriate."[10] Whatever the king or queen in power ordered was accepted because one's head was at stake. "For the most part, the country adjusted itself to these successive 'settlements' with a resilience which historians have found remarkable,"[11] but at a price. The puritan reformers had no problem with the Calvinistic 39 Articles, but they lamented the masses of people in England that appeared to them to be unregenerate. Hugh Binning represented well the puritans' view:

There is a multitude that are Christians only in the letter, and not in the spirit, that would never admit any question concerning this great matter of having eternal life; and so by not questioning it, they come to think they have it, and by degrees their conjectures and thoughts about this ariseth to the stability of some feigned and strong persuasion of it.[12]

---

[9] Thomas Shepherd, *The Works of Thomas Shepherd* (New York: AMS Press, 1967), 1:xxxvii.
[10] Philip Benedict, *Christ's Churches Purely Reformed*, 243.
[11] Patrick Collinson, *The Elizabethan Puritan Movement* (Oxford: Clarendon Press, 1967), 23. He goes on to say, "But alongside and among those who merely acquiesced in religious change, protestantism was performing its own work. Lively, rather than formal faith was generated by preaching...and by the printing presses."
[12] Hugh Binning, *The Works of Reverend Hugh Binning* (Ligonier, PA: Soli Deo Gloria Publications, 1992), 19. Thomas Case concurs: "Alas! The ignorance and misery of our

Owing to the religious instability of the times some sought further reform with evidence; division was solidified with a "puritan counter-culture" born.[13] Most saw a need for separation from the Roman Catholics, but with the puritans a new partition arose within Protestantism.

"If doctrine alone cannot reveal a regenerate nature, then what can?" was a burning question for puritans. The puritans stressed the experimental nature of real faith. Armed with scripture and Calvin's doctrine of union and communion they surmised that real faith should affect the heart and the head, as well as one's actions. They believed right doctrine must be married to correct action and proper affections; the supreme affections being love and joy. So one can see at least an indirect correlation between the Act of Supremacy and the puritan movement. The monarchy's indecision between Catholicism and Protestantism seems to have brought about a people seeking a purer form of reform, which led them to what they described as an "experimental knowledge of Christ," rather than a "speculative knowledge." [14] This experimental knowledge would gradually emphasize more and more the idea of enjoying God as an evidence of real faith as well as being a part of God's ultimate purpose for creating humans.[15]

The second factor that led to the unique situation in England was that the puritans were persecuted, but for the most part, not extinguished, as were reformers in other countries such as France, Spain and Italy. Both Mary's short reign and Elizabeth's semi-tolerance owing to her fear of the Catholics ensured an ongoing presence of dissenters willing to remain within the church.[16] Mary's

---

times is, not that people are totally destitute of the principles of Christian religion, but that they know them singly only and apart; and so they know them but by halves." James Nichols notes and translations, *Puritan Sermons: 1659-1689* (Wheaton: Richard Owen Roberts Publishers, 1981), 5:22.

[13] Tyacke describes the use of "Puritan baptismal names" as an "extreme manifestation of popular Puritanism" which "accentuate rather than distort the ethos of a movement" which he goes on to call the "Puritan counter-culture." Nicholas Tyacke, *Aspects of English Protestantism* (Manchester University Press, 2001), 105.

[14] Thomas Boston, "A Discourse on the Experimental Knowledge of Christ" in *The Works of Thomas Boston* (London: William Tegg and Co., 1853), 2:645.

[15] It should be noted that the Act of Supremacy also fostered a resentful spirit among many who thought religious power did not belong in the hands of the monarchy; this played into the hands of Parliament that also felt the monarchy had too much power, thus wedding the religious spirit of puritanism with the legitimate political concerns of Parliament.

[16] Some include the separatists of this time as puritans, but Patrick Collinson sees them as people with puritan tendencies, but not fully puritan. Once again for sake of definition with admitted ambiguity we will call those puritan who sought to purify the Church of England from within and did not see it as apostate, but rather 'halfly reformed.' Patrick Collinson, *English Puritanism* (London: The Historical Association, 1983), 18. See also Peter Toon, *Puritans and Calvinism* (Swengel, PA: Reiner Publications, 1973), 49-50. After the restoration those who, owing to conscience, could not fulfill the requirements concerning the Prayer Book, ordination, etc. will still be

reign was brutal and short. The Marian exiles fled mostly to Strasbourg and
Geneva rather than Lutheran Germany. While on the continent they were
heavily influenced by Calvin and so when Mary died they brought back new
ideas for reform. Mary's return to Catholicism and the reprisal toward the
Protestants left a lasting impression on the exiles. When they came back they
were cautious toward anything that smacked of "popery." To their dismay
Elizabeth seemed almost like a closet Catholic.[17]

During Elizabeth's long tenure two major controversies erupted: The
Vestments Controversy and the Admonition Controversy.[18] The Act of
Uniformity demanded that all pastors wear the surplice and other
accoutrements while in the pulpit; this caused friction between the more
conservative bishops and the puritans, which led to the Vestments Controversy.
What was at the heart of this disagreement was a conflicting understanding of
the nature of worship. Rather than using the unbiblical ceremonies that
appeared to appeal to the flesh, the puritans wanted a simpler form of worship
that could be justified by scripture alone. The issue of wearing the surplice
initiated the controversy, but gradually the disagreement went deeper to include
the concept of heart worship. The puritans emphasized the communion with
God Calvin taught so much about as an experience in worship. This focus may
have stemmed from the early English reformers such as John Hooper,[19] John

---

considered puritan because of their previous status as puritan, but after that generation
puritanism as a movement is affectively finished.

[17] Patrick Collinson, *English Puritanism*, 12-16. John Brown notes: "In the case of the
Queen herself but little change was made in the ritual of her own private chapel. Being
fond of pomp and magnificence in worship as in everything else, she would not part
with the altar or crucifix; the choristers and priests still appeared in their copes; the altar
was furnished with rich plate, had gilt candlesticks with lighted candles and a massive
silver crucifix in the midst; on solemn festivals there was special music; and the
ceremonies observed by the knights of the garter in their adoration towards the altar –
ceremonies which had been abolished by King Edward and restored by Queen Mary –
were now retained." John Brown, *The English Puritans* (Ross-shire, Great Britain:
Christian Focus Publications, 1998), 34-35.

[18] The Vestments controversy had a predecessor in England during Edward's reign.
John Hooper had at first refused to wear the surplice and cope for his installation as
bishop, causing division in the beginning of the Protestant reform in England. "The
whole episode had deeply divided the foreign Protestant community." Jennifer Loach,
*Edward VI*, 120.

[19] Hooper describes the true church: "I believe all the people of the world are either the
people of God, or the people of the devil. The people of God are those, that with heart
and mind know, worship, honour, praise, and laud God, according to the doctrine of the
prophets and apostles. The people of the devil are those that think they worship, honour,
reverence, fear, laud, or praise God, any other ways besides, or contrary to, the doctrine
of the prophets and apostles." John Hooper, *The Writings of John Hooper* (London:
Religious Tract Society, n.d.), 200. Notice Hooper seeks to bring out a balance of heart
and mind.

Bradford[20] and William Tyndale[21] and enhanced by the exile. The exact line of progression may be impossible to discern but for them experimental religion engaging the affections of the heart, was as important as right doctrine and holy living.[22]

In the Admonition Controversy the puritans appealed to parliament to reform the church along Presbyterian lines. Thomas Wilcox and John Field wrote *Admonition to Parliament* declaring the Book of Common Prayer an "imperfect book, culled and picked out of the that popish dunghill," and calling for a system of consistorial discipline along the lines of the reformation in France and Scotland.[23] Archbishop Whitgift replied to the first Admonition and Thomas Cartwright, Lady Margaret Professor at Cambridge, answered Whitgift point by point in the second Admonition, declaring that "a properly Reformed church contained the classic four orders of ministers, exercised its own ecclesiastical discipline to which even rulers were subject, and permitted no minister permanent jurisdiction over any other." [24] This was considered an attack on the current episcopacy and Elizabeth's authority as the supreme governor of the Church of England. After Elizabeth reprimanded the bishops for not suppressing Cartwright he was thrown into prison. There are three things to note concerning this dispute: First the appeal to parliament. Rather than going to the queen, where all attempts had proven fruitless, a new strategy developed of appealing to parliament. This strategy should not be seen as a rejection of the monarchy, but it does reveal where the puritans thought power

---

[20] Bradford describes the elect as feeling God: "As for who be the elect and who be not, because it is God's privilege to know who be his, God's people are not curious in others: but, as in themselves they feel 'the earnest' of the Lord, and have God's Spirit in possession by faith." John Bradford, *The Writings of John Bradford* (Carlisle, PA: The Banner of Truth Trust, 1979), 1:328. Ian Breward notes that Bradford's "writings were strongly marked by an experimental emphasis," suggesting that the puritan focus on the heart originated with Bradford. William Perkins, *The Work of William Perkins* (Appleford, England: The Sutton Courtenay Press, 1970), 28-29.

[21] Tyndale describes the true church as "feeling in their hearts that God for Christ's sake loveth them, and will be, or rather is, merciful unto them, and forgiveth them their sins of which they repent." William Tyndale, *The Work of William Tindale* (London: Blackie and Son Limited, 1938), 181.

[22] At the end of the Puritan age David Clarkson, successor of John Owen, wrote a polemic against Catholic worship saying, "There is nothing wherein the honour of God and the happiness of men is more concerned than divine worship. Religion provides for these great ends by obliging us to worship God; this it doth indispensably, and can do no less without abandoning itself; for this is essential to it, and gives it being. And the truth and goodness of it depends as much thereon; for no religion is true and saving but that which obligeth to worship God really. Now worship is not real unless mind and heart concur in it; whatever it hath, without this it wants its life and soul, and is no more worship really than a picture of a man." David Clarkson, *The Works of David Clarkson* (Carlisle, PA: Banner of Truth Trust, 1988), 3:9 (in part two of volume three).

[23] Philip Benedict, *Christ's Churches Purely Reformed*, 248.

[24] Ibid., 249.

should reside. Second, the contention began to take a doctrinal slant. Whitgift's theology was thoroughly Reformed as seen in his dealings with the Arminian Peter Baro. Baro had asserted that human will was able to refuse divine grace. Whitgift's Calvinism is patent in his Lambeth articles, which he exhorted Baro to study and teach nothing to the contrary. The debate continued until Baro was silenced and eventually forced out of Cambridge.[25] But immediately after Whitgift an Arminian was chosen as the Archbishop of Canterbury. Arminianism or anti-Calvinism[26] appeared to the puritans to be a further move back to Catholicism thus solidifying their suspicions that the Church of England and its leaders were largely unregenerate and in danger of reverting to the Roman fold;[27] the Admonition Controversy and later the influx of Arminianism increased their skepticism. Finally because the puritans took another loss in this debate they backed off for a while and focused on reaching England through preaching and creating a scholarly consensus in the universities, especially Cambridge.

William Perkins' time at Cambridge was a high water mark for puritanism perhaps because he set aside the political attempts at reform and was happy to acquiesce over vestments and church polity[28] being thus able to focus on Christianity as an experience of the heart. Perkins had one minor difficulty with the officials early on in his ministry because he allegedly said that kneeling to receive communion was superstitious,[29] but then focused on doctrine, preaching and the experimental aspects of religion. Perkins' writings became more popular than those of Calvin; he became the most influential religious author in seventeenth century England. The "prophesyings," which predated Perkins but became very popular during his ministry, advanced puritanism considerably. Licensed preachers would get together to preach as well as discuss theological issues; these meetings became known as "exercises of prophesying." Elizabeth ordered Grindal to suppress them, but he was not willing to do so; his refusal brought about his fall from her favour and house arrest. The prophesyings continued sporadically, gaining momentum at the time of Perkins with his simple style of preaching. The concepts of assurance, real faith and experimental knowledge came to the fore.[30] It would appear that this

[25] C. S. Knighton, 'Baro, Peter (1534–1599)', *Oxford Dictionary of National Biography* (Oxford University Press, 2004).
[26] Nicholas Tyacke states, "With reference to England, anti-Calvinism is, strictly speaking, a more accurate description than Arminianism, yet to insist upon it seems unduly pedantic." *Aspects of English Protestantism*, 159.
[27] Ibid., 145, 147. He quotes Bedford as accusing Arminianism as "the little thief put into the window of the church to unlock the door" for Catholicism.
[28] William Perkins, *The Work of William Perkins*, 21.
[29] Ibid., 4. He was cleared of all charges.
[30] See especially "A Treatise Tending Unto a Declaration whether a man be in the estate of Damnation, or in the estate of grace," "A Declaration of the True Manner of knowing

emphasis on "heart religion," especially the affections, had an impact on future puritan works including the Westminster Confession and Catechisms.

At the death of Elizabeth (and Perkins) in 1603, James I acceded to the throne. The puritans hoped for concessions because he was already the king of Scotland, religiously a Reformed kingdom with an established Presbyterian church. They presented him with the Millenary Petition asking for further reform and he called the Hampton Court Conference to discuss their differences. The puritans were dismayed that the only concession they received was the approval of a new translation of the Bible. James stated firmly, "No bishop, no king" meaning he was not interested in establishing a Presbyterian church in England and saw an attack on the bishops as an assault on the king. After James, his son Charles I brought further division between the established church and the puritans leading parliament to sever its relationship with the king and to civil war. During this time of political upheaval parliament called together the Westminster divines who would be responsible for the Westminster Confession and Catechisms. At this point it will be appropriate to define "puritan."

What is puritanism? There is a great array of opinions, both positive and negative, as to what a puritan was. Some, like J.I. Packer, give glowing accounts of puritanism,[31] whereas others refer to the "intellectual backwardness of the movement."[32] Most agree that the term "puritan" originated as a derogatory name along with other terms such as "precisians" or "disciplinarians" describing individuals of a strict and biblically based piety.[33] But many such as Richard Baxter later embraced the name because they sought to go back to a pure expression of Christianity such as was seen in the early church in the New Testament era.

Was puritanism primarily a political movement, a theological system or a shared experience? Generally puritans are defined as "The more extreme English Protestants who, dissatisfied with the Elizabethan Settlement, [who] sought a further purification of the Church from supposedly unscriptural and corrupt forms along the Genevan model."[34] Here we see a definition in which puritanism is seen as a religious if not political movement. This is a reminder that puritanism arose at the time when religion and politics were inseparable. Doctrinally in the sixteenth century those in the Church of England were in agreement for the most part, but there was a minority that saw some of the

---

Christ crucified" and "A Graine of Musterd-Seede" in *The Workes of William Perkins* (Cambridge: John Legate, 1608), 357-420, 619-634.

[31] J.I. Packer, *A Quest for Godliness* (Wheaton: Crossway Books, 1990), passim.

[32] M.M. Knappen, *Tudor Puritanism* (University of Chicago Press, 1939), 367.

[33] Patrick Collinson notes some anti-puritan satire such as "a puritan is such a one as loves God with all his soul, but hates his neighbour with all his heart." Patrick Collinson, *English Puritanism*, 9.

[34] F.L. Cross and E.A. Livingston, editors, *Oxford Dictionary of the Christian Church* (New York: Oxford University Press, 1974), 1351.

rituals of the church as remnants of "Popery." Some left the church as separatists, but the great majority stayed, seeking to change the church from within. Nicholas Tyacke says puritans were "those members of the English Church who wanted further Protestant reforms in liturgy and organization."[35] He states that this definition was used by most until the 1620s, when the doctrinal question came in owing to the appearance of Arminianism. Leonard Trinterud defines puritanism as "The Protestant form of dissatisfaction with the required official religion of England under Elizabeth."[36] "What were the elect to do about this dissatisfaction?" was the puritan's query. Alan Simpson comments, "For three generations Puritans organized, with a base in the universities, a grip on the press, a connection in the country houses and counting-houses, and a party in Parliament."[37] The use of politics was certainly a part of who the puritans were.

R.T. Kendall prefers to abandon the terms "Puritanism" and "Puritan" in favor of the phrase "experimental predestinarians."[38] Here we see an emphasis on theology. Peter Toon agrees that a commitment to Reformed theology was essential to the identity of the puritan.[39] Many who went to the continent during the Marian exile returned heavily influenced by John Calvin and others. Those who sought further reform in the Church of England, which they saw as halfway reformed, did so because of the influence of the Reformed church on the continent. They wanted Reformed theology that worked out into the practical aspects of church ritual and practice. Puritans embraced Reformed theology because they saw the Bible as their final authority "in all matters of faith, morals and worship."[40] The Bible was the driving thrust behind all puritan practice and belief. Edward Hinson says, "The greatness of Puritanism was its fidelity to the Word of God as the only source of true doctrine and right practice."[41] The use of the Bible was at the heart of the difference between puritanism and Anglicanism. Anglicans believed that if the Bible did not mention something it was non-essential. "In all 'indifferent' matters, human

---

[35] Nicholas Tyacke, *Anti-Calvinists* (Oxford: Clarendon Press, 1987), 8.

[36] Leonard Trinterud, editor, *Elizabethan Puritanism* (New York: Oxford University Press, 1971), 9.

[37] Alan Simpson, *Puritans in Old and New England* (Chicago: University of Chicago Press, 1955), 11.

[38] R.T. Kendall, *Calvin and English Calvinism to 1649* (Carlisle, Cumbria: Paternoster Press, 1997), 6-9.

[39] Peter Toon, *Puritans and Calvinism*, 9. John Goodwin is an exceptional case that should either be seen as an exception to the rule, or simply one who displayed puritan tendencies, but did not fully embrace the puritan movement. He displayed anti-predestinarian views but also opposed Arminianism. Tai Liu surmises him best: "His was a searching mind too independent to subscribe to any particular theological 'ism'." Tai Liu, 'Goodwin, John (*c.*1594–1665)', *Oxford Dictionary of National Biography*.

[40] Ibid.

[41] Edward Hinson (ed.), *Introduction to Puritan Theology: A Reader* (Grand Rapids: Baker Book House, 1976), 23.

reason and human authority and the power to devise and enforce policy"[42] was accepted. The Anglicans saw the non-essentials as practices that could be enforced on the church as a whole, so long as it was not specifically condemned in scripture. The puritans believed that if a practice was not specifically endorsed in scripture it should not be enforced. For the puritans the doctrines of predestination and scripture were essential; therefore, theology should also be included in one's definition of puritanism.

The puritan's experiential faith was at the core of his or her identity. Peter Lake notes, "Puritan religion always retained a very strong experiential bias."[43] Kendall argues that it would be better to describe puritans as "experimental" predestinarians rather than "experiential" predestinarians. He gives two reasons for using the word experimental rather than experiential. First, it is the term they used themselves. Second, it brings out their emphasis on assurance of salvation through the "practical syllogism" which they used to test whether an individual was one of the elect or not. If certain tests applied to the individual's life then he or she could be assured of their salvation.[44] Kendall gives good reasons for using "experimental" in describing the puritan, but this does not mean the term "experiential" cannot be used as well. By "experimental" the puritans meant that true Christianity could be verified by a sanctified life as well as renewed affections; the believer was not perfect in his or her sanctification or affections and desires, but these areas would be changed to some degree if the person had the right knowledge of God and a true faith in God. The puritans included "experiential" in their understanding of an experimental faith. For the puritan conversion was at the heart of Christianity, and this conversion was consciously experienced by the participant. Alan Simpson describes the "essence of Puritanism" as "an experience of conversion which separates the Puritan from the mass of mankind and endows him with the privileges and the duties of the elect."[45] For the puritan the *sine qua non* of true religion was an "inward relation to God."[46] The chief reason the puritans were dissatisfied with the *via media* of the English church was the apparent lack of an experimental/experiential faith in most of the people of England. They saw in the Bible an emphasis on an experiential relationship with Christ when true conversion came, which brought about an experimental faith – a changed life where holiness and happiness cohered; religion was an affair of the heart rather than a matter of notional orthodoxy, moral conformity or outward rituals. This did not mean that they simply embraced the notion of a

---

[42] Patrick Collinson, *The Elizabethan Puritan Movement*, 27.
[43] Peter Lake, *Moderate Puritans and the Elizabethan Church* (Cambridge University Press, 1982), 168.
[44] R.T. Kendall, *Calvin and English Calvinism to 1649*, 9.
[45] Alan Simpson, *Puritanism in Old and New England*, 2.
[46] Edwin Deibler, "The Chief Characteristic of Early English Puritanism" *Bibliotheca Sacra*, v. 129, (1972), 72.

mystical experience. But the Bible led them to expect an inner experience, which led to an outward change of life. Therefore, the puritans can be said to have been both experimental and experiential.

Geoffrey Nuttall has contributed greatly to the thesis that at the heart of puritanism is an experiential piety. He states, "The Puritan movement, in its various phases, has evinced itself to be a movement towards immediacy in relation to God."[47] Using the doctrine of the Holy Spirit as his rule, he presents a spectrum of beliefs within puritanism from moderate to radical with the unifying understanding of true Christianity as propinquity in relation to God: "Religiously, the Puritan movement was a movement towards immediacy, towards direct communion with God through His Holy Spirit."[48] Puritanism sought a balance of mind and heart with the radicals leaning more toward mysticism, rejecting reason and embracing God's voice apart from the scriptures, and the conservatives elevating reason and cessationism concerning God's voice apart from scripture. But they all could be considered mystics in some sense. Nuttall explains that the puritans did not have many of the tendencies of mysticism such as the use of symbolism in worship, the application of imagination when contemplating God or the passivity of personality, but they did experience the intimacy with God the mystics were so endeared toward. In arguing for the use of the term 'puritan mysticism' he explains: "Here, there is meant by it a sense of being carried out beyond the things of time and space into unity with the infinite and eternal, in which the soul is filled with a deep consciousness of love and peace, a unity so intimate as to make erotic terms the most natural on which to draw."[49] The puritan preoccupation with the allegorical interpretation of the Song of Songs as referring to the Christian's relationship with Christ would seem to back up Nuttall's theory. John Flavel's interpretation of the Song of Songs is typical of the puritans:

> This book is a sacred allegory: the sense thereof is deep and spiritual. Our unacquaintedness with such schemes and figures of speech, together with the want of spiritual light and experience, makes it difficult to be understood; but the allegory being once unfolded by reason of its affinity with the fancy, truth is more easily and affectingly transmitted, both to the mind and heart.[50]

Nuttall's work reveals that puritanism cannot be seen as "a mere sediment of common belief and practice," but rather "as dynamic, a process of experience

---

[47] Geoffrey Nuttall, *The Holy Spirit in Puritan Faith and Experience* 2nd ed. (University of Chicago Press, 1992), 134.
[48] Ibid., 91-2.
[49] Ibid., 146.
[50] John Flavel, *The Works of John Flavel* (Carlisle, PA: The Banner of Truth Trust, 1968), 6:450.

and experiment."[51] "The essence of Puritanism is not to be found in matters of polity, theological dogma, principles of authority, or class orientation, but, as Geoffrey Nuttall has shown us, in the deeply spiritual experience which Puritans and many sectaries shared and recognized in others."[52]

The idea of experiential faith being the essence of puritanism does propose a problem. It does not clearly pinpoint who is and who is not a puritan. It is vague and subjective, but still fits the group in question. Richard Greaves sums up the problem with this definition:

> What this means for the historian however, is that the nature of Puritanism is elusive, impossible to define, label, or catalogue with crisp precision, quantitative data, or scientific accuracy. Certain fundamental characteristics may be delineated, but in the end there can be no substitute for a careful immersing in Puritan literature in a quest to grasp what is at root experiential in nature.[53]

Puritanism should be understood as a fairly loose movement rather than a clearly defined denomination or a church. The term 'puritan' "is therefore used as a term of degree, or relative religious zeal rather than as a clear-cut party label."[54] Herschel Baker claims the most important common attribute of the puritan was what he calls "Puritan intensity." [55] Collinson mentions an Elizabethan pamphleteer who said, "The hotter sort of protestants are called puritans."[56] The movement was not centrally organized, so it had variety with certain distinct features. Because there were no controls, people could be puritan to greater or lesser degrees with a centrist rather than an exclusionist way of determining whether one was puritan or not.

On the whole puritans, whether moderate or radical, were agreed on the following points: First, was a need for further reform in the English church seeing it as their duty to bring about change if they possibly could. They were not willing to leave the English church unless forced out, but they were not willing to compromise either. Second, puritans embraced Reformed theology. They were predestinarians; they believed the Bible was their supreme authority in all matters including worship; they believed in salvation by faith alone through the finished work of Christ on the cross (as did the Arminians). Third, they were experiential and experimental in their faith. They held to an inward experience of conversion, which led to an outward experimental life of assurance in Christ. Ian Breward sums up this definition of puritanism:

---

[51] Geoffrey Nuttall, *The Holy Spirit in Puritan Faith and Experience*, xix.

[52] R. Buick Knox, ed., *Reformation Conformity and Dissent* (London: Epworth Press, 1977), 257.

[53] Ibid., 257-258.

[54] Peter Lake, *Anglicans and Puritans?* (London: Unwin Hyman, 1988), 7.

[55] Herschel Baker, *The Wars of Truth* (Gloucester, MA: Peter Smith, 1969), 203. He goes on to say that "Puritan piety... was experienced with an intensity and a passion that seemed to obliterate all else." Ibid., 204.

[56] Patrick Collinson, *The Elizabethan Puritan Movement*, 27.

Puritanism cannot be defined simply by measuring the winds of social change, because it was also a deeply religious phenomenon. It included wide varieties of opinion and practice, but can broadly be applied to those who by reason of their religious experience and theological convictions were dissatisfied with the government and worship of the Church of England, but who nonetheless refused to separate.[57]

It is helpful to see puritanism in three stages: early puritanism (1558-1603), middle puritanism (1603-1662) and later or restoration puritanism (1662 to 1702). Early puritanism is synonymous with Elizabeth's reign. This stage includes the witness of many of the Marian exiles who were not happy with what they saw as compromise when they returned. Though William Tyndale, John Bradford and John Hooper had similar practices, beliefs and values, they should be considered predecessors to the puritans rather than puritans as such. Middle puritanism characterizes the period between Elizabeth's death and the Act of Uniformity of Charles II when over two thousand puritan pastors chose to leave the Church of England rather than submit to the Act of Uniformity. William Perkins should be seen as a transitional figure from early puritanism to middle puritanism. He did much to change puritanism from a political movement to one of emphasizing personal piety and sound doctrine. He was largely responsible for drawing a new generation into the puritan fold. William Ames and Richard Sibbes were very influential at the early stages of this second period and the Westminster divines at the end. The Westminster Confession and Catechisms were products of this time, as was the Civil War and the restoration. The later puritans lived through the Civil War and wrote afterwards. This was perhaps the greatest devotional time, mirroring the end of Elizabeth's reign when the political edge had been dulled, making more room for a heart focus; this is not to say that there were no great devotional or heart focused writings in the earlier stages, but it did seem to flower at this time when political activism had been curtailed. Most of the better-known puritans wrote at this time including Richard Baxter, John Owen, Thomas Boston, John Flavel and Stephen Charnock.[58]

By 1642 civil war erupted between parliament and King Charles. Charles was later executed for waging war on his people and the commonwealth and Oliver Cromwell's lord protectorate took control. John Owen preached a sermon before parliament justifying the execution of Charles but others found it difficult to support biblically.[59] Confusion ensued and the great experiment fell apart. By 1660 parliament invited Charles II to return to England as king. Charles II, who seemed conciliatory at first, convened the Savoy Conference to get the Presbyterians and the Anglicans to compromise. The Presbyterians were not in favor of complete toleration, which would include Catholics because they feared the political influence of Rome. The Anglicans who were very sore

---

[57] William Perkins, *The Work of William Perkins*, 14.

[58] We do not include John Bunyan because he was a separatist who voluntarily left the Church of England rather than being forced out. Also because this paper deals with English puritanism, the American puritans have largely been ignored.

[59] Peter Toon, *Puritans and Calvinism*, 42.

about being ousted under Cromwell's reign, were not willing to compromise at all with the Presbyterians though a few were sympathetic namely Jeremy Taylor, Edward Stillingfleet, Archbishop Ussher and others.[60] A new liturgy was put into place that was not acceptable to many of the Presbyterians though many did remain in office. In 1662 parliament issued the Act of Uniformity with the king's approval, which made it mandatory that all clergy agree with the 39 Articles and use the Book of Common Prayer. Many left the Anglican Church because they could not accept the interference of the state in deciding proper worship. The Clarendon Code, which consisted of the Corporation Act (1661), the Act of Uniformity (1662), the Conventicle Act (1663) and the Five Mile Act (1665) brought about by the cavalier parliament forced seventeen hundred Presbyterian, 172 Independents and seven or eight Baptists to leave the church.

Dewey Wallace Jr. describes the decline of Calvinism after 1660. He finds three factions: Arminians, moderate Calvinists, and high Calvinists. As a general rule Anglicans embraced Arminianism, Presbyterians embraced moderate Calvinism and Congregationalists and Particular Baptists embraced high Calvinism.[61] At this time the puritans embraced either moderate Calvinism or high Calvinism. The high Calvinist puritans promoted tolerance, but seemed to advocate sectarian divisiveness especially with the doctrine of limited atonement.[62] The moderate Calvinist puritans emphasized unity[63] and de-emphasized or rejected particular atonement (i.e. Stephen Charnock, John Flavel, John Howe, Richard Baxter, Thomas Manton, and Thomas Boston). After seeing the execution of the king, the failure of the puritan experiment in politics, and the ejection of puritan pastors from the pulpit, it seems the moderate Calvinists grew tired of controversy (i.e. concerning the decrees) that did not directly affect the gospel of experiential (and experimental) Calvinism (i.e. the fundamental articles to be discussed in chapter five).

Seventeenth century England entered the modern age in the areas of philosophy, science and politics. Cartesian philosophy with its non-religious and non-scholastic bent swept all of Europe and was either warmly embraced, cautiously accepted or spoken against by the intellectuals in England including the puritans. The Copernican revolution was building speed and a mechanistic understanding of the universe more and more inclined to. State-centered politics began in the sixteenth century, but seventeenth century England saw the most dramatic changes with parliament controlling and even discarding the

---

[60] Harry Grant Plum, *Restoration Puritanism* (Port Washington, NY: Kennikat Press, 1972), 22.

[61] Dewey Wallace Jr., *Puritans and Predestination* (University of North Carolina Press, 1982), 159.

[62] John Owen's *The Death of Death in the Death of Christ* will be evaluated as a possible example of speculation.

[63] John Flavel, in reference to true believers, expressed the necessity of unity: "You are taken out of the world, to be a people for his name, that is, for his honour: but there is little credit to the name of Christ from a dividing, wrangling people." John Flavel, *Works*, 3:607. We will later see a difference between desiring tolerance and having an attitude of tolerance.

king – for a time. Charnock grew up in the midst of this tumultuous time at its epicenter, London, the nation's capital.

# CHAPTER ONE

# STEPHEN CHARNOCK (1628-1680)

*1. Biographical Introduction*

There is very little written by way of biography on Charnock. William Symington's "Life and Character of Charnock"[1] and James M'Cosh's "Introduction to Charnock's Works" are the two main extant resources.[2] Both Symington and M'Cosh seemed to have leaned heavily on John Johnson's funeral message for Charnock as well as Richard Adams and Edward Veal's preface to Charnock's works.[3] Bishop Parker mentions Charnock in his *History of His Own Time*[4] and A.G. Matthews includes a brief sketch of his life in *Calamy Revised*.[5] A good but brief modern biography can be found in an article written by Richard Greaves in the *Oxford Dictionary of National Biography*.[6] Charnock was born in London and entered Emmanuel College, Cambridge in 1642 receiving his B.A. in 1646 and his M.A. in 1649. Apparently while pursuing his M.A. he ministered in Southwark and then went to Oxford where he was incorporated Master of Arts and then in 1652 became Senior Proctor. In 1656 he went to Ireland, serving under Henry Cromwell, Protector of Ireland. At the restoration of Charles II in 1660 he was no longer able to minister and so moved back to London, traveling to France and Holland periodically for the next fifteen years. In 1666 his library was destroyed in the fire of London. In 1675 he co-pastored with Thomas Watson at a Presbyterian church in Crosby Hall, where he ministered until his death in 1680.

There are two important discrepancies in his life: was Charnock an Independent or Presbyterian? And was Charnock involved in a conspiracy in

---

[1] Stephen Charnock, *The Existence and Attributes of God*, 1:5-18.

[2] M'Cosh mentions a *memoir* supposedly written by John Gunter but admitted there was no trace of its whereabouts. Stephen Charnock, *Works of Stephen Charnock*, 1:vii.

[3] John Johnson, *Eklampsis ton Dikaion* (London: Thomas Parkhurst, 1680). Johnson, Adam and Veal were all apparently longtime friends of Charnock.

[4] Samuel Parker, *Bishop Parker's History of His Own Time* (London: Charles Rivington, 1727), 71-72.

[5] A.G. Matthews, *Calamy Revised* (Oxford: Clarendon Press, 1934), 111-112.

[6] Richard Greaves, 'Charnock, Stephen (1628-1680)', *Oxford Dictionary of National Biography* (Oxford University Press, 2004), article 5172.

Ireland?  As to the first question, Richard Greaves refers to him as a moderate Independent.[7]  While in Oxford Charnock attended church with Thomas Goodwin, Thankful Owen, Francis Howel, Theophilus Gale, and John Howe; most of these were independents with Howe the notable exception.  It should be noted that in the seventeenth century (and the eighteenth) there was considerable fluidity in respect of what we would call denominational allegiance.  Ministers of the 'three denominations' would float between them as they felt called.  Charnock is later implicated in the Blood Plot where Thomas Blood and others attempted to seize Dublin Castle in April 1663.  Most of those involved in the plot were Presbyterians, not Independents.  But was Charnock involved?  Most of the information appears to have come from Bishop Parker's history, a history antagonistic toward Presbyterians.  Parker portrays Charnock as fleeing to London under the alias of Clark where "he exercis'd great authority at London amongst the Fanaticks, and long presided in a large Conventicle; for he did not die till two years after, anno 1683."[8]  There are too many discrepancies in this account to hold it as true.  We know Charnock traveled extensively to France and Holland from 1660-1675 and then for five years co-pastored a Presbyterian congregation with Thomas Watson at Crosby hall in London.  He died July 27, 1680 not 1683.  M'Cosh suggests he was deeply influenced by the Thirty Year War and his biographers all describe him as quiet, mild mannered with a peaceable disposition.  It seems incredible to think he was involved in a poorly conceived attempt to take over the government.

Two possible scenarios unfold.  Either Charnock was involved in the Blood Plot and later abandoned his political attempts of reform or he never was involved.[9]  If he was an Independent earlier in life, it appears he changed to Presbyterianism.  He seems to have been influenced by both Baxter[10] and Howe and adopted their broader Calvinist outlook with the Presbyterian desire for comprehension in the restoration Church of England, rather than toleration.  He preached with his friend Edward Veal at a Presbyterian church on Wood Street in Dublin after the restoration.  A portion of a Presbyterian congregation wanted to secure him as joint pastor with Thomas Jacombe to succeed Lazarus Seaman, but John Howe was selected instead.  He then pastored a Presbyterian church at Crosby Hall for five years along with the Presbyterian Thomas Watson.  It would seem he had abandoned any possible connection with

---

[7] Richard Greaves, *God's Other Children* (Stanford University Press, 1997), 14.

[8] Samuel Parker, *Bishop Parker's History of His Own Time*, 74.

[9] M'Cosh states, "There is no evidence whatever to shew that Charnock was identified in any way with the projected rising in Dublin.  His name does not appear in the proclamation from Dublin Castle, 23d May 1663.  That the government should have proceeded against him, is no presumption of his guilt, though it may have been quite sufficient to lead Bishop Parker to propagate the story."  Stephen Charnock, *Works*, 1:xxi-xxii.

[10] He was recommended by Baxter to Matthew Sylvester for a Presbyterian church in 1674.

moderate independency in favor of moderate Presbyterianism.

## 2. *Influences on Charnock*

Because of the tremendous changes taking place in seventeenth century England and the peculiar situation of Charnock, several influences on his life need to be understood in order to evaluate his peculiar doctrine of the knowledge of God. In reviewing his life and works, especially the copious citations of authors within his works, we can discern three major influences on his beliefs: Puritanism, the Cambridge Platonists and the School of Saumur. These three inspirations helped shape what we will call a *latitude puritan* disposition.

### a. The Puritans

There are two major puritan influences that directly relate to Charnock's doctrine of the knowledge of God: The elevation of the affections and the puritan use of the scholastic method.

### i. The Affections

We have seen the puritan inclination toward an experimental/experiential faith, which Charnock wholeheartedly affirmed and propagated. Later we will see how his attention to the affections will protect him from a sterile intellectualism and fill out his doctrine of the knowledge of God. Along with the rest of the restoration puritans,[11] Charnock found himself in a similar situation as Perkins in the previous century. Just as the experiential writings of Perkins and Sibbes became especially powerful once the political impulse was thwarted, the same was true of the restoration puritans and Charnock was no exception. Throughout his writings a deep felt love for God is revealed and an unapologetic appeal to experiential Christianity encouraged. He exhorts his readers: "Let us have as strong affections of love and joy, as the devils, by their knowledge of God as discovered in Christ, have of horror and hatred…. Let the motions of your will, and the affections of your soul, rise according to the elevation of your knowledge of God in Christ."[12] Puritan writings were saturated with references to the affections and their importance in the Christian life. How did the affections become so prominent especially in restoration

---

[11] Restoration puritanism refers to the puritans who lost their positions at the return of Charles II once the Act of Uniformity was passed in 1662.

[12] Stephen Charnock, *Works*, 4:162-163.

puritanism? It would appear that John Calvin influenced the puritans greatly and their peculiar situation in history helped these ideas to flower into something new. They quote Calvin often and extensively adopt his doctrine of union and communion.[13]

The reformers and the puritans for the most part held to a dichotomist understanding of the nature of humanity as being composed of body and soul. The spirit and the soul were not seen as separate entities but rather are used synonymously for the most part.[14] Calvin resisted the complexity of the scholastics, holding to a simplified understanding of the soul as "an immortal though created essence, which is his nobler part."[15] It inhabits and animates the body as well as regulates its conduct. It is an incorporeal substance made up of two faculties: intellect and will, which continue after the body dies. To see how Calvin's view may have effected the puritan understanding, it will be helpful to look at Calvin's understanding of the faculties of the soul and whether he should be considered a voluntarist or an intellectualist.

Calvin held to the traditional faculty psychology of Aristotle and, like the other reformers, embraced the two faculties of mind and will. The faculty of the will included the inclinations and affections, and the heart was very often seen as synonymous with the will.[16] He did not tend to delve into the intricacies of the philosophers but he did know their distinctions; he simply thought their complexities were more harmful than helpful even if true.[17] T.F. Torrance notes:

---

[13] Charnock mentions Calvin in his *Existence and Attributes of God* more than any other reformer. He mentions Calvin seven times and cites him three more times, with Luther as the next runner up being mentioned only three times. Charnock rarely mentioned anyone by name, so directly referring to Calvin and adopting so much of his theology reveals his dependence on him.

[14] *Institutes of the Christian Religion*, John T. McNeill (ed.), (Philadelphia: The Westminster Press, 1960), I. 15,2. In his *Psychopannychia* he says, "We know that when the two terms are joined, 'soul' means *will*, and 'spirit' means *intellect*." John Calvin, *Selected Works of John Calvin Vol. Three, Tracts part three* "Psychopannychia" (Albany, OR: Ages Software, 1998), 385.

[15] John Calvin, *Institutes*, I. 15,2. Henry Bullinger had a similar definition bringing out the substantial aspect of the soul: "The soul is a spiritual substance, poured of God into man's body, that, being joined thereunto, it might quicken and direct the same; but being dissevered from the body, it should not die but live immortal for ever." Henry Bullinger, *The Decades of Henry Bullinger* (Grand Rapids: Reformation Heritage Books, 2004), 2:368-369.

[16] He states, "Scripture is accustomed to divide the soul of man, as to its frailties, into two parts—the *mind* and the *heart*. The *mind* means the *understanding*, while the *heart* denotes all the *disposition* or *inclinations*. These two terms, therefore, include the entire soul." John Calvin, *Commentary on the Epistle to the Philippians* (Albany, OR: Ages Software, 1998), Philippians 4:7.

[17] *Institutes* I. 15,7.

Calvin obviously makes an entire break from the Scholastic conception of creation and existence, particularly in the case of man. It represents a return to the essentially dynamic conception of God's relation to the world which we have in the Bible, but which mainly under the influence of Aristotelian thought had been translated into a logical and static relation of being.[18]

In discussing Calvin's anthropology in regard to the faculties of the soul the question arises as to whether Calvin was an intellectualist or a voluntarist? According to Thomas Aquinas the will is subordinate in function to the intellect and so the intellect had priority over the will; this became known as "intellectualism."[19] Duns Scotus opposed Aquinas and saw a priority in the will, which became the view of "voluntarism."[20] R.T. Kendall adds to the definition of voluntarism the area of faith saying that voluntarism is the idea of "faith as an act of the will in contrast to a passive persuasion in the mind."[21] When one reads Calvin, it at first appears that he was an intellectualist. He says in the *Institutes*: "The understanding is, as it were, the leader and governor of the soul; and that the will is always mindful of the bidding of the understanding, and its own desires awaits the judgment of the understanding."[22] In his commentary on Ephesians he states, "Now, *the mind* holds the highest rank in the human constitution, is the seat of reason, presides over the will and restrains sinful desires."[23] His definition of faith also reveals an element of passivity rather than an act of the will.[24] As Richard Muller points out, Calvin held to an intellectualist stance in regard to temporal priority.[25] But the issue is not as cut and dried as it might seem. Calvin himself resisted these kinds of categories because of his "anti-speculative approach to theology and his disdain for scholasticism."[26] Muller suggests that Calvin held to a temporal priority of the mind but a causal priority of the will. The will is able to accept or reject the knowledge the intellect presents to it and therefore is prior in causality.[27] In his

---

[18] T.F. Torrance, *Calvin's Doctrine of Man* (Grand Rapids: Eerdmans, 1957), 29.

[19] Richard Muller, "*Fides* and *Cognitio* in Relation to the Problem of Intellect and Will in the Theology of John Calvin," *Calvin Theological Journal* 25 (1990), 211.

[20] Ibid.

[21] R.T. Kendall, *Calvin and English Calvinism to 1649*, 3.

[22] *Institutes* I. 15,7.

[23] John Calvin, *Commentary on the Epistle to the Ephesians* (Albany, OR: Ages Software, 1998), Ephesians 4:17. He goes on to reject the view of the "theologians of the Sorbonne" in favor of Paul who "makes the mind consist of nothing else than vanity."

[24] "[Faith] is a firm and certain knowledge of God's benevolence toward us, founded upon the truth of the freely given promise in Christ, both revealed to our minds, and sealed upon our hearts through the Holy Spirit." Ibid., III. 2,7.

[25] Muller, "*Fides* and *Cognitio* in Relation to the Problem of Intellect and Will" 221.

[26] Ibid., 223.

[27] Neither position demands an Arminian point of view because faith is seen as a gift from God and the will is changed by God, not by an act of humans.

commentary on John, Calvin sees faith as synonymous with "receiving Christ" and states, "by faith they obtain this glory of being reckoned the sons of God."[28] He even went so far as to say, "Faith regenerates us, so that we are the sons of God."[29] The will takes an active part in receiving Christ.

It can also be shown that for Calvin a value priority would fit the voluntarist category because he believed it was more valuable to move the heart than the head. Knowledge is a means to the end of love and worship.[30] In discussing true and false believers he said:

> For it is a doctrine not of the tongue but of life. It is not apprehended by the understanding and memory alone, as other disciplines are, but it is received only when it possesses the whole soul, and finds a seat and resting place in the inmost affection of the heart.[31]

He stated "the chief part of faith" is "that firm and steadfast constancy of heart."[32] In speaking of a speculative faith only in the head he noted:

> And here again we ought to observe that we are called to a knowledge of God: not that knowledge which, content with empty speculation, merely flits in the brain, but that which will be sound and fruitful if we duly perceive it, and if it takes root in the heart.[33]

In his commentary on the Psalms he said, "For as our affections rise in rebellion against the will of God, so faith, restoring us to a state of humble and peaceful submission, appeases all the tumults of our hearts."[34] And in his commentary on 1 John "For faith is not a naked and a frigid apprehension of Christ, but a lively and real sense of his power, which produces confidence."[35] In all of these quotations we see that for Calvin faith was never intended to simply be *notitia* but rather should also stir the heart, which is the end of faith rather than simply filling the head. This emphasis, which qualifies him for the voluntarist camp, is magnified in the puritans.

Charnock held to the traditional faculty psychology concerning the soul, but a change should be noticed in the structure of the faculties. Whereas for Calvin

---

[28] John Calvin, *Commentary on the Gospel According to John* (Albany, OR: Ages Software, 1998), John 1:12.
[29] Ibid. He immediately qualifies himself saying that God breathes faith into us from heaven.
[30] *Institutes*, I. 2,1 and I, 12,1.
[31] *Institutes*, III. 6,4.
[32] *Institutes*, III. 2,33.
[33] *Institutes*, I. 5,9.
[34] John Calvin, *Commentary on the Psalms Vol. 1* (Albany, OR: Ages Software, 1998), Psalm 37:7.
[35] John Calvin, *Commentary on the First Epistle of John* (Albany, OR: Ages Software, 1998), 1 John 2:27.

and Aquinas[36] there were two main faculties (mind and will or cognitive and appetitive) with divisions within the two, the restoration puritans began to develop a more complex faculty psychology. The standard categories for the soul became the understanding, the will and the affections. William Perkins was a transitional figure in that he held to the two faculties of mind and will, placing conscience in the mind and affections in the will. He saw the mind as prior to the will saying the understanding "is the more principall part, serving to rule and order the whole man and therefore it is placed in the soule to be as the wagginer in the waggin."[37] He said, "Faith is a supernaturall gift of God in the minde" and "The place and seate of faith (as I thinke) is the mind of man not the will."[38] It is quite clear that he saw some priority of the mind to the will and should be considered an intellectualist in some sense. But like Calvin he also saw faith as an action that "apprehends and applies" Christ "with all his merites unto himselfe."[39] Though he pointed out two principal faculties of the soul he did call conscience a faculty within the same writing.[40] In his *Golden Chaine* he pointed out five faculties: mind, memory, conscience, will and affections,[41] and elsewhere described the three faculties of mind, will and affections.[42] The affections became prominent in his writings and so could be seen as a value priority. William Ames also saw intellect, conscience, will and affections as the parts or faculties of the soul.[43] John Owen opted for three: mind, will and affections.[44]

Thomas Boston saw five faculties with three primary ones. In some sense the mind, will, affections, conscience and memory are seen as faculties of the soul.[45] But he also referred to three main faculties as head, heart and affections,[46] or mind, will and affections.[47] And even when he mentioned the five faculties he indicated some kind of subordination of conscience and memory to the "threefold cord" of mind, will and affections.[48] For Boston faith is an act of the mind and will, and the affections, though subordinate to the mind, are what God longs to move through faith. In *The Marrow of Modern*

---

[36] Thomas Aquinas, *Summa Theologica* (Albany, OR: Ages Software, 1997), P (1) – Q (75) – A (3). Aquinas called the two faculties the sensitive faculty and the intellectual faculty.

[37] William Perkins, *Workes* 1:510.

[38] Ibid., 1:126.

[39] Ibid., 1:2.

[40] Ibid.

[41] Ibid., 1:84-85.

[42] Ibid., 1:625.

[43] William Ames, *The Marrow of Theology* (Grand Rapids: Baker Books, 1997), 120.

[44] John Owen, *The Works of John Owen* (Rio, Wisconsin: Ages Software, 2000), 3:366.

[45] Thomas Boston, *Human Nature in its Fourfold State* (Carlisle, Penn: Banner of Truth Trust, 1964), 79-129, 209-221, 230.

[46] Ibid., 134.

[47] Ibid., 40-44, 55, 128, 438.

[48] Ibid., 128.

*Divinity* written by Edward Fisher, but published with notes by Boston, he said:

> I would have you more strong in desire than curious in speculation, and to long
> more to feel communion with God than to be able to dispute of the genus or
> species of any question, either human or divine; and press hard to know God by
> powerful experience.[49]

Charnock held to the puritan view of three faculties, emphasizing the
priority and absolute necessity of the affections:

> A bare speculation will tire the soul; and without application, and pressing upon
> the will and affections, will rather chill than warm devotion. It is only by this
> means that we shall have the efficacy of truth in our wills, and the sweetness in
> our affections, as well as the notion of it in our understandings.[50]

Neither Calvin nor Charnock defined the word *affections*, but it appears that
most of those in the sixteenth and seventeenth century had the same idea when
using the word. In *A New General English Dictionary* (1740) "affections" was
defined: "Love, friendship, tenderness for, desire, inclination, passion."[51] Other
earlier dictionaries concurred.[52] In the eighteenth century Jonathan Edwards
gave a lengthy definition in *A Treatise Concerning Religious Affections*, which
will be helpful. Edwards went back to Calvin's understanding of the soul being
made up of two faculties where the affections are seen as a subset of the
inclination or will. The inclination or will can be exercised in various degrees
and when it is raised to a height where "the soul comes to act vigorously and
sensibly" and the body is "sensibly altered" the affections are said to be
moved.[53] Edwards definition was in full agreement with puritan William
Fenner (1600-1640) who defined affections in his *Treatise of Affections*: "The

---

[49] Edward Fisher with notes by Thomas Boston, *The Marrow of Modern Divinity*
(Edmonton: Stillwater Revival Books, 1991), 253.

[50] Stephen Charnock, *Works*, 5:308. He goes on to say: "Never, therefore, leave
thinking of a spiritual subject till your heart be affected with it. If you think of the evil
of sin, leave not till your heart loathe it; if of God, cease not till it mount up in
admirations of him. If you think of his mercy, melt for abusing it; if of his sovereignty,
awe your heart into obedient resolutions; if of his presence, double your watch over
yourself. If you meditate on Christ, make no end till your hearts love him; if of his
death, plead the value of it for the justification of your persons, and apply the virtue of it
for the sanctification of your natures. Without this practical stamp upon our affections,
we shall have light spirits."

[51] Thomas Dyche and William Pardon, *A New General English Dictionary (1740)* (New
York: George Olms Verlag, 1972), AFF.

[52] See Sir William Craigie, *A Dictionary of the Older Scottish Tongue: From the Twelfth
Century to the End of the Seventeenth,* (The University of Chicago Press, 1931), 1:31.

[53] Jonathan Edwards, *The Works of Jonathan Edwards,* (Carlisle, Penn: The Banner of
Truth Trust, 1974), 1:237. He goes on to describe the affections as "these more
vigorous and sensible exercises of this faculty." Ibid.

affections are the forcible and sensible motions of the heart, or the will, to a thing, or from a thing, according as it is apprehended to bee good or to bee evill."[54] The affections are not to be confused with feelings in the body though "they always accompany them in the present state."[55] They are either approving or disapproving and so can be put into the two general categories of love and hatred, but also include the auxiliary categories of "love, desire, hope, joy, gratitude, complacence" and "hatred, fear, anger, grief, and such like."[56] Fenner added that the effect of the affections is often physical manifestations such as weeping, trembling and blushing, which can lead to even greater manifestations:

> If the apprehension be deepe indeed, the affections break out into raptures as dancing and leapings of the heart, which are the raptures of joy: ravishments and enamorings, which are the raptures of love; meltings, and bleedings, and breakings of Spirit, which are the raptures of greife; astonishments, amazements, which are the raptures of feare; confusion and the like, which are the raptures of shame: the affections burst forth into such raptures as these, when the apprehension is deepe.[57]

Edwards' and Fenner's definition seems to fit what Calvin, Charnock and the puritans meant when they used the term so this will be our working definition: The deep and sensible motions of the soul that make up heart religion – experiential Christianity.

Charnock, Boston, Owen,[58] Ames,[59] and Perkins all seemed to follow Calvin in seeing a temporal priority given to the mind with the will playing a major part in the act of faith. But with the puritans a heightened recognition of importance is given to the affections, and they seem to go farther than the original reformers in giving the affections a promotion as a distinct faculty of the soul. The restoration puritans, both high Calvinist and moderate, borrowed from Calvin and the early reformers, but they were also unique in their emphasis and elevation of the affections.

---

[54] William Fenner, *A Treatise of the Affections* (London: E. Tyler, 1657), 2.

[55] Jonathan Edwards, *The Works of Jonathan Edwards,* 1:237. Fenner also said the affections are not in the sensitive or material parts of the soul which seems to be similar to the modern idea of emotions and therefore is in agreement with Edwards. He concurred that there is an intimate connection between the affections and the emotions but that they should not be confused. William Fenner, *A Treatise of the Affections*, 2-3.

[56] Jonathan Edwards, *The Works of Jonathan Edwards,* 1:237.

[57] William Fenner, *A Treatise of the Affections*, 4.

[58] Owen saw real faith affecting the will and the affections. *Works,* 5:104. He said, "Believing is an act of the heart; which, in the Scriptures comprises all the faculties of the soul." 5:115.

[59] Ames saw faith as "resting of the heart on God" residing in both the mind and will. *The Marrow,* 80.

*ii. The Scholastic Method*

The puritans were products of post-reformation Reformed scholasticism, though their ideas were not identical with that of continental Reformed orthodoxy. Gordon Wakefield defines puritans as "evangelical scholastics."[60] Like Reformed orthodoxy the puritans used the scholastic method and depended on Aristotelian logic at times, but seemed to imbibe more of the humanist emphases of the original reformers and produced a theology which had a more practical bent.

Two major ideas have developed in modern historiography concerning Reformed scholasticism, one side seeing it in a negative sense as a deviation of the original reformation, and the other side seeing it in a neutral manner as a method of teaching theology, with little if any variation from the initial group of reformers. This is germane to our study because the position taken on this issue will affect the degree of speculation seen in the puritans and thus a possible overemphasis on the mind to the neglect of the heart. The puritans, and Charnock in particular, decried the theological abuse of the medieval scholastics as needless speculation and heresy. The original reformers, especially John Calvin, made the same accusations. Were they simply misinformed, actually using the scholastic method while rejecting scholasticism? Or were some of their critiques of medieval scholasticism necessary warnings for post-reformation orthodoxy?

Brian Armstrong, R.T. Kendall and Basil Hall have presented an extraordinary theory concerning the immediate followers of Calvin – that Calvin's successor Theodore Beza slipped in a completely different theology that has more affinity with Arminianism, the nemesis of the Calvinists, than with the thought of Calvin himself, without anyone even realizing a change had taken place. Hall claims that "Calvin's disciples," including Beza, abandoned Calvin's balance of doctrines for a "restored Aristotelianism."[61]  It is scholasticism that supposedly led Beza and William Perkins toward supralapsarianism, limited atonement and a man-centered piety as the basis for assurance.[62] Kendall goes even further. The puritans, whom he prefers to call "experimental predestinarians," repudiated Calvin on a number of doctrines: the atonement (embracing limited rather than general atonement), faith (seeing it as an act of the will rather than a passive persuasion), assurance (separating it from faith and basing it on sanctification rather than on Christ alone), and repentance (placing it before faith rather than after in the *ordo salutis*). Were this the case, the nature of piety produced would effect greatly the life of a believer. The question which must be asked is whether such radical changes in doctrine, made in such a short period of time without anyone, including Beza

---

[60] Gordon Wakefield, *Puritan Devotion* (London: Epworth Press, 1957), 111. Wakefield uses the term in reference to the puritan use of casuistry.

[61] Basil Hall, "Calvin Against the Calvinists" in G.E. Duffield, editor, *John Calvin* (Grand Rapids: Eerdmans, 1963), 25.

[62] Ibid., 27, 29.

and the puritans noticing, is a tenable theory? Stephen Thorson comments: "It is hard to believe that such brilliant disciples of Calvin, far closer to his own day than we, could have dreamed up an activist aspect to faith and arbitrarily foisted it onto Calvin without anyone noticing until recently."[63]

Robert Letham brings an interesting twist to the debate. He recognizes that it is a little farfetched to see such rapid change from Calvin to Beza.[64] Richard Muller has shown the continuity of Calvin and Beza by exposing what he calls the abuse of a document, referring to the accusation that Beza's *Tabula Praedestinationis* put predestination as the driving force or central dogma of all of his doctrine.[65] Beza wrote the *Tabula* (1555) before Calvin's final edition of the *Institutes* (1559) and was a trusted ally and associate. Calvin did not point out any dramatic modification in Beza's theology and so methodological rather than theological differences are the only noticeable changes. Letham accepts Muller's findings and rightly shows the acceptance among the reformers of some theological diversity in their ranks. They saw themselves as holding to the core truths of the reformation and were willing to embrace each other as colleagues and co-religionists even if they differed on such things as the exact correlation of the Supper and feasting on Christ, the *ordo salutis* concerning predestination or the idea of covenant theology. Letham acknowledges some gradual change taking place among the reformers, but then suggests that the puritans countenanced a considerable degree of diversity concerning the idea of assurance. He agrees with Kendall that the puritans placed faith in the will rather than the understanding. However, he disagrees with Kendall's opinion that those differences were rooted in a particular view of predestination and limited atonement. Instead he blames the change on their covenant theology.[66] He argues that the puritans rather than the immediate successors of Calvin made the major modifications of Calvin.

Paul Helm addresses Kendall's thesis in his book *Calvin and the Calvinists*. He argues that Kendall distorted the teachings of both Calvin and the puritans, taking them out of context and at times making them say the opposite of what they actually taught.[67] One major area of contention is the idea that Calvin

---

[63] Stephen Thorson, "Tensions in Calvin's View of Faith: Unexamined Assumptions in R.T. Kendall's *Calvin and English Calvinism to 1649*," *Journal of Evangelical Theological Society* 37/3 (1994), 419.

[64] Robert Letham, "Faith and Assurance in Early Calvinism: A Model of Continuity and Diversity," in W. Fred Graham, editor, *Later Calvinism* (Kirksville, MO: Sixteenth Century Journal Publishers, 1994), 357.

[65] Richard Muller, "The Use and Abuse of a Document" in Carl R. Trueman and R.S. Clark, editors, *Protestant Scholasticism* (Carlisle, Cumbria: Paternoster Press, 1999), passim.

[66] Robert Letham "Continuity and Diversity in Early Calvinism" in W. Fred Graham, editor, *Later Calvinism*, 373-383.

[67] He says, "Kendall's account of Calvin's teaching is at best an exaggeration, at worst a complete misrepresentation." Paul Helm, *Calvin and the Calvinist* (Carlisle, PA: Banner of Truth Trust, 1982), 55-56.

taught a general atonement where Christ is said to have died for everyone, whereas the Calvinists held to a particular atonement where Christ only died for the elect.  Helm shows how Calvin was not as precise in his wording as his followers,[68] but definitely taught the scholastics' view that Christ's death was sufficient for all but only efficient for the elect.[69]  Christ did not simply make salvation possible but actually accomplished something definite on the cross.[70] Kendall correctly brings to light several passages from Calvin where he teaches that Christ died sufficiently for all,[71] but that is not the end of the story.  Calvin also taught that in some sense Christ only died for the elect.  In a tract written against Tileman Heshusius he said:

> But the first thing to be explained is, how Christ is present with unbelievers, as being the spiritual food of souls, and, in short, the life and salvation of the world. And as he adheres so doggedly to the words, I should like to know how the wicked can eat the flesh of Christ which was not crucified for them? and how they can drink the blood which was not shed to expiate their sins? I agree with him, that Christ is present as a strict judge when his Supper is profaned.[72]

Helm points out that Kendall was selective in his references to Calvin, and then appropriately asks the question: "Is it not natural to take Calvin to be saying, in effect, that Christ's death is sufficient for all but efficient for the elect alone?"[73]  What Helm apparently does not realize is that much of Reformed orthodoxy did not embrace the scholastic view that Christ died sufficiently for all and efficiently for the elect.[74]  Beza's particular atonement, later expounded

---

[68] Ibid., 13.

[69] Ibid., 39, 44.

[70] Calvin states, "The priestly office belongs to Christ alone because by the sacrifice of his death he blotted out our own guilt and made satisfaction for our sins" revealing something actually took place rather than simply potentially made possible concerning our forgiveness. John Calvin, *Institutes* II. 15,6.

[71] R.T. Kendall, *Calvin and English Calvinism to 1649*, 13-16.  In Calvin's commentary on Romans 5:18 he specifically references to who Christ died for: "He makes this favor common to all, because it is propounded to all, and not because it is in reality extended to all; for though Christ suffered for the sins of the whole world, and is offered through God's benignity indiscriminately to all, yet all do not receive him."  John Calvin, *Commentary on the Epistle to the Romans* (Albany, OR: Ages Software, 1998), 163.

[72] John Calvin, *Selected Works of John Calvin Vol. Two, Tracts Part Two* (Albany, OR: Ages Software, 1998), 477.

[73] Paul Helm, *Calvin and the Calvinists*, 44.

[74] This is the thesis of G. Michael Thomas in *The Extent of the Atonement* (Carlisle, UK: Paternoster, 1997), passim and 56-58 for Beza particularly.  Many of the post-reformers would agree with the scholastic statement but would then go on to reject it as inadequate.  Francis Turretin is a good representative stating: "To this purpose a distinction is made by the Fathers and retained by many divines, '*that Christ died sufficiently for all, but efficiently for the elect only*.'  This is perfectly true, if it be understood of the dignity of Christ's death, though the phrase is not accurate if it be

repeatedly by John Owen in *The Death of Death in the Death of Christ*, stated clearly that Christ died for the elect only and did not in any sense die for the non-elect.[75] We will see later that a significant group of puritans rejected particular atonement and embraced either Moise Amyraut's hypothetical universalism or the scholastic distinction noted above. Since the earliest reformers did not articulate the doctrine of particular atonement in the manner it was subsequently taught, it would seem that this might be a case of doctrinal change owing to the scholastic method.

Another major challenge Helm makes against Kendall's thesis is in reference to his understanding of Calvin's view of faith. Kendall claims that Calvin believed that faith was passive and resided in the faculty of the mind rather than the will, whereas the puritans saw faith as something a person actively wills. Because of this shift, assurance as a direct part of faith is abandoned and left to be acquired later through the believer's focusing on his or her own inner state. Once again Helm points out the selectivity of Kendall. Calvin did see an active *receiving* as a part of true faith and therefore faith is both active and passive. The puritans were not diametrically opposed to Calvin's thought on faith, in fact, they held to a very similar understanding as the Genevan reformer. Charnock explained what he meant by faith: "*Believing* here notes not only an assent, but a recumbency, 'believe in me.' You do not only believe God, but believe *in* him, i.e. rely upon him for what he hath promised."[76] Here we see Calvin's passive understanding of faith. Charnock goes on to explain that the object of faith is God, even using the same categories of Calvin's *Institutes* on the subject of the knowledge of God.[77] Helm may at times slightly overstate his case, but in general he is correct in saying, "This teaching [that of the puritans concerning the atonement, faith and assurance] is, in all essentials, the teaching of Calvin himself."[78] He admits there are nuances and new emphases in the puritans' doctrine owing to their particular situation, but for all intents and purposes it was a development consistent with Calvin.[79] Joel Beeke points out that the difference between the reformers and the puritans was not one of principle but rather that of emphasis

---

referred to the will and purpose of Christ." Francis Turretin, *The Atonement of Christ* (Grand Rapid: Baker Book, 1978), 123.

[75] Owen specifically addresses this question rejecting the "distinction of the schoolmen" stating: "It is denied that the blood of Christ was a sufficient price and ransom for all and every one, not because it was not sufficient, but because it was not a ransom," which he goes on to say is a necessary part of the phrase "to die for them." John Owen, *The Death of Death in the Death of Christ* (Carlisle, PA: Banner of Truth Trust, 1959), 184.

[76] Stephen Charnock, *Works*, 5:148.

[77] Ibid., 5:151ff.

[78] Paul Helm, *Calvin and the Calvinists*, 31.

[79] Ibid., 80.

owing to their situations.[80] "Calvin was defining faith in its assuring character" in contrast to the Roman Catholics who saw assurance as heresy, and the puritans described, "what assurance is as a self-conscious, experimental phenomenon" owing to the lack of an experiential faith in seventeenth century England.[81] Both Calvin and the puritans saw assurance in some way as a part of the essence of faith, but assurance could be attained without experiencing it subjectively. Calvin wanted to make sure assurance was included in faith and the puritans wanted to stress the fact that assurance of one's salvation could be a subjective experience, felt as well as believed.

Another aspect of the "Calvin versus the Calvinists" debate concerns the puritans' use of scholasticism. Did the scholastic method alter the doctrine of the puritans as Hall contends?[82] In his discussion of the evolution of the debate of continuities and discontinuities between the reformation and Reformed orthodoxy, Muller gives some significant help in these questions.[83] One suspects, though, that he places an excessive emphasis on the element of continuity. Hall, Armstrong and others drew from the earlier works of Alexander Schweizer, Heinrich Heppe, Hans Emil Weber and Ernest Bizer who propounded that Reformed orthodoxy made predestination a central dogma and saw this as a negative transition owing to their embracing of scholasticism. Muller first questions the idea of a central dogma among the adherents of Reformed orthodoxy and then challenges the supposed inevitability of distortion caused by scholasticism. We will need to evaluate some definitions of scholasticism and see if the use of the scholastic method necessitates doctrinal deviancy, as well as discuss the concept of *central dogma*.

Armstrong describes Protestant scholasticism as possessing four tendencies:

(1) Primarily it will have reference to that theological approach which asserts religious truth on the basis of deductive ratiocination from given assumptions or principles, thus producing a logically coherent and defensible system of belief.... (2) The term will refer to the employment of reason in religious matters, so that reason assumes at least equal standing with faith in theology, thus jettisoning some of the authority of revelation. (3) It will comprehend the sentiment that the scriptural record contains a unified, rationally comprehensible account.... (4) It will comprehend a pronounced interest in metaphysical matters, in abstract, speculative thought, particularly with reference to the doctrine of God.... The strongly biblically and experientially based theology of Calvin and Luther had, it

---

[80] Joel Beeke, *The Quest for Full Assurance* (Carlisle, PA: Banner of Truth Trust, 1999), 53.
[81] Ibid.
[82] Basil Hall, "Calvin Against the Calvinists," 20-21.
[83] Richard Muller, *After Calvin* (Oxford University Press, 2003), 63-102.

is fair to say, been overcome by the metaphysics and deductive logic of a restored Aristotelianism.[84]

Muller, in combating what he considers false definitions of scholasticism, gives his own definition:

> Scholasticism is rightly defined as a dialectical method of the schools, historically rooted in the late patristic period, particularly in the thought of Augustine, and developed throughout the Middle Ages in the light of classical logic and rhetoric, constructed with a view to the authority of text and tradition, and devoted primarily to the exposition of Scripture and the theological topics that derive from it using the best available tools of exegesis, logic, and philosophy...[85]

Two differing views for the definition of scholasticism are emerging. One opinion reveals a rather negative picture of scholasticism in general and Reformed scholasticism in particular; the other sentiment reveals a fairly positive view – that scholasticism is simply a method, rather than a theology.

The term *scholasticism* was first coined by the humanists to describe the philosophers and theologians of the Middle Ages in a pejorative manner. A. Vos says, "It was a negative, derogatory term meant to indicate a tradition-bound, logic-chopping mentality, involving a slavish adherence to Aristotle."[86] At times Calvin used this caricature of the scholastic method because of the way in which the method had been abused, mainly in the later Middle Ages, especially among the nominalists. Muller points out that Calvin's polemic against scholasticism probably referred to the School of Sorbonne at the University of Paris, which was the main obstacle to reformation in France.[87] David Steinmetz observes that even Calvin, when not in polemical mode, used aspects of the scholastic method and spoke favorably of earlier scholastics.[88] Muller and Steinmetz are correct in what they affirm, though they are probably too ready to assess the reformer according to the categories of scholasticism and claim that he was, in effect, a scholastic theologian himself. Steinmetz's article is entitled "The Scholastic Calvin."

Armand Aime LaVallee in his doctoral thesis *'Calvin's Criticism of Scholastic Theology'* strikes a reasonable balance. As Calvin was extremely critical of scholasticism, it would be inappropriate to call him a scholastic.

---

[84] Brian Armstrong, *Calvinism and the Amyraut Heresy* (The University of Wisconsin Press, 1969), 32.

[85] Richard Muller, *The Unaccommodated Calvin* (Oxford University Press, 2000), 42.

[86] A. Vos, "Scholasticism," Sinclair Ferguson, David Wright, J.I. Packer, editors, *New Dictionary of Theology* (Downers Grove: Inter Varsity Press, 1988), 621.

[87] Richard Muller, *The Unaccommodated Calvin*, 46-58. He states, "Calvin clearly tended to reserve his most angry and specified polemic for his French audience, for the sake of reminding them (if that was needed!) that the faculty of the Sorbonne was the chief theological barrier to the reform of Christianity in France." 57.

[88] David Steinmetz, "The Scholastic Calvin" in *Protestant Scholasticism*, 16-30.

LaVallee admits that Calvin was probably referring primarily to "late medieval nominalism prevalent in Paris during his student days.... Still, Calvin apparently did not make sharp distinctions among the Scholastics."[89] The vast majority of Calvin's references to the scholastics or sophists are derogatory with the reformer criticizing the theology, which he believed to be the result of the method. Since the only scholastic theologian mentioned consistently is Peter Lombard it makes sense to understand Calvin as referring to more than just the late medieval nominalists. After a thorough analysis of Calvin's references to the scholastics, LaVallee claims:

> The Scholastic as seen through Calvin's eyes is primarily interested in "speculative theology." His method is centered in the positing of subtle questions and the drawing of infinite distinctions. Theology becomes a disputatious art. Its keynote is speculation, which delves into things hidden and unknown, rather than holding strictly to the doctrine of Scripture. The Scholastic neglects the "practical" or "useful" aspects of doctrine.[90]

For Calvin the speculative nature of scholasticism creates new doctrines unwarranted by scripture. This too, is the primary accusation of Kendall and Hall. Muller correctly extrapolates scholastic tendencies from the reformers, but is he addressing the real problem?

It is probably inaccurate to speak of pure scholastics and pure humanists, but rather to speak of scholastic tendencies and degrees of the use of the scholastic method. Philip Melanchthon used the rhetorical skills of humanism as well as the elevation of the concept of *ad fontes*, but also used Aristotelian logic in order to attain clarity in argument. Calvin spoke out against the nominalists' tendency to elevate reason to equal or superior status with revelation, elitism, and speculation with no clear practical intent, but as Muller argues, these are not necessary qualities of scholasticism. If we accept the idea that scholasticism is a method rather than a theology (especially as we know there were scholastics from the eleventh century to the seventeenth century who held to widely differing theologies),[91] then we must evaluate the scholastic method as being a tendency rather than a tight scheme.

Muller argues that, "method and content need to be distinguished albeit not utterly separated."[92] Method does not determine results because the same method produces differing results in different theologians. Predestination

---

[89] Armand Aime LaVallee, *Calvin's Criticism of Scholastic Theology* (unpublished Ph.D. thesis, Harvard University, 1967), 237.

[90] Ibid., 221.

[91] Even the implication that scholasticism demands a use of Aristotelian logic might be incorrect because the earlier scholastics such as Anselm were not dependent on Aristotle, though Anselm was never attacked by Calvin or the other early reformers.

[92] Richard Muller, *After Calvin*, 81.

cannot be inherent in scholasticism[93] because the scholastics that Calvin challenged with specific vehemence were the nominalists such as Duns Scotus and Gabriel Biel, neither of whom held to an Augustinian view of predestination. It is also true that Jacob Arminius used the scholastic method even more thoroughly than the puritans yet his rejection of the Reformed understanding of election was total.

If scholasticism as a method does not necessitate adherence to any doctrine in particular, does it invoke tendencies that lead to unnecessary speculation? LaVallee says, "A good part of scholastic theology, for Calvin, is born out of vain curiosity, which leads to frivolous questions and dares to deal with things hidden and unknown."[94] This seems to be Calvin's view, but was he correct? It would appear that both the medieval scholastics and the Reformed scholastics might have had an unhealthy desire for speculation. Francis Turretin (1623-1687), a Reformed scholastic who was one of Calvin's successors in Geneva, argued for a theology that was both speculative and practical.[95] This is certainly in opposition to Calvin's desire for a completely practical theology. Did this speculative penchant lead to the espousal of any novel doctrines? In the case of definite atonement we have already seen how Helm inadvertently admits a change from Calvin to the more scholastic Beza. This issue later brought division in the Reformed church through Turretin's *Formula Consensus Helvetica*. The *Consensus* was used as a test to judge future pastors. Three areas were focused on in the *Consensus* because of the supposedly unsound teaching coming out of the School of Saumur: the extent of the atonement, the imputation of Adam's sin and the inspiration of the Hebrew vowel points. The early reformers saw none of these doctrines as valid reasons for division. Zwingli did not believe in the imputation of Adam's sin according to the view of Calvin and Luther and yet this issue, unlike that of eucharistic doctrine, did not bring separation.[96] The extent of the atonement was not made a potential doctrine of division until the Synod of Dort, but when Moise Amyraut suggested the idea of hypothetical universalism, his belief was renounced and silenced by the *Consensus*.

The supralapsarian debate would also qualify as a speculative question based on the essence of God, which also brought considerable division in the

---

[93] Contra Dewey Wallace Jr. who states: "In addition to the use of logic to achieve precise definition...great importance [is] given to predestination [in Reformed Scholasticism].... Predestination was becoming the central point of an airtight theological system." Dewey Wallace Jr., *Puritans and Predestination*, 60.

[94] LaVallee, 41.

[95] Francis Turretin, *Institutes of Elenctic Theology* (Phillipsburg, NJ: P and R Publishing, 1992), 1:20-2.

[96] Ulrich Zwingli, *On Providence and Other Essays* (Eugene, OR: Wipf and Stock Publishers, 1999), 5; G.W. Bromiley (ed), *Zwingli and Bullinger* (Philadelphia: Westminster Press, 1953), 52.

church.[97] Calvin consistently cautioned his readers about speculation concerning the divine essence. He warned:

> Here, indeed, if anywhere in the secret mysteries of Scripture, we ought to play the philosopher soberly and with great moderation; let us use great caution that neither our thoughts nor our speech go beyond the limits to which the Word of God itself extends. For how can the human mind measure off the measureless essence of God according to its own little measure, a mind as yet unable to establish for certain the nature of the sun's body, though men's eyes daily gaze upon it? Indeed, how can the mind by its own leading come to search out God's essence when it cannot even get to its own?.... Let it be remembered that men's minds, when they indulge their curiosity, enter into a labyrinth. And so let them yield themselves to be ruled by the heavenly oracles, even though they may fail to capture the height of the mystery.[98]

Another potential candidate is the order of faith and regeneration. Whereas Calvin taught that faith was logically prior to regeneration,[99] later scholastics argued that faith was a consequence of being born again. The charges of both doctrinal change and impractical diversions seem to be implicit in the thought of those whose methodology was overly scholastic. Though their doctrinal content was different, they seem to follow their medieval predecessors in devising speculative theology and then elevating these doctrines to the status of being fundamental to the faith and purity of the church.

But are Kendall, Hall and Armstrong asking the right questions? They seem to portray Calvin as embodying the ideas of a pristine age later distorted by scholasticism. A more accurate picture would be of the reformers as a group of pastor theologians who respected each other, dialogued through treatises and letters, and affirmed one another without necessarily agreeing on all aspects of theology, method or practice.[100] Ulrich Zwingli, Heinrich Bullinger, John Calvin, Theodore Beza, Peter Martyr Vermigli, John Knox and Martin Bucer should all be considered giants of their time, who collaborated with each other to advance a reformation of the church. Lesser lights such as Robert Rollock, Wolfgang Musculus, Andreas Hyperius and Amandus Polanus, who also added greatly to the cause, never regarded each other in any adversarial way. Muller's charge against the historiography of Armstrong, Hall and Kendall

---

[97] Alan Sell notes, "Dr. Strang, Principal of Glasgow College, had to relinquish his position because he veered (only) so far as infralapsarianism." *The Great Debate* (Grand Rapids: Baker Book, 1983), 33.

[98] John Calvin, *Institutes*, I. 13,21.

[99] John Calvin, *Commentary on the Gospel According to John*, 1:12. See also *Consensus Tigurinus* article 3 as well as most early reformers of the sixteenth century (i.e. Bucer, Bullinger, Ursinus, and the Belgic Confession).

[100] The exception to this was Martin Luther and his followers (with the possible exception of Philip Melanchthon) who were more zealous for the perpetuation of their own particulars than for the unity of the Protestant faith.

should be seriously considered:

> Calvin was not the sole arbiter of Reformed confessional identity in his own
> lifetime – and he ought not to be arbitrarily selected as the arbiter of what was
> Reformed in the generations following his death. Calvin himself recognized the
> need to balance his own particular theological views with those of his
> contemporaries in such confessional efforts as the *Consensus Tigurinus*, where the
> Eucharistic teaching was a compromise between Geneva and Zurich. Most of the
> major confessional documents of the Reformed churches produced in the mid-
> sixteenth century were conceived with a breadth of definition capable of including
> diverse individual theologies. Each of these individual theologies, moreover, left
> its mark on its time and on the writers of the early orthodox era, accounting for a
> series of trajectories of formulation, all within the boundaries set by the
> confessions. Given the diversity and the fact that the confessional boundaries
> were set by no single theologian, it is historically inaccurate to identify the later
> generations in a strict sense as "Calvinists" and it is quite useless to measure them
> against Calvin as if he were the standard of orthodoxy.[101]

The fact that the early reformers sought unity and were often willing to
compromise in order to preserve that unity, that they wrote confessions which
were broad enough to include a variety of thought without compromising a core
set of values and doctrines, and they refused to consider any one person as the
head of the Reformed movement, necessitates a reevaluation of the very
questions Armstrong, Hall and Kendall have asked. Reassessment becomes
essential when one considers the concept of "a central dogma."

Armstrong, Hall and Kendall borrowed the concept of a central dogma in
Calvin and Reformed orthodoxy from the "nineteenth-century dogmatic
approach that discussed the history of Reformed theology in terms of the
development of predestination as a central dogma."[102] But did any of the
reformers see a basic principle upon which their entire system was built? For
those who had been influenced by the thought of Karl Barth, it became popular
to argue that Calvin was a basically Christocentric theologian whereas his
successors saw predestination as the center of all dogmatic thought. But a
perusal of the way in which both Calvin and his successors ordered their
thought militates against the idea that any of them had a "central" dogma.
Calvin, Vermigli, Bucer and "virtually all of the theological systems of the
sixteenth and seventeenth centuries"[103] embraced the locus method of
arrangement. Muller explains:

> The place-logic of Agricola and Melanchthon emphasized the examination of the
> text of a document in order to identify the topics or central issues presented there.
> This approach led directly to a pattern of biblical interpretation and theological

---

[101] Richard Muller, *After Calvin*, 8.
[102] Ibid., 63.
[103] Ibid., 94-95.

formulation that related the exegesis of the text of Scripture to the task of eliciting *loci communes*, "standard topics" or "places," from Scripture and then using these topics as the core of theology.[104]

The *loci communes* or *theologiae* would usually begin with the doctrine of Scripture and then proceed to the doctrines of God, Christ, salvation, the church and last things. These topics could be varied in order but there was no one doctrine that could be considered the *principia theologiae*. Instead of thinking of central dogmas, one should consider emphases within the theological works as well as styles of writing. Predestination was important to Beza and Perkins, but it was also very important to Calvin. The doctrine of the Kingdom of God had a central place in Bucer and the covenant was key to Bullinger, but this does not mean it was the central dogma of all the rest of their thought and the organizing point of their entire theology.

Styles of writing were different among the reformers. As has been argued above, the use of the scholastic method was a matter of degree rather than a test that the method's adherent was exclusively either a scholastic or a humanist. Calvin and Bucer's styles were more readable than Vermigli, owing to the humanist influence on them, but Bucer was also accused of being verbose,[105] which may not have accommodated a more academic setting where the maximum amount of information in the fewest words seemed to be the goal of the scholastic.[106] The scholastic method had already proven to be effective in *disputatio* as seen in Aquinas and others and so was put to use in the academic setting. Even the more scholastic writers could write in a popular style when the occasion demanded. Donald Sinnema notes the distinction of scholastic and popular interpretations made by Hyperius as early as 1546, where Hyperius described the different settings for using a scholastic or popular style:

> No one is unaware that two ways of interpreting the Scriptures are used in the churches, the one scholastic (*scholasticam*), the other popular (*popularem*). The former is appropriate in the assemblies of learned men and young students who have advanced to some extent in scholarship; the latter is provided entirely to instruct the common people, most of whom are ignorant, uneducated, and illiterate. The former is exercised within the narrow walls of the school; the latter takes place in spacious sanctuaries. The former is concise and compact, smelling of philosophical solitude and rigour; the latter is expanded, free in expression, and diffuse, and indeed delights in the light and forum, as it were, of oratory. In the former most things are examined by the standard of dialectical brevity and

---

[104] Ibid., 10.

[105] D.F. Wright (ed.), *Common Places of Martin Bucer* (Appleford, England: Sutton Courtenay Press, 1972), 18.

[106] Calvin's *Institutes* could be seen as a balance between humanism and scholasticism because of its organization and brevity (scholastic) and its rhetorical excellence, readability and resistance to speculation (humanistic); see Richard Gamble, "Brevitas et Facilitas: Toward an Understanding of Calvin's Hermeneutic," *Westminster Theological Journal*: 47 (1985), 1-17.

simplicity; in the latter rhetorical abundance and copiousness garner the most favour.[107]

Scholasticism was a method of doing theology in the schools; it was not advocated for use in the pulpit. Calvin's *Institutes* could probably be seen as a hybrid because of its readability, polemics, and relative brevity. Perkins' *A Golden Chaine* and *An Exposition of the Symbole or Creede of the Apostles* were far more scholastic in style than his *A Declaration of the True Manner of Knowing Christ Crucified*. There were differing styles among the reformers even within their own writings, but this does not argue for difference in content.

We have noticed the following: 1) The use of the scholastic method does not necessitate a divergence from Calvin, but its speculative tendency did bring about the potential for doctrinal change. 2) The idea of a central dogma is not obvious in sixteenth or seventeenth century Reformed writings. 3) Reformed orthodoxy was not synonymous or identical with the thought of Calvin alone because Calvin was not regarded as the chief reformer in his day. It would appear therefore, that the debate concerning Calvin versus the Calvinists needs to be nuanced. The arguments used by both sides are problematic. It would appear that Calvin did have reservations concerning the use of the scholastic method because of its tendency towards speculation, which seemed to bring unnecessary division to the Reformed churches. Perhaps an intermediate definition of scholasticism is necessary. Alister McGrath states:

> Scholasticism is best regarded as the medieval movement, flourishing in the period 1200-1500, which placed emphasis upon the rational justification of religious beliefs and the systematic presentation of those beliefs. Thus 'scholasticism' does not refer to a *specific system of beliefs*, but to a *particular way of organizing theology* – a highly developed method of presenting material, making fine distinctions, and attempting to achieve a comprehensive view of theology. It is perhaps understandable why to its humanist critics, scholasticism seemed to degenerate into little more than logical nitpicking.[108]

Borrowing from McGrath, we will define scholasticism as a particular way of organizing theology that focuses primarily on getting as much information to the mind as possible in as simple a manner as allowable (ratiocination, syllogism, distinctions), rather than seeking the transformation of the heart through rhetoric (persuasion, story); the faculty of the soul it is primarily

---

[107] Quoted by Donald Sinnema, "The Distinction Between Scholastic and Popular: Andreas Hyperius and Reformed Scholasticism," in Carl R. Trueman and R.S. Clark, ed., *Protestant Scholasticism*, 129.

[108] Alister McGrath, *Reformation Thought* (Oxford: Blackwell Publishers, 1999), 67. He later adds to this definition: "This, then, is the essence of scholasticism: the demonstration of the inherent rationality of Christian theology by an appeal to philosophy and the demonstration of the complete harmony of that theology by the minute examination of the relationship of its various elements." Ibid., 68.

engaged in is the understanding rather than the will or affections.

How does this affect the Restoration puritans? The puritans attempted to use the scholastic method but with a practical intent. They spoke out against speculation as much as Calvin and insisted on a practical theology. But it appears that the more scholastic one was, the less room was allowed for diversity within one's ranks. Also, as scholasticism appealed to the mind – it was a method for the schools – it had a tendency to neglect the heart. This did not mean that scholastic theologians neglected the heart in all their writings or in their personal lives, but they did foster a sense which, given time, created an imbalance between mind and heart. The two versions of Calvinism noted in our sketch of puritanism exemplify these two propensities. Charnock was a moderate Calvinist who repudiated speculation and disunity. He maintained a balance of mind and heart by curtailing his use of the scholastic method. Two groups helped incline Charnock toward humanism along with a disinclination toward scholasticism – the Cambridge Platonists and the School of Saumur.

## b. The Cambridge Platonists

The next major influence in Charnock's life and restoration puritanism in general was a loosely associated group known as the Cambridge Platonists. Included in this group are Benjamin Whichcote (1609-1683), Nathaniel Culverwell (1619-1651), Henry More (1614-1687), Ralph Cudworth (1617-1689), John Smith (1618-1652) and Peter Sterry (1613-1672). These men grew up under puritan influence though they had to varying degrees diverged from this tradition. Apart from More, who was a fellow at Christ's College, they were all associated with Emmanuel College. Although, as its critics, they "contributed to the decline of Calvinism,"[109] they helped shape the thought and focus of moderate puritanism. To understand the Cambridge Platonists and how they helped shape restoration puritanism we will need to examine four areas: 1) a more detailed history of the time, 2) their particular theology and philosophy, 3) their influence on the Latitudinarians, and 4) how they may have helped birth the particular subgroup of restoration moderate puritans known as the latitudinarian Calvinists,[110] which we will call latitude puritans.

How could English puritanism move from dominance to near obscurity in a span of twenty years? Puritanism seemed to thrive best when political controversy was not in the ascendancy. There are two opposing views as to the influence of puritanism in England in the seventeenth century. G.R. Cragg speaks of the "eclipse of Calvinism" arguing that puritanism slipped into insignificance after the regicide debacle. "Seldom has a reversal of fortune been so complete. Within fifty years Calvinism in England fell from a position

---

[109] G.R. Cragg, *From Puritanism to the Age of Reason* (Cambridge University Press, 1966), 38-39.

[110] Dewey Wallace Jr., "Natural Theology Among the Dissenters: Richard Baxter and His Circle," 4-5.

of immense authority to obscurity and insignificance."[111]   By contrast Harry Grant Plum is more positive in his assessment of puritan vitality after the restoration.  Describing the same events as Cragg, he portrays the puritans as crucial in filling the pastoral needs created by the plague and London fire, as well as having a major impact on bringing unity among the Protestants in England, a movement which eventually led to the Toleration Act of 1689.  He depicts the beneficial affect of persecution on the English puritans: "Long suffering had purged much of the dross of the earlier authoritative Puritanism from the body, had given more emphasis to its spiritual growth, and had brought closer unity among the Protestant sects."[112]   Dewey Wallace takes an intermediary position stating: "To state the fact of Calvinism's decline in this period is accurate up to a point, but a further question must be asked: for whom did it decline?"[113]   To see which perspective is more accurate or whether some nuance to these views needs to be made, we will have to examine the events immediately before and after the restoration of Charles II.  This will also reveal possible insights into the formation of thought and attitude in the Cambridge Platonists as well as in Charnock.

During the Great Rebellion of the 1640s and 1650s puritanism may have appeared to be a monolithic and insurmountable force, but that was not the case.  J. Wayne Baker points out that the Westminster divines who were supremely representative of the puritan cause, were divided into three groups: Erastians, Presbyterians and Congregationalists.  Parliament was largely made up of two groups: Presbyterians and Independents, with the Presbyterians being the clear majority.  Three issues at stake were: "First, how the church should be governed;  second, the relationship between church and state;  and third, toleration."[114]   The Erastians were in favor of "the Christian government" wielding "complete authority over all matters in this Christian society, including ecclesiastical matters" and were opposed to any form of toleration given to dissenters; this was the view of the Church of England from its inception by Henry VIII.[115]   The Presbyterians, who were the majority of both parliament and the puritan divines, sought a Presbyterianism where the magistrate had no power over the church, but should only punish those the church deems as heretics and worthy of punishment.  They were apprehensive of toleration toward dissenters because they held to the idea of a corporate Christian society where there could only be one true religion.   After the restoration the Presbyterians would become more inclined to toleration or at least a more comprehensive church that embraced most dissenters, excluding Catholics, but not at this point.  The Congregationalists along with most of the

---

[111] G.R. Cragg, *From Puritanism to the Age of Reason*, 30.

[112] Harry Grant Plum, *Restoration Puritanism*, 62.

[113] Dewey Wallace, Jr., *Puritans and Predestination* (The University of North Carolina Press, 1982), 158.

[114] J. Wayne Baker, "Church, State, and Toleration: John Locke and Calvin's Heirs in England, 1644-1689" in *Later Calvinism* edited by W. Fred Graham, 526.

[115] Ibid., 527.

independents in parliament advocated a "popular church government, with discipline imposed by a local congregation free from every type of governmental dictation."[116] They also asked for toleration for "those who felt the need to separate from the national church."[117] Here we see three schools of thought very different from each other within English puritanism.

Most of the puritans were in favour of the Civil War, but few advocated the execution of the king. When it appeared that parliament was going to side with the Scots and bring back Charles I, Oliver Cromwell, leader of the army, stepped in. Cromwell, like most of the army, was an Independent. The Independents did not want a Presbyterian church, which would have been just as intolerant as the previous church, which became a contributing factor to Cromwell's paring down of parliament. This rump parliament had the king beheaded January 30, 1649. The Presbyterians were appalled by the idea of regicide, as was the rest of the world. Henry Sheldon describes the sentiment:

> The execution of Charles I was an event at which but few rejoiced. The groan of anguish and terror which greeted the stroke of the headsman found an echo in all Christian lands. Continental Europe was substantially unanimous in expressions of abhorrence. Among the foremost in this respect were the Protestant countries....In Germany, Denmark, Sweden, and Holland, emphatic denunciations were poured forth against the impiety and sacrilege of the regicides.[118]

The killing of the king went against the Presbyterians' more conservative viewpoint and they felt it could not be supported by scripture.

After Cromwell's death, the Presbyterians pushed for making Charles I's brother king. They were even open to an Episcopal church government just so long as they were not forced to use the Prayer Book. A new parliament made up of restored Anglicans reinstated Charles II as king. Charles II was at first conciliatory toward the Presbyterians but the Anglicans were not, with the Clarendon Acts as the result. "Even moderate Calvinism was swept away in the reaction against everything that the Interregnum stood for."[119]

The moderate puritans found themselves a persecuted minority and so began to advocate a more comprehensive church. Their working more closely with the other dissenters who espoused toleration certainly had its impact, but there were other sources for this reversal in thought. Early in the English reformation during Elizabeth's reign Cambridge became a hotbed of puritanism. Emmanuel College in particular was known for its puritan ethos from its inception. In the 1640s, Emmanuel College, the citadel of puritanism, birthed a group of original thinkers, an alternative to the dogmatic puritans and

---

[116] Ibid., 529.

[117] Ibid., 530.

[118] Henry Sheldon, *History of the Christian Church* (New York: Hendrickson Publishers, 1988), 3:523.

[119] G.R. Cragg, *From Puritanism to the Age of Reason*, 31.

rationalist Laudians – the Cambridge Platonists. Armed with Plato and other early philosophers they elevated reason as the *candle of the Lord*, while holding to a "broader and simpler"[120] form of Christianity. It is not entirely exact to refer to the Cambridge Platonists as Platonists. They had obviously read Plato's dialogues and were indebted to him in a general sense concerning "the role of ideas, the nature of the soul, the place of reason, [and] the eternity of moral concepts,"[121] but were free to diverge from Plato for instance in believing the Christian's participation in the divine nature was exclusively the gift of Christ.[122] They were among the first to read Descartes in England, but did not fully endorse his rationalist philosophy and were adamantly opposed to Hobbes' materialism.[123] Most of them repudiated the Reformed view of predestination and opted for a less scholastic theology that would combat what they considered the real enemy, atheism. Henry More stated, "And this is the true and genuine meaning of my interweaving of Platonisme and Cartesianisme so frequently as I do into these writings, I making use of these hypotheses as invincible bulwarks against the most cunning and most mischievous efforts of atheism."[124] Above all they advocated tolerance for most Protestant Christianity.

Benjamin Whichcote is considered the founder of the group. He debated with Anthony Tuckney who had accused him of potentially advocating heresy. Their debate revealed a courteous, yet convinced Whichcote. Whichcote exemplified the mild, seasonable and irenic temper of the Cambridge Platonists that contrasted starkly with the explosive polemics of the day. Whichcote supported a tolerant religion. In a compilation of his sayings entitled *Aphorisms* he stated: "Religion is unity and love: therefore it is not religion that makes separation and disaffection."[125] Whichcote also argued for a simplified religion without a preoccupation with difficult to understand doctrines.[126] For Whichcote religion was primarily ethical.

---

[120] Ibid., 39.

[121] G.R. Cragg, editor, *The Cambridge Platonists* (New York: Oxford University Press, 1968), 14.

[122] P.H. DeVries states, "These men were called Platonists because of a general interest in the metaphysical perspectives of people from the Platonic tradition, from Plato to Plotinus. They were committed not so much to particular doctrines as to a general Platonistic perspective: a love of truth, a contempt for worldliness, and a concern for justice." P.H. DeVries, "Cambridge Platonists" in Walter Elwell (ed), *Evangelical Dictionary of Theology* (Grand Rapids: Baker Books, 1984), 189.

[123] G.R. Cragg, editor, *The Cambridge Platonists*, 15. Cragg says that Plato's debate with Pythagoras "first exposed the very issues which were involved in their own controversy with Hobbes."

[124] Henry More, *A Collection of Several Philosophical Writings of Dr. Henry More* (London: James Flesher, 1662), vi.

[125] Benjamin Whichcote, *Moral and Religious Aphorisms* (London: Printed for J. Payne, 1753), 50.

[126] G.R. Cragg, *From Puritanism to the Age of Reason*, 40.

Henry More was the most philosophical of the group but his rationalism was not sterile. He promoted Descartes at first, but then later became skeptical of his thought. He demonstrated the *Platonist* attitude of Cambridge Platonism in his tempered mysticism. Though the Cambridge Platonists elevated reason, they were adamantly opposed to a mere materialistic world. More was outspoken in his attack against Hobbes. Willie Weathers is not too far off the mark in saying: "The goal of the quest was for the Cambridge Platonists a mystical religious experience."[127]  Even in his discussion of reason he used experiential and mystical language:

> That there are two Temples of God: the one the universe, in which the First-Born of God, the *Divine Logos*, or eternal Wisedome, is High Priest; the other the Rational Soul, whose Priest is the true man, that is to say the Intellect, (as Plotinus somewhere speaks) and which is the Image of the Divine Logos, as Clemens has expressed himself.[128]

Nathaniel Culverwell reveals the place of reason for the Cambridge Platonist in his interpretation of Proverbs 20:27 where he expounded the *Candle of the Lord* as being human reason. This candle was seen as a gift from God that should not be slighted.[129]  He agreed that reason was not perfect, but that did not take away from its importance.[130]  The Cambridge Platonists saw the nature of humanity in a more positive light than the puritans and so were very optimistic about the use of reason. However, they still recognized the deficiency of reason because humans are "vulneratus in ipsis naturalibus."[131] Reason was not meant to be a substitute for revelation, but rather a counterpart. It is a "derivative light" from God, so that God "might communicate more of himself to them, then he could to other more drossie and inferiour beings, and that they might in a more compleat and circular manner *redire in principium suum.*"[132]  It is difficult to tell which light was subordinate to the other by the

---

[127] Willie Weathers, *Edward Taylor and the Cambridge Platonists* (EBSCO Publishing, 2003), 6.  He suggests that Edward Taylor became a better poet because of the mysticism influence of the Cambridge Platonists.

[128] Henry More, *A Collection of Several Philosophical Writings of Dr. Henry More*, v.

[129] Nathaniel Culverwell, *An Elegant and Learned Discourse of the Light of Nature* (University of Toronto Press, 1971), 13.  He speaks of how "*Reason* and *Faith* may kisse each other" and therefore should not be seen in opposition to one another.  Ibid.

[130] Ibid., 14.  He illustrates: "Well then, because the eye of *Reason* is weakened, and vitiated, will they therefore pluck it out immediately? And must *Leah* be hated upon no other account, but because she is blear-ey'd?  The whole head is wounded, and akes, and is there no other way but to cut if off?  *The Candle of the Lord* do's not shine so clearly as it was wont, must it therefore be extinguisht presently? Is it not better to enjoy the faint and languishing light of this *Candle of the Lord*, rather then to be in palpable and disconsolate darknesse?"

[131] Ibid., 108.  Wounded in his nature.

[132] Ibid., 79.  To return to their own first cause.

Cambridge Platonists, whether reason or revelation. Culverwell seems to keep reason as an inferior but necessary help to revelation,[133] but the other Cambridge Platonists are more equivocal.

In his *True Intellectual System of the Universe* Ralph Cudworth used reason to demonstrate the existence of God. He criticized Descartes' dualism, but agreed that reason reveals God. He also attacked the atheists' position by confronting their arguments against God's existence. He was very outspoken against the Calvinist notion of predestination, calling it both divine fatalism and a rather abstruse doctrine.[134] He sought a middle ground between the materialism of Hobbes and the mechanical understanding of the universe typified by the new science, with the Reformed understanding of the continual intervention of God in providence. Cudworth developed the idea of "plastic nature," the impersonal force God put into place to accomplish his purposes so that God would not have to constantly interfere with the regular operations of the universe. This did not mean God did not directly interact with the universe at times and so it was not a form of deism, but it was clearly a compromise between the new science and the old Reformed view of providence.[135]

Because the Cambridge Platonists were not partisan they were left undisturbed in their positions at the restoration. They clearly had an impact on both the latitudinarians as well as many of the moderate Calvinists. How were they different from the latitudinarians? The latitudinarians would continue to proclaim the need for toleration, emphasize reason and exalt morality, but something was missing.[136] Cragg describes this missing element thus: "You can transmit a certain kind of rationalism, but mysticism is a subtler and more elusive matter. Something of incalculable value had faded into the light of common day."[137] By reacting so forcefully to what they called enthusiasm they became bland. The latitudinarians seem to have neglected the affections and elevated reason as near infallible; they would not countenance the fact that reason was in any way incomplete, being at odds with Culverwell who admitted:

> This faint and languishing candle-light [reason] does not always prevaile upon the will, it doth not sufficiently warme and inflame the affections. Men do not use to warme their hands at a candle, tis not so victorious and over-powering as to

---

[133] Reason is "Lumen exile & diminutum." Ibid., 110.

[134] Gerald Cragg, editor, *The Cambridge Platonists*, 10.

[135] Ralph Cudworth, *An abridgment of Dr. Cudworth's True intellectual system of the universe. In which all the arguments for and against atheism are clearly stated and examined* (London: Printed for John Oswald, 1732), 51-109. Cragg stated, "He believed that he had found a means of preserving the essential message of the Bible and yet of reconciling it with the implications of the new science that was emerging in his day." Gerald Cragg, editor, *The Cambridge Platonists*, 235. Later we will see Charnock's attempts to reconcile the new science with the Bible.

[136] G.R. Cragg, *From Puritanism to the Age of Reason*, 63.

[137] Ibid., 63-64.

scatter all the works of darknesse. It will be night for all the candle; the Moralists were not only frigid in their devotions, but some of them were very dissolute in their practices. When you think upon these things, sure you'll willingly subscribe to the forementioned particular, which you may do very safely, that the spirit of a man tis but a Candle.[138]

The latitudinarians are important to study because they helped create a consensus where toleration would become a norm. J. Tillotson, Edward Stillingfleet, G. Burnet, Edward Fowler and Simon Patrick were untypical Anglicans in that they did not harbor resentment to the views of religionists different from themselves. Stillingfleet's *Irenicum* pleaded for a comprehensive Church of England that would encompass as many as possible. The idea of a comprehensive Church of England was endorsed by some of the puritans but not others.

In two important works Dewey Wallace describes two possible reasons for division among the puritans after the restoration.[139] First he makes a good case for the antinomian controversy during the period of 1640-1660 as playing a major role in the partition. We saw earlier a disagreement at this time over the ideas of tolerance and church government. A further division came with two different reactions from the Anglicans who fell from power during the commonwealth period. The disenfranchised Anglicans began to accuse the puritans of antinomianism because of their stance on predestination and grace. The Anglicans' two accusations were: 1) Predestination made God the author of evil, and 2) It led to moral laxity because morality did not effect one's salvation. There were two responses to this view. Some saw the accusation as proof that the Arminians believed in works righteousness and so they themselves moved closer to antinomianism. John Eaton was considered the father of English Antinomianism by his detractors, but his book *The Honey-Combe of Free Justification by Christ Alone* reveals that he simply spoke out against legalism, quoting Luther on almost every page.[140] John Saltmarsh also

---

[138] Nathaniel Culverwell, *An Elegant and Learned Discourse of the Light of Nature*, 110.

[139] *Puritans and Predestination*, passim and "Natural Theology Among Dissenters: Richard Baxter and His Circle," passim.

[140] His lengthy definition of justification places him in the center of Reformation thought concerning justification and reveals he was not antinomian: "Justification is, when we feeling what lost creatures we are in our owne selves, and in all our works and holy walkings by reason of our sins, and sighing up unto Christ for help, are by the power of Gods imputation, so cloathed with the wedding garment of Christs owne perfect righteousnesse, that of unjust we are made just before God: that is, all our sinnes are utterly abolished out of Gods sight, and we are made from all spot of sinne perfectly holy and righteous in the sight of God freely. And this is Gods pardon or forgivenesse (which few understand) great above mans, and glorious, and wonderfull, like God himselfe, Acts 13.38, 39, 40. the joyfull faith wherof sanctifieth us, and makes us to doe the duties of our vocations faithfully, and to walk to the glory of God in the spirituall

spoke out against legalism in salvation and questioned the idea of looking for assurance in outward change as dangerously close to "works righteousness."[141] Both Eaton and Saltmarsh and a number of others did go beyond other puritans in teaching that justification occurred prior to the exercise of faith, in order to make sure faith was not considered a work. Wallace argues that this was "theological innovation as a consequence of extreme predestinarianism."[142] Other puritans reacted to the accusation of antinomianism by distancing themselves from the antinomians. By the time of the restoration two groups became evident among puritans on this issue: the rigid Calvinists who leaned in the direction of antinomianism and who also tended to be Independents, and the moderate Calvinists who moved in the direction of moralism and for the most part consisted of the Presbyterian party. John Owen became the chief spokesman for rigid Calvinism and Richard Baxter for moderate Calvinism.

The second reason for division among the puritans was their desire to be included within the Church of England. The Congregationalists had no desire to be a part of the Church of England, but wanted complete toleration for all expressions of Christianity. The Presbyterians still hoped for comprehension and so moderated their Calvinism. They began to downplay the importance of predestination and spoke out against the scholastic quibbling over the order of the decrees. They were "not yet ready to turn away from the intellectual currents of the larger society. The moderation of their Calvinism kept them in contact with that wider world and also with the Anglican thinkers."[143] Their desire for comprehension kept them from distancing themselves from the Anglicans and therefore some influence from the Anglicans was the natural consequence, especially from the Cambridge Platonists. Charnock favorably cites the Cambridge Platonists throughout his works, particularly More and Culverwell. How did the Cambridge Platonists affect the moderate Calvinists?

Three areas can be seen where the Platonists helped shape the views of the moderate puritans. Firstly, their more positive application for the role of reason had an impact on the puritans. The moderate Calvinists would continue to hold to the doctrine of total depravity as expressed in the Westminster Confession:

By this sin they [Adam and Eve] fell from their original righteousness and communion with God, and so became dead in sin, and wholly defiled in all the faculties and parts of soul and body. They being the root of all mankind, the guilt of this sin was imputed, and the same death in sin and corrupted nature conveyed to all their posterity descending from them by ordinary generation.[144]

Some would begin to question whether the guilt of sin was imputed, but the

---

meaning of all Gods tenne Commandements zealously, Tit. 2.14." John Eaton, *Honey-Combe of Free Justification by Christ alone* (London: R.B., 1642), 7.

[141] Dewey Wallace, Jr., *Puritans and Predestination*, 118.

[142] Ibid.

[143] Ibid., 160.

[144] Philip Schaff, *Creeds of Christendom* (Grand Rapids: Baker Book, 1977), 3:615.

depravity of every faculty of the soul, including the mind, was upheld.[145] But even though they affirmed the depravity of the mind, the moderate Calvinists elevated reason.[146] Like Culverwell, Flavel called reason "the candle of the Lord" and viewed it as the leading faculty of the soul.[147] He declared:

> Reason exalts man above all earthly beings; it is his dignity and privilege, that God hath furnished him with abilities of mind, to recollect, animadvert, compare, infer, ponder, and judge his own actions…. For though there be some mysteries in religion above the sphere and flight of reason: yet nothing can be found in religion, that is unreasonable.[148]

Bates said, "Reason is the singular ornament of the human nature."[149] They were not afraid to appeal to the mind of the unbeliever using the general revelation of God they believed was available to all. This appeal to general revelation coincided with an ecumenical spirit. Bates wrote *The Christian Religion Proved by Reason* in the same fashion as Hugo Grotius' work *The Truth of the Christian Religion.* Grotius cannot be placed in the same camp as the moderate puritans because of his lack of emphasizing heart religion and his Arminian soteriology,[150] but Howe, Bates, Baxter and Charnock emulated him. Grotius gave the reason for his writing as "not to treat particularly of all the opinions in Christianity; but only to show that the Christian Religion itself is most true and certain."[151] Bates and Charnock both quoted Grotius approvingly expressing an irenic spirit toward those who sought to promote the Christian faith based on its reasonable nature.[152]

Secondly, the Platonists' understanding of toleration had an impact on the moderate puritans. Cragg notes the Cambridge Platonists "had for some years been teaching that blend of enlightened conviction and generous forbearance

---

[145] Thomas Watson, *A Body of Divinity* (Carlisle, PA: The Banner of Truth Trust, 1965), 142-153; *Puritan Sermons: 1659-1689*, 5:104-167; William Bates, *The Complete Works of William Bates* (Harrisonburg, VA: Sprinkle Publication, 1990), 1:207-212, 218-219; John Howe, *The Works of John Howe* (New York: John Haven and Son, 1857), 2:1202-1203.

[146] *Puritan Sermons: 1659-1689*, 5:65.

[147] John Flavel, *The Works of John Flavel*, 2:502-504.

[148] Ibid., 6:472.

[149] William Bates, *The Complete Works of William Bates*, 1:263.

[150] Some would put John Goodwin in the category of puritan even though he held to an Arminian soteriology, but in accord with our definition of puritan, which includes a Reformed understanding of predestination, we would consider Goodwin as one who maintained many puritan qualities without completely fitting the puritan mold.

[151] Hugo Grotius, *The Truth of the Christian Religion* (Edinburgh: Thomas Turnbull, 1819), 77.

[152] William Bates, *The Complete Works of William Bates*, 1:118; Stephen Charnock, *The Works of Stephen Charnock*, 1:287. Charnock cites Grotius 21 times in his works.

which was so characteristic of their outlook."[153] The Platonists' acceptance of a variety of opinions and their congenial approach to discussing differences had an impact on the moderate puritans. Tim Harris depicts the hopes of the moderates: "The presbyterians, who played a prominent part in bringing back Charles II, wanted a comprehensive church settlement with a modified form of episcopacy, but no toleration for those who chose to worship outside the established church."[154] The moderate puritans were perhaps not as tolerant as the Cambridge Platonists but they did seek a comprehension by downplaying the importance of certain doctrinal and ecclesiastical positions. They asked for a modified episcopacy and would not allow the Irish Presbyterians' resolution to denounce episcopacy to be introduced in court.[155] This toleration included calmness in debate, rather than vigorous contention. Howe represents the group when he stated:

> It will therefore not be besides our present purpose, but very pursuant to it, to consider awhile, not in the contentious way of brawling and captious disputation, (the noise whereof is as unsuitable to the temple, as that of axes and hammers,) but of calm and sober discourse.[156]

Thirdly, the Platonists' discarding of the scholastic speculation concerning the being of God was adopted by the moderate puritans. The moderate puritans moved away from the scholastic tendencies of conjecture and in humanist fashion sounded warnings against the dangers of speculation.[157] Anti-scholastic rhetoric comparable to that of Calvin was revived.[158] This does not mean that they rejected the Reformed understanding of predestination, but many of those seeking comprehension became willing to say predestination was not a fundamental article of the faith. Baxter went so far as to say the Creed, Lord's Prayer and Decalogue were alone the essentials or fundamentals and "contain all that is necessary to salvation."[159] Howe asked the question, "Whether for

---

[153] G.R. Cragg, *From Puritanism to the Age of Reason*, 191.

[154] Tim Harris, Paul Seaward, and Mark Goldie, *The Politics of Religion in Restoration England* (Oxford: Basil Blackwell, 1990), 9.

[155] G.R. Cragg, *From Puritanism to the Age of Reason*, 192.

[156] John Howe, *The Works of John Howe*, 1:9.

[157] Thomas Vincent said, "True wisdom does not consist in the invention of curious and quaint notions... but the chief wisdom lies in the right placing of affections." *The True Christian's Love to the Unseen Christ* (Morgan, PA: Soli Deo Gloria, 1993), 60.

[158] Latitude puritans would have agreed with the latitudinarian Stillingfleet: "Religion hath been so much rarefied into airy notions and speculations, by the distempered heat of men's spirits, that its inward strength, and the vitals of it, have been much abated and consumed by it." Edward Stillingfleet, *Irenicum* (Philadelphia: M. Sorin, 1842), vii.

[159] Richard Baxter, *The Autobiography of Richard Baxter being the Reliquiae Baxterianae Abridged from the Folio 1696* (Mobile, AL: R.E. Publications, n.d.), 139. Howe quotes Bishop Davenant in agreement: "He that believes the things contained in the apostle's creed, and endeavours to live a life agreeable to the precepts of Christ,

any party of Christians to make unto itself other limits of communion than Christ hath made, and hedge up itself within those limits, excluding those whom Christ would admit, and admitting those whom he would exclude, be not in itself a real sin?"[160]

Within the moderate expression of restoration puritanism there appears to be a subgroup loosely called Baxterians, latitudinarian Calvinists, or simply latitude puritans who seem to take the three categories noted above to a heightened level. Reason was not seen as untainted by the *lapsus*, but this group used it extensively in proving God's existence, entertaining aspects of the new science and even enjoying God. The latitude puritans were at the forefront of attempts to bring about a more comprehensive Church of England. Finally their doctrine of the decrees was downplayed and the doctrine of limited atonement discarded.

Where does Charnock fit in this picture? Though he does not appear to have had an excessive amount of contact with Baxter, Howe, Calamy and Bates, he did attend church with Howe and Manton. He certainly had much in common with their idiosyncrasies with some slight differences. He was not afraid to speak of reason as long as it was understood to be a servant of revelation rather than master. He, like Bates, Howe and Baxter, wrote extensively on the existence of God as well as the attributes of God. He quoted the Cambridge Platonists positively as well as the latitudinarians. By studying Charnock's doctrine of the knowledge of God we will see how far this small group of puritans agreed.

*c. The School of Saumur*

If number of citations are any indication it would appear the School of Saumur in France made the largest impression on Charnock next to puritanism. In his *Works* he cited Moise Amyraut 130 times and Jean Daille 79 times. The next largest number of citations of anyone not affiliated with the School of Saumur was the Roman Catholic Francisco Suarez with 44 and Johannes Cocceius 33 times. From the School of Saumur and those affiliated with it he referred to Amyraut, Daille, Louis Cappel, Jean Mestrezat, John Cameron, Paul Testard, Michel Le Faucheur, Josue de Place (Placeus) and the *Theses Salmuriensis* a total of 254 times. It is clear from Baxter's correspondence that the School of Saumur faculty also enamored him.[161]    After the ejection

---

ought not to be expunged from the roll of Christians, nor be driven from communion with the other members of any church whatsoever." John Howe, *The Works of John Howe*, 1:476.

[160] John Howe, *The Works of John Howe*, 1:457.

[161] While approving John Davenant and Amyraut he states: "It is the mere love of truth that makes me value both the doctrine and the men." N.H. Keeble and Geoffrey Nuttall, *Calendar of the Correspondence of Richard Baxter* (Oxford: Clarendon Press, 1991), 1:118. See also 1:53 Baxter visited the School of Saumur 1:385 and recommends Philippe du Plessis-Mornay, John Cameron, Jean Daille among others 1:104, 113, 216.

Charnock visited France for an extended period and brought back the French reformers' books as well as their ideas. First we will look at how the French school came to its unique situation, then we will see its contributions to the reformation and finally the ideas that influenced the latitude puritans in general and Charnock in particular.

The French reformation modestly began through the work of the French humanists Guillaume Briconnet, Jacques Lefevre d'Etaples and Marguerite d'Angouleme known as the Meaux circle who sought to reform the French church from within. It is probably not appropriate to see these figures as Protestant reformers but they did pave the way with their calls for reform, biblical scholarship and vernacular translations of the Bible. Like Erasmus these "pre-reformers were clearly not proto-Protestants."[162] The Meaux circle most likely would not have been harassed except for the timing. The faculty of the Sorbonne, one of the most elite Roman Catholic schools in Europe, censured and condemned Luther's writings in 1521 and accused Briconnet and Lefevre of being Lutherans. This group would eventually forcibly be dissolved but the French King Francis I came to their rescue.

Francis I strongly advocated humanist scholarship even inviting Erasmus to come and head the College de France. He forbade the doctors of Sorbonne from adding Erasmus and Lefevre's books to the index of heretical works. This seems strange since he also opposed Protestantism. The king of France took an oath at his coronation to expel heretics. He was consecrated with sacred oil by the archbishop and partook of the Eucharist in both kinds. This special ceremony was unique to heads of state in Europe; Holt explains:

> For French kings as well as their subjects the anointing with the sanctified oil of the holy ampulla, the explicit promise to defend the church from heresy, and the public display of the celebration of mass in both kinds were all signifiers full of meaning, as well as evidence that in France there was a special relationship between church and state that was not duplicated elsewhere.[163]

This special relationship would produce a very different situation for reform in France than in Switzerland. The king's support of humanism shows there was a difference between humanist reform and Protestant reform, but the lines were not as clearly drawn as one might think. Many like Guillaume Farel were also imbibing in the various Lutheran writings smuggled into France. Others in the Meaux circle were in correspondence with Zwingli and Oecolampadius.[164]

By 1551 there were two clandestine groups of Protestants in Lyon meeting in informal Bible studies and singing Psalms in the streets while attending the Catholic church.[165] In 1555 Calvin encouraged them to organize into churches

---

[162] Mack Holt, *The French Wars of Religion, 1562-1629* (Cambridge University Press, 1995), 15.
[163] Ibid., 9.
[164] Philip Benedict, *Christ's Churches Purely Reformed*, 130.
[165] Ibid., 133.

and by 1567 Geneva had sent 120 pastors into France to organize churches.[166]
Between 1555 and 1565 explosive growth took place to a large extent owing to
the help of Geneva. Holt states that Calvin's *Institutes* "became, after the Bible
itself, the single most important influence on French Protestantism."[167] With
the help of Calvin's missionaries, correspondence, *Institutes*, and organizational
skills as well as Beza's many visits to France the first national synod of the
Reformed church in France met in Paris in 1559.[168] This synod adopted the
French Reformed Confession of faith, which was basically drafted by Calvin in
Geneva. Mark Greengrass estimates that by 1565 there were slightly fewer
than two million Protestants in France known as Huguenots, which was about
ten percent of the total population.[169] Mack Holt makes the case for religious
conviction being responsible for the growth and that ensuing French civil wars
were fought primarily over religion. Politicization and socio-economic
tensions certainly played significant roles, but "religion was nevertheless the
fulcrum upon which the civil wars balanced."[170]

Calvin himself was a native who fled France after his involvement in the
Cop address of November 1, 1533. Francis I stepped up his persecution of
heretics after the placard affair where a zealous Protestant placed tracts all over
Paris in the early hours of October 18, 1534. These sheets attacked the mass,
one of which was supposedly found on the door of the king's bedchamber.[171]
In 1536 Calvin dedicated his first edition of the *Institutes* to Francis I in the
hope of stemming the tide of persecution and perhaps persuade Francis toward
Protestantism. He stated in his dedicatory to the king:

> For this reason, most invincible King, I not unjustly ask you to undertake a full
> inquiry into this case, which until now has been handled with no order of law and
> with violent heat rather than judicial gravity…. I embrace the common cause of
> all believers, that of Christ himself – a cause completely torn and trampled in your
> realm today, lying, as it were, utterly forlorn, more through the tyranny of certain
> Pharisees than with your approval.[172]

There is no evidence that Francis was influenced at all by this work, but his
persecution was neither consistent nor effective. His son, Henry II, continued
the persecution using his *chambre ardente* but did not slow the growth of
churches which reached somewhere between 1200 and 2500 churches by 1562.

---

[166] Carter Lindberg, *The European Reformations* (Oxford: Blackwell, 1996), 282.

[167] Mack Holt, *The French Wars of Religion*, 23.

[168] Carter Lindberg, *The European Reformations*, 282.

[169] Mark Greengrass, *The French Reformation* (Oxford: Basil Blackwell, 1987), 43.

[170] Mack Holt, *The French Wars of Religion*, 1-2. Greengrass agrees revealing that
trying to find a materialistic explanations for the explosion of growth fails to describe
the situation. Mark Greengrass, *The French Reformation*, 59-60.

[171] Mack Holt, *The French Wars of Religion*, 19.

[172] John Calvin, *Institutes of the Christian Religion 1536 Edition* (Grand Rapids:
Eerdmans, 1986), 2.

By 1562 Henry II had died, his 15 year old son Francis II had died and his younger son Charles IX became king with his mother Catherine de Medici acting as regent. At this time the French Protestants had become well organized both politically and religiously and began to take advantage of a struggle at the court between the Guises and the Bourbons. Earle Cairns notes, "The Huguenots became so powerful and so well organized that they formed a kingdom within a kingdom."[173] They demanded the "dismantling of machinery of repression against heresy, the right to worship in their churches openly, and the summoning of a 'holy and free' council to reform the church to which they would send deputies on an equal footing with the catholics."[174] Catherine de Medici granted them toleration under the Edict of Saint-Germain. At this time few if any wanted a religiously divided kingdom and so it was inevitable that the toleration would not be tolerated. From 1562 to 1629 a series of civil wars and edicts of toleration ensued.

The civil wars impacted the French Protestants greatly. It appears that evangelism was replaced by iconoclasm; Greengrass reflects, "These were the years of the protestant church militant."[175] These aggressive tactics would backfire, seriously debilitating the movement. Greengrass notes, "As protestants attacked catholic rituals, pulled down images, stained-glass, relics and otherwise offended or ridiculed objects of catholic veneration, they forcefully provoked the considerable, popular reserves of strength in local, often lay, catholicism."[176] Tensions were rising just before the fourth civil war. The Catholics were not happy about the marriage between Catholic Marguerite de Valois and the Protestant Henry of Navarre August 18, 1572. "Parisian preachers immediately informed their Catholic parishioners that 'God would surely be avenged for the impiety of this perverse union.'"[177] While the political leaders were plotting the destruction of the Protestants, the common people were also being prepared. On August 22 the Guises[178] attempted the assassination of Gaspard de Coligny, the leader of the French Protestants. Catherine recognized the possible outcome of this botched assassination and so coordinated the murder of several Huguenot leaders on August 24, St. Bartholomew's Day. Owing to the unrest of the people over the wedding and the tumult of the murder of the Huguenot leaders "a wave of popular violence was unleashed throughout the capital."[179] 3000 to 6000 were killed in Paris and the pandemonium spread throughout France. Within a month estimates

---

[173] Earle Cairns, *Christianity Through the Centuries* (Grand Rapids: Zondervan, 1981), 316.

[174] Mark Greengrass, *The French Reformation*, 65.

[175] Ibid.

[176] Ibid., 77.

[177] Mack Holt, *The French Wars of Religion*, 81.

[178] Some have suggested that Catherine de Medici was the principal villain but Holt shows that more likely candidates were the Guises. Ibid., 83.

[179] Ibid., 85.

between 11,000 and 20,000 were killed including men, women and children.[180]

The Saint Bartholomew's Day massacre seriously hurt the Protestant movement in France.[181] With many abjuring, others fleeing to America and the death toll itself the numbers of French Protestants never again reached the 1662 mark.[182] The tragedy of the massacre and the civil wars impaired the Protestant movement, but it may have led to some more positive results as well. First, a unity among Protestants was encouraged similar to the original reformation, where differences of opinion on minor issues were tolerated for the sake of unity under the threat of a common enemy.[183] This unity begun in the midst of persecution was played out later at the School of Saumur. Second, the atrocities would eventually lead to sympathy and openness toward peaceful dialogue. Holt observes, "The Huguenots were no longer perceived as the demons and pollutants of Catholic culture they had once been."[184] The religious wars in France and Germany led many to abandon religious contention, but others embraced discourse if done affably; this also would become a trademark of Saumurian practice. Finally, seeing the failure of the military approach to bringing France to Protestantism, seventeenth century French reformers would engage in apologetics.

In 1593 the Huguenot Henry of Navarre became king of France. Henry converted to Catholicism, supposedly making the statement, "Paris is worth a mass," though it is disputed as to whether he actually said this or not.[185] Whether his abjuration was sincere or he was simply acting as a politique, he would change the course of French Protestantism. In 1598 after personally overseeing its composition and actual wording, he passed the Edict of Nantes.[186] Holt suggests that this was only a temporary measure used for political reasons to strengthen the monarchy,[187] but as Gerson points out this would weaken the monarchy, which is why Queen Elizabeth sent a special

---

[180] Greengrass states 11,000 total and Lindberg 20,000. Samuel Stiles claimed the Roman Catholic bishop Perefixe said 100,000 were destroyed, but this is probably high. Greengrass, 78; Lindberg, 292; Samuel Stiles, *Huguenots in England and Ireland* (London: John Murray, 1876), 61.

[181] It is interesting to note that Peter Ramus was killed in the Saint Bartholomew's Day massacre, which may have helped his popularity considerably among the puritans.

[182] Mack Holt, *The French Wars of Religion*, 95. Holt states, "The massacres not only put a permanent end to the growth of the Reformed faith in France; they brought about an immediate and catastrophic decline in the numbers, strength, and zeal of the Protestant movement."

[183] Benedict notes, "The proliferation of independently established churches across a broad kingdom in the face of governmental persecution suggested to those involved that they needed to cooperate with one another to maintain unity of doctrine and discipline." Philip Benedict, *Christ's Churches Purely Reformed*, 135.

[184] Mack Holt, *The French Wars of Religion*, 188.

[185] Ibid., 153.

[186] Noel Gerson, *The Edict of Nantes* (New York: Grossett and Dunlap, 1969), 16.

[187] Mack Holt, *The French Wars of Religion*, 153, 163.

messenger to register her "vehement protest."[188]  It does not appear that the strength of the monarchy was his primary objective in passing the Edict of Nantes.  Henry was a practical politician and he saw that civil war was damaging his country as well as the peasant uprisings in protest of the war,[189] but it is possible that he also still had a heart for the Huguenots.  Under the edict, Huguenots were allowed to worship in the towns they controlled as well as hold both provincial and national synods.  They were provided an annual subsidy to pay their ministers and they were allowed troops paid by the crown to protect the 200 towns they controlled.  Henry IV was assassinated in 1610 and the civil wars continued until 1629 where the Protestants were soundly defeated, but they were tolerated.  A relative peace was maintained until the revocation of the Edict of Nantes by Louis XIV in 1685.  It was during this time of peace that the School of Saumur thrived.

The School of Saumur was founded in 1598 by Philippe Du Plessis-Mornay and remained the most important Protestant school in France until its closing by royal edict in 1685.  The school maintained a humanist milieu rather than scholastic from its beginning perhaps owing to the French reformation's origin stemming from the French humanists Briconnet and Lefevre d'Etaples.[190]  In Switzerland and Germany Reformed orthodoxy moved toward scholasticism after Protestantism secured the areas, but Protestants in France never went in that direction perhaps because it was always under the threat of attack and never gained a "favored" status in France.[191]  In the seventeenth century

---

[188] Noel Gerson, *The Edict of Nantes*, 13.

[189] The poor took the brunt of the hardship caused by the war.  Gerson remarks, "The slaughter had been endless.  Every poor family mourned the loss of a husband, a son or a brother.  Men who had been maimed or injured in battle could be found in every town, village and rural district.  The poor were heartily sick of the conflict and yearned for permanent peace." Ibid., 16.  Holt quotes a handbill circulating at the time revealing the plight of the poor: "The poor farmers, who time after time have suffered from the quartering of the soldiery upon them by one side or the other, have been reduced to famine.  Their wives and daughters have been raped and their livestock stolen.  They have had to leave their lands untilled and die of starvation, while numbers of them languish in prison for failure to meet the enormous *tailles* and subsidies both parties have levied upon them." Mack Holt, *The French Wars of Religion*, 156.

[190] Jean-Claude Margolin comment on sixteenth century French humanism, "What was common to all humanists during this period was their aversion to scholastic theology, to its stronghold at the Sorbonne," was probably equally as true for the French reformers. *Humanism in Europe at the Time of the Renaissance* (Durham, NC: The Labyrinth Press, 1989), 25.

[191] Armstrong states: "This study has failed to provide any definitive answers as to why the French Calvinists remained attached to the humanist spirit while the rest of continental Calvinism slowly reverted to a religious expression more closely resembling medieval scholastic thought than the thought of the early reformers.  Yet such seems to be the case." *Calvinism and the Amyraut Heresy*, 15.  It is possible that they never embraced scholasticism because they never gained control of France and with the persecution up to 1629 their focus always remained more practical.

scholasticism began to be replaced with rationalism, largely through the influences of Cartesianism, historical criticism and scientific advances, all "lending new power to the claims of reason."[192]   Like Calvin, the Saumur theologians were also pastors and so practical concerns were always at the forefront of their thought.  The professors and graduates helped form a unique brand of Reformed Protestantism influencing Charnock and the latitude puritans.

John Cameron (1579-1625) took over the chair of theology at Saumur succeeding Franciscus Gomarus in 1618 and held that position for three years. In this short space of time he put an indelible mark on the school that would increase in his successors, especially Amyraut, Cappel and de la Place.  His major influences were his humanist tendencies, faculty psychology, threefold covenant and hypothetical universalism.

Armstrong discloses the humanist sway on Cameron.[193]  It is inappropriate to categorize people in the seventeenth century as though they were completely scholastic or humanist as if each emphasis was in opposition to the other.[194] Cameron and others at Saumur used Aristotle and syllogisms at times and favored Ramism, which, though it was a reaction to Aristotelian logic, borrowed some of the concepts of scholasticism.  Muller correctly points out the similarities of Ramist bifurcation and use of loci to the "Protestant scholastic enterprise."[195]   But there was a difference between Ramism and scholasticism.  Ramus valued logic[196] but rejected what he saw in scholasticism as being impractical and too technical for "ordinary people."[197]  Cameron was probably influenced toward humanism and Ramism by his teachers at Glasgow and continued in this direction through his friendship and correspondence with the "renowned humanist scholar, Isaac Casaubon."[198]   French Protestant humanism may have been what drew him to France.  Cameron's humanism can be seen in his placing "careful biblical exegesis before system-building."[199] This humanism would permanently affect the School of Saumur and through its influence would also compliment Charnock and the latitude puritans.[200]

Cameron's originality is seen in his threefold covenant scheme.  Whereas

---

[192] Philip Benedict, *Christ's Churches Purely Reformed*, 337.

[193] Brian Armstrong, *Calvinism and the Amyraut Heresy*, 44-46.

[194] Paul Kristeller, *Renaissance Thought* (Harper Torchbooks, 1961), 116-117.

[195] Richard Muller, *After Calvin*, 75.  Herschel Baker accuses Ramism of being "a dramatic example the Renaissance compulsion to pour old wine into new casks." *The Wars of Truth*, 99.

[196] Peter Ramus, *The Art of Logick* (London: I.D., 1626), passim.  He defines logic as "an art of reasoning well." 1.

[197] Walter Ong, *Ramus: Method and the Decay of Dialogue* (Harvard University Press, 1983), 53-54.

[198] G. Michael Thomas, *The Extent of the Atonement*, 162.

[199] L.W.B. Brockliss, 'Cameron, John (1579/80-1625)', *Oxford Dictionary of National Biography*, 5.

[200] Brian Armstrong, *Calvin and the Amyraut Heresy*, 121-127.

most Protestant reformers embraced the twofold covenant of nature and grace, seeing two parts to the covenant of grace under the old and new testaments, he separated them because passages like Jeremiah 31:31 and Luke 22:20 called them old and new covenants.   He stated, "Wee say therefore there is a Covenant of Nature, another Covenant of Grace, and another Subservient to the Covenant of Grace; (which is called in Scripture, the Old Covenant) and therefore wee will deale with that in the last place; giving the first place to the Covenant of Nature, and of Grace; because they are the chief."[201]  He separated and subordinated the old covenant probably to counteract the legalism he saw in Reformed orthodoxy.[202]   The *foedus naturale* declares God's justice and demands complete righteousness.   The *foedus gratiae* declares God's mercy and requires faith.   The *subservient* covenant or old covenant is the covenant God made with Israel to obey the moral, ceremonial and judicial law with temporal blessings and curses attached to it to lead them to the Messiah and prepare them for faith.[203]   He called it *subservient* "in that it ought to wax old, and to give place to a better Covenant, which is to succeed it, and so itselfe at length to be abolished."[204]    Amyraut continued to develop the threefold covenant idea along with its rejection of legalism and elevating the gospel as the "pinnacle of God's dealings with humanity."[205]   Though the latitude puritans would continue to hold a twofold covenant structure, Cameron and Amyraut impacted them greatly.

Moise Amyraut (1596-1664) was the most influential of the professors at the School of Saumur as well as the most controversial though he attributed his ideas to Cameron.   He was born in Gourgueil, near Saumur.   He studied theology at Saumur under Cameron beginning in 1618 and became minister at Saumur in 1626 also lecturing at the Academy.   He continued as minister and professor until his death.   In 1634 he wrote *A Brief Treatise on Predestination* where he presented in what he calls a "popular approach and language"[206] the doctrine of predestination.   In this work he presents a single predestinarian view similar to Bullinger but including a hypothetical universalism, which he believed Calvin taught.   Pierre du Moulin and Andre Rivet attacked his views and he was tried for heresy at the national synod of Alencon in 1637.   The synod decided in favor of his orthodoxy, perhaps because of "the independent spirit of the French Church," the letters of recommendation sent by five ministers in Paris and the French humanism which may have led to an openness

---

[201] John Cameron, "The Threefold Covenant of God with Man" in Samuel Bolton, *The Truebounds of Christian Freedome* (London: P.S., 1656), 356.

[202] G. Michael Thomas, *The Extent of the atonement*, 169; Brian Armstrong, *Calvinism and the Amyraut Heresy*, 55.

[203] John Cameron, "The Threefold Covenant of God with Man," 381, 401.

[204] Ibid., 381-382.

[205] G. Michael Thomas, *The Extent of the Atonement*, 169.   See Moise Amyraut, *A Treatise Concerning Religions* (London: M. Simmons, 1660), 389-458.

[206] Moise Amyraut and Richard Lum, *Brief Treatise on Predestination and its Dependent Principles* (United States: R. Lum, 1985), i.

to differences of opinion on minor issues.[207]  Rivet and du Moulin were more
scholastic in their approach,[208] and the controversy seemed to be over the order
of the decrees, when all agreed that time-sequence concepts in reference to the
eternal God are accommodations to human finitude.[209]  His most important
contributions to the French reformation as well as the latitude puritans were his
focus on Calvin, hypothetical universalism, endeavors for unity and
rationalism.

The early reformers did not elevate any one reformer as the sole
embodiment of orthodoxy, but Amyraut seems to have come close.  Armstrong
notes:

> Certainly no other seventeenth-century theologian had such a thorough working
> knowledge of Calvin's writings.  At least there can be no question but that he
> meant to make Calvin the "prince of the theologians" and that he contrasted
> Calvin's theology with orthodox theology.[210]

During the controversy over his *Brief Treatise* he published *Six Sermons de
la Nature, Estendue, Necessite, Dispensation, et Efficace de l'evangile* to
defend the *Brief Treatise*.  In *Six Sermons* he attached a 75 page *Eschantillon
de la Doctrine de Calvin* to show that he was being faithful to Calvin in his
doctrine on predestination and universal atonement.  This was unusual because
no one else at this time appealed to Calvin or any one reformer to justify his
position.  Later he wrote *Defensio Doctrinae J. Calvini de Absoluto
Reprobationis Decreto*, which defended Calvin's doctrine of election and
reprobation, but in this work he also defended his own work by revealing his
faithfulness to Calvin.  He also profusely quoted Bullinger, Musculus and
Bucer who, along with Calvin, were the more humanist of the original
reformers.  His main opponent, du Moulin confronted him on what he thought
was an overuse of Calvin, asking why he did not give equal time to other
reformers such as Martyr, Zanchius or Beza.[211]  It should be noted that du
Moulin brought up the more scholastic reformers whereas Amyraut focused on
the more humanist.  Amyraut believed he was being faithful to Calvin and that
the Reformed orthodox had strayed, especially in the matter of the extent of the
atonement.

Amyraut's doctrine of hypothetical universalism brought serious
controversy to the Reformed church throughout Europe.  Du Moulin and Rivet
attacked this doctrine in France and Francis Turretin, who was the primary
author of the Helvetic Formula Consensus 1675, would later condemn

---

[207] Ibid., ii; Brian Armstrong, *Calvinism and the Amyraut Heresy*, 96.
[208] Brian Armstrong, *Calvinism and the Amyraut Heresy*, 83.  Armstrong comments on
du Moulin, "His Aristotelianism, added to his traditionalist orientation, makes him a
premier example of the Protestant scholasticism of this century."
[209] Ibid., 92.
[210] Ibid., 265.
[211] Ibid., 87, 99-101.

Amyraldianism in Geneva. John Davenant (1572-1641) Bishop of Salisbury and British delegate to the Synod of Dort had embraced a similar view, which he brought to the synod, convincing his fellow Englishmen and making an impact on the synod's decision.[212] He wrote *A Dissertation on the Death of Christ, as to Its Extent and Special Benefits* discussing the extent of the atonement because he believed this issue was dividing the Reformed church.[213] He thought those at the synod opposed to the idea that Christ died for everyone were reacting to Cameron's views and so he defended Cameron.[214]

Amyraut, borrowing from Cameron, taught that Christ died for everyone, that his sacrifice was "intended equally for all."[215] This universal design of the atonement was dependent on a person's faith and so was only hypothetically universal. The faith necessary to appropriate the atonement was a gift from God only given to the elect so God's sovereignty in salvation is maintained. The difference in Amyraut's view compared with the scholastic view was that Amyraut believed that Christ's atonement was not only sufficient for everyone, but that it was in some sense intended for everyone. He believed this view was not as repulsive to the Catholics and Arminians and would help in attempts of union with the Lutherans.[216] G. Michael Thomas has revealed that there was never "such a thing as a coherent and agreed 'Reformed position' on the extent of the atonement."[217] Many seemed to hold the old scholastic view of the atonement being sufficient for all and efficient for the elect, but would emphasize one part of the equation over the other. Though it is not true in all cases, it seems that in the seventeenth century those with more scholastic leanings accentuated the limits of the extent of the atonement (i.e. Geneva and Netherlands reformers) and those with a more humanist bent focused on the universal aspect (i.e. non-puritan British Calvinists, latitude puritans and French reformers). This also seems to be true of the original reformers. The more scholastic reformers such as Theodore Beza (1519-1605), Peter Martyr Vermigli (1499-1562) and Girolamo Zanchius (1516-1590) focused on the particularity of the atonement.[218] They said Christ's death was efficient only

---

[212] Vivienne Larminie, 'Davenant, John (Bap.1572, d. 1641)', *Oxford Dictionary of National Biography*, 1.

[213] Davenant was very concerned about unity among the Reformed and wrote several treatises including *An Exhortation to the restoring of Brotherly Communion betwixt the Protestant Churches* discussing the concept of fundamental articles (London: R.B., 1641), passim.

[214] John Davenant, *A Dissertation on the Death of Christ, as to Its Extent and Special Benefits* (Springfield, IL: Good Books, 1995 photocopy from *An Exposition of the Epistle of St. Paul to the Colossians with a Dissertation on the Death of Christ* London: Hamilton, Adams, and Co., 1832), 561-569.

[215] Moise Amyraut, *Brief Treatise on Predestination and its Dependent Principles*, 38.

[216] Ibid., 2.

[217] G. Michael Thomas, *The Extent of the Atonement*, 250.

[218] Theodore Beze, *Propositions and Principles of Divinitie* (Edinburge: Robert Waldegrave, 1591), 112; *A Briefe Declaration of the Chiefe Points of Christian Religion*

for the elect and actually accomplished their salvation rather than simply making it potential. They placed predestination in the doctrine of God[219] and stated that the atonement was based on God's decree rather than a human response.[220] The reformers that could be categorized as more humanist in their orientation (i.e. Calvin, Bullinger and Musculus) made many more statements to the effect that Christ died potentially for all.[221] They placed predestination in the context of soteriology rather than in the doctrine of God.[222] Like Amyraut they taught that the effectiveness of the atonement was dependent on a person's faith;[223] this was not to be construed as a work of humans because faith itself

*Set Forth in a Table* (London: Tho: Man., 1613), 25. Vermigli held that Christ's death was in some sense for all mankind, but he also stated, "God gave him that by him he might save them that were predestinate." Peter Martyr Vermigli, *The Common Places* (London: Anthony Marten, 1583), 2:619, 5:131. Zanchius commented "that he by his death and passion hath expiated and purged away all our sins in his flesh" where the context clearly is referring only to the church. He later emphasized that the redemption brought about by Christ's obedience, passion, death and resurrection was only communicated to the elect. Girolamo Zanchius, *The Whole Body of Christian Religion* (London: John Redmayne, 1659), 102, 109-110.

[219] Theodore Beze, *Propositions and Principles of Divinitie*, 19-22; Zanchius, *The Whole Body of Christian Religion*, chapter 3 (in between chapter 2 "Concerning God, the Divine Persons, and Properties" and chapter 4 "Concerning God's Omnipotence and Will").

[220] Theodore Beze, *A Briefe Declaration of the Chiefe Points of Christian Religion*, 25-26; Peter Martyr Vermigli declared that grace demands that "a change or conversion should be introduced, nor should it be our will or choice to follow or cleave to the promises" seemingly taking away man's response. *Philosophical Works* (Kirksville, MO: Sixteenth Century Essays and Studies, 1996), 298. Armstrong suggests that a subtle change took place in seventeenth century Reformed orthodoxy where justification by faith became a secondary doctrine with speculative formulations of the doctrine of predestination taking the lead. *Calvinism and the Amyraut Heresy*, 223.

[221] Bullinger says, "Christ our Lord is the full propitiation, satisfaction, oblation, and sacrifice for the sins, I say, for the punishment and the fault, of all the world." *Decades*, 1:110. Wolfgang Musculus stated, "Before the constitution of the world, he willed, decreed, and purposed so, that sending his sonne at the fulnesse of the time, he wold deliver and save mankinde." *Common Places of Christian Religion* (London: Henry Bynneman, 1578), 302.

[222] Musculus places predestination in between grace and redemption. Ibid., 295-315; Calvin discussed predestination in book three of the *Institutes* after justification by faith. Bullinger discussed predestination in between grace and the Son of God (though he talks about God within this section too). One cannot make too much of this argument because the reformers did see a natural connection between providence and predestination, but it should be seen as somewhat significant because they went against the normal scholastic placing of predestination, Calvin only in his final edition of the *Institutes*; one must ask, "Why did Calvin change it?"

[223] Wolfgang Musculus, *Common Places of Christian Religion*, 493-496 on the efficacy of faith; Henry Bullinger, *Decades*, 1:97-104 on the force of faith; Calvin said, "First,

was a gift from God.[224] With few exceptions most of the reformers might have agreed with the formula "sufficient for all, efficient for the elect," but holding acute differences in detail and emphasis. With both the original reformers as well as the seventeenth century reformers, those of the more humanist persuasion did not see the extent of the atonement as a controversy worthy of dividing over, whereas the scholastics were much more likely to make it an issue of division.

Amyraut was exonerated at the synod of Alencon, but his idea divided the Reformed church even though he believed he was being faithful to Calvin and the synod of Dort.[225] Modern scholars have disagreed whether Amyraut was being faithful to Calvin concerning the extent of the atonement or not. Brian Armstrong has argued that Amyraut, though slightly more rational in his approach, authentically represented the thought of Calvin,[226] but Roger Nicole disagrees, asserting that Amyraut digressed from Calvin.[227] In fact Amyraut varied from Calvin very little. His presentation was more rationalistic than Calvin, seeing people's faith as being expressed predominantly in the area of understanding, whereas Calvin placed faith in both the understanding and the will. This though, is not as different as it might seem. Amyraut also diverged from Calvin in that he focused on the revealed will of God, whereas Calvin often deliberated on the hidden will of God. Calvin spoke of the doctrine of predestination as the *decretum quidem horribile,* [228] but he highlighted

---

we must understand that as long as Christ remains outside of us, and we are separated from him, all that he has suffered and done for the salvation of the human race remains useless and of no value for us... we obtain this by faith." *Institutes,* III. 1,1; he goes on to say that it is by the "energy of the Spirit, by which we come to enjoy Christ," maintaining the sovereignty of God without diminishing the place of faith.

[224] Henry Bullinger said, "Faith is a gift of God, poured into man from heaven, whereby he is taught with an undoubted persuasion wholly to lean to God and his word." *Decades,* 1:84; Amyraut said God "ordained to create" faith in us. *Brief Treatise on Predestination,* 56; Musculus, *Common Places,* 478-479.

[225] The Canons of the Synod of Dort actually declared the idea of sufficient for all and efficient for the elect, not the limited atonement of the Reformed scholastics. But Amyraut did go beyond the synod by saying Christ "intended" to die for all. Philip Schaff, *Creeds of Christendom,* 3:586-587. "Sufficient to expiate the sins of the whole world...effectually redeem...those only, who were from eternity chosen to salvation."

[226] Brian Armstrong, *Calvinism and the Amyraut Heresy,* passim.

[227] Roger Nicole, *Moyse Amyraut and the Controversy on Universal Grace* (published thesis for the degree of Doctor of Philosophy at Harvard University, April 1966), passim.

[228] Muller is correct in saying this phrase does not imply that God's decree is "unjust or horrifying," but to add that it is terrifying "particularly to those who are not in Christ" seems to take away from Calvin's intention because the non-elect are not in view in the context. Calvin himself is awestruck by the decree and so "dreadful" is an appropriate translation. Richard Muller, *Dictionary of Latin and Greek Theological Terms* (Grand Rapids: Baker Books, 1985), 88; *Institutes,* 3. 23,7.

reprobation and the hidden will of God throughout his writings.[229] It cannot be said that predestination was his central dogma, but he did not shy away from the doctrine either. Amyraut believed in the Reformed teaching on predestination, but he wanted to take away some of the harshness he saw in the scholastic presentation of the doctrine. Like Calvin he underscored the mystery involved in the doctrine but took this a step further, seeking to put the secret will of God in the background, stressing the revealed will of God;[230] this is seen in the emphasis on hypothetical universalism as the revealed will of God in *A Brief Treatise on Predestination*. He embraced Calvin's two-will perspective, but chose to focus on the revealed will. Amyraut's apologetic concerns were always at the forefront of his thought. Lum notes that the purpose of his *Brief Treatise* was to "present the reformed doctrine of predestination in a manner which would give the least offense to Catholics who had been scandalized by misunderstanding and misrepresentations."[231] His position of hypothetical universalism and single predestination helped alleviate some of the tension between the Reformed and the Catholics as well as the Lutherans. He also took

---

[229] He covers election in the *Institutes* in chapters 21-24 of book three. He brings up reprobation several times throughout and focuses on it almost exclusively in chapter 23 even going beyond most of the reformers by rejecting the idea of God's permissive will (3. 23,8). In book one chapter eighteen is entitled: "God So Uses The Works Of The Ungodly, And So Bends Their Minds to Carry Out Hs Judgments, That He Remains Pure From Every Stain" and once again rejects the idea of *mere permission* specifically referring to his dealings with the reprobate. He also ends book three with a final note on the lot of the reprobate. He covers the secret will of God in 1. 17, 1-2, his comments in his commentary on Ezekiel 18:23, and Romans 9:6-13, his sermon on Job 26:14 where he speaks of the "owtleets" of God's will which we can attain and the "depths" which we cannot. *Sermons on Job* (London: Impensis Georgii, 1574), 453. He also fully expounds on the secret will of God in election and reprobation in *Secret Providence* (Albany, OR: Ages Software, 1998), passim. Though Calvin did not shy away from reprobation his treatment of this doctrine was different than that of many of the post-reformers. McNeill reveals the reason: "The doctrine of double predestination is a forbidding one, and a ruthless emotional oratory may make it terrifying and damaging to tender minds. It would seem that such results did not follow from Calvin's own preaching. This may have been partly because he treated the doctrine with the reticence he recommended to other teachers. Another reason may well be the fact that he did not treat it in isolation from the body of his soteriology. He led men to wonder and worship before God's majesty, power, and grace, so that they escaped the psychological trap set by the mere doctrine of reprobation." John McNeill, *The History and Character of Calvinism* (Oxford University Press, 1954), 212.

[230] Armstrong notes Amyraut's use of the two-will theory in his idea of the *foedus gratiae* which highlights his unique Amyraldian theology: "For while using [the covenant of grace] to emphasize the hidden and revealed nature of God's will, the absolute, incomprehensible and the conditional, accommodated work of God in grace, he shifts his emphasis decidedly to the latter as the proper object of religious contemplation." *Calvinism and the Amyraut Heresy*, 200.

[231] Ibid., i.

a clear sublapsarian position going so far as to say that the fall "changed not only the whole face of the universe but also the very design of the first creation and, if one should speak thus, have induced God to take new counsels."[232] Amyraut did not mean that God changes his mind, but this kind of language helped take away some of the offense the doctrine brought to the Catholics. Armstrong argues that this is a consistent teaching of Amyraut but is simply a use of anthropomorphism.[233] Amyraut varied slightly from Calvin in these points but mostly in emphasis rather than substance because of his apologetic concerns.

Nicole is right in bringing out the differences between Amyraut and Calvin, but Armstrong also correctly identifies the similarities between them as well as the dissimilarities between Calvin and Reformed orthodoxy. The humanism of Calvin, Bullinger, Musculus and Bucer kept them from some of the speculations of the more scholastic reformers such as deliberating on the order of the decrees and preserved their focus on unity in diversity and the same can be said for Amyraut and the French reformers. Calvin knew of Beza's supralapsarianism and particular atonement, but did not reveal that he embraced it. Thomas claims that Calvin was simply being inconsistent whereas Beza systematized him,[234] but this would indicate that Calvin was not aware of Beza's departures. It would seem to be more likely that Calvin simply wished to remain biblical without speculating on issues on which the Bible is silent, while at the same time accepting Beza with his more scholastic bent because he did not feel it was an issue worth dividing over; this, as we have seen, was a trait of the humanist reformers.

Concerning the extent of the atonement the latitude puritans would follow Amyraut in varying degrees. They all embraced some form of the scholastic formula, "sufficient for all, efficient for the elect," with different nuances. With the exception of the prolific Baxter, most of them shied away from the subject, as they tended to do with predestination.[235] Baxter covered the subject of the extent of the atonement briefly in *Catholick Theologie*[236] and more extensively in *Universal Redemption of Mankind*.[237] Like Amyraut he saw that

[232] Moise Amyraut, *Brief Treatise on Predestination*, 4.

[233] Brian Armstrong, *Calvinism and the Amyraut Heresy*, 181-182.

[234] G. Michael Thomas, *The Extent of the Atonement*, 59, 251.

[235] Only Baxter wrote an entire treatise on the extent of the atonement. Neither Bates, Howe or Charnock wrote a treatise on predestination; Charnock never mentions predestination in his *Existence and Attributes of God* and there isn't even a listing for it in the index of his *Works*. He speaks of election from a thoroughly Reformed position, mentioning it 33 times in *The Existence and Attributes of God*; this seems to be the pattern of the other latitude puritans. Bates touches on predestination in one place in his *Works* emphasizing the mystery of it. Howe does not mention predestination in his index, though he does have a lengthy section on the decrees.

[236] Richard Baxter, *Catholick Theologie* (London: Robert White, 1675), 2:51-54.

[237] Richard Baxter, *Universal Redemption of Mankind* (London: John Salisbury, 1694), passim.

the atonement was intended for all people in some sense, but he went on to say that this is not an absolute intention.[238] In *Universal Redemption of Mankind* he wrote 480 pages discussing the question in Aristotelian fashion stating hundreds of propositions and answering objections, concluding that Christ's sacrifice was a satisfaction made to God for all of humanity. He attached to the book "Disputation of Special Redemption," and proceeded to argue in the affirmative the point: "Whether Christ Died with a Special Intention of bringing Infallibly, Immutably, and Insuperably certain Chosen Persons to Saving Faith, Justification, and Salvation?"[239] God's conditional intention was for Christ to die for all of humanity, making satisfaction for all of the sins of the world, but his absolute or special intention was to bring his elect to faith, justification and salvation as the *causa totalis*. One could easily be confused if these two sections were read separately, but he masterfully presented the scholastic view as summed up in his statement: "Christ therefore died for all, but not for all equally, or with the same intent, design or purpose: So that the case of difference in the matter of Redemption, is resolved into that of Predestination; and is but Gods different Decrees about the effects of Redemption."[240]

The rest of the latitude puritans were in agreement with the scholastic formula on the extent of the atonement. Bates could speak of how Christ died for men but they could "frustrate the blessed methods of grace," and that "the blood of Christ was a price so precious that it… might worthily have redeemed a thousand worlds" but "the effects of it are to be dispensed according to the eternal covenant between the Father and the Son."[241] Howe believed that the atonement was extended to all, even the devils, and the sacrifice was "of no less value than if every single transgressor was to have his actual, sealed pardon," but that it depends on God's sovereign election. Charnock quoted Amyraut in reference to Christ's death taking away the sins of the world.[242] He said, "There is a sufficiency in it to cleanse all, and there is an efficacy in it to cleanse those that have recourse to it."[243] He elaborated on the infinite value and sufficiency of the atonement: "It is absolutely sufficient in itself, so that if every son of Adam, from Adam himself to the last man that shall issue from him by natural descent, should by faith sue out the benefit of it, it would be conferred upon them."[244] Thomas Jacombe stated:

> There is a sufficiency of virtue and merit in Christ's Sacrifice to expiate the sins of all men in the world. Yet in point of efficacy it extends no farther than to true believers; others may receive some benefits by a dying Christ, but this, of the full and actual expiation of sin, belongs only to those who have saving faith wrought

[238] Richard Baxter, *Catholick Theologie*, 2:51, 53.
[239] Richard Baxter, *Universal Redemption of Mankind*, 481-502.
[240] Richard Baxter, *Catholick Theologie*, 2:53.
[241] William Bates, *The Complete Works of William Bates*, 1:338-339, 384.
[242] Stephen Charnock, *The Works of Stephen Charnock*, 4:507.
[243] Ibid., 3:503.
[244] Ibid., 4:564.

in them. As this (which I here assert) is a matter of controversie I have no mind to engage in it.[245]

The moderate puritans were in agreement with the humanist reformers, but not everyone was content over the doctrine of the extent of the atonement. In the quotation stated above, Jacombe pointed out the controversy over the extent of the atonement. The original reformers as well as the moderate puritans did not see the extent of the atonement as a divisive issue. Calvin could work with Beza and Charnock could work with Thomas Watson.[246] But the more scholastic John Owen along with others stepped up the disagreement because they felt the idea of universal redemption was too close to Arminianism. In his book *The Death of Death in the Death of Christ* Owen argued against universal redemption, hypothetical universalism and the scholastic understanding of "sufficient for all, efficient for the elect," in an inflammatory style that amplified the controversy.[247] The middle ground of peace that held a universal redemption as well as a particular atonement was rejected by Owen who stated: "It is denied that the blood of Christ was a sufficient price and ransom for all and every one, not because it was not sufficient, but because it was not a ransom."[248] This is an important distinction because it appears that the seventeenth century Reformed scholasticism, with its minute distinctions, seemed to bring division rather than unity in the church. The humanist French reformers agreed to disagree with their opponents, but the scholastics brought heresy charges against them. In England Baxter and Davenant wrote in a conciliatory fashion, whereas the scholastics seemed to attack those who differed from them. Amyraut and the School of Saumur worked tirelessly to bring unity into the Protestant church in France,[249] an endeavor also pursued by the latitude puritans in England, which appears to be a byproduct of their humanism.

---

[245] Thomas Jacombe, *Several Sermons Preach'd on the whole Eighth Chapter of the Epistle to the Romans* (London: W. Godbid, 1672), 511.

[246] Thomas Watson was a moderate Presbyterian who shared the pulpit with Charnock for five years. Watson believed that Christ shed his blood "only for the elect," but never made it an issue of controversy. Thomas Watson, *A Body of Divinity*, 178.

[247] The work is prefaced with the attestation of Stanley Gower who states: "There are two rotten pillars on which the fabric of late Arminianism (an egg of the old Pelagianism, which we had well hoped had been long since chilled, but is sit upon and brooded by the wanton wits of our degenerate and apostate spirits) doth principally stand" revealing that this treatise was not given in a latitude spirit. *The Death of Death in the Death of Christ*, 35.

[248] Ibid., 184.

[249] The French Reformed church at their national synod in 1631officially decided to allow Lutheran and Reformed believers to marry, join in communion and have their children baptized in the Reformed churches without recanting their beliefs because they saw them as agreed in "The fundamental points of veritable religion." Richard Stauffer, *The Quest for Church Unity* (Allison Park, PA: Pickwick Publications, 1986), 25-26.

Another issue where the latitude puritans followed Amyraut, digressing from
Calvin but not necessarily the other humanist reformers, was the belief in a
single predestination.  Calvin taught a double predestination of election and
reprobation:

> We call predestination God's eternal decree, by which he compacted with himself
> what he willed to become of each man.  For all are not created in equal condition;
> rather, eternal life is foreordained for some, eternal damnation for others.
> Therefore, as any man has been created to one or the other of these ends, we speak
> of him as predestined to life or to death.[250]

By double predestination it is meant that both election and reprobation were
based on God's decree rather than any acts of humanity: "Therefore, those
whom God passes over, he condemns; and this he does for no other reason than
that he wills to exclude them from the inheritance which he predestines for his
own children."[251]  Bullinger wanted to soften the harshness of predestination
through the concept of a single predestination.[252]  He agreed with Calvin that
the only cause of election was God's will, but he said the cause of reprobation
was based on his foreknowledge of man's sin and his judgment on that sin.[253]
He saw reprobation as a passive hardening where God passes over some, but he
hardens them because of their sin.  In his teaching on predestination he exalted
God's grace, but warned against curious and contentious disputing.[254]  Bullinger
attempted to remain biblical and so did not shy away from what he believed the
scripture taught, but he did not want to go beyond the clarity of scriptural
teaching.  Muller sums up the differences between Bullinger and Calvin on the
question of predestination: "Bullinger differed with Calvin specifically over the
inclusion of the fall in the eternal divine decree and over the extent to which
predestination ought to be preached – but he consistently assumed that only the
elect would be saved and that election did not rest on divine foreknowledge of
human choice."[255]  Not many followed Bullinger, but rather opted for the idea
of a double predestination.  Even Musculus said that God "refused whom he
would, not for any merites which he saw to come, but yet upon a most right

---

[250] John Calvin, *Institutes*, 3. 21,5.
[251] Ibid., 3. 23,1.
[252] J. Wayne Baker details an ongoing debate through correspondence Bullinger had
with Calvin where he criticized Calvin's doctrine of predestination. *Heinrich Bullinger
and the Covenant* (Ohio University Press, 1980), 34-38.
[253] In the Second Helvetic Confession which Bullinger composed in 1561 he stated,
"Therefore when God is said in the Scripture to harden (Exod. Vii. 13), to blind (John
xii. 40), and to deliver us up into a reprobate sense (Rom. I. 28), it is to be understood
that God does it by just judgment, as a just judge and revenger." Philip Schaff, *Creeds
of Christendom*, 3:844.
[254] Henry Bullinger, *The Decades of Henry Bullinger*, 2:185.
[255] Richard Muller, *After Calvin*, 11-12.

truth, and hidden from our senses."[256] But Bullinger would not be forgotten.

Similar to Bullinger, Amyraut desired to ameliorate some of the austerity of predestination in order to make the doctrine more palatable to the Catholics and Lutherans. He believed he was being faithful to scripture, Calvin and the Canons of Dort, but neither did he want to unnecessarily offend those outside Reformed circles. For Amyraut God passively hardens the unbeliever by leaving them in their corruption and so "is not the cause of the unbelief and damnation of the [reprobate]."[257] He rejected what some saw as a logical inference that if some are predestinated to life, the others are predestinated to death by default: "Although he has predestined some to believe, that is, concluded to give them faith, he has nevertheless not predestined the others not to believe, that is, concluded to prevent them from believing."[258]

In agreement with Amyraut, Howe said unbelievers are "barred only by their non-acceptance or refusal, which appears in the general tenor of the gospel-covenant itself."[259] He believed the impenitent perish solely because of their refusal to receive God's offer, not because Christ's atonement was not sufficient for them or God elected them to be damned. Howe, like all of the latitude puritans, held to a single predestination scheme, seeing reprobation only in the permissive will of God.[260] Charnock agreed with Howe stating, "Reprobation, in its first notion, is an act of preterition, or passing by.... And though it be an eternal act of God, yet, in order of nature, it follows upon the foresight of the transgression of man, and supposeth the crime."[261] Election is not based on God's foresight of the person's faith or works, but reprobation is. Because God is not the cause of either evil or our sins, "our salvation is of him, and our Destruction of ourselves," stated Baxter.[262]

A final contribution of Amyraut that had an impact on the latitude puritans was his rationalism. Armstrong refers to Amyraut's theology as *latent* and *incipient* rationalism.[263] Amyraut gave a larger place to reason in people's

[256] Wolfgang Musculus, *Common Places*, 515; he went on to say they were reprobate first because they were reprobate of God and only secondly because of their evil nature; Contra Baker who claimed Musculus was a single predestinationist, *Heinrich Bullinger and the Covenant*, 201-202. Peter Viret seemed to hold to a single predestination schema in that he saw the cause of election as God's grace, but the cause of reprobation as God leaving the reprobate in their "corrupted and perverse nature" as his just judgment on their sin. *A Christian Instruction, conteyning the law and the Gospell, Also a Summarie of the Pricipall Poyntes of the Christian Fayth and Religion* (London: Abraham Veale, 1573), 160.

[257] Moise Amyraut, *Brief Treatise on Predestination*, 54-55.

[258] Ibid., 85.

[259] John Howe, *The Works of John Howe*, 1:96.

[260] See also William Bates, *The Complete Works of William Bates*, 2:269.

[261] Stephen Charnock, *The Existence and Attributes of God*, 2:146.

[262] Richard Baxter, *The Protestant Religion Truly Stated and Justified* (London: John Salusbury, 1692), 100. He goes on to say, "Sin he permitteth, but Faith he effecteth."

[263] Brian Armstrong, *Calvinism and the Amyraut Heresy*, 79, 178.

relationship to God than the original reformers.[264]  In *A Treatise Concerning Religions* he made a case against the idea that it does not matter what one believes about religion.   Armstrong believes he is addressing Catholic apologists who have embraced a radical fideism,[265] but it appears that a form of incipient deism was surfacing in France.  He stated, "There are three kinds of men that esteem the exterior profession of all Religions indifferent" and categorized them as those who reject all providence, those who hold to providence but reject revelation and those who assent to providence and revelation but do not believe any form of religion is necessary.[266]  This is a highly rational treatise seeking to "undeceive, if possible, such as are already mislead into [this error], and to pre-arm others against its poyson."[267]  He attempted to fight their rationalism with rationalism, proving to the first group that reason requires providence, to the second group that providence demands a revelation, and to the third group that revelation cannot allow indifference in profession of religion.  In this work Amyraut displayed a trust in reason that goes beyond the original reformers.  He still held to total depravity where, owing to the fall, the understanding has been blinded,[268] and often opted for mystery when reason seemed to go against revelation.[269]  Amyraut, however, was a pure intellectualist whereas Calvin and many of the puritans were a hybrid of intellectualist and voluntarist, as we saw above.  Moreover, he believed that all revelation, including general revelation, could be used by God to draw the elect, even those who never hear the gospel.[270]  He also described reason and truth, aspects of the mind, in superlative fashion. "I do not conceive there is any person so brutish and unworthy the name of man, as to think it indifferent what sort of Philosophy to embrace," and then goes on to describe truth: "Truth is so beautiful and admirable that she ravishes the minds of men into her love; and the more purified and sublime they are the more violent is the love they bear naturally to her."[271]  Finally he seemed to have been influenced by Descartes in starting with reason and ending with revelation, rather than starting with revelation as his basic presupposition.

Apologetics was very important to the French reformation, especially the School of Saumur.  Louis Cappel propounded the idea that the Hebrew vowel points in the Old Testament were not original and corrected passages in the Masoretic text on the basis of earlier translations and as such is considered one

[264] Richard Lum in Moise Amyraut, *Brief treatise on Predestination*, xii.

[265] Brian Armstrong, *Calvinism and the Amyraut Heresy*, 79.

[266] Moise Amyraut, *A Treatise Concerning Religions*, preface.

[267] Ibid.

[268] Moise Amyraut, *Brief Treatise on Predestination*, 25.

[269] Ibid., 19, 55, 58. This reveals his humanism as opposed to the scholastic tendency to speculate.

[270] Ibid., 39-41. He did believe that the elect who never hear the gospel are saved by faith in God's mercy and repentance, not works of any kind.

[271] Moise Amyraut, *A Treatise Concerning Religions*, 299.  He makes the highest affections as pertaining to the mind.

of the first textual critics. Alongside his textual criticism he was an apologist, writing *The Hinge of Faith and Religion; or, A Proof of the Deity against Atheists and Profane Persons, by Reason, and the Testimony of Holy Scripture*.[272] Like Amyraut he recognized the presence of a growing number of atheists in France. He stated that he did not write in order to convert the atheists, but rather to sway those who were considering atheism, to "beat down" the pride of the atheist and to present a foundation for faith and religion to the believer.[273] John Daille and John Mestrezat also wrote defending the Reformed faith against Catholicism.[274] These intellectual attempts to bolster the faith of the Reformed believer and persuade those not yet committed elevated the faculty of the understanding above the will and affections.

Amyraut's treatise is similar to the work done by Bates in *Considerations on the Existence of God, and the Immortality of the Soul, with the Recompences of the Future State, to which is now added, The Divinity of the Christian Religion Proved by the Evidence of Reason, and Divine Revelation*,[275] Howe's *The Living Temple*,[276] Baxter's *The Reasons of the Christian Religion*,[277] and Charnock's *The Existence and Attributes of God*.[278] Bates also held to intellectualism seeing that God first enlightens the understanding, which moves the will and affections.[279] He attempted to prove the existence and providence of God, the immortality of the soul, and an eternal state of happiness or misery in the hereafter by the use of nature alone.[280] Like Amyraut he gave knowledge and understanding a very high stature saying:

> Knowledge is a quality so eminent, that it truly ennobles one spirit above another. As reason is the singular ornament of the human nature, whereby it excels the

---

[272] Louis Cappel, *The Hinge of Faith and Religion; or, A Proof of the Deity against Atheists and Profane Persons, by Reason, and the Testimony of Holy Scripture* (London: for Thomas Dring, 1660), passim.

[273] Ibid., author's preface.

[274] John Daille, *An Apologie for the Reformed Churches* (University of Cambridge: Th. Buck, 1653), passim; John Mestrezat, *The Divine Portrait* (London: A.M., 1631), passim.

[275] William Bates, *The Complete Works of William Bates*, 1:1-176.

[276] John Howe, *The Works of John Howe*, 1:1-113.

[277] Richard Baxter, *The Reasons of the Christian Religion* (London: R. White, 1667), passim.

[278] Stephen Charnock, *The Works of Stephen Charnock*, 1:121-257.

[279] William Bates, *The Complete Works of William Bates*, 1:xxi. Amyraut also taught that the other faculties were necessarily moved by the understanding: "If they had their understanding so well disposed that they were capable of clear and certain understanding, all their affections would be caught up and their wills necessarily determined to follow these things." *Brief Treatise on Predestination*, 71-71.

[280] William Bates, *The Complete Works of William Bates*, xxiii.

brutes; so in proportion, knowledge, which is the perfection of the understanding, raises those who are possessors of it, above others that want it.[281]

He went beyond Amyraut in stating, "The corruption of the will is more incurable than that of the mind,"[282] seemingly acknowledging less depravity on the mind than the will. He had some affinity to Cartesian philosophy, but he was not a complete rationalist seeing that sense, reason and faith are all necessary though in different degrees:

> Sense, reason and faith, are the instruments of our obtaining knowledge. Sense is previous to reason, and reason prepares the way to faith. By our senses we come to understand natural things, by our understandings we come to believe divine things. Reason corrects the errors of sense, faith reforms the judgment of reason.[283]

The School of Saumur, alongside the Cambridge Platonists, also had an effect on Howe's rational tendencies. Similar to the puritans in general, Howe combined the necessity of the stirring of the affections with the proper apprehension of God, but he saw the "contemplative delight" or meditation of God in the understanding as superior to the "sensitive delight."[284] The more radical puritans tended to devalue the place of the mind in preference to what they called the spiritual senses.[285] Howe's Cartesianism surfaced when he spoke of how special revelation needs the foundation of natural reason.[286] He embraced the adequacy of reason to discover truth, even though he held to the total depravity of humanity.[287] He referred to Descartes as "the great and justly admired master," though not agreeing with all his principles.[288] Baxter spoke favorably of Descartes in his writings, seeing reason as superior to the senses for gaining knowledge, even touching on his famous *cogito ergo sum*.[289] None of the French reformers or latitude puritans went as far as Descartes in his first

---

[281] Ibid., 1:263.

[282] Ibid., 1:219.

[283] Ibid., 2:371.

[284] John Howe, *The Works of John Howe*, 1:375.

[285] Walter Cradock, *The Saints Fulnesse of Joy* (London: Matthew Simmons, 1646), passim. Cradock said, "Faith is not wrought so much in a rationall way, (I mean in a way of ratiocination) as by the Spirit of God coming upon the soules of people by the relation, or representation of Christ to the soule." 8. Though seeing a subordinate place for natural reason later in his work, Francis Rous, in his preface, commends those "who have taught and professed a denial of their own wits and reasons, though acute and excellent; and have (as it were) quenched their owne naturall lamps, that they might get them kindled above by the Father of lights." *The Heavenly Academie* (London: Robert Young, 1638), The Preface.

[286] John Howe, *The Works of John Howe*, 1:9.

[287] Ibid., 2:1202-1203.

[288] Ibid., 1:20-21.

[289] Richard Baxter, *The Reasons of the Christian Religion*, 544, 548-549.

rule of logic accepting nothing as true "unless it presented itself so clearly and distinctly to my mind that there was no reason or occasion to doubt it;"[290] this concept elevated reason above revelation, which they were not willing to do, but the latitude puritans were some of the most open to Descartes. Cartesianism and Ramism spread throughout Calvinism, though there were detractors such as Gisbertus Voetius. It seems the more scholastic one was, the less likely he or she would favor Descartes.

Charnock cited Descartes favorably in his works three times. He believed thought, the work of the mind, ruled the other faculties.[291] He also referred to *cogito ergo sum* as the first principle in the new philosophy, agreeably adding: "We know that we have souls by the operations of them."[292] He concurred with Descartes that it is a sin for the believer not to use reason in ascertaining the things of God.[293] He mentioned Amyraut's *A Treatise Concerning Religions* multiple times, recognizing a place for natural theology and a need to show the reasonableness of Christianity. But Charnock does show an element of uniqueness among the latitude puritans. His view of depravity seems to be more thorough than the others, being more skeptical of reason apart from revelation.[294] Whereas Bates saw that natural reason can lead to true though partial worship,[295] Charnock stated: "Since, therefore, nature cannot represent God in his brightest apparel to us, we cannot worship God by all our natural knowledge of him; for as by nature we rather know what God is not than what he is, so by nature we may rather tell what worship is not worthy of him than what is."[296] Unlike the others he used a presuppositional approach, starting from scripture. Though puritanism, the School of Saumur and the Cambridge Platonists played an important role in the formation of his thought, the Bible had the greatest influence. There is some truth to his biographer, William Symington's statement: "Charnock may not have...all the metaphysical

---

[290] Rene Descartes, *Discourse on Methods and Meditations* (Indianapolis: The Bobbs-Merrill Co., 1960), 15, 117, 120. Though Baxter did use similar vocabulary saying, "We have all great need of the clearest evidence, and the most suitable, and frequent and taking explication of them, that possibly can be given us." Richard Baxter, *The Reasons of the Christian Religion*, Preface.

[291] Stephen Charnock, *The Complete Works of Stephen Charnock*, 5:290.

[292] Stephen Charnock, *The Works of Stephen Charnock*, 4:489.

[293] Ibid., 4:362. In this passage Charnock notes that some think Descartes makes "too great an occasion to the atheism of our times," probably referring to Voetius, but reveals that Descartes ideas enhance true Christianity.

[294] He presented depravity as thorough, resulting in the absolute necessity of regeneration in his treatise "The Necessity of Regeneration." Ibid., 7-81 see especially 16-19. He did not give room for less depravity concerning the mind than the will as Bates appears to have done (see above).

[295] William Bates, *Works*, 1:106.

[296] Stephen Charnock, *The Works of Stephen Charnock*, 4:28. We will cover Charnock's understanding of reason more thoroughly below.

acumen and subtle analysis of Howe…but he is…more theological."[297]  With
all of his works he began with an exposition of a text and proceeded in Ramian
fashion to organize thoughts coming from the text.  He was influenced by Peter
Ramus in that he did not reject the scholastic method wholesale, but rather
tempered it by seeking to produce practical theology rather than speculative.
What Walter Ong said of Ramus could also be said of Charnock: "He was a
kind of humanist-scholastic who stood on the middle ground between
linguistics and metaphysics."[298]  His humanism is revealed in the way he
illustrated his points with biblical and natural images, always concluding with
practical application.  He combined biblicism with rationalism revealing that
natural reason justifies scripture and that atheism goes against nature, being
corrupt owing to the depravity of humanity.[299]

## 3. The Latitude Puritans

A small, yet influential group of puritans emerged during the time between the
restoration and the glorious revolution.  Richard Baxter, William Bates, John
Howe and Stephen Charnock seem to have had affinities to Presbyterian
puritanism, the rational tendencies of the Cambridge Platonists, and the
humanist propensity of the School of Saumur.  Edmund Calamy, Thomas
Manton and Thomas Jacombe could also be considered affiliates.  These
latitude puritans helped shape the landscape of English Protestantism for years
to come by promoting a balance of heart and mind.

There were two major kinds of intellectualism in seventeenth century
England – scholasticism and rationalism.  Scholasticism was on the wane with
its tendency toward speculation concerning doctrine and the relative neglect of
practical theology.  On the continent there was a move for more practical
theology as seen in Gisbert Voetius, but he remained a scholastic and resisted
the new philosophy.[300]  In England scholasticism had been resisted by a variety
of writers since Tyndale.  During Edward's reign the scholastic Peter Martyr
Vermigli was brought over to teach at Oxford, but the puritans in Elizabeth's
reign and after helped tone down the scholastic tendencies.  Rational theology

---

[297] Stephen Charnock, *The Existence and Attributes of God*, 1:17-18.

[298] Walter Ong, *Ramus: Method, and the Decay of Dialogue*, 4.

[299] Ibid., 1:25-27.

[300] John Beardslee (ed.), *Reformed Dogmatics* (New York: Oxford University Press,
1965), 12.  In his introduction to Voetius' *Selectae Disputationes Theologicae* Beardslee
states: "His controversy with Descartes must be understood in the same way.  Bizer
quotes Voetius as saying, 'Doubt can never and in no way be the right method for
finding the truth.'  As he saw it, to compromise on such an issue*s* was to betray the
Truth incarnate, and Voetius would not compromise.  He adhered to an almost Thomist
ideal, even upholding, rather uncritically, the authority of 'Aristotle' in philosophy;
which is one reason why he is an excellent example of the 'scholastic.'"

became the prevailing thought in England in the seventeenth century with its inclination to downplay doctrine. The puritans were caught somewhere in the middle, rejecting the speculation of scholasticism in varying degrees, but upholding the importance of doctrine. The latitude puritans embraced the move toward rational theology and attempted to cut ties with scholasticism, without discarding doctrine. Their focus on the mind necessitated both reason and the Bible. Right thinking meant right doctrine and a correct use of logic.

Muller correctly points out that most of the Reformed world, scholastic or otherwise, held to similar ideas concerning the use of philosophy and reason in that they were seen as necessary in the theological enterprise as a servant to revelation.[301] However, he challenges the theories that put blame on scholasticism for the change that took place in the eighteenth century where reason took priority over revelation. He presents Reformed orthodoxy as virtually unchanged from start to finish until J.A. Turretin and others embraced Cartesianism leading to Wolffian dogmatics, where there was no longer a subordination of reason to revelation. He seemingly places the blame for the demise of Reformed theology on Cartesianism.[302] Muller concludes:

> The decline of Protestant orthodoxy, then, coincides with the decline of the interrelated intellectual phenomena of scholastic method and Christian Aristotelianism. Rationalist philosophy was ultimately incapable of becoming a suitable *ancilla* and, instead, demanded that it and not theology be considered queen of the sciences. Without a philosophical structure to complement its doctrines and to cohere with its scholastic method, Protestant orthodoxy came to an end.[303]

The huge thrust of the scientific and philosophical revolutions of the seventeenth and eighteenth centuries certainly greatly impacted theology, but does this mean scholasticism had no negative impact on Reformed theology? Could scholasticism have been partially causative to the fall of Reformed theology? Scholasticism may have been a contributing factor to disunity when unity was needed most to counter the effects of rationalism. It may have also led to legalism, particularly acute to the scholastic spectrum of puritanism. The puritan balance of mind and heart regulated the potential negative affects of rationalism and so rationalism may not have been the primary reason for the downfall of Reformed theology.[304] A divorce of mind and heart made possible

---

[301] Richard Muller, *Post-Reformation Reformed Dogmatics* (Grand Rapids: Baker Academic, 2003), 1:360-405.

[302] Ibid., 1:81-84.

[303] Ibid., 1:84.

[304] Michael Heyd says, "The new mechanical philosophy in Geneva was not a drastic and revolutionary event." He does not see Descartes' rational or scientific contributions as the offender. He continues, "Yet, it should be stressed that the theology of J.A. Turrettini was also the culmination of a long process in which the rational and ethical elements in Reformed theology became progressively more important." He correctly

by the scholastic method seems to have had an effect on Geneva that was not as pronounced in seventeenth century England because of the puritan elevation of the affections. To say rationalism or scholasticism caused the downfall of Reformed theology goes too far because it does not take into account the multiple influences and various nuances of persuasion on the people of that time. Rationalism seems to have been held in check by the equal emphasis of the affections by the puritans, whereas scholasticism was ultimately incapable of becoming a suitable *ancilla*.

The latitude puritans sought to advance the mind in religion without neglecting the heart. They did not abandon the deep, personal communion with God that was typical of puritanism. Howe exalted spiritual contact with God as essential to the true Christian in his treatise *Of Delighting in God*. He presented the proposition: "That all delightful enjoyment of God supposes some communication from him. Nothing can delight us, or be enjoyed by us, whereof we do not, some way, or by some faculty or other, partake somewhat." He believed that God "communicates himself" to all true believers and gives to them "the sweet relish and savour thereof, wherein God is actually enjoyed."[305] Bates spoke of how our deep affections toward God enable us to endure any hardship:

> By love we enjoy God, and love will make us willing to do or suffer what he pleaseth, that we may have fuller communion with him.... His infinite goodness can supply all our wants, satisfy all our desires, allay all our sorrows, conquer all our fears. One beam of his countenance can 'revive the spirit dead in sorrow, and buried in despair.'[306]

The latitude puritans should not be placed on the radical end of Nuttall's spectrum. He places them in the middle party between the radical and conservative.[307] They were cautious concerning extra-biblical words from God and tended to be more cerebral than affectionate in their language than the radical party. They were open to both extempore and read prayers.[308] Whereas the radical puritans became more and more opposed to education and in favor of lay preaching, the latitude puritans elevated the need for education. Nuttall notes that in describing the experience of the Spirit a variety of terms are used:

> Sometimes, as in the passages quoted from Cradock and Thomas Goodwin, the experience is described in visual terms; sometimes, as in those from Sterry and

---

reveals a gradual process of change under the oversight of the Reformed orthodoxy in Geneva, not a dramatic and sudden alteration. Michael Heyd, *Between Orthodoxy and the Enlightenment* (Jerusalem: The Magnus Press, The Hebrew University, 1982), 236, 240.

[305] John Howe, *The Works of John Howe*, 1:353.

[306] William Bates, *The Complete Works of William Bates*, 2:189.

[307] Geoffrey Nuttall, *The Holy Spirit in Puritan Faith and Experience*, 62.

[308] Ibid., 70.

Rous, it is terms of taste; most frequently, perhaps because of the Hebraic influence upon their minds through Scripture, the Puritans preferred auditory terms.[309]

It is true that all three groups of terms are used by radical, middle and conservative puritans, but Nuttall's stated preference of auditory terms such as the voice of the Spirit seem to be true more for the radical puritans than the middle and conservative. The latitude puritans and middle puritans in general often used the idea of tasting the Lord and relishing his presence, rather than hearing his voice. To taste, relish, feel, and see the sweetness and savor of the Lord was encouraged far more than hearing his voice unless hearing him referred to the Bible. Because the radical puritans were open to new revelation apart from Scripture they used this terminology more frequently, but the middle puritans, especially the latitude puritans were far more skeptical when it came to new revelation. In latitude puritan thinking God's voice was heard almost exclusively from scripture. But they did have elaborate descriptions of experiencing the Spirit. Charnock encouraged encountering the Lord using terms of sense to describe that experience in order to avoid atheism:

> View God in your own experiences of him. There is a taste and sight of his goodness, though no sight of his essence. By the taste of his goodness you may know the reality of the fountain, whence it springs and from whence it flows; this surpasseth the greatest capacity of a mere natural understanding. Experience of the sweetness of the ways of Christianity is a mighty preservative against atheism.[310]

Charnock combined the rational faculty with the affections by stating, "a rational creature only can understand and relish spiritual delights, and is capable to enjoy God, and have communion with him."[311] His preference for terms of taste over auditory seems to be typical of the middle puritans and the latitude puritans in particular probably because of their more conservative view of revelation.[312]

It seems that a balance of heart and head was at the forefront of the vision of the latitude puritans. By balance it is not meant that they used a little of each and were cautious of going overboard in either area. Without hesitation they embraced the elements of rational theology that they believed coincided with

---

[309] Ibid., 139.

[310] Stephen Charnock, *The Existence and Attributes of God*, 1:86. Charnock uses the term *taste* to describe one's experience of God 51 times in *The Existence and Attributes of God* and *relish* 16 times.

[311] Ibid., 2:27.

[312] Thomas Watson stated: "Divine joys are so delicious and ravishing, that they put our mouth out of taste for earthly delights; as he who has been drinking cordials tastes little sweetness in water." *A Body of Divinity*, 270. See also his conservative view of revelation 26-38.

scripture and continued the puritan promotion of deep affections in the experience of God. This attempted balance of head and heart, reason and affections was especially true in Stephen Charnock.

# CHAPTER TWO

# KNOWLEDGE OF GOD: HOLISTIC

Charnock set out to write an extensive systematic theology beginning with the existence and attributes of God, but never finished. In this work as well as all of Charnock's other publications an holistic approach can be detected where all of the major doctrines are interweaved. He could not conceive of separating one aspect of belief from the rest; this is especially true with the knowledge of God and the doctrine of humanity. This holistic approach was common among puritans as well as the original reformers, but appears to be less highlighted by the non-puritan post-reformers, especially the scholastics who tended to compartmentalize each doctrine. To understand the different nuances we will observe Charnock's four kinds of knowledge and examine the enthusiasm controversy of the seventeenth century.

*1. Four Kinds of Knowledge*

Charnock wrote two treatises on the doctrine of the knowledge of God, *The Knowledge of God*, and *The Knowledge of God in Christ*. He began *The Knowledge of God* in humanist fashion with an exposition of John 17:3, "And this is life eternal, that they might know thee the only true God, and Jesus Christ, whom he has sent." He spent the first fourteen pages explaining the context of the passage and advanced some doctrinal considerations. He contrasted true knowledge, which he also called saving knowledge, with theoretical knowledge. For Charnock true knowledge of God was always "joined with ardent love" for Christ and included faith in him.[1] This knowledge could not just be noetic; "It must be therefore such a knowledge which descends from the head to the heart, which is light in the mind and heat in the affections."[2] Like most puritans he made a conscious effort to balance head and heart, recognizing each sphere had its place. The affections played a crucial part in his doctrine of the knowledge of God. This did not mean that doctrine was not important. He went on to discuss the two things that constituted the knowledge of God: 1) The biblical notion of God in contrast to false gods, namely "that he is spiritual, just, powerful, merciful, faithful." 2) The triune relationship of the Father, Son and Holy Spirit.[3] For Charnock the affections and the understanding were not in opposition to each other, but rather coessential and symbiotic. He deliberated on how God can be called the *only*

---

[1] Stephen Charnock, *Works*, 4:10.
[2] Ibid.
[3] Ibid., 4:10-11.

God without denying the deity of Christ, giving several orthodox options and concluded with his own. He discussed the position of Gerhard, Zanchius and others, to reveal a consensus of truth. Truth was important to Charnock, but not simply for truth's sake; truth concerning God led to "the life and happiness of the soul."[4] He believed happiness was holistic in that "the understanding is satisfied, the will filled with love, and all the desires of the soul find the centre of their rest."[5] This knowledge for Charnock was presently imperfect because our vision of God is imperfect, but will be faultless in heaven. He finished his introduction to each of these treatises by stating the two doctrines which he intended to elaborate upon: "The knowledge of God, and Christ the mediator, is the necessary means to eternal life and happiness," and "The true and saving knowledge of God is only in and by Christ."[6]

In the rest of the first treatise he described four kinds of knowledge; he stated why this knowledge is necessary; he elucidated the properties of this knowledge; and he concluded, in typical puritan fashion, with some practical uses of this information. In the second treatise he briefly introduced the second doctrine and developed four ideas: that there are different means whereby a person can know God including nature and law, though both are insufficient to inculcate a saving knowledge of him; that clear, saving knowledge of God only comes by Christ; that Christ is the only necessary medium for the true and saving knowledge of God; and that all the attributes of God are discovered and harmonized in Christ.

Throughout these treatises an holistic understanding of the knowledge of God is evident, especially in his discussion of the four kinds of knowledge. Before discussing the four kinds of knowledge it will be helpful to see how the early reformers, particularly Calvin, also held a multifaceted understanding of the knowledge of God. A comparison of the early reformers to the post-reform scholastics will also provide a contrast with the holistic approach of the puritans, especially the latitude puritans, and bolster the view that in varying degrees the scholastic method may have truncated Reformed theology.

*a. Calvin and Other Early Reformers*

We have seen that despite the propensity of earlier commentators to assign to Calvin or other reformers a single dogma as a means of expressing their system, that this is not appropriate. Those who do so usually are reading nineteenth and early twentieth century theology back into the sixteenth and seventeenth century reformers.[7] Calvin embraced the *loci* structure and

---

[4] Ibid., 4:14.
[5] Ibid. He goes on to say, "True happiness ariseth from truth known and goodness beloved."
[6] Ibid., 4:15.
[7] Richard Muller, *After Calvin*, 92-94. Muller states, "The central dogma thesis stands as a more or less suitable description of the theologies of Schleiermacher, Schweizer,

therefore saw theology as consisting of many parts, all of which are essential to an adequate revelation of God. But one could argue for certain doctrines being highlighted by Calvin owing to their perceived importance by him. Election, sovereignty and providence certainly come to the fore in Calvin's theology, not as a key to understanding the whole of his doctrine of God, but because they reflect what he saw as the need of the day owing to the downplaying of God's power and majesty in late medieval thought. Concerning humanity's purpose he raised the knowledge of God, faith in God and communion with God to a place of great significance. John Hesselink makes a good case for considering the doctrine of the Holy Spirit as a key to Calvin's thought, not as a central dogma, but rather as a doctrine intricately related to almost every other doctrine Calvin discusses.[8] In all of these doctrines he brought in a holistic understanding, including the place of the affections in each.

Calvin has been accused of intellectualizing Christianity, especially because of his emphasis on knowledge, but when we see what he meant by the knowledge of God "some of the sting of this rebuke – some, if not all – will be removed."[9] Edward Dowey explains why this is true: "The word knowledge, we may say in anticipation and apparent contradiction, is not purely noetic in Calvin's theology, and therefore its ubiquity is not *ipso facto* evidence of an intellectualized faith."[10]

Dowey exposes a crucial aspect of the knowledge of God in Calvin, what he calls "the existential character of all our knowledge of God." He states: "The knowledge of God in Calvin's theology is never separated from religious and moral concerns."[11] We see this in Calvin's definition of the knowledge of God:

> Now, the knowledge of God, as I understand it, is that by which we not only conceive that there is a God but also grasp what befits us and is proper to his

---

Thomasius, Ritschl, and Barth – not of the theologies of the sixteenth and seventeenth centuries." Ibid., 97.

[8] John Hesselink, *Calvin's First Catechism* (Louisville: Westminster John Knox Press, 1997), 177-187. He concludes, "My hope is that this survey of a few aspects of Calvin's doctrine of the Spirit does indeed confirm the thesis that Calvin is a theologian of the Holy Spirit. Focusing on this dimension of his theology reveals a personal, dynamic, and experiential side of the Genevan reformer that is often overlooked." Ibid., 187.

[9] Edward Dowey Jr., *The Knowledge of God in Calvin's Theology* (New York: Columbia University Press, 1952), 3.

[10] Ibid.

[11] Ibid., 24. Benjamin Warfield similarly stated: "The knowledge of God with which we are natively endowed is therefore more than a bare conviction that God is: it involves, more or less explicated, some understanding of what God is. Such a knowledge of God can never be otiose and inert; but must produce an effect in human souls, in the way of thinking, feeling, willing. In other words, our native endowment is not merely a *sensus deitatis*, but also a *semen religionis* (I. Iii.1,2; iv. 1,4; v.1)." Benjamin Warfield, *The Works of Benjamin Warfield* (Grand Rapids: Baker Books, 2003), 5:37.

glory, in fine, what is to our advantage to know him. Indeed, we shall not say that, properly speaking, God is known where there is no religion or piety.[12]

For Calvin piety (*pietas*; euvse,beia) was essential to a real knowledge of God. He defined piety as "that reverence joined with love of God which the knowledge of his benefits induces."[13] He did not advocate a purely speculative knowledge divorced from a relationship to God. Calvin's "belief that knowledge is 'for use' dissolved the boundary between the contemplative and active life; it brought biblical scholarship and theological reflection out of the study and into the world."[14] Knowledge of God was not true knowledge unless it was a practical knowledge:

> What help is it, in short, to know a God with whom we have nothing to do? Rather, our knowledge should serve first to teach us fear and reverence; secondly, with it as our guide and teacher, we should learn to seek every good from him, and, having received it, to credit it to his account.[15]

There was no room in Calvin's theology for 'ivory tower' thinking, especially when considering who God is. For Calvin the knowledge of God could not be speculative, but rather involved the whole person; true knowledge always led to worship, and ultimately was a major means of fulfilling our eternal purpose.

Speculation only involved the mind and therefore was deficient knowledge in Calvin's thought. He believed that true knowledge involved the whole person. After rejecting a false and pretended knowledge, he said true knowledge "is not apprehended by the understanding and memory alone, as other disciplines are, but it is received only when it possesses the whole soul, and finds a seat and resting place in the inmost affection of the heart."[16] True knowledge involved all the faculties of the soul and therefore could be considered experiential and involved a personal relationship with God.[17]

---

[12] John Calvin, *Institutes*, I. 2,1.

[13] Ibid.

[14] William Bouwsma, *John Calvin* (Oxford University Press, 1988), 159.

[15] John Calvin, *Institutes*, I. 2,2.

[16] John Calvin, *Institutes*, III. 6,4. In his commentary on Colossians he brings out how both the mind and will are involved in true knowledge: "He shews in the *first* place, that newness of life consists in *knowledge* — not as though a simple and bare knowledge were sufficient, but he speaks of the illumination of the Holy Spirit, which is lively and effectual, so as not merely to enlighten the mind by kindling it up with the light of truth, but transforming the whole man. And this is what he immediately adds, that we are *renewed after the image of God*. Now, the *image of God* resides in the whole of the soul, inasmuch as it is not the reason merely that is rectified, but also the will." *Commentary on the Epistle to the Colossians* (Albany OR: Ages Software, 1998), Colossians 3:10.

[17] This is what Martin Bucer called "a true and living knowledge of the eternal God." Martin Bucer, *Work*, 78. William Perkins described two kinds of knowledge saying, "Man must know Christ, not generally and confusedly, but by a lively powerfull, and

For Calvin the experiential knowledge of God included an intimate association with God.[18]  He believed that the Spirit was responsible for enflaming the affections of the believer, drawing him or her into an ever increasing familiarity with Christ; "persistently boiling away and burning up our vicious and inordinate desires, he enflames our hearts with the love of God and with zealous devotion."[19]  Though this intimacy is imperfect in this life it is not an option.  For Calvin true knowledge led to a real experiential relationship of love.  There is a saving knowledge and a false knowledge and the saving knowledge affected the whole person – mind, affections and will - inevitably resulting in an intimate relationship of love, imperfect but real now and complete in heaven.

Another aspect of the existential character of our knowledge of God according to Calvin was that it would lead to obedience.  "Because [true knowledge of God] acknowledges him as Lord and Father, the pious mind also deems it meet and right to observe his authority in all things, reverence his majesty, take care to advance his glory, and obey his commandments."[20]  This obedience stemmed from the prior love from God, and resulted in love toward him.  A realization of who God is inevitably terrifies a person because of the divine justice and also draws that person to God via the divine love.  The pious mind, that which fears and loves God, "restrains itself from sinning, not out of dread of punishment alone; but, because it loves and reveres God as Father, it worships and adores him as Lord.  Even if there were no hell, it would still shudder at offending him alone."[21]  Once again true knowledge was not static for Calvin, but inevitably led to obedience.  This was not a perfect obedience because the Christian is always in process, but it was there if saving knowledge was present.

For Calvin knowledge of God was existential in nature in that it involved the whole person, led to obedience and produced correct worship.  "Calvin is not first preoccupied with formulating correct propositions about God as if this need be or could be perfected prior to a subsequent expression of it in worship."[22]  True knowledge induced fear and love, reactions of worship to his

---

operative knowledge: for otherwise the divels themselves know Christ." He then said this operative knowledge must be applied to each faculty of the soul: "That he enlightens thy mind, and by degrees reformes thy will and affections, and gives thee both the wil and the deed in every good thing." About the affections specifically he says, "Lively knowledge is, that by all the affections of our hearts, we must be carried to Christ, and as if were, transformed into him." William Perkins, *Workes*, 1:625, 619. Vermigli saw two kinds of knowledge, effectual and cold, the former requiring at least "moderate affections." Peter Martyr Vermigli, *Common Places*, Part 1: 13, 16.

[18] John Calvin, *Institutes*, I. 6,1. He said that Adam, Noah and Abraham, with the help of the Scriptures, "penetrated to the intimate knowledge" of God.

[19] Ibid., III. 1,3.

[20] John Calvin, *Institutes*, I. 2,2.

[21] Ibid.

[22] Edward Dowey Jr., *The Knowledge of God in Calvin's Theology*, 29.

presence. Calvin asked the question, "What is God?" and after rejecting "idle speculations" described a practical knowledge:

> What help is it, in short, to know a God with whom we have nothing to do? Rather our knowledge should serve first to teach us fear and reverence....  Here indeed is pure and real religion; faith so joined with an earnest fear of God that this fear also embraces willing reverence, and carries with it such legitimate worship as is prescribed in the law.[23]

He believed true knowledge of God ultimately led to the proper worship of God.

Finally Calvin held to an holistic understanding of the knowledge of God, which fulfilled the ultimate purpose of glorifying and enjoying God in a relationship that touched the mind, will and affections. He said, "The final goal of the blessed life, moreover, rests in the knowledge of God," and then speaks of this knowledge as "access to happiness."[24] He wrote two catechisms, the first in French (1538) and the second in French and Latin (1541, 1545) called the *Geneva Catechism*. The 1538 catechism was in the form of a summary of Christian religion and the second in the format of question and answer like the Westminster catechisms. According to his first catechism a true knowledge of God was the end of our existence, but this knowledge entailed felicity.

> No human being can be found, however barbarous or completely savage, untouched by some awareness of religion. It is evident, consequently, that all of us have been created in order to acknowledge our Creator's majesty and to receive it and esteem it, once acknowledged, with all fear, love, and reverence.... Nowhere but in God can one find eternal and immortal life. Hence the chief concern and care of our life ought to be to seek God, to aspire to him with our whole heart, and to rest nowhere else but in him.[25]

Here, in his first catechism, we see that the purpose of humans according to Calvin is to know God. We are to acknowledge God in such a way as to bring him glory.[26] For Calvin the main purpose in life is to glorify God and enjoy him forever. In his second catechism he made the same points:

> 1. Minister. What is the principall and chief end of man's life? Childe. To know God. 2. M. What moveth thee to say so? C. Because he hath created us, and placed us in this world, to set foorth his glory in us. And it is good reason that we employ our whole life to his glorie, seeing he is the beginning and fountaine

---

[23] John Calvin, *Institutes*, I. 2,2.

[24] John Calvin, *Institutes*, I. 5,1.

[25] I. John Hesselink, *Calvin's First Catechism* (Louisville: Westminster John Knox Press, 1997), 7.

[26] "To acknowledge our Creator's majesty...with all... reverence" – and to receive him "with all love." Later he says, "By faith we grasp Christ.... Therefore, Christ is *enjoyed* only by believers" Ibid., 16-17. (emphasis mine).

thereof. 3. M. What is then the chief felicitie of man? C. Even the self same; I meane, to know God, and to have his glorie shewed foorth in us.[27]

Here we see Calvin's concern for God's glory and our *felicitie*, or our good. God has his glory and our best interest in mind and so our chief concern should be his glory, which brings our highest benefit. Calvin combined God's glory and our enjoyment of him in his opening questions. He continued to solidify this symbiotic relationship saying:

> 7. M. Which is the way to honor God aright? C. It is to put our whole trust and confidence in him; to studie to serve him in obeying his wil; to call upon him in our necessities, seeking our salvation and all good thinges at his hand; and finally to acknowledge both with hearte and mouth that he is the lively fountaine of all goodnesse.[28]

He taught that we honor God or give him glory by trusting in him, serving him, seeking him with our whole being recognizing he is the source of our ultimate goodness.

To know God was to enjoy God for Calvin. His catechisms were very similar to the later puritan Westminster Larger Catechism. Its first question asks, "What is the chief and highest end of man?" and answers, "Mans chief and highest end is, to glorifie God, and fully to enjoy him for ever."[29] Most would agree that Calvin had a significant influence on the puritans. Phillip Schaff compares the first question of Calvin's catechism with the first question of the Westminster catechisms and states:

> Calvin's Catechism... prepared the way and furnished material for... the Westminster Catechisms.... The first question of the Westminster Catechism makes the glory of God 'the chief *end* of man,' and is a happy condensation of the first three questions of Calvin.[30]

But others have a different opinion. R.T. Kendall boldly states: "Westminster theology hardly deserves to be called Calvinistic – especially if that term is to imply the thought of Calvin himself."[31] Kendall mainly attacks the supposed changes in the Westminster Divines' doctrines of faith and atonement, but he also puts the blame on their "experimental knowledge."[32] But, as we will see, the experimental knowledge of the puritans was very similar to that of Calvin.

Knowledge of God for Calvin was existential in that it was experiential for him. There was no room for speculative knowledge because it did not

---

[27] Horatio Bonar, *Catechisms of the Scottish Reformation* (London: James Nisbet and Co., 1866), 5.

[28] Ibid., 6.

[29] Philip Schaff, *Creeds of Christendom*, 3:675.

[30] Ibid., 1:469-470.

[31] R.T. Kendall, *Calvin and English Calvinism to 1649*, 212.

[32] Ibid., 8-9.

accomplish God's ultimate goal for humans – to glorify him and enjoy him in a relationship of love that affected the whole person. This knowledge led to obedience and worship because it involved all the faculties of the soul, including the chief affections of love and joy.

Out of all the early reformers Calvin seemed to tie in the affections to his doctrine of the knowledge of God most extensively. Though Bullinger, Musculus and Vermigli wrote specifically on the knowledge of God, none of them elaborated on the place of the affections concerning a true knowledge of God to the extent Calvin did.[33] Vermigli described two kinds of knowledge, recognizing that not all knowledge of God was true knowledge. He said, "One is effectual, by which we are so changed that we try to express what we know in works; Scripture ascribes this knowledge of God to the faithful alone. The other is frigid, by which we do not become better people."[34] Though he does not demand a place for the affections, he does see that true knowledge of God affects the will.[35] The more scholastic works of Vermigli, Beza, Zanchius and Polanus fail to discuss the place of the affections in our understanding of who God is.

Musculus embraced a more thoroughly holistic view of the true knowledge of God than Vermigli. In his loci on God, Musculus declared that God created us for the purpose that "we should know and glorifie God."[36] Similar to Calvin, Musculus understood knowing God in a practical and experiential way.[37] This knowledge was not for curiosity, but for the "studie of true godlinesse" where the believer is "able to serve, call upon, love and honor God in perfect faith."[38] In his loci on the knowledge of God he discussed eight degrees of knowledge, where the true knowledge of God must embrace all eight. The seventh reveals that true knowledge demands that the person sees God as his or her father particularly in a loving and merciful relationship. His eighth degree brings out both the ethical and affectionate parts of true knowledge where knowledge of God changes the person's actions and affections.[39] This special knowledge from God given to the elect by the Spirit through the word always included "some familiarnesse and love."[40] Throughout his section on the knowledge of

---

[33] Beza does mention the connection between our happiness and our knowledge of God, "Seeing that the whole summe of all wisedome and felicitie, doth consist in the true knowledge of God: it is most meet that all our endevors should be spent, in seeking to attain unto that knowledge, as far as we may be capable of it." *Propositions and Principles of Divinitie*, 1.

[34] Peter Martyr Vermigli, *Philosophical Works*, 23. Bucer uses the phrase "true and living knowledge" in the same way. *Common Places*, 78.

[35] We will discuss the similarity with Calvin concerning his *duplex noticia* later.

[36] Wolfgang Musculus, *Common Places*, 1.

[37] He says we can know the nature of God by faith and experience. Ibid., 891-892.

[38] Ibid., 9, 1068.

[39] Ibid., 1069-1070.

[40] Ibid., 1073. Casper Olevianus contrasted historic knowledge with heart knowledge where heart knowledge alone saved when the believer experienced "all the kindes of that

God he spoke of how this knowledge works in the heart, changing our will and desires. Though the believer's knowledge of God is imperfect "in this Pilgrimage" there is a partial experience of "felicitie" which brings hope for "the full knowledge of God [where] there is full felicitie."[41] Knowledge of God was not merely focused in the mind for Musculus.

Most of the early reformers advocated the idea that a true knowledge of God went beyond information and affected the person involved in practical ways, but the more humanist Calvin, Musculus and Olevianus brought out the experiential aspects more thoroughly. Their refusal to become entrenched in scholastic speculations freed them to give equal standing to the mind and heart concerning the doctrine of the knowledge of God as is seen by their inclusion of the affections in this doctrine. Muller argues for continuity between the original reformers and codifiers with the later Reformed scholastics, revealing similarity in doctrine under the broad umbrella of Reformed theology,[42] but this observation needs to be nuanced when considering the place of the affections in the doctrine of the knowledge of God. These reformers may not have recognized this subtle difference, but it was there nonetheless; this divergence becomes more acute in the seventeenth century.

*b. Seventeenth Century Reformed Theology*

The English puritans and the *Nadere Reformatie* Dutch reformers maintained to various degrees the original reformers' holistic approach to the knowledge of God while also using either an Aristotelian scholastic method or Ramean bifurcation. Reformed theology in the rest of Europe followed the more scholastic of the original reformers in a relative neglect of the affections in the doctrine of the knowledge of God. The puritans and Dutch reformers saw a need for more emphasis on piety and the affections because of what they perceived as dead orthodoxy among their peers.[43]

Those who appear to have followed Beza, Vermigli and Zanchius using a more pure scholastic method would include Johannes Wollebius (1586-1629), Amandus Polanus (1561-1610), William Bucanus (d.1603) and Francis

---

wonderfull union that we have with the father, with the sonne Jesus Christ, and with the holy Ghost, which throughout all the Gospell is promised and given to the beleever." Casper Olevianus, *An Exposition of the Symbole* (London: H. Middleton, 1581), 60. Lyle Bierma sees Olevianus as a transitional figure between Calvin and the orthodox dogmatics, neither scholastic nor anti-scholastic; "a systematic yet nonspeculative theologian." Lyle Bierma, *German Calvinism in the Confessional Age: The Covenant Theology of Caspar Olevianus* (Grand Rapids: Baker Books, 1996), 167-168.

[41] Ibid., 1077.

[42] Richard Muller, *Post-Reformation Reformed Dogmatics*, 1:46-81.

[43] Joel Beeke in the series preface of *Spiritual Desertion* says, "The proponents of the *Nadere Reformatie* offered a balance of doctrine and piety as well as theology and life that has seldom been equaled in church history." Gisbertus Voetius and Johannes Hoornbeeck, *Spiritual Desertion* (Grand Rapids: Baker, 2003), 7-8.

Turretin (1623-1687). Wollebius defined the knowledge of God as "The act by which we recognize as the one and only true God that God who offers knowledge of himself in Scripture."[44] In book one titled "The Knowledge of God" he gave several propositions on God with the design of increasing knowledge alone, though in his prolegomena he included as a subordinate end of theology "salvation, which consists of communion with God, and enjoyment of him."[45] In similar style Polanus described the knowledge of God in cognitive terms, neglecting the affections. Even when he mentioned comfort, it is a comfort that "doth strengthen our minds" with no mention of the heart or affections in the entire discussion accept to define the love of God as "that whereby he being moved doth bestow his gifts on his creatures."[46] When discussing what it means to be created in the image of God he mentioned two parts, perfect reason and perfect blessedness where perfect blessedness is experienced when the natural creature, "through an excellent joy, taking pleasure in God alone, doth enjoy perfect felicity."[47] Yet even here this joy is described in a detached way, revealing no emotion on the writer's part. This style where the writer is removed from his subject, showing no emotion or affection of his own seems to be a part of the scholastic method. Bucanus, professor of divinity at the University of Lausanne, was no exception where after describing the knowledge of God using the question format, he asked, "What use make you of the knowledge of God?" and answered, "Surely this, that he alone may be rightly worshipped, to which purpose man was created: and that we being guided by this knowledge, may pray to him, and acknowledge that from him we have every good thing."[48] In the first common place of his theology entitled "On God" there is no integration of the affections in knowing God. Wollebius, Polanus and Bucanus are relatively short systems of theology, but all with similar content and style and a relative neglect of the affections and experiential faith.[49]

Francis Turretin is one of the last true post-Reformed scholastics in Geneva. The 1992 edition of his *Institutes of Elenctic Theology* is three volumes with a total of 2085 pages. The editor of this new edition, James T. Dennison Jr., describes Turretin's manner of writing as "the scholastic style with its awkward

---

[44] John Beardslee (ed.), *Reformed Dogmatics*, 197.

[45] Ibid., 35.

[46] Amandus Polanus, *The Substance of Christian Religion* (London: R.F., 1597), 1-14.

[47] Ibid., 21-22.

[48] William Bucanus, *Body of Divinity* (London: Printed for Daniel Pakeman, 1659), 8.

[49] Wollebius' 1660 edition, *The Abridgement of Christian Divinity*, (London: T. Mabb, 1660) is 431 pages with a schematic chart at the end with similarities to Beza; Polanus' work is 300 pages with a catechism and schematic chart at the end; it is interesting that the catechism has the same detached scholastic style as the main work has; Bucanus has 858 pages which does include a brief recognition of the affections in his doctrine of faith where real faith includes "a lively and assured feeling of Gods love towards us, diffused in our hearts." *Body of Divinity*, 340.

phrasing, bulky subordinate clauses and stilted form."[50]  This massive work
used an elenctic or polemical style used for debate in order for the author to
defeat his opponent with intellectual argumentation.  He gave a series of
questions and answered them in opposition to various antagonists such as
Pelagians, Socinians, papists, Anabaptists or Remonstrants.  Turretin's work is
very heavy on the cognitive side owing to the style and purpose of the writing,
but it does not completely neglect the affections.  Though in his section on the
knowledge of God there is no mention of the necessity of the affections,[51] he
touched on them in his segment on the soul[52] and highlighted them when
discussing the topic of faith.  He discussed six aspects of faith in contrast to the
usual three (*notitiam*, *assensum* and *fiduciam*) and concluded with a necessary
affect that must touch the affections:

> But seventh, an act of consolation and confidence follows this act – consisting in
> that joy, tranquility, peace, acquiescence and delight which arise from the
> possession of Christ, by which the believing soul leaning upon its beloved (Cant.
> 8:5) and conscious of its own most intimate union with Christ through faith and
> sure of its own mutual communion and love with him, piously exults and rejoices
> in the Lord, glories in adversity and courageously challenges and despises all
> enemies whatever (Rom. 8:38, 39); rejoices with joy unspeakable and glorious (1
> Pet. 1:8); rests under the shade of the tree of life and satiates itself with its
> sweetest fruits (Cant. 2:3), certain that he who began the good work, will
> infallibly carry it on to perfection.  We have an example of this in the spouse
> (Cant. 2:16; 7:10); in David (Pss. 16:7, 8; 116, 118); in Paul (Rom. 8:38, 39) and
> in all believers (Rom. 5:1, 2).[53]

So far we have seen that the more scholastic writers tended to neglect the
affections and the more humanist included them in their understanding of the
doctrine of the knowledge of God, but we have also seen some exceptions.  In
scholasticism it appears that there was a propensity to neglect the heart in their
writings because the method did not call for it.  This method for the schools
with the idea that more information was better, simplified language by taking
out what they considered unnecessary rhetoric which included the absence of
illustration so that more information could be given in the same amount of
space (writing) or time (lecture).  Humanist scholars were more apt to include
the affections but this also was not inevitably the case where their absence is

---

[50] Francis Turretin, *Institutes of Elenctic Theology*, xxvii.
[51] He does mention the need for both a practical as well as theoretical knowledge of God
in theology. Ibid., 1:20-23.
[52] He holds to two faculties, the intellect and the will, but then describes the soul in its
original righteousness as "embracing wisdom in the mind, holiness in the will, and
rectitude and good order (*eutaxian*) in the affections." Ibid., 1:466.
[53] Ibid., 2:563.  He calls this last act of faith "a necessary consequence and an
inseparable effect." Ibid., 2:564.

seen in Bullinger's work on the doctrine of the knowledge of God.[54]  Though there is nothing inherent in the humanist method that would demand a holistic understanding of the knowledge of God, the use of rhetoric may have facilitated it in many of the reformers.  Pictures and illustrations, a main device of the rhetorician's art, did not just aid the understanding at a cognitive plane alone, but also at an emotive level.  The method played a part in how much emphasis was placed on the affections and experiential Christianity, but the theologian's personal faith also played a key role, as we will see in the puritan and non-puritan writers of seventeenth century England.

All puritans elevated the affections to a prominent place in their life and teaching, but their use of the scholastic method did seem to affect their writings, even in the more devotional genres, not by neglecting the affections and an experiential emphasis, but by somewhat obscuring that focus with detailed analysis and speculation; this obfuscation was lessened by those who consciously attempted to avoid unnecessary speculation such as the latitude puritans.  A textual comparison of sermons preached by the more scholastically oriented Thomas Goodwin and the latitude puritan Charnock reveals this distinction.

Both Goodwin and Charnock wrote a sermon on the intercession of Christ in heaven with many similarities but also some distinct differences.  In discussing Christ's intercession both men examined Romans 8:34, 1 John 2:2 and Hebrews 7:25.  Both took a scholarly approach, breaking down the doctrine and passages into sub-points in order to more thoroughly understand the issues at hand.  Goodwin used a more scholastic approach, whereas Charnock favored a humanist style; by this we do not mean there were no scholastic tendencies in Charnock nor do we mean Goodwin completely neglected the use of rhetoric, illustration or the original sources, but in general this evaluation seems true that Goodwin attempted to present as much information as possible with relatively few illustrations and used far more Latin than Greek, whereas Charnock used the art of persuasion with an abundance of analogy and a thorough use of the Greek.

Goodwin discussed two major truths concerning Christ's prayers in heaven: "First, the concurrency of influence that Christ's intercession hath into our salvation.  Secondly, the security that faith may have therefrom (sic) for our justification."[55]  Under the first head he described the necessity of Christ's

---

[54] In his lengthy section on the doctrine of the knowledge of God there is no mention of the affections, but in his sermon on the force of faith he stated that true faith brings happiness and "maketh us to enjoy the chief goodness, that God may dwell in us and we in God." Henry Bullinger, *The Decades*, 1:103. Martin Bucer does not have a separate treatise on the doctrine of God, but he did call for "a true and living knowledge of the eternal God" and "a true and living knowledge of ourselves" in his brief summary, and he rejected the idea of a true faith "which exists apart from love and zeal for God." *Common Places*, 78, 179.

[55] Thomas Goodwin, *The Works of Thomas Goodwin* (London: James Nichol/Ballantyne, 1861), 4:56.

prayers in order for Christ to have been a complete priest and the influence his prayers have on the believer's salvation. Goodwin believed that Christ's intercession "was as necessary as oblation itself," and that it was a part of the "golden chain of the causes of our salvation."[56] Appealing frequently to the book of Hebrews and its discussion of the high priest, he declared that, like the high priest, his death is the *"medium impetrationis,* that is, the means of procurement," and his intercession is the *"medium applicationis,* the means of applying all unto us," also calling it "the applying cause of salvation."[57] He concluded this section defending God, stating he didn't need the prayers of Jesus, but that it was "only for a formality sake," and so that Christ would not be out of work as high priest.[58]

Goodwin's second major point was that Christ's intercession brings security to the believer. He revealed how it is both the father and the son's love that brought about the elect's salvation and so the father is not seen as a reluctant God, whereas the son is willing to save his people, but rather both the father and the son equally love the elect.[59] There were moments of devotion and practical use in this sermon, but interspersed throughout were his more scholastic arguments. Though briefly touching on the golden chain in the last section, he highlighted God's limited atonement as seen in his particular intercession, which makes a *"procuratio ipsius salutis."*[60] His argument concerning Christ's prayer was very similar to John Owen's discussion in reference to Christ's death in that both must actually accomplish what they are intended for otherwise they are not perfect actions and Christ fails in some sense.[61] Owen tied together Christ's oblation and intercession and claimed that since his intercession is only for the elect, then his sacrifice was also only for the elect; the oblation procured what the intercession conferred and so there is "an inseparable conjunction" between them.[62] Like Owen, Goodwin used tedious philosophical argumentation to show how owing to the greatness of his deity, Christ's intercession was completely sufficient to accomplish exactly what he set out to accomplish and was a necessary compliment to his oblation:

---

[56] Ibid., 4:60-61.

[57] Ibid., 4:63.

[58] Ibid., 4:65-66. "It became him, and was for his honour, that none of his offices should be vacant or lie idle, and he want employment in them."

[59] Ibid., 4:86. This truth of the unity of the father and son in Christ's intercession is not brought out in the latitude puritan Thomas Manton, who seemed to promote Christ as our friend who was necessary "to prevent breaches between him[the father] and us." Thomas Manton, *Works* (London: William Brown, 1845), 12:371, 373. This is not the case for Charnock who uses similar examples as Goodwin to reveal the love of both the father and the son. Stephen Charnock, *Works,* 5:94-95, 123.

[60] Thomas Goodwin, *The Works of Thomas Goodwin,* 4:68-69.

[61] Ibid.; John Owen, *The Death of Death in the Death of Christ,* 194, 210.

[62] John Owen, *The Death of Death in the Death of Christ,* 72-73.

Whereas his obedience, though perfect, was but once offered up, and its existence
is but virtual; but he continues a Son for ever, not virtually only, but actually.
And therefore it is added in that 7ᵗʰ to the Hebrews, ver. 28, that the 'gospel
ordained the Son, *perfected for ever.*' The meaning whereof is, that he is not only
a priest, perfected in the time past by that perfect offering once made, but in that
he is the Son, he remains a perfect priest for ever, for time to come; whom
therefore no imperfection in his office, no failing or missing of his suits can
befall.[63]

Goodwin went so far as to add his own comment into his quotation of scripture
to promote limited atonement and intercession: "So John iii. 16, 'God so loved
the world (of elect), that he gave his only begotten Son to die.'"[64]    This
philosophical argumentation promoting the doctrine of limited atonement is
noticeably absent in Charnock.

　　Charnock's sermon, in typical humanist fashion, brought out the original
language throughout and used multiple illustrations and basic logic to persuade
the readers/hearers of the comfort of knowing that Christ is interceding for
them at all times.  All through the sermon he used the language of the heart,
advocating the deep affections Christ and the Father have for people, and the
experiential relationship with God made possible by the death and prayers of
Jesus.  The Father's "pleased countenance" toward believers on account of
Christ's passion, brings joy to Jesus and is expressed in "active joy in his
intercession," which in turn is to fill God's people with joy in knowing of the
benefits of his "mediatory prayer."[65]  There was no concept of a passionless
God in Charnock's sermon, but rather an affectionate God was displayed, one
who hates sin and loves righteousness to such an extent that he changes his
people "by utterly dispossessing out of the hearts of his people what he hates,
both root and branch, and perfecting what he loves, in all the dimensions of
it."[66]    Though both Goodwin and Charnock are puritans and include the
affections, the expressions of the heart were far more prevalent in Charnock's
sermon than Goodwin's.[67]

　　Directly connected to his emphasis of experiential Christianity, Charnock
rejected any form of antinomianism because of the nature and efficacy of
Christ's intercession.  The true believer does commit sins, but his or her faith is

---

[63] Thomas Goodwin, *The Works of Thomas Goodwin*, 4:73.

[64] Ibid., 4:86.

[65] Stephen Charnock, *Works*, 5:108-109, 140.

[66] Ibid., 5:132.

[67] Charnock concludes his sermon: "Glorify and love this advocate. If Christ presents
our persons and prayers in heaven, it is reason we should live to his glory upon earth. If
he carries our names on his breast near his heart as a signal of his affection to us, we
should carry his name upon our hearts in a way of ingenuous return. We should empty
ourselves of all unworthy affections, be inflamed with an ardent love to him, and behave
ourselves towards him as the most amiable object. This is but due to him, as he is our
advocate." Ibid., 5:144.

a faith that is manifested "by their holiness, and walk in his commands."[68] The difference between the believer and the unbeliever is the attitude of his or her heart. Charnock explained:

> Christ is not an advocate for all men, but only for them that believe, and strive, and watch against sin; for those that are invaded by it, not for those that are affected to it; for those that slip and stumble into sin, not for those that lie wallowing in the mire.... He intends not this comfort for all, but for those that are in fellowship with God, and strive against temptation. Intercession, being the application of the propitiation, implies the accepting the propitiation first.... He 'lives for ever to make intercession for those that come to God by him;' so that the coming to God by him is previous to the intercession he makes for them.[69]

While holding firmly to the doctrine of salvation and sanctification by grace alone, he believed that through the prayers of Jesus for believers, they would be experimentally changed.[70]

In his message Charnock pointed out how Christ's intercession is both like and dissimilar to his sacrifice. It is like it in that it is a necessary part of the work of a priest. Like Goodwin, he thoroughly covered the biblical discussion of Hebrews concerning Christ's high priesthood as well as all the types found in the Old Testament pointing to Christ's death and intercession. Christ's intercession is dissimilar to his oblation in that the sacrifice was potentially for all of humanity, whereas the prayers of Christ in heaven are only for believers; this point is the most striking difference between Charnock's and Goodwin's sermons on this subject. Charnock said, "His propitiation belongs in some sort to the world, his intercession to his church, to those that are children new begotten by the Spirit."[71] In several places he emphasized the sufficiency of Christ's death for the whole world even if they refuse its benefits.[72] This did not mean he supported an Arminian view of free will, but he simply attempted to remain biblical.[73] He believed the Bible taught that Christ died potentially for everyone, but interceded only for the believers.

Charnock concluded by discussing what Christ prayed for concerning the believers. In this section we see a rich, multifaceted intercession, much like his view of the atonement. He prayed for all the privileges his atonement purchased.[74] These benefits include justification, the defeat of Satan the accuser, daily pardon, sanctification, strength against temptation, perseverance in grace, and the happiness of the believer's soul.[75]

---

[68] Ibid., 5:96, 143.

[69] Ibid., 5:97-98. For Charnock Christ's intercession was not for the unbelieving elect's salvation, but rather for the believer, contra Goodwin.

[70] Ibid., 5:98.

[71] Ibid., 5:92.

[72] Ibid., 5:95-96, 127.

[73] Ibid., 5:134. Here he refutes free will.

[74] Ibid., 5:129.

[75] Ibid., 5:129-136.

By comparing these two sermons we see that the amount of use of the scholastic method affected both the manner of presentation as well as the content of the sermon. Goodwin promoted an experiential faith, but labored his points with somewhat tedious argumentation. Charnock's presentation was much easier to follow and made a much greater attempt to stir the affections of the reader/hearer toward a holistic understanding of the intercessory work of Christ.

## c. Stephen Charnock and the Latitude Puritans

Charnock, and puritans in general, elaborated on the place of the affections in the doctrine of the knowledge of God as well as the rest of his doctrinal works. It would appear that after Calvin and prior to the puritans, few works included any lengthy discussion on the doctrine of the knowledge of God. The puritan focus on a holistic understanding of knowing God along with a tempered scholastic interest to break down doctrines for better understanding led them to elucidate the believer's knowledge of God in a variety of ways; this is clearly seen in Charnock's four kinds of knowledge.

## i. Speculative Knowledge

The first kind of knowledge he mentioned he called a speculative knowledge. Charnock used *speculative* in two senses; non-salvific knowledge, or knowledge that goes beyond Scripture. Later he will condemn speculative knowledge in the second sense, but here he sees it as necessary but insufficient to lead to salvation. Speculative knowledge is a natural knowledge apart from the Spirit, where people may profess Christianity but not really know Christ. He spoke of mere professors as knowing God "in the bark of the letter, not in the sap of the Spirit."[76] Natural or historical knowledge is not the same as spiritual knowledge, because everyone has some of the natural knowledge, but only those who are spiritual can know God because he is spiritual. A cure of the soul is necessary.

Speculative knowledge is not enough. For Charnock this kind of knowledge actually torments us because it is "without affections."[77] He used the popular puritan analogy of light to represent knowledge and heat to represent the affections, especially love, stating: "Light without heat preserves not a man from chillness and shaking."[78] He argued that if information alone could save

---

[76] Stephen Charnock, *Works*, 4:15. He likened them to those who have a picture of someone without any acquaintance of them.

[77] Ibid., 4:16.

[78] Ibid. David Clarkson used this analogy: "Content not yourselves with light without heat. Let every spark of knowledge beget some spiritual and heavenly heat, let it kindle you into more zeal for him, more ardent desires after him, more flames of love to him, more fervour of spirit in seeking, in following him. If the light whereby you discover anything of Christ be not accompanied with spiritual heat, it will prove but a fruitless

then the devil must be "seated in the highest happiness."[79] This kind of knowledge was not enough, but it is also not an option. It was seen by Charnock as a prerequisite to spiritual knowledge: "It is the foundation of a spiritual: though a speculative might be without a spiritual, yet a spiritual cannot be without a speculative; a foundation may be without a superstructure, but a superstructure can never be without a foundation."[80] He goes farther than the radical puritan was willing to go. Francis Rous agreed that there does not have to be a division between the lower and higher academies, but he did not see natural knowledge as a prerequisite to spiritual knowledge.[81] He later called for the "heavenly scholler" to "put off his owne earthly and carnall wisedome, and goe up to God for a new Principle, even a new mind, by which hee may truly see and know the things of God." For him spiritual wisdom could not have a natural foundation;[82] in fact, the more one had natural wisdom the harder it would be for that person to overcome sin.[83] Though at times he seems to allow natural wisdom, most often Rous saw it in a negative light using the terms 'natural wisdom', 'sight', 'earthly wisdom', 'human' or 'carnal wit' as synonymous. Saltmarsh was equally harsh on human wisdom saying that if one's own reason or wisdom is still alive then he or she has never seen God.[84] The latitude puritans did not see human wisdom in such a negative light, though it did need to be kept in proper perspective. Baxter believed human wisdom to be true knowledge, but it was still "a poor, low, insufficient light."[85]

Charnock's category of speculative knowledge as being useful but not sufficient is similar to the Reformed and puritan category of historic faith. For the reformers, historic faith was preliminary to saving faith but not identical to it. Calvin claimed that most understood faith as "a common assent to the gospel history," because the schools neglected the other essential aspects of

---

blaze, which will soon go out, and end in smoke, come to nothing or worse. Satisfy yourselves with no knowledge of Christ, but such as makes you in love with him, Cant. I. 3." *Works*, 1:265. George Swinnock commented: "The soul without knowledge is not good, Prov 19:2. There may be a clear head without a clean heart, the light of knowledge without the heat of grace; but a gracious heart in a grown person not distracted, was ever accompanied with a competency of knowledge in the head. And indeed knowledge is so near akin to grace, that it is often in the word of God put for it: John 17:3, 'It is life eternal to know thee to be the only true God, and Jesus Christ whom thou hast sent.'" *The Works of George Swinnock* (Edinburgh: James Nichol, 1868), 3:333.

[79] Ibid.

[80] Ibid., 4:17.

[81] Francis Rous, *The Heavenly Academie*, 91-92.

[82] Ibid., 108-109.

[83] Ibid., 110.

[84] John Saltmarsh, *Sparkles of Glory* (London: Printed for Giles Calvert, 1648), 208-210. He even equated "the meer letter or scriptures, and light of nature or reason" with this human wisdom that must die before one can know God. Ibid., 207.

[85] Richard Baxter, *The Practical Works of Richard Baxter* (Morgan, PA: Soli Deo Gloria Publications, 2000), 4:556.

faith.[86] Calvin, Vermigli, Bucer, Bullinger, Beza and Tyndale were remarkably unified in their basic understanding of faith. Calvin's definition of faith is typical of all the reformers: "[Faith is] a firm and certain knowledge of God's benevolence toward us, founded upon the truth of the freely given promise in Christ, both revealed to our minds and sealed upon our hearts through the Holy Spirit."[87] For Calvin and the reformers there was a certainty and assurance inherent to true faith because it is founded on the promises of Christ and the word of God, though there are degrees of faith.[88] Real faith was seen in contrast to the schoolmen's truncated version of faith because it embraces Christ rather than simply assenting to a list of facts.[89] It is a gift of the Holy Spirit and affects the whole person, including the affections of the heart.

For Calvin true faith affected the whole person. Even the aspect of assent in faith "is more of the heart than of the brain, and more of the disposition than of

---

[86] John Calvin, *Institutes*, III. 2,1. He goes on to say that the schoolmen, with their speculations, "lead miserable souls astray, rather than direct them to a definite goal." Ibid. In his commentary on Romans 10:9 he says Paul requires more than "an historical faith." John Calvin, *Commentary on the Epistles to the Romans*, 304. He goes on to comment on verse 10, "The seat of faith is not in the head (*in cerebro* – in the brain.) but in the heart... [and so] is not a bare notion only."

[87] John Calvin, *Institutes*, III. 2,7. Vermigli defined faith: "Faith is a firm assent of the mind to the divine promises concerning Christ, through the persuasion of the Holy Spirit to salvation." Peter Martyr Vermigli, *Early Writings* (Kirksville, MO: Sixteenth Century Journal Publishers, 1994), 106. Bullinger defined faith: "Faith is a gift of God, poured into man from heaven, whereby he is taught with an undoubted persuasion wholly to lean to God and his word; in which word God doth freely promise life and all good things in Christ, and wherein all truth necessary to be believed is plainly declared." Henry Bullinger, *Decades*, 1:84. Bucer defined faith: "Faith is the sure persuasion through the Holy Spirit of God's love and fatherly kindness towards us, in reliance upon our Lord Jesus Christ, who by his death has expiated our sins, and by his life through which he now reigns, makes us partakers of his righteousness." Martin Bucer, *Common Places*, 196. Beza defined faith: "We doe define [faith] to bee that assurance whereby, beyond the former assent, the godlie are carried unto Christ, and so particularlie apply unto themselves the promise of salvation offered in him." Theodore Beza, *Propositions and Principles of Divinitie*, 48.

[88] The definitions above all reveal a firm assurance that is integral to real faith but the reformers also allowed for degrees of certainty that they called *weak faith* and *strong faith* depending on the measure of light, sin, etc. Bucer, *Common Places*, 175; William Tyndale, *Work*, 176; Henry Bullinger, *Decades*, 1:88; John Calvin, *Institutes*, III. 2,12 and 20; Peter Martyr Vermigli, *Early Writings*, 133. Weak faith is true faith as opposed to transitory faith.

[89] Faith rests on knowledge of Christ but also embraces, receives and trusts in Christ. John Calvin, *Institutes*, III. 2,2,5,8; William Tyndale, *Work*, 173; Martin Bucer, *Common Places*, 191, 195. Beza said, "We say that by faith alone we are justified, insomuch as it embraces Him who justifies us, Jesus Christ, to whom it unites and joins us." Theodore Beza, *The Christian Faith* (East Sussex, England: Focus Christian Ministries Trust, 1992), 18.

the understanding."[90]    Although using metaphorical rather than precisely physionomical language, Calvin saw the heart as the seat of faith rather than the brain because for him the heart represented the place of the affections.[91]    For Calvin "faith is the principal work of the Holy Spirit"[92] where "persistently boiling away and burning up our vicious and inordinate desires, he enflames our hearts with the love of God and with zealous devotion."[93]    "Faith *embraces* Christ, as offered to us by the Father" and "*rests* upon the knowledge of Christ (emphases mine)."[94]    Real faith entailed a love for God,[95] not "a frigid and bare knowledge of God,"[96] and therefore was experimental.[97]    There is no indication from Calvin's works that he believed any differently than the puritans concerning the experiential nature of true faith except perhaps in emphasis. This does not make Calvin a mystic because he did not seek experience for experience sake; he embraced experience, which affirmed God's word and the

---

[90] John Calvin, *Institutes*, III. 2,8.

[91] In his commentary on Romans 10:10 he stated: "But let us observe this, — that the seat of faith is not in the head, *(in cerebro* — in the brain,) but in the heart. Yet I would not contend about the part of the body in which faith is located: but as the word *heart* is often taken for a serious and sincere feeling, I would say that faith is a firm and effectual confidence, *(fiducia* —trust, dependence,) and not a bare notion only." John Calvin, *Commentary on the Epistle to the Romans*, Romans 10:10. Bullinger saw faith in both the mind and the heart saying, "Faith, therefore, according to the definition of Paul, is in the mind a most evident seeing, and in the heart a most certain perceiving of things invisible, that is, of things eternal; of God, I say, and all those things which he in his word setteth forth unto us concerning spiritual things." Henry Bullinger, *The Decades*, 1:82.

[92] John Calvin, *Institutes*, III. 1,4.

[93] Ibid., III. 1,3.

[94] Ibid., III. 2,8.

[95] Martin Bucer agreed with Calvin on this point against the scholastics stating: "The Schoolmen are in agreement with us to the extent of acknowledging that faith is the gift of God and a divinely granted faculty, and also of understanding belief to be assent to the teachings of Scripture on the explicit basis of their being divine revelation.  But in one respect they have apparently failed to understand their own position; they teach that this assent, though given to the words of God out of an ingrafted faith, can exist without the love of God." Martin Bucer, *Common Places*, 178.

[96] John Calvin, *Commentary on the Epistle of James* (Albany, OR: Ages Software, 1998), James 2:14.

[97] William Tyndale rejected what he calls a "story faith" because mere assent is not experimental: "There is a story faith, without feeling in the heart, wherewith I may believe the whole story of the bible, and yet not set mine heart earnestly thereto, taking it for the food of my soul, to learn to believe and trust God, to love him, dread him and fear him by the doctrine and ensamples thereof; but to seem learned, and to know the story, to dispute and make merchandise, after as we have examples enough." *Work*, 179. Bullinger said, "Faith maketh us happy." Henry Bullinger, *The Decades*, 1:103.

testimony of the Spirit. Joel Beeke describes the place of experience in faith for Calvin:

> Thus, bare experience (*nuda experientia*) is not Calvin's goal, but experience grounded in the Word, flowing out of the fulfillment of the Word. Experimental knowledge of the Word is essential. For Calvin, two kinds of knowledge are needed: the knowledge of faith (*scientia fidei*) that is received from the Word, "though it is not yet fully revealed," and the knowledge of experience (*scientia experentiae*) "springing from the fulfilling of the Word."[98]

The puritans also recognized degrees of faith, referring to several types usually including historic, temporary, miraculous and justifying faith.[99] They would then divide justifying faith into its component parts, differing in their lists but usually covering the same material. John Flavel separated true faith into assent, acceptance and assurance where assent was seen as necessary but not sufficient for salvation and assurance as available but not necessarily experienced.[100] The puritans fully agreed with the reformers that the assent held to be true faith by the papists was not real faith but rather belonged to the category of historic faith. Knowledge and an assent to certain facts are a preliminary necessity,[101] but if not combined with a receiving of Christ they are no more salvific than the faith possessed by the demons. Receiving Christ, which is described as trusting in, cleaving to, leaning on and depending on him, is at the heart of true faith. For Flavel

> Our receiving Christ necessarily implies our hearty *approbation,* liking and estimation; yea, the acquiescence of our very souls in Jesus Christ, as the most excellent, suitable, and complete remedy for all our wants, sins, and dangers, that ever could be prepared by the wisdom and love of God for us: We must receive him with such a frame of heart, as rests upon, and trusts in him, if ever we receive him aright.[102]

For the latitude puritans assurance was not seen as being as closely knit to the essence of faith as it had been for the reformers, but it was still considered a part of faith. Seventeenth century England was filled with those the puritans saw as having only a historic faith so they focused on assurance to convince the masses of their need for Christ. This emphasis on assurance may have increased anxiety for some who had legitimate but weak faith. Like the reformers they maintained that a true believer, though devoid of assurance, may yet have weak faith, consequently strong assurance, for them, could be

---

[98] Joel Beeke, *The Quest for Full Assurance,* 46.

[99] Thomas Watson, *A Body of Divinity,* 215; see also Thomas Boston, *Works,* 2:400 who gives the exact same list only calling justifying faith saving faith.

[100] John Flavel, *Works,* 2:114-115.

[101] David Clarkson stated: "If knowledge be not faith, yet there can be no faith without knowledge." David Clarkson, *Works,* 1:64.

[102] John Flavel, *Works,* 2:107-108.

separated from initial faith. For some puritans assurance became a fruit of faith that was granted to a very few,[103] but was available to all. In this matter, on which they tended to elaborate extensively, they moved beyond Calvin considerably at least in emphasis.

For the puritans as well as the reformers, true faith was "an act of the whole person"[104] involving the understanding, will and affections. There was some debate on whether faith was seated in the mind or the will but most saw it encompassing both.[105] It was through the mind that the individual was convicted of his or her need for Christ and his provision, while receiving Christ took place through the consent of the will. An abhorrence of sin and self, combined with a love and strong desire for Christ were the initial affections experienced.[106] Like speculative knowledge, historic faith was necessary but not enough.

Charnock believed there were two major categories of knowledge, head knowledge and heart knowledge: "The thinking of God and Christ with the head, and embracing Christ with the heart, are two distinct things; as the seeing a country in a map, and by traveling over it with our feet, are different kinds of knowledge."[107] The next three kinds of knowledge he lists (practical, experimental and knowledge of interest) all fit in the heart category and are considered as being germane to saving knowledge.

## ii. Practical Knowledge

Charnock's second kind of knowledge was practical knowledge which for him was "not a floating knowledge in the head, but a knowledge sinking to the

---

[103] Flavel remarked on assurance as "being found only in some eminent believers." Ibid., 2:114.

[104] William Ames, *The Marrow of Theology*, 80. The Dutch reformer Herman Witsius stated, "[Saving faith] implies a change of the whole man...[and is] a principle which pervades all the faculties of the soul." *The Apostles Creed* (Phillipsburg, NJ: Presbyterian and Reformed Publishing, 1993), 1:35.

[105] Flavel called the debate a "fruitless dispute." John Flavel, *Works*, 2:109. Boston said, "Not only the understanding, but the heart and will of such a one, is the subject of faith, where it has its seat." Thomas Boston, *Works*, 2:402. William Perkins argued that the seat of faith was only in the mind, but seems to be the exception to the rule. William Perkins, *Workes*, 1:126.

[106] Clarkson said, "The sinner thus affected, apprehends he cannot speak bad enough of himself and of his sins. This makes him abhor himself, this makes him sick of sin. That which was before as a sweet morsel, it is now nauseous to his soul, it lies heavy on his stomach, he is sick of it." David Clarkson, *Works*, 1:86.

[107] Stephen Charnock, *Works*, 4:17. Matthew Poole concurred with Charnock, commenting on John 17:3: "Knowing, in this verse, signifies not the mere comprehending of God and of Christ in men's notions; but the receiving Christ, believing in him, loving and obeying him, etc." Matthew Poole, *A Commentary on the Holy Bible* (Carlisle, PA: Banner of Truth Trust, 1962), 3:368.

heart; not a knowledge in the brain, but efficacious to make an union with him."[108] Faith must be "melted into an affectionate practice, and not lie like a hard lump in the head."[109] Practical knowledge is an enlivening knowledge and a likening knowledge; that is it both "enflames the heart," "driving away cold affections toward God"[110] (enlivening knowledge), and this delight in God or "mighty pleasure in God and Christ" actually begins to make the believer like Christ (likening knowledge). Saving faith makes the rational faculty of the soul, which has been enlightened with truth, dominant over the will and affections, leading them to submit to Christ. "Such a knowledge, which ravisheth the mind, quickens the prayers, seasons the converse, and fortifies against temptations... shaping the whole man according to its own mould."[111] Righteousness is not only imputed through faith, it is imparted if the faith is real. Sanctification does not save the person, but the saved person is inevitably sanctified. The latitude puritans were opposed to the antinomians within the more radical branches of puritanism.[112]

For Charnock, as for Calvin as we saw above, practical faith leads to good works, holiness and worship. The puritans described this obedience as conformity to the likeness of Christ. When one truly knows God, the believer sees him in such a way that he or she is transformed gradually into God's image, which is an image of righteousness.[113] In fact obedience is impossible without true knowledge of God.[114] Charnock described the process where, first, knowledge of God's beauty occurs, which then stirs the affections, which in turn changes the subject into his image.[115] In fact, "without affection, our knowledge of God may have, and will have, base and corrupt ends."[116]

---

[108] Stephen Charnock, *Works*, 4:17.

[109] Ibid.

[110] Ibid., 4:18

[111] Ibid.

[112] William Lamont states: "[Baxter] wrote *The aphorisms of justification*, having been traumatized by the shock of his experiences as an army chaplain in the Civil War. There he encountered the doctrine of Free Grace in its rawest form: chaplains like Saltmarsh and Dell who were telling the soldiers that the elect were justified and could not fall." *Puritanism and Historical Controversy* (Montreal: McGill-Queen's University Press, 1996), 167.

[113] Boston said, "All true religion is the creature's conformity or likeness to God, made by virtue of divine influences, transforming the soul into the divine image." Thomas Boston, *Works*, 2:648. Clarkson said, "The seeing of Christ will make those that see him like unto him." David Clarkson, *Works*, 1:256.

[114] Stephen Charnock, *Works*, 4:28. Witsius said, "When God communicates himself to the soul, he not only makes it happy, but also holy." *The Apostle's Creed*, 1:107.

[115] Ibid., 4:46. He said, "We are not changed into his image till we behold his beauty so as to love and adore him.... He cannot be said, therefore, to have any sound apprehension of God, who hath not a choice affection to him, and delight in him."

[116] Ibid., 4:48.

Knowledge, affections and obedience are inseparable for the puritans, as they were for Calvin.[117]

For both Calvin and the puritans knowledge of God is not static in nature, but rather involves choice and action by the whole person, leading to obedience and generating proper worship. True knowledge of God in due course leads to the suitable worship of God. Like Calvin the puritans saw correct worship taking place with a right knowledge of God, but they took it a step further in emphasizing the experiential nature of that worship, which they felt the Anglicans neglected. The main concern of the puritans was that the religion of their day seemed to be just enough to anesthetize the people from wanting the real thing. The puritans felt that the set liturgies kept the people from experiencing God in worship.[118] J.I. Packer defines puritan worship: "It is essentially doxology, a giving of glory, praise, honour, and homage to God;"[119] this is in agreement with Stephen Charnock: "Worship is nothing else but a rendering to God the honor that is due to him."[120] William Perkins also concurred: "The worship or service of God is, when upon the right knowledge of God, we freely give him the honour that is proper to him, in our hearts, according to his owne will."[121] The primary focus of worship is to honor or glorify God. A secondary aspect of worship is to commune with or enjoy the presence of God. Charnock revealed that since God requires spiritual worship, mere bodily worship is a "dead sacrifice." Spiritual worship entails a connection of our soul with God; to truly honor God "such a worship wherein the mind thinks of God, feels a sense of God, has a spirit consecrated to God, the heart glowing with affections to God" is what is pleasing to God; "it is else a mocking God with a feather."[122] Richard Sibbes saw worship as "comprehending our fear, love of God, and joy in him, issuing from the knowledge of the true God."[123] So for the puritans worship was the response of the saints to honor and glorify God, which entailed the experience of

---

[117] Clarkson anticipates the twentieth century Lordship salvation controversy by stating those "who take notice of Christ as a Saviour, but not as Lord" do not have the knowledge of Christ. *The Works of David Clarkson*, 1:251.

[118] William Perkins spoke on the times he lived in: "The sinne [of our times] is noted by the Prophet, *There is none that understandeth, and seeketh after God*. This we see by daily experience. Men content themselves with that knowledge of God which nature affoardeth and they endeavour not to know and acknowledge, him as he hath revealed himself in the written word, specially in the covenant of grace.... Thus most men present a worship unto God, but it is without ground or foundation." William Perkins, *Workes*, 1:683.

[119] J.I. Packer, *A Quest for Godliness*, 249.

[120] Stephen Charnock, *The Existence and Attributes of God*, 1:212.

[121] William Perkins, *Workes*, 1:687.

[122] Stephen Charnock, *The Existence and Attributes of God,* 1:212.

[123] Richard Sibbes, *Works of Richard Sibbes* (Carlisle, Pennsylvania: Banner of Truth Trust, 1983), 5:70.

communion and enjoyment of God in order to fully glorify God; this was a rejoinder to a proper, holistic knowledge of God.

The puritans brought two significant contributions to the subject of worship: how our knowledge of God affects our worship, and the concept that in worship the people of God find God.[124] First our knowledge of God is crucial to proper worship. The less knowledge of God we have the less adequate our worship will be because we will be less impressed with God and therefore our response will be small. The puritans were not impressed with knowledge for knowledge's sake, but they did see it as an essential means to a deeper communion with Christ.[125] In his treatise "On Spiritual Worship" Charnock stated: "We cannot give him a worship unless we judge him worthy, excellent, and deserving a worship at our hands; and we cannot judge him worthy of a worship, unless we have some apprehensions and admirations of his infinite virtues."[126] In another place he says, "Now it is impossible to honor God as we ought, unless we know him as he is; and we could not know him as he is, without divine revelation from himself."[127]

There is a certain polemic running throughout the puritan writings against the Roman Catholic Church, but there is also the positive teaching of what it means to obey the first two commandments. William Perkins portrayed this negative and positive treatment in his treatise on worship. He wrote his treatise in two parts: "A Warning Against the Idolatrie of the Last Times" and "An Instruction Touching Religious or Divine Worship." The first part is a polemic against the Roman Catholic Church where he addressed the sin of idolatry in worship, where he accused "popish" worship of being idolatry. He said that the Bible is the only source for the Christian's knowledge of God and how he desires to be worshipped: "God is to be conceived as he reveales himselfe unto us, and no otherwise: if otherwise, God is not conceived, but a fiction or idol of the braine." Then later he remarked: "The second way of erecting an idol is, when God is worshipped otherwise, and by other meanes, then he hath revealed in the word. For when men set up a devised worship, they set up also a devised God."[128] In other words the Bible gives us the true knowledge of God and his preferred ways of worship, in order for us to be able to worship him properly. The second part of his treatise covers the positive aspects of worship as described in the New Testament. His definition reveals his understanding of our dependency on knowing God for proper worship: "The worship or service of God is, *when upon the right knowledge of God*, we freely give him the honour that is proper to him, in our hearts, according to his owne will (emphasis mine)."[129]

---

[124] J.I. Packer, *A Quest for Godliness*, 245-257. Packer gives three contributions including the place of the ordinances.

[125] Thomas Boston, *Works*, 2:645.

[126] Stephen Charnock, *The Existence and Attributes of God*, 1:207.

[127] Ibid., 1:209.

[128] William Perkins, *Workes*, 1:658-659.

[129] Ibid., 1:687. (emphasis mine).

The second significant contribution the puritans brought to worship was the idea that a felt communion with God should be expected as part of the everyday Christian life. David Clarkson spoke of how God "does in a special manner manifest himself present" in public worship, where believers experience "the intimacy of his presence."[130] For the puritans communion with God in worship was something that affected the entire soul including mind, will and affections. Clarkson declared: "The sweetest pleasures are in fellowship with the Father and the Son. Every step in communion with God is a paradise.... He holds forth himself as delightful to every faculty of man that is capable of pleasure."[131] He later described how experiential communion with God in public worship is the norm that should be longed for when absent.[132] The puritans were not esoteric mystics, but they did hold to a deep experience of Christ in worship. The early reformers emphasized the experience of communion during the Lord's Supper to varying degrees, but the puritans seemed to take it a step further in making the entire worship service an avenue for experiential communion with God as the expected encounter.

The puritans believed in the experiential nature of their worship as well as how true worship stems from our knowledge of God and fulfills our eternal purpose of glorifying and enjoying God. Their emphasis on experience does seem to go beyond Calvin, but it is not radically different from the reformer's view because Calvin also included the experiential aspect of worship in his scheme; the difference is not in kind, but only in degree. Calvin and the puritans seem to be in agreement that practical knowledge of God leads to obedience and worship, including the affections in communion with God, revealing a holistic understanding of what it means to know God.

*iii. Experimental Knowledge*

Charnock described how the soul has spiritual senses just like the body has physical senses. The experimental knowledge of God involves tasting Christ in the soul as well as relishing, smelling, feeling and seeing him, which is necessary for true happiness. He draws out several Bible passages that use this multisensory imagery of our relationship with God, including Philippians 1:9; 1 Peter 2:3; Matthew 16:23; 2 Corinthians 2:14 and 1 John 1:1.[133] We have already noted that for the puritan *experimental* referred to both a sanctified life as well as renewed affections; in his third type of knowledge Charnock used *experimental* almost completely as *experiential* where contact is made and the affections stirred. He used illustration after illustration to make the point that spiritual knowledge is experienced by the whole soul:

---

[130] David Clarkson, *Works*, 3:190.
[131] Ibid., 3:176.
[132] Ibid., 3:199.
[133] Stephen Charnock, *Works*, 4:19.

> This is such a knowledge that can better describe God, from his spiritual illapses (sic) into the soul, than the clearest reasons of men with all their speculative notions. A blind man may know something of the reasons of colours, but he cannot know them so feelingly as he that hath eyes in his head. A man may know wine by the sight and smell, but not so clearly as when he tastes the sweetness, and feels the cordial warmth of it in his stomach.[134]

Saving knowledge of God is felt as well as understood and the experiential feeling of Christ is more important than the bare knowledge of him. For Charnock, "God and Christ felt, refresh the soul more than the lifeless notions of them."[135] This did not mean that knowledge was dispensable. The "saving knowledge of God" entailed both knowledge in the mind and affections in the heart; one without the other did not simply make the knowledge inferior, it took away its saving quality.[136] "Both must go together; knowledge without affections is stupid, and affections without knowledge are childish."[137] The light of knowledge and the heat of the affections increase or decrease together in experimental knowledge; "the diviner the light in the mind, the warmer will love be in the soul."[138]

The affections usually associated with saving knowledge include delight, love and joy toward God along with hatred for sin. In writing on "The Excellent Knowledge of Christ" Clarkson described how this knowledge "kindled his affections, ardent desires after him, intense delight in him," affections which exalt Christ over everything else.[139] Experiential knowledge "has a powerful efficacy upon the affections, to kindle desire, and raise joy in Christ, as the object transcendently desirable and delightful."[140]

The puritans did not seek this knowledge for selfish motivations, but rather for God's glory. Their joy and delight were not based on circumstances, but

---

[134] Ibid., 4:21.

[135] Ibid.

[136] He states, "If knowledge in the head doth not work spiritual affections in the heart, it can never be put upon the account of a saving knowledge; it is not really knowledge, but only a pretence to it." Ibid., 4:47.

[137] Ibid., 4:45.

[138] Ibid. Manton asked the question: "Wherein, you say, lies the happiness of the soul? In knowledge or love? Ans. Divines are divided; certainly in both. Our happiness consists in the love of God, and knowledge of God, from whence results union with God, and fruition of God. It is hard to say which is to be preferred, to know God, or love God.... By knowing we come to love, and by loving we come to know. As light is, so is love, and so is enjoyment. Here we love little because we know little...and the more we love, the more we know." Thomas Manton, *Works of Thomas Manton* (London: William Brown, 1845), 2:466.

[139] David Clarkson, *Works*, 1:251-252.

[140] Ibid. 1:252.

rather on experiencing God in the midst of bad or good conditions.[141]   The puritan culture was not materialistic because their joy came from their inner experience of Christ.  This did not mean that they denigrated material things, but rather that they simply regarded material things as being subservient to the things of the spirit.[142]  They believed that God was glorified by their enjoyment of him and he was more glorified when their joy, love, delight and happiness in him were increased.  Charnock believed that God's ultimate purpose through this experimental knowledge was for the believer's affections to be focused on God.  "God's end is not so much to be known by us, as to be loved by us, and the discovery of himself is in order to a return of affections from us."[143]  Our thoughts, actions and affections were to be focused on God and all three were essential to make sure that selfish motivations did not undermine true piety.  Knowledge of God's beauty comes first, which stirs the affections to love him, which in turn changes the believer into his image, which is love.  In fact, "without affection, our knowledge of God may have, and will have, base and corrupt ends."[144]

Not everyone focused on the affections as much as the puritans.  In Geneva, for instance, Francis Turretin and his Reformed successors gave little prominence to an experiential encounter with God that moved the affections as well as mind.  Turretin's immediate successor was Benedict Pictet, professor of divinity at the University of Geneva.  He was a transitional figure, moving away from the scholastic focus of his predecessors, leaning more in the direction of Cartesian rationalism.[145]  He wrote in his preface to *Christian Theology* that the *schoolmen* "obscured rather than illustrated Theology," and recommended that the church should banish scholastic theology.[146]  His purpose was to write a simple theology leaving out doctrinal discussions he felt were not important.  He abandoned the scholastic method of his uncle, Francis

---

[141] Clarkson spoke of how this knowledge of Christ was capable of "lifting him up, not only out of the state of sin, but also above all pressures, incumbrances of life and the world, to seek those things that are above, and enjoy him who is exalted." Ibid., 1:253.

[142] Clarkson said, "The enjoyment of outward comforts, and the enjoyment of Christ, are not inconsistent; many times both may be enjoyed together.  Christ does not always require every one that has interest in him actually to part with their earthly enjoyments, but he always requires a heart fully resolved to quit them, in case they cannot be enjoyed without the dishonour or displeasure of his Lord." Ibid., 1:268.

[143] Stephen Charnock, *Works*, 4:45.

[144] Ibid., 4:48.  He seems to have a priority of the affections because even the holiness received in this experimental knowledge is subordinate to the affections and dependent on them: "We are not changed into his image till we behold his beauty so as to love and adore him.... Though the light of the fire attends the heat of it, yet it is not the light, but the heat, transforms combustible matter into fire." Ibid., 4:46.

[145] His incipient rationalism is especially seen in his *True and False Religion Examined* (Edinburgh: J. Ogle, 1797), 1-104.  Also *Christian Theology* (Philadelphia: Presbyterian Board of Publication, n.d.), 17-24.

[146] Benedict Pictet, *Christian Theology*, vi.

Turretin, but did not opt for the affectionate style of the puritans. In book one of his *Christian Theology* entitled "Of the Existence of God and His Word" there is no doctrine of the knowledge of God or any mention of an experimental knowledge. He embraced the classical view of God as having no affections, claiming the affections were a sign of weakness.[147] Later he spoke of the affections being stirred in the inward calling of the Holy Spirit and included joy as both a part of real faith and a test for assurance of faith.[148] His doctrine did not change from standard orthodoxy and he did include the affections, but he clearly moved toward a more rational faith. In *True and False Religion Examined* he criticized the masses that "follow their senses, their imagination, their inclinations, and their passions, rather than reason."[149] In *Christian Theology* he condemned enthusiasm, seeing the Holy Spirit as primarily affecting the mind and the will and only negatively keeping the passions from perverting reason.[150] The affections are relegated to a minor part and rationalism plays a leading role in his theology. This neglect of an experiential understanding of the knowledge of God and move toward rationalism continued in Pictet's successor Jean Alphonse Turretin, the son of Francis Turretin.[151]

England had a wide variance of opinion as to whether an experiential faith should be included within the doctrine of the knowledge of God. We have seen how the puritans saw the affections as extremely important in the true knowledge of God; this was true for the radical puritans, the moderate including Presbyterian and Independent, as well as the latitude puritans. In their doctrinal works, the Anglicans rarely included a separate section on the doctrine of the knowledge of God and seldom emphasized an experiential

---

[147] Ibid., 84. "With regard to what are called *affections*, although they do not properly exist in God, seeing they are connected with the ideas of passion or emotion, which argues weakness and mutability, and therefore would be contrary to the supreme happiness of God, yet are they attributed to him in the scripture, which speaks to men in their own style; but they do not designate any passions or emotions."

[148] Ibid., 296, 304, 308. Concerning assurance he stated: "If our faith be such as stirs up within us the love of Christ and the desire of enjoying him...if we feel peace and joy unspeakable – if we delight in reading, meditation on the word, and prayer. From all these effects we shall be able to ascertain real faith." 308.

[149] *True and False Religion Examined*, 4. He also fully endorsed Descartes' method where only that which is found "so evidently true, that one cannot refuse to admit it without incurring the secret reproaches of his reason" should be accepted. Ibid., 3-4.

[150] *Christian Theology*, 295. The doctrine of union and communion so prominent in Calvin's theology is noticeably absent.

[151] Jean Alphonse Turretin, *Dissertations on Natural Theology* (Belfast: James Magee, 1777). For the move toward rationalism in Geneva in what Klauber calls *enlightened orthodoxy* see Martin Klauber, "Theological Transition in Geneva from Jean-Alphonse Turretin to Jacob Vernet" (Portland: Theological Research Exchange Network, n.d.).

faith.[152]   Lancelot Andrewes (1555-1626), bishop of Winchester, was an exception to this rule, including in his catechism a section entitled "Of the Knowledge of God and Its Opposite."[153]   But for Andrewes knowledge was only in the mind and when love is mentioned it is described in terms of obedience and duty rather than an experience or feeling of the soul.[154]   Henry Hammond (1605-1660) included a section on the affections in his work, but only in a negative sense.   He recommended that one should regulate the affections by "sober education" and "moderating and tempering their passions."[155]   A number of Anglicans composed *A System of Divinity and Morality: Compiled from the Works of the Most Eminent Divines of the Church of England* where a systematic presentation of doctrine is presented from an Anglican perspective.[156]   Its teaching is staunchly orthodox, but any mention of what it means to know God in an experiential way is noticeably lacking. Francis Atterbury mentions "passions and affections" in his treatment of faith, but saw them only as hindrances to knowing God.[157]   The Anglicans were very leery of any form of enthusiasm.

---

[152] In Jeremy Taylor's (bap. 1613, d. 1667) catechism and exposition of the creed there is no mention of the doctrine of the knowledge of God or the affections being a part of our knowing God.   *The Golden Grove* (London: J. Leake, 1713), see also *A Moral Demonstration of the Truth of the Christian Religion* (London: Printed for T. Cadell, 1775).   In his *Rules for Holy Living* he speaks of practicing the presence of God with no *mention* of affections or an experiential faith until one gets to heaven, using the idea of God's presence only to stir one on to holiness rather than to enjoy God.   *The Rules and exercises of Holy Living* (London: J. Heptinstall, 1703), 22-49.   The following also have no section on knowing God in their works, John Tillotson, *Several Discourses upon the Attributes of God* (London: Ralph Barker, 1699), as well as *The Remaining Discourses on the Attributes of God* (London: Ralph Barker, 1700), passim; Henry Hammond, *A Practical Catechism: whereunto is added The Reasonableness of Christian Religion* (London: Printed for J. Nicholson, 1715); Gilbert Burnet, *An Exposition of the Thirty-nine Articles* (London: R. Roberts, 1699).

[153] Lancelot Andrewes, *The Pattern of Catechistical Doctrine at Large* (London: Printed for M.G., 1675), 102-110.

[154] Ibid., 103.

[155] Henry Hammond, *A Practical Catechism: whereunto is added The Reasonableness of Christian Religion*, 388.   In his catechism he represents joy in rational terms alone. Ibid., 69-70.

[156] What they call "a regular system of doctrinal and practical divinity, in the method of sermons."   Compiled by Ferdinando Warner, *A System of Divinity and Morality* (London: Printed for R. Griffiths, 1750), 1:v.   Contributing authors include Gilbert Burnet, Edward Stillingfleet, John Tillotson, Francis Atterbury and Charles Hickman.

[157] Ibid., 1:21.   His definition of faith also lacked any experiential quality: "Faith in general is an assent of the mind to some proposition, upon the authority of another person, who affirms the truth of it."   Ibid., 1:14.   Peter Heylyn also defined faith as assent alone, specifically differentiating it from any kind of "experience."   *Theologia Veterum, or, The Summe of Christian Theologie, Positive, Polemical, and Philological,*

Those Reformed puritans who had conformed to the establishment in 1662 for the most part held to an *intermediate* emphasis on the affections and an experiential understanding of true knowledge of God; representatives of this group would include Ezekiel Hopkins, Edward Reynolds and Edward Leigh. [158] Ezekiel Hopkins, bishop of Raphoe and then Derry, wrote a treatise "On Glorifying God in His Attributes" where he discussed knowing God in experiential terminology. In discussing "what is our happiness and felicity" he stated: "Our objective happiness, is the infinite and boundless good, even God himself; our formal happiness, is our clear vision of and full fruition of him, and the near conjunction of our souls unto him by love and inherence." [159] He argued that it is good and not selfish to seek our own happiness just so long as we seek it in knowing and enjoying God. In fact, "The more intensely we thus love our own souls [in loving ourselves by loving and enjoying God] the more supremely do we love God, while we breathe and pant after the fruition of him with the holy impatience of an amorous spirit." [160] For Hopkins, to truly know God meant more than a cognitive recognition of God, but rather in taking notice of "the emanations and beamings-forth of God's attributes" one has his "heart affected with them" and his life "conformed to them." [161] In other words, knowing God changes one's mind, affections and will in such a way that the person honors God. We honor and glorify God with the "whole man" or not at all. "[God] will interpret all to be but a solemn mockery, if thy soul fall not as prostrate before him as thy body, and if thy affections be not elevated unto heaven as well as thy hands and eyes." [162] Leigh agreed encouraging all Christians to "labour for an experimentall practicall knowledge of God and Christ." [163]

---

*contained in the Apostles Creed, or Reducible to it according to the tendries of the antients both Greeks and Latines* (London: E. Cotes, 1654), 1-3.

[158] Leigh was not ejected but, preferring a primitive episcopacy, became disillusioned with Charles II and so retired. James Ussher (1581-1656) bishop of Armagh would have fit into this category if he had lived longer. *A Body of Divinitie* (London: R.J., 1702), 1-4, 23, 170-172, 179-180.

[159] Ezekiel Hopkins, *The Works of Ezekiel Hopkins* (Philadelphia: The Leighton Publications, 1874), 2:595. Edward Leigh stated: "The excellency of divine knowledge is seen…in the delight and sweetness of it." *A Treatise of Divinity* (London: E. Griffin, 1647), 1:6-7.

[160] Ezekiel Hopkins, *Works*, 2:596.

[161] Ibid., 2:623. He went on to say that those who admire God by reflecting on his attributes sing "with ravished and inflamed hearts." Ibid., 2:625.

[162] Ibid., 2:672. He went on to say that "if their hearts and affections correspond not with their outward semblances, they do but play the antics, they do but grin and make mouths at God." Ibid., 2:673. Hopkins embraced the puritan view of three faculties of the soul, understanding, will and affections seeing that we are to glorify God with each faculty. Ibid., 2:679-682.

[163] Edward Leigh, *A Treatise of Divinity*, epistle dedicatory.

*iv. Knowledge of interest*

In this fourth type of knowledge Charnock is referring to the idea of human happiness. The question "What is man's happiness or felicity?" was discussed throughout the reformation and post-reformation by Christians of every theological background. Charnock included happiness as part of the believer's knowledge of God in that the true knowledge of God "renders us as happy as we can be in this world."[164] Knowledge of interest is when we know Christ died for *us*, and in that knowledge is our felicity. Charnock frequently discussed the puritan idea of the Christian's end or ultimate purpose being to glorify God and enjoy him forever. He tied this concept in with knowledge in that the more we truly know God the more we enjoy him and thus fulfill the end for which God made us; in other words, a true knowledge of God fulfills the purpose of the believer's existence.

Though most of the theologians of this time referred to the idea of human happiness and joy, the puritans made a significant contribution in including it in God's ultimate purpose for creating humans and describing this purpose in such demonstrative terms. The puritans, as seen in the Westminster Shorter Catechism, seemed to have added a second part to God's supreme intention for creating humans by stating that a person's chief end was not only to glorify God but also to enjoy him forever.[165]

We have already noted how Calvin taught something very similar to the puritans with regard to the chief end of humans. But the reformers after Calvin seemed to focus solely on the aspect of glorifying God as the principal reason for our existence. Theodore Beza was typical, recording in his Little Catechism: "For what purpose [did God place us in this world]? So that we might worship Him, and so that He might be glorified by granting us eternal life."[166] It is not that the reformers did not see that the Christian's supreme happiness is to be found in Jesus, and they certainly taught an experiential faith to some degree, but the level of emphasis on enjoying God presently was lower than the typical puritan emphasis. The immediate influence for the specific phrasing of the first question in the Westminster Catechism was probably the puritan Richard Sibbes. Sibbes was well read by the Westminster divines and

---

[164] Stephen Charnock, *Works*, 4:22.

[165] The catechism asks, "What is the chief end of man?" and answers, "Man's chief end is to glorify God, and to enjoy him forever." Philip Schaff, *Creeds of Christendom*, 3:676.

[166] Theodore Beza, *A Little Book of Christian Questions and Responses* (Allison Park, PA: Pickwick Publications, 1986), 5. He also stated in *The Christian Faith*, "There shall be those saved and those damned, and all of them for the glory of God, as all Scripture testifies. Since nothing happens by chance and God never changes His mind, it follows therefore that God has not only foreseen, but eternally decreed to create man in order to manifest His glory (1 Cor 11:7), in saving by His grace those whom He is pleased to (Rom 9:23; Eph 1:5-7), and condemning the others by His just judgement (Exod 9:16; Rom 9:22; 2 Tim 2:20)." Theodore Beza, *The Christian Faith*, 6.

so it is not surprising to see the close comparison between the Westminster Catechism's answer to the question, "What is the chief end of man?" and Sibbes writing "The Christian End" originally printed (1639) only eight years before the Shorter Catechism was completed (1647). Sibbes stated:

> Though it must be our chief aim to look to Christ, yet God allows us to look also to our own salvation, how to be saved and happy in another world. God hath joined these two together as one chief end and good. The one, that he might be glorified; the other, that we might be happy: and both these are attained by honouring and serving him. And this is no self-love; for we cannot seek our salvation but in honouring God and yielding! the means that he hath sanctified for us, which is to cast ourselves on him for our salvation in his way. Thus our happiness and God's chief end agree together.[167]

The divide seems to have been widened by the second half of the seventeenth century with the puritans and second reformation Dutch focusing on an experiential component to people's chief end, whereas the post-reformers in Geneva and the Anglicans in England centered on glorifying God, especially in holy living. Pictet stated: "Man was designed for the glory of God, for his knowledge and worship."[168]  Tillotson asserted, "The design and aim of all things that are made, is the illustration of God's Glory some way or other, and the manifestation of his Perfections."[169]  Even when there is some mention of enjoying God there is not any elaboration on the theme as had become characteristic of the puritan writings.[170]

The puritans' embellishment on the experiential nature of enjoying God as a part of the primary reason for existence is seen in the many commentaries on the first question of the Westminster Catechism. In these commentaries they explained what it means to enjoy God. Another element of discussion is the nature of enjoyment of God. In *A Short and plain Explication Of the Shorter Catechism Composed by The Reverend Assembly of Divines*, it stated:

> Q. How doth man enjoy God? A. Two wayes. 1. Here in this life, by an holy communion with him, in the Duties of his worship, and in an upright conversation. 2. Hereafter, in the life to come, in a Glorious and Immediate Communion with him, in his Kingdom.[171]

The puritans spoke of an imperfect enjoyment of God in this life and a perfect enjoyment of the divine presence in heaven. In this life God is understood and

---

[167] Richard Sibbes, *Works*, 5:298-299.
[168] Benedict Pictet, *Christian Theology*, 136.
[169] John Tillotson, *The Remaining Discourses, on the Attributes of God*, 407.
[170] Jeremy Taylor asked the question, "Wherefore did God create and make us?" and answers, "That we might do him honour and service, and receive from him infinite felicities." But he does not go into detail on what these felicities are and seems to indicate that they are mainly experienced in heaven. *The Golden Grove*, 3.
[171] S.W., *A Short and plain Explication of the Shorter Catechism* (London: 1667), 2.

experienced only in part because our "communion with God here is clogged with sin."[172] Puritans were pilgrims on a journey longing for the fuller experience of delight in God that will come in heaven. In this life God is enjoyed through the ordinances. The ordinances are not magical and can be used in such a way that no real communion is experienced, but they are the normal way a believer experiences and enjoys God. When combined with faith and the Spirit varying degrees of "sensible manifestations of God's special love"[173] are enjoyed.[174] The chief ordinances are the word and sacraments: "In the Word we hear God's voice, in the sacrament we have his kiss."[175] But the puritans were careful to reveal that the treasure is Christ not the ordinances, though they are the ordinary avenues to Christ.

The believers' life here is as if he or she has one foot in heaven and one foot on earth,[176] but in heaven it will be perfect joy.[177] The beatific vision of God in heaven will bring perfect conformity to his will and "perfect joy will result from hence."[178] Though we cannot experience God's fullness now, God will "capacitate us for glory" where we will continuously feel his presence in the fullest measure.[179] The pleasure will not be sensual, but it will be a sensory experience of infinite joy.[180]

> God will be enjoyed hereafter by his people, when they shall be admitted into his glorious presence, have an immediate sight of his face, and full sense of his love in heaven, and there fully and eternally acquiesce and rest in him with perfect and inconceivable delight and joy.[181]

Another question the puritans tried to answer was, "How does enjoying God fit with glorifying God?" They believed that enjoying God was the chief means of glorifying God and therefore inseparable.[182] It is impossible to glorify God apart from enjoying him since God is our supreme happiness; seeking ultimate

---

[172] John Flavel, *Works*, 6:216.

[173] Thomas Vincent, *An Explanation of the Assembly's Shorter Catechism* (Escondido, CA: Ephesians Four Group, 1998), 13.

[174] Watson said, "This sweet enjoyment of God, is, when we feel his Spirit co-operating with the ordinance, and distilling grace upon our hearts." He went on to say, "The higher we fly by the wings of faith, the more we enjoy of God." Thomas Watson, *A Body of Divinity*, 21-22.

[175] Ibid.

[176] Edward Fisher, *The Marrow of Modern Divinity*, 259.

[177] Anthony Tuckney said, "In nearest approach, to see him as he is, and in closest Communion to enjoy him, there alwayes to be experimenting, and yet ever learning the truth of this Text [Psalm 73:28] to all Eternity." Anthony Tuckney, *Forty Sermons* (London: J.M., 1676), 505.

[178] John Flavel, *Works*, 6:216.

[179] Thomas Watson, *A Body of Divinity*, 24.

[180] Ibid., 24 and 301.

[181] Thomas Vincent, *An Explanation of the Assembly's Shorter Catechism*, 14.

[182] Ibid.

happiness in any other place would detract from God's glory. To enjoy God is not a matter of selfishness because it is found precisely when we do not seek it, but rather seek to glorify God. The enjoyment of God is subordinate to glorifying God, but it should not be seen as being dispensable.[183] Some had speculated whether a person should even wish his own damnation in hell if that would bring God glory, but the puritan answer was that the question reveals an ignorance of God's glory as seen in his goodness.[184] God's glory and people's happiness fit together like a hand and a glove.[185]

Finally the puritans saw the enjoyment of God as an experiential encounter. Boston described two kinds of joy in Christ; the first is *habitual joy*, which every believer has at all times, a seed of joy even in the toughest of times. But there is also an *actual joy*, which acts upon the habitual joy at times in varying degrees. The actual joy is either a sensible joy or a rational joy. The sensible joy may be rare, but the rational joy, which consists of a satisfaction of the soul based on the experience of love from God, is common.[186] Two words the puritans used frequently in relation to their affections toward God were satisfaction and happiness. The prevalence of superlative language used when referring to satisfaction and happiness in connection with communion with God suggests that these concepts were central to the puritan experience of God. Boston had intricate categories for describing what satisfaction means,[187] and happiness was the central theme of the commentators of the catechism as to what it means to enjoy God.[188] In seventeenth century England the puritans had many ways of describing delight in God and satisfaction of the soul revealing the heightened value to them of this commodity.[189] Charnock's description of

---

[183] John Howe, *The Works of John Howe*, 1:377.

[184] Howe said, "For it were a most injurious and vile supposition of somewhat inconsistent with his own most blessed nature, and eternal, essential felicity, (for his happiness cannot but be much placed in the benignity of his nature,) to imagine that he ever can be pleased, or esteem himself glorified, by the everlasting miseries of any one that truly loves him." Ibid., 1:407. God can be glorified by punishing the wicked in hell, but his glory would be lessened by allowing someone who loves him through Christ to suffer hell.

[185] John Flavel said, "Because no man can glorify God, that takes him not for his God; and none takes him for his God, that takes him not for his supreme good; and both these being essentially included in this notion of the chief end, are therefore justly put together." John Flavel, *Works*, 6:142.

[186] Thomas Boston, *Works*, 4:494-495. Howe agreed. John Howe, *Works*, 1:369, 375. Howe differentiated between affections and emotions, ibid., 1:373.

[187] Ibid., 4:518-524.

[188] Flavel said, "The chief happiness of man consisteth in the enjoyment of God.... The chief happiness of the creature consisteth in the enjoyment and blessed vision of God." John Flavel, *Works*, 2:280.

[189] Arrowsmith stated: "Creature-comforts are but lean blessings in comparison, there is a fatness in Gods house, such as satisfies, and that abundantly. They afford but drops, Christ a river of pleasures. Look as when an Army of men comes to drink at a mighty river, a Jordan, a Thames, they all go satisfied away, none complaining of want, none

"knowledge of interest" as being a part of our eternal purpose where "our felicity" derives from this "happy knowledge" and is necessary for all true knowledge of God was typical of the puritan emphasis,[190] but not necessarily that of the rest of post-reformation Europe. The enthusiasm controversy uncovered this difference.

## 2. The Enthusiasm Controversy

A major divide occurred in seventeenth century England which centered on the issue of enthusiasm. Enthusiasm was understood to be both a disposition prone to ecstatic behavior and rash zeal as well as a theological perspective that embraced extraordinary manifestations such as prophecies, healing or divination. The issues of new revelation from God and extreme behavioral expressions were discussed from the beginning of the reformation. The reformers considered the Zwickau prophets, Thomas Müntzer and Andreas Carlstadt as dangerous because of their adherence to direct divine inspiration that was often accompanied by ecstasies and convulsions. They also saw the Anabaptists as the direct successors of these groups and called them all "Schwarmer" or "Enthusiastae."[191]

In seventeenth century England the puritans and Anglicans further parted ways over the underlying issues of enthusiasm. Though the term enthusiasm was not clearly defined at that time,[192] it can be seen to have two key components: the claim to divine revelation and emotionalism. Within puritanism the radical element advocated contemporary divine revelation and they all promoted an experiential faith to varying degrees.[193] Similar to the reformers who uncritically put all Anabaptists into the mold of Schwarmer, some of the Anglicans saw all puritans as enthusiasts.[194] Very much like the time of the sixteenth century reformation, there was a real fear of civil unrest,

---

envying another, because there was water enough for them all: whereas had they come to a little brook there would not have been found enough to quench the thirst of every one. So here. The creatures are small brooks that have but a little water in them, yea broken cisterns that hold no water: No wonder if souls return empty from them. But Christ hath a river for his followers, able to give them all satisfaction." John Arrowsmith, *Armilla Catechetica* (Cambridge: John Field, 1659), 20-21.

[190] Stephen Charnock, *Works*, 4:22.

[191] Michael Heyd, *Be Sober and Reasonable* (Leiden: E.J. Brill, 1995), 11-13.

[192] Heyd notes, "The label 'enthusiasm' was thus rather loosely used by Reformed theologians in the sixteenth and seventeenth centuries as far as its specific denotations were concerned.... They used the term to designate a cluster of claims made by some of the their radical opponents (prophecy, apocalyptic prediction, direct divine inspiration unmediated by Scripture), as well as a certain behavioural pattern (ecstasies, convulsions, raptures, shouting)." Ibid., 22.

[193] Geoffrey Nuttall, *The Holy Spirit in Puritan Faith and Experience*, 20-33.

[194] Theophilus Evans, *The History of Modern Enthusiasm, From the Reformation to the Present Times* (London: W. Owens, 1752), 5-18.

even of violent revolution.    Some of the Commonwealth sectaries had advocated extreme apocalypticism that seemed to promote anarchy (i.e. Fifth Monarchism);[195] these same groups received their information from supposed new revelations and ecstatic experiences.[196]   These real dangers helped move others to reject all forms of enthusiasm.[197]

Two major works on enthusiasm were produced in the latter part of the seventeenth century which represented Anglican thought; the Cambridge Platonist Henry More wrote *Enthusiasmus Triumphatus*[198] and Meric Casaubon wrote *A Treatise Concerning Enthusiasme*.[199]   Though primarily attacking contemporary revelation, both of these works undermine all exuberant expressions of religiosity, advocating instead a placid, reasonable faith; in them the balance shifts heavily toward the mind.[200]   More began his work by showing similarities between atheism and enthusiasm and argued how the one complements the other.   They each reject true knowledge of God and they work together against true religion.   Atheism, for its part, makes the enthusiast reject reason as a guide to God and enthusiasm makes an atheist reject God as a product of melancholy and nothing more.[201]   More made a psychological assessment of the enthusiasts claiming their imagination has such an overwhelming effect on the senses that it deems things to be true even if they are wholly contrary to reason.   For him the senses cannot be a source of knowledge and therefore reason alone can be trusted.   The senses cannot be relied upon because they can be distorted by wine, Tarantula poison, meat,

---

[195] Austin Woolrych "Fifth Monarchy men" *The Oxford Companion to British History*. Ed. John Cannon. Oxford University Press, 1997.

[196] Christopher Hill, *The World Turned Upside Down* (London: Penguin Books, 1991), 87-98.

[197] The fear of enthusiasm persisted for a long time as can be seen in the addition of a chapter on enthusiasm by John Locke in his *Essays* in the fourth edition as late as 1700. John Locke, *An Abridgment of Mr. Locke's Essay Concerning Human Understanding* (London: Printed for J. and J. Knapton, 1731), 355-366.

[198] Henry More, *A Collection of Several Philosophical Writings* (London: James Flesher, 1662), 2:1-48.

[199] Meric Casaubon, *A Treatise Concerning Enthusiasme* (London: R.D., 1655), passim.

[200] Heyd states, "This shift [from supernatural to natural arguments] is also noticeable in the increasing reliance on individual human reason, alongside, if not instead of, Scripture." *Be Sober and Reasonable*, 10.

[201] More stated, "For the atheist's pretence to Wit and natural Reason (though the foulness of his Mind makes him fumble very dotingly in the use thereof) makes the Enthusiast secure that Reason is no guide to God: And the Enthusiast's boldly dictating the careless ravings of his own tumultuous Phansy for undeniable Principles of Divine knowledge, confirms the Atheist that the whole business of Religion and Notion of a God is nothing but a troublesome fit of over-curious Melancholy." *A Collection*, 2:1-2.

disease and especially melancholy, all of which can provoke "the distemper of enthusiasm."[202]

In this treatise More was not simply confronting those who claimed to have divine revelations, but also anyone who is overzealous or experiences too much joy. Zeal is seen as a fruit of "melancholy when it is heated."[203] He described the melancholy person as one who ebbs and flows between excitement and depression, a description similar to the modern diagnosis of bipolar disorder.[204] He heavily depended on Aristotle and mentioned no scriptures in this discussion, whereas the puritans encouraged zeal and supported their contention with scripture.[205] Not only did he caution against zeal but also excessive joy. More believed that "Ecstasies and Raptures with triumphant joy and singing" was a result of heat rather than God overcoming the "Heart and Blood".[206] He described the enthusiast as one who is full of zeal, joy and ability to persuade, as well as possessing a romantic nature though blighted by pride that leads to supposed revelations from God. The tremendous highs and lows which accompanied such suppositions reveals that it is not the Spirit but rather the combination of melancholy and sanguine personality traits that in fact controls the one who has undergone such fits.

More explained away all the proofs which the enthusiasts used to show they were from God. Revelations, visions, ecstasy and quakings were all products of melancholy, he claimed, rather than being of the Spirit. It was only by chance that the enthusiast occasionally got some of their prophecies correct and even dramatic healing could be attributed to "boiled blood and spirits" rather than the Holy Spirit.[207] He also said that the overcoming of sin and a life of self-denial was no proof of divine sanction because it could simply be the victory of the "sanguine temper" over the melancholy.[208]

More blamed melancholy on vapors and fumes and for him the cure was quite simply temperance, humility and reason. Those suffering from melancholy should first practice temperance:

> By Temperance I understand a measurable Abstinence from all hot or heightening meats or drinks, as also from all venereous pleasures and tactuall delights of the Body, from all softness and effeminacy; a constant and peremptory adhesion to the perfectest degree of Chastity in the single life, and of Continency in wedlock, that can be attain'd to. For it is plain in sundry examples of Enthusiasm above

---

[202] Ibid., 2:4-10. Later he compared enthusiasm with the affects of wine in its distorting of reason, stating, "A man in wine will kisse such persons as a sober man would scarce touch with a pair of tongs, by reason of their age and uglinesse." Ibid., 2:14.
[203] Ibid., 2:12.
[204] Ibid., 2:12-13. He called this fluctuation between joy and despair "a Paroxysme of Melancholy."
[205] I.e. William Bates, *Works*, 3:426.
[206] Henry More, *A Collection*, 2:17. He called this "enthusiastical joy" which is just heated melancholy.
[207] Ibid., 2:18-21, 40-41.
[208] Ibid., 2:25.

named, that the more hidden and lurking fumes of Lust had tainted the Phansies of those Pretenders to Prophecy and Inspiration.[209]

He advocated abstinence of pleasure in order to be able to reason properly; the elevation of the mind over the heart and body is evident. Even in his definition of humility he included "a privation of all desire" revealing that the rational elements of the soul can only work to their full potential when the affectionate parts of the soul are resisted.[210]

He concluded with a test on how to discover "pure religion and complexion."[211] Here he admitted that some affection is necessary in religion, even calling for "a delicious sense of the divine life."[212] He disclosed with approval that Plato and Plotinus had "more then ordinary sensible visits of the divine Love and Beauty descending into their enravished Souls."[213] These rational affections must pass three tests before they should be considered as having come from God. The first test was the "goodness" or holiness test; did the person's lifestyle match their experience? The second test was biblical; did the experience line up with the teaching of the Old and New Testaments? The final test was the rational, "whereby a man neither admits nor acts any thing but what is solidly rational at the bottom."[214] For More reason appears to be elevated to an equal status with scripture in order to determine the validity of true spiritual experience.

Meric Casaubon was an Anglican minister who lost his living in 1644 and was imprisoned, fined and accused of popery and ecclesiastical innovation. He recovered his living at the restoration and wrote several treatises advocating a rational faith.[215] In his book *A Treatise Concerning Enthusiasme* he sought to reveal how modern manifestations of prophecy, ecstasies, visions, trances and healings could be understood as natural rather than supernatural phenomena. He defined enthusiasm as "an extraordinary, transcendent, but natural fervency, or pregnancy of the soul, spirits, or brain, producing strange effects, apt to be mistaken for supernatural."[216] Expressions of enthusiasm, whether some sort of divine revelation or ecstatic behavior, stem from melancholy, which he saw as a disease.[217] He listed several examples, both contemporary to him and historic, of supernatural phenomena including healing and gave natural

---

[209] Ibid., 2:37.

[210] Ibid.

[211] Ibid., 2:44-47.

[212] Ibid., 2:45. Heyd notes, "It is only at this point, toward the very end of his text, that More hints at a positive role of melancholy, thus linking himself with the Platonic tradition of the Renaissance." *Be Sober and Reasonable*, 102.

[213] Henry More, *A Collection*, 2:45.

[214] Ibid.

[215] R.W. Serjeantson, "Casaubon, Meric", *Oxford Dictionary of National Biography*.

[216] Meric Casaubon, *A Treatise Concerning Enthusiasme*, 17.

[217] Ibid., 28.

explanations for them.[218] He admitted that not all ecstasies or dreams were necessarily natural, and therefore was open to the possibility of God or Satan being the author, but the thrust of the book endorsed skepticism toward contemporary supernatural behavior and phenomena.[219] He argued for a taming of the passions and advocated doubt concerning anything beyond a calm rational experience.[220] This was all based on his belief that those affected by melancholy producing enthusiasm "hath attained to a good degree of Madnesse, without rapture, which makes him so much to undervalue the highest gift of God, (Grace excepted, which is but a perfection of Reason, or a reformation of corrupt Reason;) sound reason."[221] Reason seems to be elevated above all other faculties and becomes the arbitrator as to whether any phenomena is from God or not. For Casaubon even grace is "a perfection of reason" and "sound reason" is the highest gift of God. Thus the Anglicans moved away from the affections and toward the mind in their understanding of enthusiasm.[222]

There were various beliefs among puritans concerning the cessation of the supernatural gifts of the Spirit and a range of experiential expressions; therefore the label of enthusiast was not always unwarranted. In the seventeenth century several treatises were published from radical puritan and Quaker tendencies which exalted the supernatural, their titles alone revealing an extreme experience-oriented faith: *A True Relation of an Apparition in the likeness of a Bird with a white brest, that appeared hovering over the Death-Beds of some of the children of Mr. James Oxenhame of Sale Monachorum, Devon. Gent.;*[223] *The Spirits Voice Concerning Himselfe: or, A Faithful and Clear Discovery Of the Operations of the Spirit in The Hearts of the Saints;*[224] *A True Relation of A Yong Man About Seventeen Years of Age, who was struck Dumb for the space of Twenty Four Hours, Because he would not believe what was said unto him;*[225] *Wonderful and Strange NEWS from Scotland, being A true and full Relation of a Person lately Deceased at the Town of Dumfreez, whose Corps could by no Art of Man, or Strength of Cattle, be Removed from the Place where it Lay. And when the House wherein it was, was wholly Burnt down to the Ground, the Body, Coffin, and Table whereon it stood, remained Whole and*

---

[218] Ibid., 34-35, 66-71. He also said that some people can naturally do extraordinary things, what he calls *idosycrisiae*, such as cry, sweat, swoon or go into a trance at will, which may even be contagious. Ibid., 96-98.

[219] Ibid., 34-35, 60-61.

[220] Ibid., 62-63.

[221] Ibid., 47.

[222] See also Matthew Hole, *The True Reformation of Manners, or the Nature and Qualifications of True Zeal: in a Sermon* (Oxford: L. Lichfield, 1699), passim, and George Hickes, *The Spirit of Enthusiasm Exorcised* (London: Printed for Walter Kettiiby, 1680), passim.

[223] Anon, (London: I.O., 1641), passim.

[224] Peter Atkinson, (London: Thomas Lock, 1659), passim.

[225] Thomas Astry, (London: Printed for the Author, 1671), passim.

*Untoucht, and so Continues to the great Astonishment of all Spectators.*[226]
However many of the puritans were cessationists or semi-cessationists partially
because of what they saw as superstition in Roman Catholicism and unchecked
fanaticism in the Quakers.[227]   Charnock believed that the extraordinary works
of miracles were used by God to establish the church, but once established he
took care of it "in an ordinary way of providence."[228]   The Westminster
Confession rejected new revelation stating, "Unto which [the scriptures]
nothing at any time is to be added, whether by new revelations of the Spirit, or
traditions of men."[229]   Flavel said, "But now, all are tied up to the ordinary
standing rule of the written word, and must not expect any such extraordinary
revelations from God,"[230] but prior to this he described with approval a divine
premonition of one Mr. Dod that brought about the rescue of a man about to
commit suicide.[231]  It is also noted in his biography that he was rescued from
death twice through the mediation of dreams.[232]   Bates believed that new
miracles could only be expected "when the gospel is first preached to a nation"
but not subsequently.[233]   There were varying opinions among the puritans
concerning new revelations from God, from complete openness to the
phenomena, partial acceptance to certain types of revelation such as dreams and
premonitions, acceptance in certain cases such as new territories for missions,
to complete cessation of all the supernatural gifts.

For the latitude puritans the balance of head and heart had become a
precarious thing when the issue of enthusiasm was involved.  On the one hand
they sought the respect of the latitudinarians in their effort to obtain a

---

[226] Faithfully Communicated by a Person of Quality, (London: Printed for B.H., 1673),
passim.

[227] Charnock claimed the papacy "imposed their own dreams with as much force as the
revelations of God…turn[ing] the simplicity of the gospel into pagan pomp." *Existence
and Attributes of God*, 1:588.

[228] Stephen Charnock, *Works*, 3:8.  He goes on to say, "We have now rational ways to
introduce us to a belief of the Christian doctrine; and…there are no sensible miracles as
before." See also 1:113.

[229] Philip Schaff, *Creeds of Christendom*, 3:603.

[230] John Flavel, *The Works of John Flavel*, 4:468.  See also 4:124, 173.

[231] Ibid., 4:399.  "And I find it recorded…of that holy man, Mr. Dod, that being late at
night in his study, he was strongly moved (though at an unseasonable hour) to visit a
gentleman of his acquaintance; and not knowing what might be the design of providence
therein, he obeyed and went.  When he came to the house, after a few knocks at the
door, the gentleman himself came to him, and asked him whether he had any business
with him?  Mr. Dod answered, No; but that he could not be quiet till he had seen him.  O
sir, (replied the gentleman) you are sent of God at this hour, for just now (and with that
takes the halter out of his pocket) I was going to destroy myself.  And thus was the
mischief prevented."

[232] Ibid., 1:iv, viii.

[233] William Bates, *Works*, 1:164.  Baxter appears to have been even more open to the
"age of miracles" continuing into the present day.  William Lamont, *Puritanism and
Historical Controversy*, 171.

comprehensive church and therefore showed an appreciation for their concern over the wild enthusiasm of some of the sects in England. In his autobiography Baxter warned, "That we must very much take heed lest we ascribe melancholy phantasms and passions to God's Spirit; for they are strange apprehensions that melancholy can cause."[234]   Howe warned against those who saw reason as necessarily evil and described their view negatively: "As if reason and judgment were utterly execrated, and an unaccountable, enthusiastic fury, baptized and hallowed, the only principle of religion."[235]   Even Charnock, who seems to have been slightly less on the rational side of the head/heart balance than Baxter and Howe, warned: "All truth is to be drawn from Scripture.... [God] doth not send us for truth, to the puddles of human inventions, to the enthusiasms of our brain."[236]

On the other hand the latitude puritans fully embraced an experiential faith like the rest of the puritans.   Though Charnock warned against an ignorant zeal,[237] he promoted an ardent zeal for God expressed in the affections and will:

> To have a zeal for the glorifying of God, and an overruling design for his honor...to have a heart full of the fear of God...to have a sense of his power, an eye to his glory, admiring thoughts of his wisdom, a faith in his truth...to have a hatred of his habitual lusts...to loath them as much as he loved them; to cherish the duties he hated; to make a stout wretch willingly fall down, crawl upon the ground, and adore that Saviour whom before he out-dared is a triumphant act of Infinite Power.[238]

Bates said the human passions "are of excellent use, when subordinate to the direction of the renewed mind, and the empire of the sanctified will.... And when sanctified, transport the soul to the divine world, to obtain felicity above."[239]   He described the importance of zeal in the minister:

> Zeal for the glory of our Saviour, if it inflame our hearts, will fire our lips, and animate our sermons.  Let knowledge be the breath to blow the sacred fire, and the most burning zeal is not excessive.  But our affections at the highest are very defective: how many preach the word so coldly, as if they had no desire to save souls from eternal death?[240]

---

[234] Richard Baxter, *The Autobiography of Richard Baxter*, 216-217.

[235] John Howe, *Works*, 1:8.

[236] Stephen Charnock, *The Existence and Attributes of God*, 1:504.

[237] He said, "Nothing is so great an enemy to true Christianity as ignorant zeal; nothing so hurtful as passion, clothed with the purple of a seeming piety." *Works*, 4:165.

[238] Stephen Charnock, *The Existence and Attributes of God*, 2:77.  Concerning our will he said, "If his goodness hath such an influence upon us as to make us love him, it will also move us with an ardent zeal to imitate him in it." Ibid., 2:353.

[239] William Bates, *Works*, 2:74.

[240] Ibid., 4:164.  He also saw zeal in every Christian as crucial to their growth in grace and evidence of filial love toward God.  "From filial love proceeds a zeal for his glory.... Those who with an indifferent eye see the cause, the truth, the interest of God

The differences between the puritans and the Anglicans relating to enthusiasm reveal a difference in focus concerning the head and the heart. In seventeenth century England the Anglicans were shying away from certain expressions of heart religion, settling for a more rational faith.[241] The latitude puritans tried to maintain a balance of heart and head while recognizing the inherent dangers in focusing on the heart. They maintained that an experiential and zealous faith was possible and desirable if subordinate to the truths of scripture. They did not pursue new revelations from God and so should not have been placed within the same category of enthusiasm as the more radical puritans and Quakers.[242]

---

depressed in the world, do renounce the title of his children." Ibid., 4:320; see also 2:524.

[241] Michael Heyd includes Anglicans and continental reformers when he states, "In confronting the enthusiasts, Protestant theologians on the eve of the Enlightenment thus reversed the traditional relationship between faith and reason, and turned the latter into a judge of the former." *Be Sober and Reasonable*, 180.

[242] This debate over enthusiasm will continue into the eighteenth century with the old lights accusing the new lights of enthusiasm and the new lights defending themselves as seen in the original title of Joseph Bellamy, *True Religion Delineated; or, Experimental Religion, as Distinguished from Formality on the One Hand, and Enthusiasm on the Other* (Ames, IA: International Outreach, 1997), passim.

# CHAPTER THREE

# KNOWLEDGE OF GOD: NATURAL THEOLOGY

In seventeenth century England a heightened interest in natural theology appeared to occur though the radical puritan camp seems not to have partaken of it. This intense concentration on finding evidences for God's existence in nature may be attributed to the scientific revolution, which naturally encouraged the use of the mind.[1] At this time science and philosophy went hand in hand as seen in the writings of Descartes, Francis Bacon, Robert Boyle, John Locke, Isaac Newton and the members of the Royal Society. Although they were scientists and philosophers, they felt that religion, within the sphere of rationality, was a valid sphere of endeavor.[2] The range of perceptions between the heart and the head can be illustrated in the study of natural theology in seventeenth century England. There were two major areas of natural theology that reflect the great variations of importance given to the mind or heart: the limits of natural theology and reason in general, and the proofs for the existence of God. Stephen Charnock and the latitude puritans attempted to balance the puritan focus on the heart with the Anglican accent on the mind in the area of natural theology.

## 1. The Limits of Natural Theology

The original reformers held a natural theology that was enough to condemn all of humanity if they did not receive Christ, but not enough actually to lead anyone to Christ. Natural theology was derived from general revelation where God has spoken to all of humanity through an innate knowledge as well as by outward observation of creation through the use of God-given reason. Throughout the sixteenth and seventeenth centuries proofs for the existence of God were taken for granted as well as the existence of an innate understanding of God in all people, though it was believed that this general revelation was severely limited in its scope. With the dawning of the new science and a

---

[1] G.R. Cragg, *From Puritanism to the Age of Reason*, 110; Jonathan Hill, *Faith in the Age of Reason* (Downers Grove: Inter Varsity Press, 2004), 51-72.

[2] Francis Bacon, *Essays* (Hertfordshire: Wordsworth Editions, 1997), 9-12, 45-47; *A Confession of Faith* (London: Printed for William Hope, 1641), passim; Isaac Newton, *Four Letters from Sir Isaac Newton to Doctor Bentley containing some Arguments in Proof of a Deity* (London: Printed for R. and J. Dodsley, 1756), passim; Robert Boyle, *The Theological Works of the Honourable Robert Boyle*, (London: W. Tatlor, 1715), passim, especially 1:375-432; John Locke, *The Reasonableness of Christianity* (Stanford University Press, 1958), passim.

gradually more positive view of humanity, these limitations were lifted and natural theology was elevated to varying degrees. A comparison of the views of the original reformers with those of the radical puritans on one side and the Anglicans, philosophers and scientists on the other, with the latitude puritans somewhere in between, will reveal this progression.

Calvin, Bullinger, Beza, Vermigli, Zanchius and other reformers believed that God had spoken to all of humanity in some sense, but that sin had curtailed people's ability effectively to hear his speech. Calvin arranged his *Institutes* in what has been called the *duplex cognitio Domini*.[3] He first wrote of God as creator and then as redeemer. This ordering principle is not identical with the familiar pairing of general and special revelation because God as creator is revealed in both general *and* special revelation.[4] For Calvin God has spoken in general revelation in two ways, through a *sensus divinitatis* and by observation of the external world. The *sensus divinitatis* is an innate knowledge of God placed within every human person.[5] Coupled with this "seed of religion" "sowed in men's minds" God also "daily discloses himself in the whole workmanship of the universe."[6] This revelation is so obvious to all that "even unlettered and stupid folk cannot plead the excuse of ignorance."[7] Later he described this revelation as a "dazzling theatre" of his glory.[8] But even though these two types of knowledge are religiously valid, for Calvin they serve no other purpose than to condemn the unbeliever; this is true because of the depravity of sin. People have consciously turned away from God[9] and embraced "empty speculations" instead of the truth about God.[10] But even their idolatry proves the reality of this revelation, firstly in that religion exists everywhere, and secondly, that overwhelming evidence of creation forces even human pride to bow to some form of deity.[11] "The function of the *opera Dei* as revelation is therefore negative, to take away any excuse for sin and so to make men guilty before God."[12]

The other reformers were equally as negative concerning the limits of natural revelation. They believed that every aspect of the soul, including reason, was corrupted by the fall and therefore incapable of leading individuals

---

[3] Edward Dowey, Jr., *The Knowledge of God in Calvin's Theology*, 42. Dowey claims that the *duplex cognitio Domini* is a more "significant ordering principle of the *Institutes* in the 1559 edition" than its order in terms of the Apostle's Creed.

[4] Ibid., 43.

[5] John Calvin, *Institutes*, I. 3,1. Calvin stated, "God himself has implanted in all men a certain understanding of his divine majesty."

[6] Ibid., I. 5,1.

[7] Ibid.

[8] Ibid., I. 5,8. In I. 5,5 he said the universe was "founded as a spectacle of God's glory."

[9] Ibid., I. 5,2.

[10] Ibid., I. 5,1.

[11] Ibid., I. 3,1.

[12] T.H.L. Parker, *The Doctrine of the Knowledge of God: A Study in the Theology of John Calvin* (Edinburgh: Oliver and Boyd, 1952), 39.

to God. Bullinger said "that God cannot be rightly known but by his word" even though "the workmanship of the world" does reveal his existence.[13] Beza believed that human reason should be able to recognize some basic facts about God, that he exists and that he is one. Rather than being refuted with words, therefore, atheists "ought to bee cleane rooted out of the societie of men by the Magistrate" because of their "raving madness."[14] He also embraced Calvin's idea of the innate knowledge of God "imprinted in the mind of every man, which cannot altogether be put out."[15] But due to the depravity of humans', natural revelation only leaves them without excuse, and unless further revelation is attained "they leave man straying and groping in the darke, and are smallic (sic) or nothing behoofull unto him."[16] Ussher was slightly more positive in allowing general revelation to both "make men void of excuse" and "to further unto salvation; and that by preparing and inducing men to seek God...whereby they are made more apt to acknowledge him when he is perfectly revealed in his word."[17] Ussher opens the possibility that general revelation can be used as a help to lead the unbeliever to Christ when combined with the special revelation of the Bible, but is not sufficient of its own accord; it can be a supplement to the Bible but not a substitute. When asked about the sufficiency of general revelation concerning our salvation he responded, "They may leave us without excuse and so are sufficient unto condemnation; but are not able to make us wise unto salvation."[18]

In seventeenth century England the idea of the two 'books' of God, namely general and special revelation, was amplified with a much more positive view now being afforded to the first book. George Becker notes "scientists and virtuosi-theologians alike urged exploration of 'the vast library of creation' as a necessary compliment to the knowledge of the Scriptures."[19] Here we see that natural revelation is no longer seen as a handmaid to the Bible, but rather it becomes more or less equal to special revelation.[20] In other words, general revelation is now transforming itself into a wholesale scheme of natural

---

[13] Henry Bullinger, *Decades*, 2:125.
[14] Theodore Beza, *Propositions and Principles of Divinitie*, 2.
[15] Ibid. He called this knowledge "certain motions and sparks of the knowledge of God."
[16] Ibid.
[17] James Ussher, *A Body of Divinity*, 3-4. William Perkins made similar statements: "For the light of nature is onely a way of preparation to faith; But this light [the writings of the prophets and apostles] serves to beget faith, and causeth us to believe there is a God." *The Works of That Famous and Worthy Minister of Christ in the Universitie of Cambridge, M. William Perkins* (London: John Legatt, 1631), 2:52.
[18] James Ussher, *A Body of Divinity*, 4.
[19] George Becker, "Pietism's Confrontation With Enlightenment Rationalism: An Examination of the Relation Between Ascetic Protestantism and Science" in *Journal for the Scientific Study of Religion* (1991) 30:141.
[20] Becker states, "They were complimentary and harmonious endeavors where the rationality of science concurred with the 'oracles of God.'" Ibid., 142.

theology. Richard Westfall argues for "the rise of natural science to a position of intellectual dominance over Christianity" where the reconciliation of science and religion "came more and more to mean the adjustment of Christian beliefs to conform to the conclusions of science."[21]

There were three major opinions concerning the limits of natural theology at this time: the radical puritan understanding, the Anglican view and the moderate puritan perspective. Whereas the latter two views were more positive than those of the original reformers discussed above, the radical puritan viewpoint was more negative. Christopher Hill describes the emerging of the radical party within puritanism comprised of a number of subgroups including levelers, diggers, fifth monarchists, seekers, ranters, Baptists, Muggletonians and Quakers. These groups differed in many respects but all seemed to come from the lower classes, having been given a newfound freedom of speech due to the egalitarian nature of life within the New Model Army.[22] Both political and religious innovations were prolific at this time with a general consensus among the radicals that reason, at least the reason beloved of the philosophers and clergy, was suspect. For many in these parties natural theology was the result of human pride and consequently useless whereas revealed theology was the only valid way of gaining a real knowledge of God and his ways.

Many of those in the radical camp of puritans argued against a university trained clergy, seeing natural truth in opposition to spiritual truth and spiritual truth being available to everyone who has the Spirit.[23] William Dell believed "The Power of the Holy Ghost" brought a spirit of knowledge, truth and wisdom that remedied the problem of ignorance and false doctrine; this truth was received directly from the Spirit rather than a process of ratiocination.[24] The digger, Gerrard Winstanley, had a peculiar understanding of the inner witness of the Spirit. Because of his pantheistic tendencies[25] he believed everyone had an inner light which he called 'Reason'. Reason for Winstanley was the common man's reason, similar to the Quaker's inner light, not the reason of the philosophers. He believed the sin of Adam was the desire to be "a

---

[21] Richard Westfall, *Science and Religion in Seventeenth Century England* (University of Michigan Press, 1973), 3.
[22] Christopher Hill, *The World Turned Upside Down*, 13-38. He says, "The free discussion which was permitted in this unique army led to a fantastically rapid development of political thinking." Ibid., 25.
[23] William Dell, "A Testimony Against Divinity Degrees in the Universities" in *Select Works of William Dell* (London: Printed for John Kendall, 1773), 552-577. See Christopher Hill, *The World Turned Upside Down*, 300-305.
[24] William Dell, *Select Works*, 19-21.
[25] He called the creation "the clothing of God." Gerrard Winstanley, *Fire in the Bush* (London: Printed for Giles Calvert, 1650), 2. He also spoke of how "man is made spirituall, and swallowed up in life, or taken up into the Being of God." *The Mystery of God Concerning the Whole Creation, Mankinde* (London: I.C., 1649), 18. By this he meant all of creation, embracing a form of universalism. Ibid., 14, 46, 50.

more knowing man then God made him."[26]  Like most of the radicals he had little faith in natural reason; he stated, "You must be dead to your customes before you can run in the Sea of truth, or the River of the water of life."[27] Because of this emphasis on immediate revelation from the Spirit available to everyone, there was little mention of revelation through nature.  A radical would downplay the use of reason, a device for the intellectual elite, in favor of the spirit which was available to all including the uneducated.  This may be why mystery was appealed to so often,[28] whereas those influenced by the new philosophy shied away from mystery.[29]

The few examples of radicals referring to natural theology portrayed it in a negative light.  Saltmarsh agreed that in another dispensation "the light of nature, or reason" revealed the existence of God, but went on to say that in this dispensation "God's own light" can only be seen when the person has died to his own natural abilities.[30]  Thomas Collier contrasted natural reason with God's wisdom.  Before the fall humans had reason, wisdom and understanding, not equal to God, but in his image it was a "perfection of reason above all other creatures."[31]  After the fall "Philosophy, Logic and Rhetorick" became "corrupted reliques" with no useful purpose.[32]  He rebuked the supposed Christians that see human reason as necessary and contrasted the gospel with human wisdom, not seeing any value in the latter.[33]  He criticized those who think "philosophy is the mother of theologie," saying they should be ashamed to make such claims.[34]  There was no gray area for Collier or any blending or borrowing; there are two types of wisdom, that of the first Adam and that of the second Adam, and only the second wisdom is true.[35]  Natural theology was limited to complete uselessness and was considered harmful to many in the radical camp.

In direct contrast to the radicals, many Anglicans and scientists elevated reason and natural theology, seeing few if any limitations in it.  This was not simply a more thoroughgoing rationalism of scholastic thought, but rather a revolt against scholasticism itself.[36]  The rationalism of the new science sought

---

[26] Ibid., 4.

[27] Ibid., 35.

[28] John Saltmarsh, *Sparkles of Glory*, 146-152.

[29] John Toland, *Christianity Not Mysterious* (London: Printed for Sam. Buckley, 1696), passim.

[30] John Saltmarsh, *Sparkles of Glory*, 207-210.

[31] Thomas Collier, *The Marrow of Christianity* (London: Printed for Giles Calvert, 1646), 3.

[32] Ibid.

[33] Ibid., 4.

[34] Ibid.

[35] Ibid., 5-12, 34-37.  He stated that the wisdom of the world "could not help to the knowledge of God," and the Christian is to "despise the worlds wisdome." Ibid., 35.

[36] G.R. Cragg, *From Puritanism to the Age of Reason*, 89; Richard Westfall, *Science and Religion in Seventeenth Century England*, 187-188.

to free religion from the shackles of dogma, making reason the deciding factor for truth. The new science and philosophy rejected scholasticism because of what their practitioners perceived as a misuse of reason. Both systems focused attention on the mind, but the new philosophy rejected detailed doctrines for a simple God of the machine.[37] This did not mean that they rejected the authority of the Bible, but its revelation was interpreted through the lenses of rational thought and "opened the door to a demand for serious changes."[38] Natural theology was advanced to such a place that it became the judge of revealed theology, at least in practice. A progression is discernable in much of Anglicanism in the direction of deism as a reaction to puritanism. Many Anglicans embraced the new "philosopher's method" for at least two reasons: "It promised to replace the weight of dusty authorities with the simple process, accessible to all, of logical argument from clear and distinct ideas to the most complex and yet certain knowledge," and it provided an alternative to "what was regarded as the irrationalism of the Puritan Revolution."[39] The Anglican reaction to the puritan revolution was to reject their scholasticism and enthusiasm, opting for a more cerebral, reserved and simplified theology.[40]

Alongside the Anglican clergy were the *virtuosi* defined by Westfall as "those who took an active interest in promoting the growth of natural science."[41] The virtuosi were those involved in the newly founded Royal Society. They did not reject religion, in fact they actually opposed atheism "demonstrating the existence of God with unanswerable proofs."[42] Natural religion was their source for apologetics and was promoted as a supplement to Christianity. "In practice it tended to displace it."[43] Several scientists also wrote works on religion with the same emphases as the Anglicans, but moving further toward unorthodox beliefs.

Francis Bacon (1561-1626) was a pioneer in the new science and philosophy and maintained good standing with the Church of England. Although he was

---

[37] Westfall describes the virtuosi's view of the schoolmen: "To cover their ignorance they invented endless subtle distinctions without counterparts in reality and employed words that did not have clear ideas behind them. The litigious and disputatious philosophy of the Schoolmen had only confused men's minds without increasing their knowledge." Richard Westfall, *Science and Religion in Seventeenth Century England*, 187.
[38] G.R. Cragg, *From Puritanism to the Age of Reason*, 111.
[39] John Spurr, "Rational Religion in Restoration England" in *Journal of the History of Ideas* (1988), 564.
[40] The Anglicans did not throw out scholasticism completely, especially early Anglicans. Cf. Gabriel Powel, *De Adiaphoris. Theological and Scholastical Positions, Concerning the Nature and Use of Things Indifferent* (London: Felix Kyngston, 1607), passim; Peter Heylyn, *The Summe of Christian Theologie*, passim.
[41] Richard Westfall, *Science and Religion in Seventeenth Century England*, 14.
[42] Ibid., 106.
[43] Ibid.

"preoccupied with the things of this world rather than those of the next,"[44] he wrote *A Confession of Faith* that was orthodox, even reformed in content.[45] What is conspicuously absent, however, is any mention of justification by faith or any kind of experiential piety. In the introduction to Bacon's *Essays* John Strachan says, "It is undeniable that there seems to be a distrust of human emotion in Bacon."[46] Bacon exemplified the latter Anglican tendencies of questioning enthusiasm and overemphasizing religion of the heart and of moving towards a simplification of doctrine. He also believed that providence was not immediate or in violation of natural law.[47] His ideas influenced Locke and Newton greatly as well as the early deists Charles Blount and John Toland.

Robert Boyle (1627-1691) has been called the father of chemistry[48] but his contemporaries were equally impressed by his piety.[49] He wrote voluminously on theological subjects as well as scientific.[50] Boyle sought to make religion reasonable without denying orthodoxy in any way, but like Descartes before him as well as the rest of the virtuosi, he made reason his starting point.[51] Unlike the reformers, the virtuosi made reason and natural religion rather than special revelation the foundation for faith. Boyle does not reject the Bible, but places its interpretation under the rule of reason. He defended the fundamental articles of the faith,[52] but did not say what those articles consist of. He advocated a suspension of belief in the truth or falsehood of any particular doctrine in areas "attended with difficulty."[53] In his system the fundamentals alone remained unsuspended. Without stating any specific doctrines he suggested,

> That if we lay aside all the irrational opinions, that are unreasonably fathered on the Christian Religion, and all erroneous conceits repugnant to Christianity, which

---

[44] Francis Bacon, *Essays*, xii.

[45] Francis Bacon, *A Confession of Faith*. He covers the doctrine of God including the Trinity, election, creation, humanity, the law of God, the Spirit, the church and heaven.

[46] Francis Bacon, *Essays*, xv.

[47] He stated, "Though his working [God's providence] be not immediate and direct, but by compasse; not violating nature, which is his owne law upon the creature." Francis Bacon, *A Confession of Faith*, 4.

[48] Richard Westfall, *Science and Religion*, 40.

[49] Michael Hunter notes: "The central fact of Boyle's life from his adolescence onwards was his deep piety, and it is impossible to understand him without doing justice to this." Michael Hunter, 'Boyle, Robert (1627-1691)', *Oxford Dictionary of National Biography*.

[50] Robert Boyle, *Theological Works*, passim.

[51] See especially "Considerations About the Reconcileableness of Reason and Religion" in his *Works*, 1:375-432; Joseph Glanville stated, "For if reason must not be heard, the being of a GOD, and the authority of Scripture can neither be proved, nor defended; and so our faith drops to the ground, like a house that hath no foundation." *Reason in the Affairs of Religion* (London: E.C. and A.C., 1670), 1.

[52] Robert Boyle, *Theological Works*, 1:426-429.

[53] Ibid., 1:419.

have been groundlessly fathered upon philosophy, the seeming contradictions betwixt Divinity and true philosophy, will be but few, and the real ones none at all.[54]

He believed that the passions get in the way of pure reason, polluting it, and were the means that led astray the different sects of Christianity.[55] He blamed the affections and the will for distorting the understanding, seemingly seeing the mind as being less affected by the fall than the other faculties.[56] Boyle had a devotion to God and like the rest of the virtuosi had no desire to abandon the Christian faith, but this faith becomes more and more "an affair of the head."[57]

John Locke (1632-1704) took the affairs of the mind a step further in his book *The Reasonableness of Christianity*. Whereas the previous virtuosi did not reject any fundamental doctrines of the faith and could be seen at least intellectually as orthodox, Locke discards many of the doctrines important to the original reformers. He denied hell and any form of original sin, embracing a form of Pelagianism.[58] The one article of faith necessary for salvation was the belief in Jesus as the Messiah; by this Locke did not mean that one only needed to agree that Jesus was the Messiah to be considered a Christian, but it was certainly a minimalism compared with the early reformers. [59] He denied the puritan distinction of historical faith and saving faith, claiming a simple intellectual assent is all that is necessary.[60] He admitted a limitation to reason, but only that it needed Christ's help in the area of morality:

> It should seem, by the little that has hitherto been done in it, that 'tis too hard a task for unassisted reason, to establish morality, in all its parts, upon its true foundations, with a clear and convincing light.  And 'tis at least a surer and shorter way to the apprehensions of the vulgar, and mass of mankind, that one manifestly sent from God, and coming with visible authority from him, should, as a King and law-maker, tell them their duties, and require their obedience, than

---

[54] Ibid., 1:398.

[55] Ibid., 1:387.

[56] Ibid., 1:389-390; Joseph Glanville, *Reason in the Affairs of Religion*, 21.

[57] Richard Westfall, *Science and Religion*, 214.

[58] John Locke, *The Reasonableness of Christianity*, 26-27.  He did not deny that Adam fell or that he brought death upon the world, but he specifically rejected the idea that "the corruption of human nature" was in any way passed on to "his posterity," arguing that this idea is not found in the New Testament and is a defamation of the righteousness of God.  Alan Sell reveals that it would not be proper to call Locke a Pelagian and so our understanding of him must be nuanced.  It is perhaps best to consider Locke an inconsistent semi-Pelagian. Alan Sell, *John Locke and the Eighteenth-Century Divines* (Eugene, OR: Wipf and Stock Publishers, 1997), 229-239.

[59] Ibid., 32-43. Sell points out that Locke understood the doctrine of Jesus as Messiah as implying "a range of doctrines," namely the kingdom of God, the death, resurrection and ascension of Christ, and the coming judgment.  Alan Sell, *John Locke*, 188.  Even with this explanation Locke's minimum belief was far less than orthodox Christianity.

[60] John Locke, *The Reasonableness of Christianity*, 43.

leave it to the long, and sometimes intricate deductions of reason, to be made out to them.[61]

"Locke made reason the final arbiter even of those doctrines above reason," and ended up neglecting the doctrine of the Trinity and the deity of Christ, as well as the substitutionary atonement of Christ.[62] Alan Sell points out that Locke never denied the doctrine of the Trinity and even used Trinitarian language informally and so one should be willing to give him the benefit of the doubt.[63] He avoided discussing the doctrine of the Trinity because of his distaste for scholastic wrangling, the fact that the word "Trinity" is not in the Bible, and his expressed purpose of reaching deists,[64] but all of this reveals that the doctrine was not very important to him. When he was accused of denying the Trinity by his peers he never affirmed it, and as Sell comments, "It must, however be conceded that Locke's interpretation of relevant passages of Scripture were, to put it mildly, less than full-bloodedly pro-trinitarian."[65] Locke's rationalist faith focused on Christ as an exalted human that came to be a good example, and belief in his Messiahship was the only fundamental rule of the faith necessary for salvation. His idea of Christianity was a truncated version of the orthodox view largely due to an overemphasis on the mind to the neglect of the heart.

With the virtuosi the elevation of reason was accompanied by the devaluation of doctrine. With Locke one can see a "complete and detailed overthrow of the accepted systems of theology."[66] Natural religion started out as a help to defend Christianity, but "culminated in virtually displacing Christianity in their religious thought."[67] The virtuosi were only a few steps removed from others who severed the heart completely from religion, embracing a religion of the mind alone. The early deists completely abandoned the elements of mystery and miracle. Whereas the virtuosi believed in the initial miracles of the biblical times, the deists held that God would not go against his own laws. Charles Blount (1654-1693) wrote *Miracles, No Violation of the Laws of Nature* and John Toland wrote *Christianity not*

---

[61] Ibid., 60-61.

[62] Westfall states, "Locke rejected the Trinity and the divinity of Christ. Since he excluded the articles of faith that traditional Christianity had considered to be above reason, his category of doctrines above reason was little more than a gesture simulating orthodoxy. It did not lift his conception of Christianity beyond the judgment of the unaided faculties of man." *Science and Religion*, 189, 137. Westfall also reveals that Isaac Newton took a similar religious path as Locke, rejecting the doctrine of the Trinity and the substitutionary atonement. Ibid., 211; Cragg, *From Puritanism to the Age of Reason*, 101.

[63] Alan Sell, *John Locke*, 185, 212-229.

[64] Ibid., 213.

[65] Ibid., 212-215.

[66] G.R. Cragg, *From Puritanism to the Age of Reason*, 126.

[67] Richard Westfall, *Science and Religion*, 192.

*Mysterious.*[68] When no limitations were placed on reason and natural religion, Christianity eventually gave way to deism for many.

With the Anglicans leaning in the direction of the mind and therefore seeing few limitations on reason and natural theology and the radicals inclining toward the heart, placing severe limits on reason, the moderate puritans attempted a balance of heart and head by viewing reason as a handmaid to religion. Charnock's view of reason and natural theology was more positive than the original reformers as seen in his extensive use of reason in his *Existence And Attributes of God.* He leaned more toward Descartes' rationalism than Locke's empiricism, but put restraints on reason. He encouraged his readers to study providence with certain restrictions:

> By faith: we many times correct our sense by reason; when we look through a blue or green glass, and see all things blue or green, though our sense represents them so, yet our reason discovers the mistake. Why should we not correct reason by faith? Indeed, our purblind reason stands in as much need of a regulation by faith, as our deceitful sense doth of a regulation by reason.[69]

Charnock was not afraid to use reason, but only as help and under the direction of faith. Like the Cambridge Platonists he saw reason as "the candle of the Lord," but put more restrictions on it than they.[70]

First, reason was insufficient without revelation because it is blind to the things of God and uncertain, even for the Christian. His doctrine of depravity included the mind and so for the unbeliever it was useless without revelation in the matters of religion. Even for the believer sanctification is a process in both the mind and the heart:

> Since the fall there is as little of pure reason in our minds, as there is of an exact holiness in our will, and the Spirit is as necessary to enlighten the one as to incline the other, the one being as full of prejudices and mistaken principles as the other

---

[68] Blount said that miracles that were supposedly affected by the immediate power of God are "not only inconsistent with, but point blank repugnant to the fundamental Laws and constitutions of Nature, which he in his infinite wisdom hath made, and made so ample and fertile as to extend to the certain production of whatever events he hath will'd and decreed." He claimed this would put God in opposition with God. *Miracles No Violation of the Laws of Nature* (London: Printed for Robert Sollers, 1683), preface. Toland called himself a Christian but rejected all mystery saying "Religion must necessarily be reasonable and intelligible." *Christianity not Mysterious*, xxv. He goes on to rebuke those who claim we should "adore what we cannot comprehend." Ibid., 26. He did not see any limitation to reason and saw the idea of mystery as the root of all superstition including the doctrine of the Trinity. Ibid., 26-27.
[69] Stephen Charnock, *Works*, 1:60.
[70] In reference to "the insufficiency of reason without revelation" he stated, "Reason, though it be 'the candle of the Lord,' Prov. Xx.27, yet it is but a candle, and can no more discover the nature of God as he is to be known in Christ, than a candle can help us to see the sun when it is masked by a thick cloud." Ibid., 4:154.

of corrupt and perverse habits. Hence man is represented in Scripture, Eph. iv. 17-19, with a mind as vain as his will is crooked, an understanding as much darkened towards God as his will is alienated from the life of God, as great a blindness of heart as there is madness of affection, and therefore the apostle gives it no better a title than darkness, Eph. v. 8, comprehending thereby the race of all mankind naturally.[71]

The believer's mind is still corrupted and in process of renewal by the Spirit, but the unbeliever's mind is in complete bondage concerning the things of God.

Second, reason is a servant to revelation, and, if properly submitted to God, can be an assistant to religion by bringing clarity and evidence to those things revealed in scripture.[72] As long as reason was seen as subservient to revelation, it could and should be useful in the kingdom. Charnock was careful to maintain the doctrine of depravity and so did not elevate reason too highly, but he also did not swing in the opposite direction by rejecting reason out of hand. The radical puritans seemed in part to have embraced their anti-intellectual approach as a reaction to the new philosophy, and in turn the Anglicans steered away from a more emotionally based religion due in some measure to their antagonism toward the enthusiasm of the radical puritanism they observed during the interregnum. However, Charnock, along with the latitude puritans and moderate puritans as a whole, acted according to what he understood as scriptural norms, rather than responding to an opponent. They were able to gain from both the radical puritans and the Anglicans in deciding what they believed was the proper place of reason.

Finally, Charnock put limitations on reason without rejecting it in order to ensure special revelation's status as the supreme authority concerning the things of God. An important difference between the moderate puritans and the Anglicans and virtuosi is that they did not start with reason, but rather with God. Charnock presupposed God's revelation and therefore demanded the submission of reason to it; this is especially seen in his evidences for the existence of God.[73]

---

[71] Ibid., 4:155. Baxter stated: It is most certain that when God calls us at first to the knowledge of his truth, he findeth us in darkness; and though he bring us thence into a marvelous light (Acts 26.18. 1 Pet. 2.9) yet he doth this by degrees, and not into the fullest light or measure of knowledge at the first; so that we are at the beginning but babes in knowledge. Richard Baxter, *The Practical Works of the Late Reverend and Pious Mr. Richard Baxter* (London: Printed for Thomas Parkhurst, 1707), 2:356.

[72] Ibid., 4:157.

[73] Charnock rebuked as pride the idea that one must start with reason and proceed to revelation: "Reason exalts itself, and will not submit to revelation, unless it finds marks upon it suitable to its own principles." Ibid., 4:355. Baxter also admonished those who doubt God's truth when difficulties arise, revealing a presuppositional embracing of God's revelation over the use of reason. *The Practical Works of Richard Baxter*, 2:355-358. But then he seems to place reason as the foundation of truth stating, "You must believe nothing but what you have sufficient reason to believe. But then you must know what is sufficient reason for belief. Prove but the thing to be the testimony of God, and

## 2. Proofs for the Existence of God

There are few if any radical puritan works on the existence of God, but for the moderate puritans, Anglicans and virtuosi a plethora of treatises were published in the seventeenth century defending the reality of God against atheism.[74] "On the surface it appears strange to find a vivid apprehension of atheism in an age not noted for its disbelief,"[75] but in view of eighteenth century developments it appears their fears were warranted. Westfall notes that the idea of atheism for the seventeenth century theologian was not the same as today. The atheist was not so much someone who rigorously argued denial of God, but rather "were materialists, Epicureans, those who held that the universe is the chance concourse of atoms in motion."[76] The atheist was the immoral person who lived as if God did not exist, whereas the divines held that since God was the fount of morality a blatantly immoral lifestyle was a form of atheism. There were similarities and differences in the way the different groups sought to defend the existence of God with a natural theology. The Anglicans, virtuosi and puritans had a high confidence in the evidence for God's existence, but the Anglican and virtuosi tended to have an equally high confidence in human potential to discern the evidence. The puritans, for their part, continued the

---

then you have sufficient reason to believe it, whatsoever it be." Ibid., 2:361. Howe had a similar view to the new philosophy seeing natural theology as the foundation to special revelation: "And any one that considers, will soon see it were very unseasonable, at least, to allege the written, divine revelation, as the ground of his religion, till he have gone lower, and fore-known some things (by and by to be insisted on) as preparatory and fundamental to the knowledge of this." John Howe, *Works*, 1:9. He believed that we are to use reason to discover that revelation is trustworthy and then submit our reason to that revelation.

[74] Isaac Newton declared a major purpose for his *Principia* was for men to believe in a deity, because the universe could not "spring from any natural cause alone, but were impressed by an intelligent agent." Isaac Newton, *Four Letters*, 1, 5.

[75] Richard Westfall, *Science and Religion*, 107. They apparently felt atheism was prolific. Charnock stated, "How lamentable is it that in our times this folly of atheism should be so rife! That there should be found such monsters in human nature, in the midst of the improvements of reason and shinings of the gospel." *Works*, 1:175. Tillotson echoed the belief that atheism was on the rise, "We live in so profane and skeptical an age as to call in question the most universally received principles both of reason and religion." *A System of Divinity and Morality*, 1. Bates said there were few public atheists, but probably many "who conceal themselves in secret, and dare not appear in open view." *Works*, 1:3.

[76] Richard Westfall, *Science and Religion*, 108. John Howe described his opponent in his apologetic work *Living Temple*: "I speak of such as deny the existence of the ever-blessed Deity; or (if they are not arrived to that express and formed misbelief) whose hearts are inclined, and ready to determine, even against their misgiving and more suspicious minds, there is no God: who, if they cannot as yet believe, do wish there were none; and so strongly, as in a great degree to prepare them for that belief." *Works*, 1:7.

position of the reformers in denying human ability to perceive God in any valid sense through reason. Most Anglicans and virtuosi were Arminian in their theology and owing to an espousal of the new science an optimism of the future led to a general overall confidence in humanity. The puritans maintained the reformers view that general revelation mainly increased the culpability of unbelievers, rather than leading them to God.[77] Some, though, did not close the door completely. Baxter discussed the question of whether an unbeliever could be saved on the basis of general revelation alone. He stated that there was no proof of it in scripture, but there was no specific scriptural passage which precluded the idea either.[78] This optimism among some puritans can be traced to Amyraut who claimed that one who never hears the gospel could be saved if he or she placed their faith in God's mercy and repented of their sin.[79] The Anglicans may also have influenced the latitude puritans as they sought common ground for possible comprehension. In a collection of essays by Anglican divines, Richard Bentley sounded very similar to Baxter: "We do acknowledge it to be true, that faith in Christ Jesus is the only way to salvation since the preaching of the gospel. But we do not determine the case of those who never heard of the Lord of life; because in this, God and Scripture are silent."[80]

Another noticeable difference between the three groups was the style of writing. The virtuosi tended to be very technical and used detailed scientific examples to prove their points.[81] The Anglicans tended to be more

---

[77] Thomas Boston summed up the typical puritan understanding of natural theology: "Though the light of nature directs us to many excellent moral duties, as to honour our parents, to do to others as we would have them to deal with us, etc. yet it cannot teach us to perform these duties in an acceptable manner. The apostle tells us, that 'the natural man receiveth not the things of the Spirit of God.' The mind of man by nature hath not only a native blindness, by reason of which it cannot discern the things of the Spirit, but also a natural enmity that it hates the light; so that till the mind be healed and enlightened by Christ, the natural faculty can no more discern the things of the Spirit, than the sensitive faculty can discern the things of reason." Thomas Boston, *Works*, 1:424. Charnock stated, "It is the knowledge of God as discovered, not in the creatures, but in the Scripture; a knowledge of God through faith in Christ, which is able to make us wise to salvation." *Works*, 4:15.

[78] Richard Baxter, *The Practical Works of Richard Baxter*, 4:627. He went on to say that Catholics and heretics could even be saved if they were a true lover of God. Elsewhere he seemed to indicate that a few philosophers may have appropriated natural revelation, but few had the "leisure for so deep and long a search into nature, as a few philosophers made," and therefore needed the special revelation of the Bible as a "clearer light." *The Practial Works of Richard Baxter*, 2:71.

[79] Moise Amyraut, *Brief Treatise on Predestination*, 40.

[80] *A System of Divinity and Morality*, 1:181.

[81] Boyle used the properties of a loadstone and magnetism to prove his point. Robert Boyle, *Theological Works*, 408-412 Walter Charleton uses vegetables to disprove the idea of chance: "Nor doe animals alone, but vegetables also, though of an inferior classis, amply and sensibly testifie the divinity of their founder, and confute the

philosophical than the puritans, but more readable for the average reader than the virtuosi.[82] The puritans were more inclined toward a devotional treatment, seeking to be practical and influence both the mind and heart.[83]

---

apotheosis of fortune. Thus, when the aliment of a plant, being the aqueous irrigation of the earth insensibly prolected, ascends from the lowest filament of the shaggy root up to the trunck, and thence works up to the extremities of every branch and twigge; can we imagine, that this thin, insipid juice can be so inspissated, and so ingeniously moulded into a bud; that bud discriminated and variegated into a larger particoloured blossom; that blossom gradually expanded into a determinate flower, which gratifies our eyes with the beauty of its embroidery, and our nostrils with the fragrancy of its odour; that flower lost in the richer emergencie of a fruit, which hath its figure, colour, magnitude, odour, sapour, maturity, duration, all certain and constant; and the abridgement, or epitome of this included in the seed of that fruit, which being insperst upon the earth, is impregnate with a faculty to expand it self into a second plant, in all things rival to the former, and empowered to act all those several metamorphoses over again, to a perpetuall rejuvenescence of the peculiar species: can we, I say, imagine, that all this could arise from a spontaneous range of atoms, or that necessity which ensued upon the casual disposition of the first matter; and not rather with devout hymns proclaim the efficiency of a glorious and eternall cause, whose essence being incomprehensible, and attributes infinite intelligence, goodness, power, beatitude, glory, etc. must therefore be the ordainer, creator, and consecrator of all things?" *The Darkness of Atheism Dispelled by the Light of Nature: A Physico-Theologicall Treatise* (London: J.P., 1652), 56.
[82] Tillotson began his treatise, "We live in so profane and skeptical an age as to call in question the most universally received principles both of reason and religion. The bold cavils of perverse and unreasonable men are such, as to oblige us to prove and defend those principles, which can hardly be made plainer than they are of themselves; even, that there is a God, by whom all things were made. I shall therefore endeavour to shew from the reason of things the great folly of atheism." *A System of Divinity and Morality*, 1:1.
[83] In speaking of philosophical principles in the puritan theology James M'Cosh, Charnock's biographer stated in his introduction to Charnock's *Works*, "[The puritans] never proposed, as some in our day have done, to make reason the sole discerner and judge of religion. With the puritan, religion was an affair of the whole man, including head and heart, and the heart having not only emotive sensibility and attachment, but a conscience to discern good and evil, and a will to choose." *Works of Stephen Charnock*, 1:xl. As an example of his more devotional style Charnock declared, "The evidence of a God results from the vastness of desires in man, and the real dissatisfaction he hath in everything below himself. Man hath a boundless appetite after some sovereign good; as his understanding is more capacious than anything below, so is his appetite larger. This affection of desire exceeds all other affections.... Whence should the soul of man have those desires?... Every affection of his soul hath an object, and that in this world; and shall there be none for his desire, which come nearest to infinite of any affection planted in him? This boundless desire had not its original from man himself; nothing would render itself restless; something above the bounds of this world implanted those desires after a higher good, and made him restless in everything else.... There is, therefore, some infinite being that can only give a contentment to the soul, and this is God. And

Another difference between the puritans, Anglicans and virtuosi was their starting point. Whereas the virtuosi attempted to prove the atheists wrong by beginning from a common place of doubt, the puritans and second reformation Dutch assumed the existence of God and proceeded to confirm what they already believed. The virtuosi followed Descartes' system of doubt and for the most part favorably embraced his new philosophy,[84] though many rejected his strict mechanical view of creation.[85] They believed God sustained his creation through secondary means and at times described the world as a machine, but were not willing to abandon "the medieval conception that nature is the product of divine goodness."[86] Puritans and Anglicans were mixed in their reaction to Descartes for differing reasons. Voetius, from whom many puritans learned, reacted against Descartes' starting point of doubt, which seemed to place the focus on humankind.[87] Some Anglicans opposed Descartes for what they saw

---

that goodness which implanted such desires in the soul, would not do it to no purpose, and mock it in giving it an infinite desire of satisfaction, without intending it the pleasure of enjoyment, if it doth not by its own folly deprive itself of it. The felicity of human nature must needs exceed that which is allotted to other creatures." *The Existence and Attributes of God*, 1:73-74. This argument sounds very similar to Pascal in style and content. Charnock does not cite Pascal here, but he does elsewhere revealing he has read Pascal's *Pensees*. *Works*, 1:235; see Blaise Pascal, *Pensees* (New York: E.P. Dutton, 1958), 113.

[84] In differentiating dictates and propensities from the light of nature, Walter Charleton stated, "Whatever things are declared unto me, by the light of nature; as this, that I am, because I doubt, that 2 and 3 make 5, etc. can never, on any pretence, be doubted of, in regard there can be no other faculty, or criterion to whose judgment or decision, I can afford so ample and firme credit, as to that of the light of nature, which onely can teach me, whether those things are true or false." *The Darkness of Atheism Dispelled by the Light of Nature: A Physico-Theologicall Treatise*, 7; Robert Boyle, *Theological Works*, 1:386, 394, 407.

[85] John Ray spoke against the "mechanical philosophers" who seemed to describe the world as a machine and rejected the "consideration of final causes." *The Wisdom of God Manifested in the Works of the Creation* (London: Printed for D. Williams, 1762), 16-29.

[86] Richard Westfall, *Science and Religion*, 51. Westfall elaborates: "Spurning the rigorous implications of the mechanical conception of nature which Descartes and Spinoza drew in rejecting the investigation of final causes, the English virtuosi, almost without exception, refused to look upon nature as an impersonal machine. Inconsistent though they may have been, they combined the mechanical view of nature with the medieval conception that nature is the product of divine goodness. A deep-seated conviction that creation is a benevolent order reflecting divine goodness meant that in their minds the seemingly inexorable cosmic machine lost its harsh and inhuman aspect because it ran with the lubricant of infinite love. Thus the virtuosi's conception of nature was an amalgam of the new mechanical hypothesis and the Christian philosophy of the Middle Ages, an amalgam which made it possible for them to employ the arguments of teleology without conscious inconsistency."

[87] Richard Muller, *Post-Reformation Reformed Dogmatics*, 1:397.

as a type of enthusiasm.[88]  Though Charnock was more favorable to Descartes than Voetius or Casaubon, he rejected his starting point of doubt and held instead to a presuppositional view:

> We ought therefore to submit our reasonings to God's declaration.  The rational creature was made to serve God.  His reason, then, ought to be held in the rank of a servant; the light of reason ought to veil to the author of reason, and the light in the mind ought to veil to him who enlightened it when man came into the world.  Reason ought to follow faith, not precede it.  The stars borrow their light from the sun, not the sun from the stars.  Reason, indeed, may come in with an auxiliary force after a revelation is made, for the maintaining the truth of it, and clearing it up to the minds of others, and may be a servant to revelation now under Christ, as well as it should have been to any revelation in the state of innocence.  We ought therefore to submit our reason to God, not think to mate him in knowledge any more than we can in majesty and infiniteness, nor set up a spark to vie with the sun.  Pride put out Adam's eye at first; and the pride of reason cherished will continue us as blind as beetles in the things of a heavenly concern.[89]

It appears that the Anglicans and virtuosi had moved away from the reformers' presuppositional stance that God exists, and sought to prove his existence by reason.[90]  Even Bates and Baxter followed this line of argumentation, whereas Charnock assumed his existence as well as the trustworthiness of the biblical account of religion.[91]

The different works defending theism against atheism all had common themes with slight variations and nuances.  As was typical in seventeenth

---

[88] Michael Heyd, *Be Sober and Reasonable*, 109-143.

[89] Stephen Charnock, *Works*, 4:157.

[90] *A System of Divinity and Morality*, 1:1-14; Glanville placed reason above the existence of God and the authority of the Bible, making it foundational to the two. *Reason in the Affairs of Religion*, 1; virtuosi Walter Charleton began his work defending God's existence with the ontological argument similar to Descartes, proving the innate idea of God: *The Darkness of Atheism Dispelled by the Light of Nature*, 1-38, compare to Rene Descartes, *Discourse on Method and Meditations*, 24-30; virtuosi John Wilkins revealed how reason alone leads us to God's existence, our future state, basic morality and virtue; any "external and extraordinary revelation" is not needed for this and scripture itself cannot contradict natural revelation: "Nothing being more incredible, than that Divine Revelation should contradict the clear and unquestionable dictates of natural light." *Of the Principles and Duties of Natural Religion: Two Books* (London: Printed for R. Bonwicke, W. Freeman, etc., 1715), preface.  He does admit the excellency of the Christian religion "above the mere light of nature" in his last chapter.

[91] William Bates, *Works*, 1:3-55; Richard Baxter, *The Practical Works*, 2:5-70; very similar to Descartes' famous maxim Baxter stated: "By my actions I know that I am; and that I am a sentient, intelligent, thinking, willing and operative being; or a wight that hath these powers." Ibid., 2:5. Stephen Charnock, *The Existence and Attributes of God*, 1:23-88.

century England, Charnock discussed three main proofs for God's existence.[92] The first evidence he gave was the universal belief in a deity: "Tis a folly to deny or doubt of that which hath been the acknowledged sentiment of all nations, in all places and ages. There is no nation but hath owned some kind of religion, and, therefore, no nation but hath consented in the notion of a Supreme Creator and Governor."[93] He argued that if the existence of God were not true there would be some places that did not have this belief, especially considering the idea that many people would like to get rid of the idea of a god: "The wickedness of the world would never have preserved that which was a perpetual molestation to it, had it been possible to be razed out."[94] Wilkins, borrowing from Aristotle, reasoned that if some wise philosophers believed something, it may be deemed probable, but if many wise men embraced something as true, it would be even more likely, and if all men, both wise and unwise, consent to some truth it has "the highest degree of evidence...that anything is capable of."[95]

Charnock argued that the reason for the universality of the belief in a deity is that it is "natural and innate."[96] Tillotson agreed:

> The reason of such universal consent in all places and ages of the world, among all sorts of persons can no way be accounted for, unless we suppose the notion of a Deity, is by nature imprest on the minds and understandings of men, which by the free use and exercise of itself, will find out God. And it is most reasonable to think, that God should set this mark of himself, on all his rational creatures, that they may know and acknowledge the author of their beings.[97]

If it is natural then it must be true, because "it is impossible that nature can naturally and universally lie."[98] Its innate quality also "pleads strongly for the perpetuity of it."[99] Not all agreed with the idea of innate ideas, but most at this time still held to some form of the notion that God placed knowledge of his

---

[92] Bates gives a similar list; *Works*, 1:4; Wilkins, *Of the Principles and Duties of Natural Religion*, 35.

[93] *Existence and Attributes*, 1:29. Wilkins quoted Tully stating, "There is no nation so immensely barbarous and savage, as not to believe the existence of a Deity, and by some kind of services to express their adoration of him." *Of The Principles and Duties of Natural Religion*, 37; John Howe, *Works*, 1:10.

[94] *Existence and Attributes*, 1:35. Similarly he asked, "How comes it therefore to pass, that such a multitude of profligate persons that have been in the world since the fall of man, should not have rooted out this principle, and dispossessed the minds of men of that which gave birth to their tormenting fears?" Ibid., 1:34.

[95] Wilkins, *Of The Principles and Duties of Natural Religion*, 36.

[96] *Existence and Attributes*, 1:35. Bates spoke of a "sense of the Deity indelibly stamped on the minds of men." *Works*, 1:32-33.

[97] *A System of Divinity and Morality*, 1:9.

[98] *Existence and Attributes*, 1:33.

[99] Ibid., 1:35.

existence within human beings.[100]   Charnock saw the inadequacy of innate knowledge and therefore also embraced sensationalism, but did not see a contradiction.   Charnock advanced two reasons for the concept of innate knowledge.  First he promoted Augustine's maxim that everyone is "born with a restless instinct" for God.[101]   Human desire exceeds anything in this world and it makes sense that it comes from God since all other desires have an actual source for their fulfillment.[102]   Second he believed that the conscience was an example of innate knowledge.  He pointed out that the conscience is something humans would not put up with if they had the choice, therefore God must have planted it in them.[103]   The universal notion of a conscience also contends for a deity: "It must be confessed by all, that there is a law of nature writ upon the hearts of men, which will direct them to commendable actions, if they will attend to the writing in their own consciences.  This law cannot be considered without the notice of a Lawgiver."[104]

Charnock anticipated certain objections and answered them.   Thomas Hobbes suggested two possible causes for the origination of religion.  First anxiety over the future and fear in general may have been the natural cause of religion.   It is not found in the rest of the animal kingdom because "it is peculiar to the nature of man to be inquisitive into the causes of the events they see."[105]   His second hypothesis was that religion came from "the first founders and legislators of commonwealths" in order to keep the people obedient to the state.[106]   Hobbes was not an atheist and so made an exception to Christianity in

---

[100] Wilkins queried, "It seems very congruous to reason, that he who is the great Creator of the world, should set some such mark of himself upon those creatures that are capable of worshipping him, whereby they might be led to the author of there being, to whom their worship is to be directed." *Of the Principles and Duties of Natural Religion*, 48; Walter Charleton, *The Darkness of Atheism*, 4-7. Baxter argued that some laws of God were innate while others were learned. *The Practical Works*, 2:29; Spurr declares Locke as the first to publicly jettison "the doctrine of innate ideas," but he argues that it had already become untenable for many.  "Rational Religion in Restoration England" in *Journal of the History of Ideas* (1988), 573.

[101] *Existence and Attributes*, 1:35.

[102] Ibid., 1:73.

[103] "No man would endure a thing that doth frequently molest and disquiet him, if he could cashier it.  It is therefore sown in man by some hand more powerful than man, which riseth so high, and is rooted so strong, that all the force that man can use cannot pull it up." *Existence and Attributes*, 1:36.

[104] Ibid., 36. Wilkins agreed seeing the conscience as an internal witness complimentary to the external witness of the world: "I might here add another argument to the same purpose, from Natural Conscience, which is Gods deputy, and doth internally witness for him, as other creatures do externally." *Of the Principles and Duties of Natural Religion*, 79.

[105] Thomas Hobbes, *Leviathan* (Indianapolis: Bobbs-Merrill Educational Publishing, 1958), 93.  His book was originally published in 1651 and so may have had an influence on Charnock.

[106] Ibid., 99-100.

his proposals, but his ideas would later be used by deists as being true for all religion.[107] Charnock rejected the suggestion that fear was the cause of humans creating a deity because "the object of fear is before the act of fear; there could not be an act of fear exercised about the Deity, till it was believed to be existent, and not only so, but offended."[108] Wilkins agreed stating that it was "much more probable, that the fear of a supreme Being, is rather the consequence and effect of such a belief, than the cause of it."[109] Charnock also argued against the proposal that religion originated due to state policy because if that were the case there would be some places that rebelled against the notion of a deity. The universal success of religion is more likely to have been caused by God placing it in the nature of humanity, than it having been created through some political conspiracy.[110]

The second evidence Charnock gave for the proof of God's existence was that God is manifest in creation. He is the first cause of all else and therefore eternal and infinitely perfect.[111] The universe, including all substance and time, had a beginning and could not have brought itself into being; therefore some eternal element external to the universe must have created it.[112] Nehemiah Grew elaborated on the necessity of time having a beginning:

> Moreover if matter and motion were not made, then they are eternal. But this we cannot suppose; for if motion were eternal, then time, wherein motion is made, must be eternal: And so, there must always have been infinite time past: And therefore time always past, which was never present: For how could that ever be present which was always past? To avoid which contradiction, it must be granted that there was a beginning of time; and so of motion; and therefore also of matter. For to what end should matter have been eternally without motion? And consequently, that the world was made, and that God did make it, or think it into being.[113]

Typical of the apologists of seventeenth century England, Charnock argued against the epicurean idea of atoms producing the universe by chance.[114] Tillotson illustrated what he considered the unreasonableness of

---

[107] Ibid., 97, 101, x; Noel Malcolm, "Hobbes, Thomas (1588-1679)," in *Oxford Dictionary of National Biography*.
[108] *Existence and Attributes*, 1:41; *A System of Divinity and Morality*, 1:9.
[109] *Of the Principles and Duties of Natural Religion*, 46.
[110] *Existence and Attributes*, 38-41; Wilkins, *Of the Principles and Duties of Natural Religion*, 46-47; *A System of Divinity and Morality*, 1:9-10.
[111] *Existence and Attributes*, 1:50-51; John Howe, *Works*, 1:12-14.
[112] Ibid., 1:43-51; Bates, *Works*, 1:24; Baxter, *The Practical Works*, 2:8-11; Nehemiah Grew, *Cosmologia Sacra: or a Discourse of the Universe as it is the Creature and Kingdom of God* (London: W. Rogers, S. Smith, and B. Walford, 1701), 1-5; John Ray, *The Wisdom of God Manifested in the Works of the Creation*, 10-11.
[113] *Cosmologia Sacra*, 5.
[114] He stated, "If it were, as some fancy, made by an assembly of atoms, there must be some infinite intelligent cause that made them, some cause that separated them, some

imputing an effect to chance: "Is it possible for a man by shaking a number of letters in a bag, and then throwing them on the ground, to make a good discourse on any subject? And yet may not a book be as easily made by chance, as this great volume of the world?"[115] Ray argued that if chance could produce such a marvelous work as the universe it should be able to produce less complex works such as a house, but since we do not observe chance constructing "a temple, or a gallery, or a portico, or a house, or a city" it is even less likely it produced the "whole world."[116]

Charnock not only appealed to the first cause as proof that God is manifest in creation, but also how the extraordinary design of the universe demands a designer. The order, harmony and purpose observed in the world calls for an architect.[117] Not only the design and beauty observed, but also the purpose manifest in all creation argues for a designer.[118] The virtuosi used the new

---

cause that mingled them together for the piling up so comely a structure as the world. It is the most absurd thing to think they should meet together by hazard, and rank themselves in that order we see, without a higher and a wise agent." *Existence and Attributes*, 1:50; Bates, *Works*, 1:20; Grew, *Cosmologia Sacra*, 17; John Ray, *The Wisdom of God*, 11-15; Walter Charleton, *The Darkness of Atheism*, 40, 61; Howe, *Works*, 1:16-17, 24-27.

[115] *A System of Divinity and Morality*, 8.

[116] *The Wisdom of God*, 15. He challenged: "Should any one of us be cast, suppose upon a desolate island, and find there a magnificent palace artificially contrived according to the exactest rules of architecture, and curiously adorned and furnished, yet it would never once enter into his head, that this was done by an earthquake, or the fortuitous shuffling together of its component materials: or that it had stood there ever since the construction of the world, or first cohesion of atoms; but would presently conclude that there had been some intelligent architect there the effect of whose art and skill it was." Charleton argued similarly, *The Darkness of Atheism*, 66.

[117] He explained, "The multitude, elegancy, variety, and beauty of all things are steps whereby to ascend to one fountain and original of them. Is it not a folly to deny the being of a wise agent, who sparkles in the beauty and motions of the heavens, rides upon the wings of the wind, and is writ upon the flowers and fruits of plants? As the cause is known by the effects, so the wisdom of the cause is known by the elegancy of the work, the proportion of the parts to one another." *Existence and Attributes*, 1:52; John Howe, *Works*, 1:14-30.

[118]*Existence and Attributes*, 1:60. Bates also argued that the order, beauty, regularity and purpose found in creation proves a "designing agent." *Works*, 1:21; John Ray, *The Wisdom of God*, 10; Nehemiah Grew, *Cosmologia Sacra*, 30; Wilkins summarized, "From that excellent contrivance which there is in all natural things. Both with respect to that elegance and beauty which they have in themselves separately considered, and that regular order and subserviency wherein they stand towards one another; together with the exact fitness and propriety, for the several purposes for which they are designed. From all which it may be inferred, that these are the productions of some Wise Agent." *Of the Principles and Duties of Natural Religion*, 69.

discoveries in science to bolster their design argument, especially the findings from the microscope and telescope.[119]

The puritans, Anglicans and virtuosi used forms of the cosmological and teleological arguments to prove the existence of a deity (some also invoked the ontological argument with less success[120]), but they varied in their levels of certainty attributed to God's existence which could be gleaned from these arguments. Baxter was the exception to most. He claimed that natural revelation proved both God's existence and attributes including his omnipotence, omniscience, omnipresence, holiness, goodness, happiness and triune nature.[121] Bates was more tempered, stating there was enough evidence to convince the sincere, but not enough to force the unwilling into faith:

> There is a veil drawn over the eternal world for most wise reasons. If the glory of heaven were clear to sense, if the mouth of the bottomless-pit were open before men's eyes, there would be no place for faith, and obedience would not be the effect of choice but necessity, and consequently there would be no visible discrimination made between the holy and the wicked.[122]

He attributed this ambiguity to God's wisdom. Wilkins pointed out that there were different levels of certainty, with mathematical certainty being the highest. The type of certainty whether physical, mathematical, or moral depended on the subject. It is not appropriate to demand a level of certainty from a subject where that level becomes impossible due to the very nature of the subject. For instance, history does not need to be abandoned simply because it relates to a past to which no-one living presently has access.[123] Different subjects of truth will have different levels of probability so the wise person will "incline to the greater probabilities."[124] This argument is similar to

---

[119] John Wilkins, *Of the Principles and Duties of Natural Religion*, 70-74; Grew, *Cosmologia Sacra*, 39-84; Baxter, *The Practical Works*, 2:15.

[120] John Howe, *Works*, 1:12.

[121] Baxter, *The Practical Works*, 2:11-16; concerning the Trinity he stated, "This Unity in Trinity, and Trinity in Unity is to be acknowledged as undeniable in the Light of Nature, and to be adored and worshipped by all." Not many others were willing to say natural revelation proved the Trinity.

[122] *Works*, 1:87.

[123] Wilkins, *Of the Principles and Duties of Natural Religion*, 19-33.

[124] Ibid., 30. He also stated, "There may be an indubitable certainty, where there is not an infallible certainty: And that a meer possibility to the contrary, is not a sufficient cause of doubting.... If it be supposed, that notwithstanding all that hath been said, there may yet be some probabilities to the contrary. To this it may be answered, that unless these probabilities were greater and stronger than those on the other side, no man who acts rationally will incline to them. And if there be any such why are they not produc'd? Where are they to be found?" Ibid., 83-84.

Pascal's wager; one must consider both the probability and the consequences when considering the evidence for God.[125]

Charnock's final argument was based on providence. Judgments, miracles and prophecies all reveal that God is active in the world and therefore he must exist.[126] Providence had always been an important topic among the reformers, but in the seventeenth century it became the means of a popular apologetic. While each group used providence to reveal the existence of a deity, they diverged in the specifics of how providence worked. Although most still claimed that God was actively sovereign within creation, they began to use language that would later be interpreted as implying less involvement by God toward his world. This would culminate in the deists' view that God made the world, but has little contact with it since its inception.[127]

The puritans spoke of God's intricate participation in the workings of creation. Though they were open to the idea of secondary causes, they still saw God's hand directly involved in the life of all things.[128] Charnock targeted the mechanical view of the universe stating:

> God upholds the world, and causes all those laws which he hath impressed upon every creature, to be put in execution: not as a man that makes a watch, and winds it up, and then suffers it to go of itself; or that turns a river into another channel, and lets it alone to run in the graff he hath made for it; but there is a continual concurrence of God to this goodly frame.[129]

It was obvious that Charnock was well versed in the beliefs of his times and was willing to embrace the new science and philosophy if it did not go against what he believed to be scriptural. He did not want unnecessarily to ignore what could be learned through a thorough use of the mind, but he was not willing to forego the heart, which in this case seemed to be endangered by making God a distant ruler rather than a close friend.[130] He did not reject the laws of physics

---

[125] Ibid., 85. "If it be supposed yet farther, that the probabilities on each side should be equal, or that those on the other side should somewhat preponderate; yet if there be no considerable hazard on that side which hath the least probability, and a very great and most apparent danger in a mistake about the other; in this case every rational and prudent man is bound to order his actions in favour of that way which appears to be most safe and advantageous for his own interest." See Blaise Pascal, *Pensees*, 152-162.

[126] *Existence and Attributes*, 1:74-77; *Works*, 1:6-120.

[127] Westfall sums up the views of Locke stating, "Although he still used the name 'Christianity,' the differences separating his religion from deism were essentially semantic. Natural religion had displaced Christianity almost completely in his thought." *Science and Religion*, 138.

[128] "The Westminster Confession of Faith" in Philip Schaff, *Creeds of Christendom*, 3:612-614.

[129] Stephen Charnock, *Works*, 1:13. He also stated, "If God should in the least moment withhold the influence of his providence, we should melt into nothing."

[130] In his treatise "God the Author of Reconciliation" Charnock revealed how friendship is at the heart of reconciliation stating: "Reconciliation makes us friends." *Works*,

as means of God's providence, but "God never left second causes to straggle and operate in a vagabond way; though the effect seem to us to be a loose act of the creature, yet it is directed by a superior cause to a higher end than we can presently imagine."[131]

The virtuosi rejected a completely mechanical view of the universe, but they used the language of machines to describe the world. Charleton called the universe an "ingenious machine" and tied in this view to promote an intelligent designer.[132] Grew described the world as both a machine and a work of art: "As the several parts of the universe, are so many lesser engines: so the whole, is not a meer aggregate, or heap of parts, but one great engine, having all its parts fitly set together, and set to work: or one entire movement of divine art."[133] Their devotion to God is evident in their writings, but the secondary causes seemed to be the primary focus of the virtuosi. Cudworth had previously promoted the concept of plastic nature where God is in control, but most occurrences in the universe are due to secondary means, laws of nature; the virtuosi embraced this notion.[134] The virtuosi did not abandon providence, but their ideas of providence changed from the typical Reformed view as held by the puritans. The differences between the virtuosi and the puritans in their

---

3:340. He goes on to show how reconciliation makes our friendship with God even closer and more affectionate than before sin came into the world. Ibid., 3:342.

[131] Ibid., 1:17. Baxter also saw God as immediate everywhere governing the world, using means but "so that which he doth by any creature is as truly and fully done by Himself, as if there were no created instrument or cause in it." *The Practical Works*, 2:26-27.

[132] Walter Charleton, *The Darkness of Atheism*, 64-65. He stated, "Now we cannot but observe, that in the great engine of the universe, nothing is with less order, decency, beauty, uniformity, symmetry, constancy, in a word, with less wisdom, either designed, or finished; then in the smaller organ of an animal, in the perfection of its integrality."

[133] Nehemiah Grew, *Cosmologia Sacra*, 87.

[134] Cudworth defined plastic nature: "There is a plastick nature in the universe, as a subordinate instrument of divine providence, in the orderly disposal of matter; but yet so as not without a higher providence presiding over it, forasmuch as this plastick nature cannot act electively or with discretion. Those laws of nature concerning motion, which the mechanick theists themselves suppose, really nothing else but a plastick nature." Ralph Cudworth, *The True Intellectual System of the Universe* (London: Printed for J. Walthoe, D. Midwinter, etc., 1743), 178. He also defined it as a life "operating fatally and sympathetically, according to laws and commands prescribed to it by a perfect intellect, and imprest upon it." Ibid., 172. John Ray displayed the different possibilities for motion: "Therefore there must, besides matter and law, be some efficient, and that either a quality or power inherent in the matter itself, which is hard to conceive, or some external intelligent agent, either God himself immediately, or some plastic nature." *The Wisdom of God*, 24; Walter Charleton, *The Darkness of Atheism*, 53; Grew wrote, "We are not to think, that God doth any thing immediately or by himself alone: but that he doth every thing, by the mediation of some one or more instruments." *Cosmologia Sacra*, 87.

belief in the specifics of providence can be seen in the three areas Charnock described, judgments, miracles and prophecies.

First Charnock appealed to prodigies, or "extraordinary judgments" as proof of providence. God's active participation in the world can be seen "when a just revenge follows abominable crimes, especially when the judgment is suited to the sin by a strange concatenation and succession of providences, methodized to bring such a particular punishment."[135] Ronald VanderMolen suggests that the puritans changed Calvin's view of providence by excluding the element of mystery, seeing history as a second form of special revelation and overemphasizing negative, judgmental providences.[136] The insufficiency of this idea is presented when one recognizes the variety of responses among puritans toward prodigies. VanderMolen's thesis appears to be true of many of the radical puritans, but not the moderates. Alexandra Walsham is closer to the truth when she calls puritans "the 'hotter sort' of providentialists":

> To adapt one of Patrick Collinson's most classic formulations, the difference between their beliefs about divine activity and those of their neighbors and peers was essentially one of temperature rather than substance. Providentialism was not a marginal feature of the religious culture of early modern England, but part of the mainstream, a cluster of presuppositions which enjoyed near universal acceptance.[137]

But even this view needs to be nuanced. The more radical puritans appealed to prodigies, among other reasons, to support the revolution and to oppose the restoration. The most famous radical treatment of prodigies was Thomas Beard's *The Theatre of Gods Judgements*, which is used by VanderMolen to represent all of puritanism. This work was very negative but does not represent the mainstream of puritanism at that time.[138] William Burns reveals how an attempt to regulate prodigies was made by moderate puritan Matthew Poole because they were getting out of hand and appearing much like the superstitions the Protestants accused the Catholics of promoting.[139] John Beale and Baxter supported this effort of regulation but it never came to fruition.[140] The moderate puritans, like Charnock, believed in prodigies, but sought to

---

[135] Stephen Charnock, *Existence and Attributes*, 74-75.
[136] Ronald VanderMolen, "Providence as Mystery, Providence as Revelation: Puritan and Anglican Modifications of John Calvin's Doctrine of Providence" in *Church History* (March, 1978), 47:27-47.
[137] Alexandra Walsham, *Providence in Early Modern England* (Oxford University Press, 1999), 2.
[138] Thomas Beard, *The Theatre of Gods Judgements* (London: Adam Islip, 1631). For another radical puritan work on prodigies see also Francis Rous, *Oile of Scorpions* (London: W. Stansby, 1623); anon, *A Most Notable Example of an Ungracious Son, Who in the Pride of His Heart Denyed His Owne Father, and How God for His Offence, Turned His Meat into Loathsome Toades* (London: Printed by M. Parsons, 1638).
[139] William Burns, *An Age of Wonders* (Manchester University Press, 2002), 12-19.
[140] Ibid., 19.

order them. They did not overemphasize negative prodigies, reject mystery in providence, or see history as special revelation. Works such as Flavel's *The Mystery of Providence* and Charnock's "A Discourse of Divine Providence" reveal great similarities to Calvin concerning the doctrine of providence. Calvin did derive "the justice and mercy of God from history,"[141] and Flavel and Charnock both emphasized mystery in providence and were very open to the positive use of providence.[142]

The Anglicans and virtuosi also embraced prodigies to a degree, but tended to explain them away, using natural reasons for their existence. John Gadbury wrote extensively on prodigies but also "was at pains to emphasize that no prodigy, not even the Star of Bethlehem, was actually a violation of a law of nature."[143] The virtuosi did not reject prodigies, but when prodigies were presented to them they usually found a natural explanation, even if the explanation seemed bizarre.[144]

VanderMolen was correct in seeing providentialism as a form of non-cessationism and new revelation. Although the moderate puritans and Anglicans would probably not have seen prodigies in the same category as miracles and prophecies, they did gain new insights from God by viewing them. As a general rule the more one tended to focus on the mind, as the Anglicans and virtuosi did, the less open to prodigies one became, and the more

---

[141] Edward Dowey, Jr., *The Knowledge of God in Calvin's Theology*, 78; John Calvin, *Institutes*, 1. 5, 7-9; Calvin advocated the idea that the stars actually influence humans, though are not "the chief cause of such things." John Calvin, "A Warning Against Judiciary Astrology and Other Prevalent Curiosities" translated by Mary Potter in *Calvin Theological Journal* (November, 1983), 18:169-170.

[142] John Flavel noted, "And yet, though our present views and reflections upon Providence are so short and imperfect in comparison to that in heaven, yet such as it is under all its present disadvantages, it has so much excellence and sweetness in it that I may call it a little heaven.... It is certainly a highway of walking with God in this world, and a soul may enjoy as sweet communion with Him in His providences as in any of His ordinances." *The Mystery of Providence* (Carlisle, PA: The Banner of Truth Trust, 1963), 22; Thomas Watson, co-pastor with Charnock at Crosby House, said, "Here we see but some dark pieces of God's providence, and it is impossible to judge of his works by pieces; but when we come to heaven, and see the full body and portrait of his providence drawn out into its lively colours, it will be glorious to behold." *A Body of Divinity*, 127; Charnock stated, "God reveals often to his people what he will do in the world, as if he seemed to ask their advice; and therefore surely all his providences shall work for their good." But he also warns that we should not use providence to prove our position, only scripture should do that. *Works*, 1:80, 109-112.

[143] William Burns, *An Age of Wonders*, 40; John Gadbury, *Natura Prodigiorum: or, a Discourse Touching the Nature of Prodigies* (London: Printed for Fr. Cossinet, 1665), passim.

[144] William Burns, *An Age of Wonders*, 70-77. Burns gives an illustration where Boyle explained a rain of wheat in Norwich as birds excreting ivy berries that when removed from their husk looked identical to a grain of wheat. Ibid., 74. See also Nehemiah Grew, *Cosmologia Sacra*, 95-96.

one was inclined to focus on the heart, such as the radical puritans and Quakers, the more receptive to prodigies one became. The latitude puritans forged a middle ground, being amenable to prodigies but seeking to regulate them and use them more positively.

After appealing to prodigies to prove providence, Charnock called on miracles and prophecies to make his case. His explanation of miracles was typical of the moderate puritans:

> The course of nature is uniform; and when it is put out of its course, it must be by some superior power invisible to the world; and by whatsoever invisible instruments they are wrought, the efficacy of them must depend upon some first cause above nature.[145]

The moderate puritans saw a difference between the natural and supernatural. Miracles did not break the laws of nature, but they occurred when God suspended the laws of nature.[146]

The virtuosi continued to support the miracles of the Bible but with a great distinction. More and more they saw that God only worked through secondary causes, resting after creation.[147] Grew saw all miracles as natural; the only difference was the natural cause was unknown to the people.[148] After having defined a miracle, he presented how the ten plagues in the Bible could be naturally understood by suggesting angels or demons may have used unknown natural causes to bring these things about. For instance, Moses stick turning into a serpent was probably an imaginary serpent that only *seemed* to swallow the magician's rod.[149] They questioned how God could break his own laws, referring to miracles acting contrary to the laws of nature. Their understanding of miracle was not very different from the deists and proto-deists' views they opposed. Benedict Spinoza, whom Grew vehemently opposed,[150] similarly argued against the idea that miracles broke the laws of nature:

---

[145] Stephen Charnock, *Existence and Attributes*, 1:76.

[146] Charnock stated, "That which cannot be the result of a natural cause, must be the result of something supernatural: what is beyond the reach of nature, is the effect of a power superior to nature; for it is quite against the order of nature, and is the elevation of something to such a pitch, which all nature could not advance it to." Ibid.

[147] Nehemiah Grew, *Cosmologia Sacra*, 195.

[148] Ibid. Locke's definition of miracle was similar, "A miracle then I take to be a sensible operation, which, being above the comprehension of the spectator, and in his opinion contrary to the established course of nature, is taken by him to be divine." *The Reasonableness of Christianity*, 79. He later rejects the idea that a miracle should be defined as "contrary to the fixed and established laws of nature." Ibid., 86.

[149] Nehemiah Grew, *Cosmologia Sacra*, 196.

[150] Ibid., preface. He began his work: "The many leud opinions, especially those of anti-scripturists, which have been published of late years; by Spinosa and some others, in Latin, Dutch, and English; have been the occasion of my writing this book."

Now, as nothing is necessarily true save only by Divine decree, it is plain that the universal laws of nature are decrees of God following from the necessity and perfection of the Divine nature. Hence, any event happening in nature which contravened nature's universal laws, would necessarily also contravene the Divine decree, nature, and understanding; or if anyone asserted that God acts in contravention to the laws of nature, he, *ipso facto*, would be compelled to assert that God acted against His own nature – an evident absurdity.[151]

He went on to show how all miracles had natural explanations and were only seen by the masses as opposing natural laws. For "the students of science," however, "Miracles were natural occurrences, and must therefore be so explained as to appear neither new (in the words of Solomon) nor contrary to nature, but, as far as possible, in complete agreement with ordinary events."[152] Westfall observes, "The virtuosi were concerned more with intellectual systems than with emotional experiences; their religion aimed at the head instead of the heart."[153] He then concludes:

The virtuosi originally turned to natural religion to demonstrate the rational foundation of Christianity, and most of their religious writings were devoted to the proof of the fundamentals of religion from the world of nature. With Newton the growth of natural religion reached its culmination. Early virtuosi thought of it as the foundation demonstrable by reason on which the superstructure of revealed Christianity rests. Newton followed Locke in confounding the superstructure with the foundation and embracing natural religion as the whole of Christianity.[154]

The emphasis on reason and the mind, to the relative neglect of the heart appears to have swayed the virtuosis' opinion of miracles and of Christianity itself.

---

[151] Benedict de Spinoza, *A Theologico-Political Treatise and a Political Treatise* (New York: Dover Publications, 1951), 83.

[152] Ibid., 81-97. Both Toland and Blount make similar points. John Toland, *Christianity not Mysterious*, 144-151; Charles Blount, *Miracles, no Violations of the Laws of Nature*, passim.

[153] Richard Westfall, *Science and Religion*, 206.

[154] Ibid.

# CHAPTER FOUR

# KNOWLEDGE OF GOD: SPECIAL REVELATION

Stephen Charnock and the puritans in general held to the necessity of the special revelation of scripture in order to obtain what they called saving knowledge, but this was not the case for all in seventeenth century England. With the heightened interest in natural theology, English Protestant theologians displayed a variety of opinions toward special revelation. These estimations ranged from seeing the Bible as being superior to natural revelation on the one hand to the rejection of the Bible's divine authorship on the other. Whereas the virtuosi tended to downplay the necessity of scripture as a mode of revealing God and his plan, and the rationalists began to treat it as an ordinary book, the Anglicans and puritans held the scriptures with high esteem, but varied in their approaches to it. This was true of the radicals as well, though the extreme radicals had comparable views to the rationalists. Differing convictions concerning human depravity as well as variations in the understanding of the doctrine of the Spirit influenced how individual theologians discerned special revelation and what it revealed about God. An analysis of three major areas concerning special revelation will reveal the various positions on scripture as well as the range of stances concerning the balance of head and heart: i. The significance given to scripture; ii. the place of the Spirit in the comprehension of scripture; iii. the appreciation of mystery in knowing God while attempting to interpret scripture.

## 1. The Significance Given to Scripture

The significance given to scripture by the various groups in England can be seen by looking at how they answered two questions: i. Is the Bible superior, equal or inferior to other means of revelation? ii. What does the scripture reveal about God and how does this revelation affect the reader? The rationalists, virtuosi, Anglicans, puritans and radicals answered these questions differently, revealing their diverse emphases on the head and heart.

## a. The Superior Authority of Scripture

The question "Is the Bible superior, equal or inferior to other means of revelation?" elicited a variety of different responses in seventeenth century England, whereas the original reformers would have answered with a resounding "superior." Calvin recognized a general revelation from God that "ought not only to arouse us to the worship of God but also to awaken and encourage us to the hope of the future life."[1] He did not believe there was any defect in the revelation through nature, but rather a deficiency in humanity due to the fall. The inability to see God is the fault of humanity, not God, and therefore, according to Calvin, all are culpable.[2] Because of human depravity, God gave the scriptures as a "better help...added to direct us aright to the very Creator of the universe."[3] Calvin understood the scriptures to be superior to general revelation because of its power and clarity.[4] His controversy was with those he called "fanatics" and "rascals" who apparently abandoned the Bible for the Holy Spirit. Out of this he developed his "Word and Spirit" theology where the scriptures and the Spirit are inseparably linked.[5] Both the Spirit and the Bible are necessary for true revelation according to Calvin. On the one hand he stated, "We ought zealously to apply ourselves both to read and to hearken to Scripture if indeed we want to receive any gain and benefit from the Spirit of God," and on the other hand, it is "through the Spirit [the word] is really branded upon hearts...converting souls."[6] Although Calvin believed that there were rational evidences for the divine trustworthiness of scripture,[7] nevertheless it was the inward testimony of the Spirit which provided scripture with its ultimate authority.[8] Whatever the vagaries of the modern debate over

---

[1] John Calvin, *Institutes*, I. 5,10.

[2] I. John Hesselink, *Calvin's First Catechism: A Commentary*, 49; Donald McKim (ed.), *Readings in Calvin's Theology* (Grand Rapids: Baker Book House, 1984), 50-53; Calvin stated, "But although we lack the natural ability to mount up unto the pure and clear knowledge of God, all excuse is cut off because the fault of dullness is within us." *Institutes*, I. 5,15.

[3] Ibid., I. 6,1.

[4] He stated, "So Scripture, gathering up the otherwise confused knowledge of God in our minds, having dispersed our dullness, clearly shows us the true God." Ibid. Donald McKim notes, "Calvin, then, was firmly convinced that there is an innate persuasiveness in God's divine truth." Donald McKim (ed.), *Readings in Calvin's Theology*, 47.

[5] *Institutes*, I. 9. McKim explains Calvin's position, "The Spirit does not witness apart from the Word; the Word without the work of the Spirit has no power or efficacy." *Readings in Calvin's Theology*, 58.

[6] *Institutes*, I. 9,2-3.

[7] Ibid., I. 8. He appealed to the antiquity, miracles, prophecies, preservation and "heavenly character and authority" of the *scriptures* to verify its inspiration and authority; Donald McKim, *Readings in Calvin's Theology*, 56.

[8] Francois Wendel, *Calvin* (London: William Collins Sons, 1963), 158. Calvin stated, "Therefore Scripture will ultimately suffice for a saving knowledge of God only when its certainty is founded upon the inward persuasion of the Holy Spirit. Indeed, these human testimonies which exist to confirm it will not be vain if, as secondary aids to our feebleness, they follow that chief and highest testimony. But those who wish to prove to unbelievers that Scripture is the Word of God are acting foolishly, for only by faith can this be known." *Institutes*, I. 8,13. See also I. 7,4-5. "Let this point therefore stand: that those whom the Holy Spirit has inwardly taught truly rest upon Scripture, and that Scripture indeed is self-authenticated; hence, it is not right to subject it to proof and

Calvin's view of inspiration,[9] his writings indicate he held to the absolute authority of the Bible over general revelation and the tradition of the church.

The reformers commonly held the idea that the Bible was superior to general revelation and unique in its authority over humankind. Bullinger argued that "God himself [was] the author of holy Scripture" and it was "inspired by the holy Ghost" and therefore teaches "nothing but that which is holy, no prophane thinge, no errors."[10] He appealed to its supreme authority over all other books, which should be clearly seen "so that no man that was well in his wyttes ever doubted of them or gainsaied them."[11] The church did not give the Bible its authority, but simply recognized its authority over its own life.[12]

Like Calvin, Bullinger believed the Bible contained an internal witness to its own authority; therefore rational arguments for its divine origin were unnecessary:

> For as much as the holy scripture of the Bible must without all gainsaying be beleved, bycause it is the true word of God, here of firmely and surely ensueth that it hath sufficient authoritie of it self, and needeth no allowance of men to become autentike. For the bookes of the Bible are of an other sort than the other bookes or doctrines, for the things which are in these written, must be confirmed and proved by reason, but such things as are conteined in the scriptures, neede not any further confirmation.[13]

Also like Calvin, he appealed to the miracles of the apostles as a secondary witness, verifying they were "inspired from God out of heaven by the Holy Spirit of God."[14] He explained how this inspiration worked stating: "For it is God, which, dwelling by his Spirit in the minds of the prophets, speaketh to us

---

reasoning. And the certainty it deserves with us, it attains by the testimony of the Spirit."

[9] For three differing opinions on the exact nature of inspiration held by Calvin see J.I. Packer, "Calvin's View of Scripture," in John Warwick Montgomery (ed.), *God's Inerrant Word* (Minneapolis: Bethany Fellowship, 1974), 95-112; Jack Rogers and Donald McKim, *The Authority and Interpretation of the Bible: An Historical Approach* (San Francisco: Harper and Row, 1979), 89-116; Karl Barth, *The Gottingen Dogmatics* (Grand Rapids: Eerdmans, 1991), 1:221-225. Packer is probably correct in seeing the different views concerning Calvin's doctrine of inspiration as anachronistic: "Scholars have inevitably brought their own preoccupations to Calvin, asking him to answer questions which are more theirs than his and seeking to show either, if they are Reformed men, that they can quote him in substantial support of the views they already espouse or, if they stand in non-Calvinist traditions, that he really is guilty of holding positions which they themselves have already rejected." *God's Inerrant Word*, 97.
[10] Henry Bullinger, *Common Places of Christian Religion* (London: Tho. East and H. Middleton, 1572), 2.
[11] Ibid., 7.
[12] Ibid., 13-14. He also speaks of tradition as inferior to the bible in 26-31.
[13] Ibid., 10.
[14] Henry Bullinger, *Decades*, 1:50.

by their mouths."[15] Bullinger held to a verbal inspiration of the scriptures. In confronting those who so emphasized the Spirit that they ridiculed the Bible as fleshly and therefore untrustworthy he warned:

> Holy men, and such as beleve in Christ, must not be troubled with subtill tatlinges of curious persones in the which they saye that God is a Spirit, which can neyther bee comprehended, neyther is subject to any courruption, and that the scripture is fleshe, may be comprehended, and understanded, is in daunger of corruption, and therefore the Scripture cannot bee the true word of God. For God himselfe against the opinion and fantasie of these men, calleth those sermons which the Prophets and Apostels dyd, first preach alive, and afterward put in writing, his, that is to say, the word of God.... Because the sentences which are spoken by the voice of men, and with pen and inck are put in writing, beegan not of men, but are the word and wyll of God.[16]

He understood the very words of the Bible to be authoritative because they came from God's inspiration and therefore constituted the word of God.[17]

For both Calvin and Bullinger the special revelation of scripture is superior to general revelation and absolutely necessary for a saving knowledge of God since the fall.[18] The other reformers, whether they leaned more toward scholasticism or humanism, were in substantial agreement with them both.[19]

---

[15] Ibid.

[16] Henry Bullinger, *Common Places*, 8. In the *Decades* he reiterated this point: "Although therefore that the apostles were men, yet their doctrine, first of all taught by a lively expressed voice, and after that set down in writing with pen and ink, is the doctrine of God and the very true word of God. For therefore the apostle left this saying in writing: 'When ye did receive the word of God which ye heard of us, ye received it not as the word of men, but, as it is indeed, the word of God, which effectually worketh in you that believe.'" 1:54.

[17] He stated, "Al these things, I say, do very evidently prove, that the doctrine and writings of the prophets are the very word of God: with which name and title they are set forth in sundry places of the scriptures." *Decades*, 1:51. Packer notes that Calvin held to the bible as the word of God, appealing to his use of the concept of *os Dei* and *doctrina*, quoting from his commentary on 2 Timothy 3:16. He states, "The first notion is *os Dei*, 'the mouth of God,' a biblical phrase pointing to the Creator's use of human language to address us. The second notion is *doctrina*, 'doctrine' or 'teaching,' which is the instruction that these verbal utterances convey. 'Teaching from God's mouth,' or putting it more simply and dynamically, 'God *speaking – teaching – preaching*,' is the heart of Calvin's concept of Holy Scripture." *God's Inerrant Word*, 102.

[18] Bullinger declared, "Therefore let this stand as it were for a continual rule, that God cannot be rightly known but by his word; and that God is to be received and believed to be such an one as he revealeth himself unto us in his holy word. For no creature verily can better tell what, and what kind of one God is, than God himself." *Decades*, 2:125.

[19] Beza said, "That knowledge of God, which we attaine unto, by his written word, doth far surpas al that, whatsoever it be, whereunto the light of nature doth or can lead us." *Propositions and Principles*, 3; Girolamo Zanchius, *The Whole Body of Christian Religion*, 1-2. Zanchius contrasted the revelation from nature with that of the bible

As was often true with the reformers Bucer contrasted the Reformed beliefs to the Anabaptist beliefs believing that the Reformed were firmly established in scripture "which alone is infallible."[20] As a basic article of faith concerning the knowledge of God and of Christ he stated, "We confess and teach that from these Scriptures, by the aid of the Holy Spirit and a true faith there is to be taught and learned a true and living knowledge of the eternal God, of the unity of his divine substance, and the Trinity of the Persons."[21] To counteract what he saw as an over-emphasis of the Spirit alone based on a subjective experience, the Bible was elevated as an objective authority. The reformers did not reject experience and actually elevated the things of the heart to be primary as far as the chief end of humans was concerned, but they balanced experience with understanding which came from the Bible. One could say for the reformers the heart was chief in the sense of a primacy of importance, and the mind was paramount in the sense of a predominance of order.[22]

Besides the Anabaptists, the Roman Catholics were also opposed in the reformers writings concerning their understanding of the importance of the Bible. In confronting Hosius, Vermigli proclaimed the supremacy of the Bible over the church.[23] Though embracing a natural revelation,[24] he believed the Bible alone to be the word of God. It did not need evidence of its veracity because the Spirit persuades people of its divine origin.[25] Neither the church nor reason can be supreme over the Bible because that would make human beings superior to God. After stating, "We cannot ascribe to the Church the inerrancy we associate with Scripture," he proceeded to show how both pope and councils had erred in the past.[26] Believing the word of God and the scriptures to be synonymous, he concluded, "We see the true Church as

---

saying, "He hath in a more peculiar manner, that is by his prophets and apostles, who spake and wrote as they were moved by the holy Ghost, revealed himself and his will more clearly and fully unto his Church, and therefore, that in the writings of the prophets and apostles are the very word of God."

[20] Martin Bucer, *Common Places*, 78.

[21] Ibid.

[22] For a similar contemporary statement see R.C. Sproul, *Essential Truths of the Christian Faith* (Wheaton: Tyndale, 1992), xvi.

[23] Peter Martyr Vermigli, *Early Writings*, 179-187; Zanchius, *The Whole Body of Christian Religion*, 6-9.

[24] Peter Martyr Vermigli, *Early Writings*, 131. He stated, "There are two kinds of knowledge of God, one common and called natural, which is also attributed to the ungodly; the other is full and effectual, followed by obedience to divine Law and at last eternal life, and belongs only to the elect." Here we see the superiority Vermigli gives to special revelation over general revelation; the inferior revelation is seen even by the ungodly, but the other is the only one that is effectual and embraced by the elect.

[25] Ibid., 180. He said, "Moreover, the Spirit of God helps believers. He persuades us that these writings are of divine origin, and not counterfeits concocted by men."

[26] Ibid., 180-185.

circumscribed by the Word of God, which is its infallible rule and immovable foundation."[27]

There was a concord between the reformers concerning the supremacy of the Bible over natural revelation because of the need of humans since the fall. They disagreed with the Anabaptists and Catholics over these points seeking to put God above both reason and experience because they believed the fall so affected both head and heart that only God could restore a balance.[28]  But various groups shifted this balance in the seventeenth century. The Anglicans, puritans, virtuosi, rationalists and radicals held different views concerning the relative importance of general revelation and scripture partially because of their prior commitment to either a more cognitive or a more experiential faith.

The Anglicans, virtuosi and rationalists departed from the original reformers' attempt to balance head and heart toward a more rational faith with the virtuosi and especially the rationalists departing the most.  The Anglicans maintained a firm belief in the supremacy of scripture over natural revelation, but in practice they elevated reason and natural revelation to a place of near equality with scripture.  Henry McAdoo argues that the essence of Anglicanism in seventeenth century England was its theological method "which combined the use of Scripture, antiquity and reason," with reason seen as "an ultimate factor in theology."[29]  Like the reformers they battled against the fideism of the Roman Catholics on the one side and the enthusiasm of the radicals on the other.  To counter the Catholic elevation of tradition and papal authority and the radicals' amplification of the subjective experience of the Spirit, they maintained the scriptures as supreme over church and experience, but the underpinning of their reasons occurred in a more rationalist way.[30]

The Anglican position on scriptures can be seen as having departed from the original reformers due to an element of rationalism in three areas.  Firstly, the scriptures were not seen as superior to general revelation because the effects of the fall on the mind necessitated a more direct revelation from God (the position of the reformers), but rather because they revealed more information about God.[31]  This alternate reasoning reveals a softening of their position on

---

[27] Ibid., 185.

[28] Zanchius said, "As concerning God, and divine matters pertaining to the kingdome of Christ and our salvation, we believe that none can teach us better and more certainly then God himself; who can neither deceive nor be deceived." *The Whole Body of Christian Religion*, 1.

[29] Henry McAdoo, *The Spirit of Anglicanism: A Survey of Anglican Theological Method in the Seventeenth Century* (New York: Charles Scribner's Sons, 1965), 1, 5, 26, 49.

[30] John Tillotson, *The Works of the Most Reverend Dr. John Tillotson* (London: Printed for R. Ware, etc., 1743), 2:214-341; Edward Stillingfleet, *Origines Sacrae: Or a Rational Account of the Grounds of Natural and Revealed Religion* (Oxford: At the Clarendon Press, 1797), 2:198-221; *A System of Divinity*, 1:77-119.

[31] Edward Stillingfleet, *Origines Sacrae*, 2:198-221.  He argued that the scriptures "do not at all contradict those prime and common notions which are in our natures concerning him but do exceedingly advance and improve them." Ibid., 2:206; Francis

the extent of corruption due to the fall. They held to a milder form of depravity due to both their Arminian theology as well as their escalation of the importance of the mind over the heart. Most of the reformers did not believe anyone could be saved through general revelation because of the radical nature of human depravity, but the Anglicans were more lenient. Gibson said, "As to the heathens, tho' the light of reason is but dim, yet they who honestly make use of that, as the only guide God has given them, cannot fail to be mercifully dealt with, by infinite justice and goodness."[32] Certain phrases concerning the necessity of scripture relay a softening of the reformers' position of the absolute necessity of special revelation for salvation. Tillotson said the scriptures were "the best means in the world of acquainting them with the will of God and their duty, and the way to eternal happiness" rather than being the only means to salvation.[33] Gibson said scripture was only "highly needful" rather than essential.[34] This does not mean that the Anglicans did not have a doctrine of depravity, but they did not seem to think the mind was affected by the fall to the same extent as the reformers claimed. For them natural religion, which Tillotson described as, "Obedience to the natural law, and the performance of such duties as natural light, without any express and supernatural revelation, doth dictate to men," was the foundation of Christianity.[35] Tillotson said that the truths discovered by natural light "are the great and fundamental duties which God requires of all mankind."[36] He does

---

Gastrell similarly noted, "He has in a more extraordinary manner, viz. by immediate revelation from himself made known his mind to us; by which means he has given us a clear and intire (sic) view of the fore-mentioned rational truths, render'd our knowledge of them more certain, plain, and particular, discovered a great many new truths which the unassisted force of human faculties could not have found out, and established new rules and measures of duty, over and above those our reason was before, by its utmost efforts, able to inform us of." *The Certainty of the Christian Revelation, and the Necessity of Believing it, Established* (London: Printed for Thomas Bennet, 1699), 2-3. Gastrell saw great power in the unassisted mind, with little negative affect from the fall. Special revelation was superior because of the larger content of information about God one could receive from it, not because it was needed to overcome the power of sin since the fall. He did embrace depravity (p.36), but apparently not concerning the mind; Matthew Hale, *A Discourse of the Knowledge of God, and of our Selves, I. By the Light of Nature. II. By the Sacred Scriptures.* (London: Printed for William Shrowsbery, 1688), 117-119.

[32] *A System of Divinity and Morality*, 1:81. Not all Anglicans were this positive. Robert South didn't reject the idea that God could save someone apart from the gospel, but he said it would have to be by extraordinary means, and the bible didn't give any assurance that any were actually saved any other way than through Christ. Robert South, *Sermons Preached on Several Occasions* (London: Printed for H. Lintot, 1737), 2:237-270.

[33] John Tillotson, *Works*, 2:319.

[34] *A System of Divinity and Morality*, 1:77.

[35] John Tillotson, *Works*, 6:1680.

[36] Ibid.

not give any indication in this treatise that the Spirit is needed in order to acquaint people with those duties, nor that depravity affects this revelation.[37]

It also seems that for Tillotson the will was not affected to any serious degree by the fall because of his insistence on human ability to choose God's light rather than Satan's blindness.[38] For Tillotson the only faculty of the soul that appears to be acutely influenced by the fall is the affections. In his comments on the rich man and Lazarus he indicated that the revelation given by Moses and then the Apostles should be enough to convince someone of the gospel, unless their lusts have so overwhelmed their mind and will that they cannot understand it.[39] If this is the case, miracles would hardly be more effective, so there was no need for new miracles in the presentation of the gospel. Miracles verified the original revelation but now the revelation is sufficient to convince people unless they are "obstinately addicted to their lusts."[40] This view seems to indicate that the gospel only works on those who are not too far-gone in depravity, but for those who have "a mind strangely hardened, and obstinately bent on a course of wickedness" there was no hope.[41] The original reformers saw everyone in this state, and therefore in need of God's gracious call, but with the effectual call even the most obstinate sinner would respond to the gospel. The Anglican doctrine of depravity does not appear to have been systematized, but their emphases seem to indicate that in practical thought depravity influenced the affections, which then in turn could captivate the mind and will, which seem to have gone unscathed by the fall, except perhaps in that they could be weakened somewhat to sometimes allow the affections to take control. This more rational approach to scripture and moderation of depravity was a clear move away from the reformers method.

Secondly, the Anglicans tended to see two levels within scripture, that which was clear and therefore worthy of debate and that which was ambiguous and lent toward needless division. Gerard Reedy correctly defines the Anglican position when he states, "The hard core of revelation, that which revelation specifically reveals, is always above, though not contrary to, reason."[42] In this he is seeking to distance the Anglicans from the virtuosi and rationalists in

---

[37] He will speak on the place of the Spirit in revelation later in volume 11, discussed below.

[38] Ibid., 11:202. John Balguy, in his contribution to *A System of Divinity and Morality* described the soul as synonymous with the mind and even in the present state of depravity doesn't seem to be adversely affected by the fall and is therefore fully capable of functioning normally and able to will that which is good. 1:53-64.

[39] *A System of Divinity and Morality*, 1:91-104.

[40] Ibid., 1:96.

[41] Ibid., 1:100. Contrast this view with Charnock who believed election was "not for an moral perfection, because he converts the most sinful: the Gentiles, steeped in idolatry and superstition." Stephen Charnock, *Existence and Attributes*, 2:400.

[42] Gerard Reedy, *The Bible and Reason: Anglicans and Scripture in Late Seventeenth-Century England* (Philadelphia: University of Pennsylvania Press, 1985), 10; Henry McAdoo, *The Spirit of Anglicanism*, 61-63.

regards to their place of reason in theology, but even this departs from the views of the original reformers in that the "core of revelation" or the plain and understandable parts of revelation are separated from the obscure passages of scripture. The Anglicans maintained the doctrines of the Trinity and incarnation, arguing these beliefs were not contrary to scripture, but they shied away from what they saw as controversial beliefs, while the rationalists such as Herbert of Cherbury and Spinoza simply took this a step further in developing even more "minimal lists of those truths clearly taught in Scripture,"[43] which did not include the doctrines of the Trinity and the incarnation. The Anglicans repudiated the idea of a canon within a canon held by the rationalists, but a mild form of this thought was already present in their writings, at least in embryonic form. In discussing the perspicuity of scripture Stillingfleet placed limits on its extent saying, "But all those things which concern the terms of man's salvation, are delivered with the greatest evidence and perspicuity."[44] The Anglicans embraced the inspiration of all of scripture, but they seemed to ignore parts they relegated as "hard to be understood,"[45] only viewing the parts pertaining to salvation as clear and profitable for discussion.[46] The neglect of certain portions of scripture for rational reasons was a digression from the reformers' use of the Bible.

Finally, the shift away from the original reformers can also be seen in the area of presuppositions. The Anglican expansion of the use of reason is exposed in that such a large percent of their writings were apologetic, including their view of scripture. Reedy describes this rational tendency:

> Anglican scriptural interpretation at this time was deeply controversial. Mark Pattison's nineteenth-century caricature is only slightly exaggerated: "Every one who had anything to say on sacred subjects drilled it into an array of argument against a supposed objector. Christianity appeared made for nothing else but to be 'proved'; what use to make of it when it was proved was not much thought about."[47]

The reformers engaged in polemics similar to the Anglicans, but began their doctrine of scripture with the presuppositional belief that scripture was of divine origin.[48] For them to argue for the divine nature of scripture was to put human reason above God's revelation and therefore make human beings superior to God. The Anglicans began with the idea that scripture was inspired by God, but they sought to prove it before expecting their readers' acquiescence. In *A System of Divinity and Morality* bishop Gibson gave a

---

[43] Gerard Reedy, *The Bible and Reason*, 15.
[44] Edward Stillingfleet, *Origines Sacrae*, 2:213.
[45] Ibid.
[46] John Tillotson, *Works*, 2:321.
[47] Gerard Reedy, *The Bible and Reason*, 16.
[48] Bullinger was typical of the reformers using the bible to prove that the bible was true. *Decades*, 1:37; Donald McKim, editor, *Readings in Calvin's Theology*, 55.

logical explanation of why there would be a divine revelation and then several reasons why the Bible is that revelation.[49] William Clagett taught how the fulfillment of the Old Testament prophecies in the life of Jesus "do prove the Divine authority of the Scriptures, and this without the help of the Church's authority."[50] John Tillotson used the miracles of the Bible to demonstrate its divine nature; this was the most common proof among Anglicans of his time.[51]

Reedy argues that the Anglican use of the biblical miracles to prove that God was the author of the Bible is circular reasoning:

> One of the great conundrums of Anglican scriptural interpretation in this period concerns the proof at issue. For the proof is hopelessly circular. The goal of the proof was to affirm the truth of at least the central books of Scripture. Yet the entire burden of the proof – the character of an author, his reputation, and his miracles – can be found only in the apposite book, whose very truthfulness cannot yet be assumed.[52]

Tillotson attempted to answer this potential difficulty by appealing to the place of testimony as a valid source of knowledge: "If we have the credible report of eye-witnesses of those miracles, who are credible persons, and we have no reason to doubt of their testimony; that is, if we have the reports of them immediately from the mouth of those who were eye-witnesses of them."[53] He differentiated between "infallible assurance" and "undoubted assurance," arguing that we cannot have the first, but we can have the second based on reason.[54] Tillotson seems to be cleared from the accusation of circular reasoning, but it is also clear that he has elevated reason to a higher importance

---

[49] *A System of Divinity and Morality*, 1:77-91; similarly Edward Stillingfleet, *Origines Sacrae*, 1:411-414. Stillingfleet stated, "So that from the general principles of the existence of God, and immortality of the soul, we have deduced, by clear and evident reason, the necessity of some particular Divine revelation, as the standard and measure of religion. And according to these principles we must examine whatever pretends to be of Divine revelation; for it must be suitable to that Divine nature from whom it is supposed to come, and it must be agreeable to the conditions of the souls of men; and therefore that which carries with it the greatest evidence of Divine revelation, is a faithful representation of the state of the case between God and the souls of men, and a Divine discovery of those ways whereby men's souls may be fitted for eternal happiness." Ibid., 1:414.

[50] William Clagett, *Seventeen Sermons* (London: Printed for W. Rogers, 1704), 243. He said that the prophecies fulfilled were an even more convincing testimony to the scriptures than Jesus' miracles. Ibid., 242. Matthew Hale held an intermediary position, using prophecy as a proof, but also including "a secret and immediate work of the power of God upon the soul" as testimony of its divine nature. *A Discourse of the Knowledge of God, and of our Selves*, 99-115.

[51] John Tillotson, *Works*, 11:167-203.

[52] Gerard Reedy, *The Bible and Reason*, 53.

[53] John Tillotson, *Works*, 11:182.

[54] Ibid., 11:188-190.

in faith than the original reformers. This heightened estimation of the rational faculty is made apparent in his conclusion:

> Upon these grounds we can easily resolve our faith. We believe the doctrine of Christian religion, because it is revealed by God; we believe it to be revealed by God, because it was confirmed by unquestionable miracles; we believe such miracles were wrought, because we have as great assurance of this, as any matter of fact, at such a distance from the time it was done, is capable of. Now if the Papists say, this doth at least amount to no more than moral assurance; I grant it doth not: but then I have proved this assurance to be as much as in reason can be expected, and as much as is sufficient to the nature and ends of a divine faith, and that an infallible assurance is not agreeable to human understanding; but an incommunicable attribute and prerogative of the divine nature, which whoever pretends to, he hath not the modesty of a creature, but does by a sacrilegious ambition attempt the throne of God, and equal himself to the most High.[55]

He stated that it is impossible for humans to have an infallible assurance of the divine nature of scripture because reason is not capable of that kind of assurance, not allowing any other possible way for this kind of assurance to come other than through the use of reason; this is a far cry from Calvin's opinion.

Calvin's view of the divine nature of scripture and his definition of faith would have opened him to Tillotson's accusation of "sacrilegious ambition." The Reformer's claim that "We ought to seek our conviction in a higher place than human reasons, judgments, or conjectures, that is, in the secret testimony of the Spirit,"[56] potentially downgraded reason in order to emphasize the role of the Spirit. His definition of faith also brought out a full assurance similar to Tillotson's infallible assurance:

> Therefore our mind must be otherwise illumined and our heart strengthened, that the Word of God may obtain full faith among us. Now we shall possess a right definition of faith if we call it a firm and certain knowledge of God's benevolence toward us, founded upon the truth of the freely given promise in Christ, both revealed to our minds and sealed upon our hearts through the Holy Spirit.[57]

Both Calvin and Tillotson embraced the supreme authority of scripture, but it seems that Tillotson's starting point was reason rather than revelation, which brought about the different conclusions concerning assurance of truth. Tillotson was able to start with reason rather than revelation because of his different understanding of human depravity, which was not as severe as Calvin's; in this we see that the Anglicans moved away from the reformers toward a more rational and less experiential faith.

---

[55] Ibid., 11:190.

[56] John Calvin, *Institutes*, I. 7,4.

[57] Ibid., III. 2,7.

The rationalists completed the journey the Anglicans began which led them away from the reformers' perspective on reason and the Bible. The reformers maintained that reason was a servant of revelation and always in submission to it. The Anglicans elevated the status of reason to equality with revelation, at least in practice when viewed alongside their doctrine of depravity. The rationalists downgraded revelation, understanding it as the marred opinions of the prophets, which therefore should always defer to the superior rank of reason. They placed reason above revelation, altering the reformers and Anglicans views of depravity, miracles and the nature of revelation.

One of the explanations given by the rationalists for seeing reason as being superior to revelation was their skepticism of enthusiasm. Hobbes can be seen as an intermediary between the rationalists and puritans. He never renounced God or the church and had puritan sympathies.[58] He revered the scriptures, though clearly placed reason as the final arbiter seeing reason as the supreme word of God.[59] In promoting the skill of reasoning concerning the understanding of the Bible, he warned against any need for "enthusiasm or supernatural inspiration," seeing these as more harmful than good.[60] Spinoza similarly warned against superstition as coming from too much emotion, which he described as "prayers and womanish tears to implore help from God."[61] Their neglect of the heart in order to properly promote the head helped move them toward an unorthodox understanding of scripture.

The rationalists' distrust or at least neglect of emotions can also be seen in their doctrine of depravity. Rene Descartes wrote almost entirely neglecting any possible adverse affects on the mind due to the fall. His perspective was that the mind was able to discern clear and distinct ideas, unaided by revelation and without any need of supernatural assistance.[62] He stated, "For in truth, whether we are asleep or awake, we should never allow ourselves to be

---

[58] Herbert Schneider introduced Hobbes' *Leviathan* describing Hobbes' religious beliefs: "Despite his intellectual aggressiveness and his contentious style, Hobbes Was a sober, pious person, who never broke with the Church of England though he had decided Puritan leanings. His opposition to Arminianism and to freewill doctrine indicates his Calvinist leanings and his departures from Anglican theology.... He was certainly neither an atheist nor a materialist. He believed in the essentials of the Christian revelation and in the doctrine of personal salvation." Introduction in Thomas Hobbes, *Leviathan: Parts One and Two*, x.

[59] He stated, "We are not to renounce our Senses, and Experience, nor (that which is the undoubted word of God) our naturall Reason." Thomas Hobbes, *Leviathan, or The Matter, Forme, and Power of a Common-Wealth Ecclesiasticall and Civill* (London: Printed for Andrew Crooke, 1651), 195.

[60] Ibid., 198. Charles Blount also wrote against the dangers of "Enthusiastick times." *Religio Laici* (London: Printed for R. Bentley, 1683), Preface.

[61] Benedict de Spinoza, *A Theologico-Political Treatise*, 4. He wrote against superstition, including any rejection of human wisdom as superstition.

[62] Rene Descartes, *Discourse on Method and Meditations*, 120.

convinced except on the evidence of our reason."[63]   The rational faculties apparently escaped all harm caused by the fall.  Locke denied the concept of original sin or any depravity inherited from Adam, though he did not deny the fall of Adam or that it incapacitated humanity to some extent.[64]  According to Locke, Adam's penalty for sin was simply forfeiting the state of immortality and becoming mortal.[65]  If depravity affected the mind, then one would not be able to discern truth from error.  Even Hobbes, who had a strong view of depravity, saw it as based on human equality rather than the fall, and seemingly not affecting the ability to reason.[66]   Blount rejected the idea of depravity totally, believing that God "Implant[ed] the love of goodness and truth in the soul, that he hath made them a part of common reason, and conspicuous by their own light;" in other words, God has given us the ability to discern what is good and true, rather than having taken away that ability.[67]   They were suspicious of emotions, but saw no problems with the human ability to reason, even after the fall.

In placing reason above revelation, the rationalists not only moved away from the reformers view of depravity, they also diverged from the orthodox understanding of the miraculous.  Hobbes and Locke embraced biblical miracles solely as a means to confirm revelation, but rejected any notion of miracles after the first century.[68]   Blount and Spinoza rejected miracles as confirmation of scripture because false prophets could also at least appear to do miracles and what appears to be a miracle to some might in fact be revealed to have a natural explanation, therefore miracles cannot prove anything.[69] Most of the rationalists seem to have been in agreement that miracles did not actually

---

[63] Ibid., 30.  In this section he was skeptical of imagination and empirical evidence, holding reason to be supreme.

[64] John Locke, *The Reasonableness of Christianity*, 26-27.  See footnote 58 in chapter three for more detail.

[65] Ibid., 45.

[66] Thomas Hobbes, *Leviathan: Parts One and Two*, 104-105.  He believed that the near equality of humans led them to compete for scarce resources bringing about conflict and fighting; this would have resulted in annihilation except humans saw the need to give up their rights in order to form societies where peace and defense were possible but at the expense of freedom; therefore the forming of societies was for selfish gain and so a product of depravity.

[67] Charles Blount, *Religio Laici*, 30.

[68] Thomas Hobbes, *Leviathan*, 198, 233-235; John Locke, *The Reasonableness of Christianity*, 80.

[69] Spinoza, *A Theologico-Political Treatise*, 100; Blount, *Religio Laici*, 35-36.  Blount referred both to biblical and extra-biblical miracles stating, "It is no good argument to say that such a man did miracles therefore I believe all he saith: Since those things may seem miraculous to my weak capacity, which appear not so to wiser men.  Besides, things may be done by natural means, which some may mistake for miracles."

break the laws of nature.[70]   Spinoza explained why miracles could not go
contrary to natural law:

> Now, as nothing is necessarily true save only by Divine decree, it is plain that the
> universal laws of nature are decrees of God following from the necessity and
> perfection of the Divine nature.   Hence, any event happening in nature which
> contravened nature's universal laws, would necessarily also contravene the Divine
> decree, nature, and understanding; or if anyone asserted that God acts in
> contravention to the laws of nature, he, *ipso facto*, would be compelled to assert
> that God acted against His own nature – an evident absurdity.[71]

With the elevation of the mind came the fascination of natural theology with a
concurring neglect of special revelation, especially anything that seemed to
contradict natural law.

The rationalists also seriously altered the orthodox notion of prophecy.
Hobbes believed there were two types of prophets, sovereign or supreme
prophets and subordinate prophets.   Only Jesus was a sovereign prophet in the
New Testament and only Moses and high priests qualified as sovereign
prophets in the Old Testament; all other prophets were subordinate.[72]   Hobbes
then elaborated on this idea stating that the Christian is to test all subordinate
prophets according to his own "naturall reason" to detect how much of the
prophecy is reliable; this test was even to be exacted on the biblical prophets
such as Joseph, Paul or Peter.[73]   Blount gave no credence to the miraculous
nature of prophecy and so rejected the validity of a doctrine just because it
claimed to have come from a prophet. He said the only suitable claim of truth
was its moral nature; only "the goodness of the doctrine itself" gave it
authority.[74]   By stating this he was rejecting the need for supernatural
revelation.[75]   Spinoza was in agreement with Blount and believed that the
prophets contradicted each other and so could not be completely trustworthy.[76]
Since the prophets simply spoke their opinions and were ignorant in many

---

[70] Locke, *The Reasonableness of Christianity*, 79, 86.   Hobbes was an exception.
*Leviathan*, 233-238.

[71] Spinoza, *A Theologico-Political Treatise*, 83. He went on to say, "We may, then, be
absolutely certain that every event which is truly described in Scripture necessarily
happened, like everything else, according to natural laws." Ibid., 92.

[72] Hobbes, *Leviathan*, 227-229.

[73] Ibid., 230-231. He said, "Every man then was, and now is bound to make use of his
naturall reason, to apply to all prophecy those rules which God hath given us, to discern
the true from the false."

[74] Blount, *Laici*, 13-14.

[75] He said, "Neither would it be sufficient to say, that their knowledge was supernatural
or Divine, since as that is more than could be known in following times, so, when it
were granted, it would infer little to me, but that which I would believe without it."
Ibid., 13.

[76] Spinoza, *A Theologico-Political Treatise*, 30, 40, 104.

cases, Spinoza concluded: "It therefore follows that we must by no means go to the prophets for knowledge, either of natural or of spiritual phenomena."[77]

The rationalists deviated considerably from the original reformers concerning the nature of revelation due to their esteem of reason and subsequent devaluing of scripture. Firstly this is seen in their radical separation of revelation and reason, faith and science. Whereas the reformers and puritans held the Bible and reason together, the rationalists divorced these two concepts, isolating them into completely separate categories. In discussing whether the Bible and science or philosophy contradict each other Hobbes stated, "The Scripture was written to show unto men the kingdom of God and to prepare their minds to become his obedient subjects, leaving the world and the philosophy thereof to the disputation of men for the exercising of their natural reason."[78] Spinoza completed this separation:

> It remains for me to show that between faith or theology, and philosophy, there is no connection, nor affinity. I think no one will dispute the fact who has knowledge of the aim and foundations of the two subjects, for they are as wide apart as the poles. Philosophy has no end in view save truth: faith, as we have abundantly proved, looks for nothing but obedience and piety.[79]

Spinoza believed that the Bible's only purpose was to encourage people toward lives of godliness. He argued that the prophets were not wise and the wise men were not prophets; this was mainly due to personality.[80] For a person to have visions he needed a great imagination rather than a keen intellect: "The prophets were endowed with unusually vivid imaginations, and not with unusually perfect minds."[81] The personalities of the prophets determined their prophecies, rather than God revealing information to them. This is why some prophets were cheerful and positive, while others were melancholy and negative; their disposition determined their message.[82] But if prophecies came from the prophet's demeanor rather than the inspiration of God, they could hardly be regulators of truth.[83] Like the other rationalists he cautioned against

---

[77] Ibid., 40.

[78] Hobbes, *Leviathan, Parts One and Two*, 73.

[79] Spinoza, *A Theologico-Political Treatise*, 189. Spinoza stated that the purpose of his writing was to show this separation, "Although the points we have just raised concerning prophets and prophecy are the only ones which have any direct bearing on the end in view, namely, the separation of Philosophy from Theology." Ibid., 42.

[80] Ibid., 27. He said, "Men of great imaginative power are less fitted for abstract reasoning, whereas those who excel in intellect and its use keep their imagination more restrained and controlled, holding it in subjection, so to speak, lest it should usurp the place of reason."

[81] Ibid., 27.

[82] Ibid., 30.

[83] Ibid., 27. He said, "Treating the question methodically, I will show that prophecies varied, not only according to the imagination and physical temperament of the prophet,

the imagination and enthusiasm of the more emotional sort.  Reason is the only trustworthy faculty.   He concluded, "From thence I shall conclude that prophecy never rendered the prophets more learned, but left them with their former opinions, and that we are, therefore, not at all bound to trust them in matters of intellect."[84]  The separation of revelation and reason was complete; but this also revealed a divorce of mind and heart in the focus of the rationalists.  The rationalists as well as the virtuosi and to a lesser degree the Anglicans had a propensity to neglect the heart because of its perceived inferiority to the mind.

With the severance of revelation from truth, portions of the Bible could be discarded without dire consequences according to the rationalists.  Clear and distinct ideas mattered more than what they considered as superstition.[85]  Locke and Blount abandoned the idea of eternal punishment in hell.[86]  Spinoza and Hobbes rejected the reality of demons.[87]  Westfall makes a case for the idea that Locke implicitly denied the concept of the Trinity in his vindications of the *Reasonableness of Christianity* and Cragg reveals Newton's Arianism in his unpublished letters.[88]  They believed that the scriptures were not trustworthy and were only needed for the masses of ignorant people in order to keep them devoted to God and morally upright since they did not have the capacity or the time to discover rationally the moral truths found in natural religion.[89]

The rationalists' understanding of the nature of the Bible led to some of the earliest attempts of biblical criticism.  Because they believed it was of human origin and therefore errant, they treated the Bible as they would any other type of literature, which included a critical analysis of its contents.  Hobbes and

---

but also according to his particular opinions; and further that prophecy never rendered the prophet wiser than he was before."

[84] Ibid., 33.

[85] Spinoza, *A Theologico-Political Treatise*, 28, 112 borrowing from Descartes, *Discourse on Method and Meditations*, 120.

[86] John Locke, *The Reasonableness of Christianity*, 26; Blount, *Religio Laici*, 70.

[87] Spinoza, *A Theologico-Political Treatise*, 41; Hobbes, *Leviathan*, 215.

[88] Richard Westfall, *Science and Religion*, 137; G.R. Cragg, *From Puritanism to the Age of Reason*, 101; see also James Force and Richard Popkin, editors, *The Books of Nature and Scripture: Recent Essays on Natural Philosophy, Theology, and Biblical Criticism in the Netherlands of Spinoza's Time and the British Isles of Newton's Time* (Dordrecht, The Netherlands: Kluwer Academic Publishers, 1994), ix.   Westfall also noted, "Although he [Locke] still used the name 'Christianity,' the differences separating his religion from deism were essentially semantic." *Science and Religion*, 138.   Sell convincingly makes the case that Locke was very different from the deists and actually attempted to bring them into Christianity.  Alan Sell, *John Locke and the Eighteenth-Century Divines*, 206-212.  It would be inappropriate to call Locke a deist, but his rationalist brand of Christianity downplayed the importance of the doctrines of the Trinity and the substitutionary atonement so highly prized by the original reformers.

[89] Spinoza, *A Theologico-Political Treatise*, 91; Locke, *The Reasonableness of Christianity*, 60-61.

Spinoza questioned the Mosaic authorship of the Pentateuch.[90] Spinoza said, "The method of interpreting Scripture does not widely differ from the method of interpreting nature."[91] With this hermeneutic combined with the idea of the supremacy of natural reason he was able to claim Daniel's dreams were imaginary, question the historical accuracy of the account of Joseph and his brothers, even claiming the Pentateuch as being "set down promiscuously and without order" and "that all the materials were promiscuously collected and heaped together," and pronounce multiple errors in numerical details, genealogies, history and prophecy.[92] Though "in many historical accounts, Spinoza's critical examination of Scripture is taken as the beginning of modern biblical scholarship," Richard Popkin asserts that Quaker Bible scholar Samuel Fisher (1605-65) was the originator of biblical criticism.[93]

Many of the radicals followed the rationalists in their devaluation of the scriptures, but for different reasons. Whereas the rationalists elevated the mind and subsequently suspected the affections of the heart, the radicals distrusted the mind in their high esteem for the heart, especially emphasizing the place of the Spirit. It appears that for the seventeenth century Englishman either extreme led to a rejection of scripture as the authoritative word of God.[94] Gerrard Winstanley discussed in his work *Truth Lifting up its head above Scandals* how the Bible had errors and was not the word of God. He declared that the Spirit was all that a person needed in this dispensation:

> Therefore learne to put a difference betweene the report, and the thing reported of. The spirit that made flesh is he that is reported of. The writings and words of saints is the report. These reports being taken hold of, by corrupt flesh that would rule, are blemished by various translations, interpretations and constructions, that King flesh makes; but those sons and daughters in whom the Spirit rests, cannot be deceived, but judgeth all things.[95]

---

[90] Hobbes, *Leviathan*, 200; Spinoza, *A Theologico-Political Treatise*, 120-132.

[91] Spinoza, *A Theologico-Political Treatise*, 99.

[92] Ibid., 32, 134-135, 153.

[93] James Force and Richard Popkin, editors, *The Books of Nature and Scripture*, vii, 1-22. Popkin also argues that Spinoza joined with Fisher after his excommunication, both claiming the word of God was separate from the bible and would survive "even if all physical books disappeared. For Fisher, the Word would be recognized by the Spirit or Light within, for Spinoza by reason." Ibid., 9. Hill notes, "Fisher's is a remarkable work of popular Biblical criticism, based on real scholarship. Its effect is to demote the Bible from its central position in the protestant scheme of things, to make it a book like any other." *The World Turned Upside Down*, 267.

[94] Hill points out how to varying degrees, Winstanley, John Milton, Ranters and Quakers such as Fox and Fisher either treated the bible as myth or severely criticized its contents, denying its infallibility and submitting it "to close textual criticism." *The World Turned Upside Down*, 261-268.

[95] Gerrard Winstanley, *Truth Lifting up its head above Scandals* (London: s.n., 1649), 34-35. He later said, "Qu. But are not those Scriptures the Law and Testimony for people to walk by in these dayes? Answ. No: For this is to walke by the eyes of other

Here we see the Quaker differentiation between the word of God and the scriptures; the scriptures have errors, but the word revealed by the Spirit is discernable by those who have the Spirit. Fisher also made this demarcation, stating the Bible was not identical with the word of God and was corrupt, though still useful having been written by those who were filled with the Spirit.[96] Fisher sparked a controversy with short treatises being written in response to his *The Rustic's Alarm* both opposing it and justifying it. It seems that in the heat of the moment using inflammatory accusations against each other, neither side understood the other.[97] The early Quakers did not reject the Bible, but did see it as inferior to the light of the Spirit.

George Keith wrote in order to exonerate the Quakers from what he saw as a misunderstanding of the Quaker position on the scriptures. He admitted that there were two extremes concerning the issue, arguing for a balance. He believed those who "embrace the letter of the Scripture, but reject and cast off the Spirit of God" held the first extreme, and those "under a pretence of following the Spirit inwardly, do either altogether, or at least too much neglect and lay aside, and cast off the use and exercise of the Holy Scriptures" held the second extreme.[98] He confronted John Bajer and George Hicks specifically, but also referred to anyone rejecting the place of the Spirit in giving revelation. In addition he challenged those in his own ranks who seemed to completely abandon the Bible in preference to the immediate revelation of the Spirit. In his understanding of balance he described two groups of powers or faculties of the soul. The inferior part of the soul was the imaginative and discursive, which are the faculties that are used for the "use and exercise of the Scripture words."[99] The superior faculty is the intuitive whereby the "inward operations, inspirations, and illuminations of the Holy Spirit" are experienced.[100] Keith

---

men, and the spirit is not so scanty, that a dozen or 20 pair of eyes shall serve the whole world; but every sonne and daughter as they are called children of light, have light within themselves." Ibid., 39.

[96] Samuel Fisher, *The Rustic's Alarm to the Rabbies* (London: Printed for Robert Wilson, 1660), preface.

[97] Thomas Danson spoke of Quakerism as a "deformed monster" of whose opinions Christians should hold with "hatred and detestation." *The Quakers Folly Made Manifest to all Men* (London: J.H., 1659), epistle to the reader. An anonymous Quaker who called himself "the Abused Quaker" sought to exonerate Fisher, calling the opposition "unstable Athenians." Abused Quaker, *The Holy Scripture Owned, and the Athenians Injustice Detected, by the Abused Quaker* (London: s.n., 1692), 1-2. He also defended the idea that the Bible contains the word of God but is just a book, differentiating the word from the words, the divine truths from the letters or writings.

[98] George Keith, *Divine Immediate Revelation and Inspiration, Continued in the True Church* (London: s.n., 1685), Preface.

[99] Ibid., 18.

[100] Ibid., 17. He went on to say, "In respect of that supreme power of his soul, whereby he reacheth unto God, and apprehendeth him, with faith, hope and love, far beyond and

described the immediate experience of the Spirit apart from the scriptures as better than the revelation received from the scripture, making the scripture revelation inferior.[101] He saw a need for the scriptures, especially for the immature, but did not see the absolute necessity of them for the more mature.[102] Neither was he willing to test the inner witnesses of the spirit by the outward witness of scripture or natural reason; Robert Barclay, who held similar views to Keith, made this clear stating:

> These divine inward revelations, which we make absolutely necessary for the building up of true faith, neither do nor can ever contradict the outward testimony of the scriptures, or right and sound reason. Yet from hence it will not follow, that these divine revelations are to be subjected to the examination, either of the outward testimony of the scriptures, or of the natural reason of man, as to a more noble or certain rule or touchstone: for this divine revelation, and inward illumination, is that which is evident and clear of it self, forcing by its own evidence and clearness, the well-disposed understanding to assent, irresistibly moving the same thereunto, even as the common principles of natural truths move and incline the mind to a natural assent.[103]

Barclay went on to say that if the inner witness should be examined by the Bible and reason, then the Bible and reason should also be tested by the inner witness; here he made the subjective inward experience of the Spirit equal to scripture and reason. But later he made the Spirit the first and principal rule over other testimonies, calling the scriptures "a secondary rule, subordinate to the Spirit."[104] An interesting comparison can be made between the Anglican clergyman and philosopher John Norris and Barclay in their view of the inner light. Partially because some had mistaken Norris for a Quaker, he wanted to distance himself by examining the view of the Quakers Barclay and Keith concerning the divine light.[105] He agreed with the Quakers that everyone has this light, but disagreed with what this light is. Norris quoted Barclay and Keith, revealing they believed the light was only for spiritual understanding and that it was not divine, but rather a material creature, a middle nature between

---

above all manner or measure of words, he needeth not the scriptures, although he needeth them in regard of his inferiour powers." Ibid., 21.

[101] Ibid., 31. He stated, "The Scriptures are a subordinate and secondary principle of knowing Divine doctrines and truths, as concerning God and Christ; but still we contend for the Holy Spirit, inlightning, inspiring, and by its life giving vigour, and vertue, effectually working in the souls of men, as principal or primary."

[102] Ibid., 12, 18.

[103] Robert Barclay, *Theses Theologicae: or The Theological Propositions, which are Defended by Robert Barclay, in his Apology for the True Christian Divinity as the Same is Held Forth and Preached, by the People Called Quakers* (London: s.n., 1675), 2-3.

[104] Ibid., 4.

[105] John Norris, *The Grossness of the Quaker's Principle of the Light Within, with Their Inconsistency in Explaining it. Discours'd in a Letter to a Friend* (London: Printed for Sam. Manship, 1692).

God and humanity. Norris believed the light was for both natural and spiritual understanding and could only be divine. It doesn't appear that Norris fully understood Barclay, but he did bring out some interesting statements made by Barclay such as his belief that Christ had two bodies, fleshly and spiritual and that he always had the spiritual body which is what the inner light or divine seed consists of.[106] Norris's main point was that the divine light cannot be a creature because it is both needless and impossible. Though these two seem to be polar opposites concerning their views on the inner light, they did hold a common perspective. Both Norris and Barclay (and Keith) believed that all people had an inner light or seed from divine union with God;[107] because of the universality of this divine light, it appears the Bible was not viewed as being critical for spiritual understanding. Norris did not repudiate the Scriptures in any way, but the relative absence of biblical references in the entire treatise is telling of his leanings.[108]   Whereas the virtuosi and rationalists made the scriptures inferior to general revelation, at least in practice, the Quakers made the scriptures secondary to the immediate revelation of the Spirit.

Not all radicals rejected the authority or supremacy of the Bible.[109]   J.C. Brauer contends for a difference between spiritualism and mysticism in seventeenth century puritanism, highlighting the mystic puritan Francis Rous.[110] Spiritualism as exemplified by the Quakers placed the person of the Holy Spirit as central to theology and practice.   Their attitudes toward externals such as the sacraments or the Bible were either indifferent or hostile; the Spirit was all that really mattered. On the other hand, mystics focused on intense, transitory moments of union and communion with Christ brought on by practicing the mystic path of purgation, illumination and union and resulting in activity for Christ and renewed preparation for another encounter with Christ.[111] He argues that the puritan mystic's attitude toward the externals was not as drastic as the Quakers, but not as necessary as non-mystics. It is not clear whether those in the seventeenth century recognized this differentiation, but there were degrees of emphasis on the Spirit and subsequently a gradation of attitude toward the Bible.   The stronger the emphasis on immediate revelation from the Spirit, the less respect was held for the written scriptures.

There were a number of radicals who maintained a high view of the scriptures, while advocating a deep experience of God either through the Spirit

---

[106] Ibid., 14-15.
[107] Ibid., 21-22.
[108] He only mentions two passages and then only referring to the Quakers' position. He does not use the Bible at all to prove his case. Ibid., 9, 15-18.
[109] Henry Walker, an independent with anti-Episcopal leanings is an example of a radical who embraced the authority of the Bible while elevating the place of the Spirit. *The Protestants Grammar* (London: Robert Ibbitson and John Clowes, 1648), 2-31.
[110] J.C. Brauer, *Francis Rous: Puritan Mystic 1579-1659: An Introduction to the Mystical Element in Puritanism* (Ph.D. dissertation for the University of Chicago Divinity School, December, 1948), passim.
[111] Ibid., 26.

or communion with Christ in the mystical sense. Whether the emphasis was on the Spirit or a mystical communion, those who maintained an appreciation for the authority of the Bible also held a doctrine of depravity similar to the reformers. Francis Rous is a case in point. His mystical side can be seen in his treatise *The Mysticall Marriage* where he described the relationship of the Christian and Christ as a marriage with "experimentall discoveries" that go beyond the rational understanding or ability to make clear cognitively.[112] He did not neglect the doctrine of the Spirit, but his focus was clearly on communion with Christ. In describing this union he resorted to analogy over and over:

> And being thus united and married to him, his spirit flowes into thy spirit, and the sappe of the Deity sheds it selfe into the soule. For as man and wife in a corporall marriage, are one flesh, so in this spirituall and mysticall marriage, Christ and his spouse are one spirit.[113]

He used analogy because he admited that union with Christ cannot be explained:

> One taste of it [marriage-happiness] wil tell thee more, than all that is or can be said. The true knowledge of the sweetnes of God is gotten by tasting, and therefore taste first, and then see how sweet and gracious the Lord is. The taste of it will truly tell him that tasteth it, how sweet it is; but hee that knoweth this sweetnes by tasting, cannot deliver over the full and perfect image of this sweetnes to him that hath not tasted it. For this sweetnes surmounts all knowne sweetnesse of the creatures, and by that which is knowne must that which is unknowne be made knowne.[114]

Rous used similar themes as other puritans before him, but with a much more elaborate employment.[115] Richard Sibbes and other puritans used language which was comparable to that used by Rous, but not to the same degree.[116] It would appear that Brauer is correct in calling Rous the first puritan mystic[117] if certain stipulations are made. He didn't describe the experiences of spiritual marriage as transitory as much as other mystics and so did not understand life as a series of highs and lows.[118] Neither did he reject reason as unnecessary.[119]

---

[112] Francis Rous, *The Mysticall Marriage* (London: William Jones, 1631), Passim.

[113] Ibid., 9-10. Another example he used was an extended analogy of the carnal person being married to concupiscence and needing to divorce him before she can be married to Christ. Ibid., 18-43.

[114] Ibid., 53-55.

[115] J.C. Brauer, *Francis Rous Puritan Mystic*, 31-44.

[116] Richard Sibbes, *Works*, 2:1-248; Ralph Robinson, *Christ All in All* (Ligonier, PA: Soli Deo Gloria Publications, 1992), 275-287.

[117] J.C. Brauer, *Francis Rous Puritan Mystic*, preface.

[118] Francis Rous, *The Mysticall Marriage*, 62-63. He did describe "the spouses estate in desertions" as miserable, but in no different way than other puritans understood. Ibid.,

He also did not devalue the word and its authority in judging spiritual experiences.[120]

Rous believed in the supreme authority of the scriptures while embracing an experiential union with Christ. He recognized that spiritual experiences could be counterfeits and so the Christian needed to test the mystical encounters he or she had with the word of God. If the "heavenly visitations" do not agree with the Bible or are not confirmed by the Bible, then they are suspect.[121] In his work *The Great Oracle*, he combined a high view of scripture, even adopting a dictation view of inspiration, alongside a thoroughly Reformed view of depravity.[122] He believed that the fall of Adam affected every aspect of human nature, with the understanding being the first faculty of the soul to be seduced.[123] At the fall the image of God was broken in such a way that though there was a remnant of the original image in the understanding, will and conscience of themselves, humans were hopelessly lost, needing God's effectual grace for deliverance.[124] Rous was attacking the Arminian position of free will, but especially argued against the philosophers of his day who advocated free will and the salvific possibility of general revelation. He said:

> And now assemble your selves together, all yee Phiosophers and Wizzards, and behold Man thus dressed up in corruption and miserie, and heale him, if you have any medicine equivalent to his disease. The truth is, you have taken great paines to make something of this wretched nothing, called man: you would faine have restored him to the use of reason, the ancient image of his Maker.[125]

He believed both Arminianism and philosophy had exalted humans too much and did not take seriously enough the depravity of humankind after the fall.[126] Unlike the Anglicans, virtuosi and rationalists who tended to see the mind somewhat intact even after the fall, Rous understood the mind to have been completely corrupted by sin. He saw little value in science and philosophy and

---

102ff. Compare with the German mystic Jacob Beheme, *A Brief Explanation of the Knowledge of God and of All Things* (London: M.S., 1661), 1-12; *The Way to Christ Discovered* (London: M.S., 1648), 4:1-48.

[119] When reason was seen as a "lesser light" to the Spirit and took a place of "homage" it was accepted and seen as useful. *The Mysticall Marriage*, 252-255.

[120] Ibid., 248-252.

[121] Ibid.

[122] He stated, "For the highest Spirit, when he dictated them [the scriptures], did put his mind and meaning into them; and so in them we may discern the mind of God." Francis Rous, *The Great Oracle: Or, the Main Frame and Body of the Scriptures, Resolving the Question, Whether in Man's Free-will and Common Grace, or in God's Special and Effectual Grace, stands the Safety of Man, and the Glory of God by Man's Safety?* (London: S. Palmer, 1718), 7.

[123] Ibid., 12.

[124] Ibid., 32-44, 62.

[125] Francis Rous, *The Arte of Happines* (London: W. Stansby, 1619), 115.

[126] Francis Rous, *The Great Oracle*, 38, 83-85.

spoke against "fleshly and sensual wisdom" which was the only kind of wisdom available to the unregenerate.[127] The knowledge of the unregenerate only led them away from God and his truth:

> Yea, the sway of this knowledge is so mightie, that in may plaine and evident causes of good and evil, the poore ruines of reason, even the broken remnants of Gods image in the soule, are put out of countenance, and are ashamed to give up their verdict; wherefore, many times, by men of understanding, for feare or flatterie, evill is called good, and good, evill.[128]

Like the reformers, Rous believed that salvation brought a measure of restoration as far as the shattered image of God is concerned, but unlike them he believed the transformation "is felt chiefly in the will and affections."[129] His mystical leanings caused him to downplay the mind in the regenerate in that there was no real place for natural wisdom, logic and reasoning in the believer's life. In his writings he emphasized the heart and emotional experiences and subsequently neglected the mind, though not to the extent of those who de-emphasized the mind so much that they also rejected or at least neglected the Bible. His view of depravity kept him from abandoning the supreme authority of scriptures, because one needed God's revelation to test experiences due to one's mistake prone mind.[130] However, the radicals who were willing to abandon the reformers' view of depravity did not always maintain this preservation of the reformers' outlook on scripture.

Numerous citations from the writings of the Anglicans, virtuosi and radicals show the degree to which Stephen Charnock and the latitude puritans were clearly influenced by these groups, but were seemingly unaffected by them concerning the superiority of special revelation over other types of revelation.[131] Charnock recognized value in general revelation, but he also noticed its imperfection due to depravity.[132] Because of human corruption the Bible is all the more superior to natural reason: "The revelations of God tower above reason in its purity, much more above reason in its mud and

---

[127] Francis Rous, *The Arte of Happines*, 31-35, 91-115.

[128] Ibid., 94-95.

[129] Ibid., 170-176.

[130] Francis Rous, *Treatises and Meditations* (London: Robert White, 1657), 506-507; *The Mysticall Marriage*, 248-252.

[131] Charnock cited the rationalists and virtuosi Rene Descartes, Francis Bacon, Pierre Gassendi and Walter Charleton a total of nineteen times in his *Works*, and he cited the Anglicans Edward Stillingfleet, Richard Montague, Matthew Wren, Richard Hooker, Gilbert Burnet, Henry Hammond, John Pearson, Jeremy Taylor, and Lancelot Andrewes a total of twenty one times. William Bates recognized the value of reason stating: "Reason is the singular ornament of the human nature, whereby it excels the brutes," but went on to say, "the doctrine of the gospel excels the most noble sciences." *Works*, 1:263.

[132] Stephen Charnock, *Works*, 3:119. He said it was "defaced by the fall."

earthiness."[133]   Even in the regenerate state the law of nature restored to its original condition and placed within the Christian by the Spirit still needs to be tested by the outward law because "it is imperfect as yet" whereas the written law is perfect.[134]

He not only saw scripture as superior to general revelation but also to any "enthusiasms of our brain."[135]   Here he is speaking against placing immediate revelations or traditions above the written word of God.   Boston seemed to have been writing against George Keith in saying, "It is but the blindness of enthusiasts to pretend, that it [the Bible] is only for the weaker, and that the more perfect must follow the Spirit: for if that Spirit teach any thing contrary to the written word, it is a spirit of darkness."[136]   Boston and Thomas Jacombe specifically wrote against the Quaker idea of immediate revelation being superior to the written revelation of the Bible and warned against their enthusiasm.[137] Charnock and puritans in general held a middle position between the rationalists, virtuosi and Anglicans on the one side and the radicals on the other.   He agreed with the Anglicans that all truth must be subject to the scriptures, but also agreed with the radicals that real truth affects the heart as well as the mind.   He agreed with the virtuosi that even the unbeliever easily understands some truths in the Bible, but he also qualified that idea by stating that unless those truths are grasped by the heart as well as the mind they will soon be lost.[138]   He disagreed with the philosophers and Socinians, arguing: "It is base to set up reason, a finite principle, against an infinite wisdom; much baser to set up a depraved and purblind reason against an all-seeking and holy

---

[133] Stephen Charnock, *Existence and Attributes*, 1:590.

[134] Stephen Charnock, *Works*, 3:119-120.

[135] Stephen Charnock, *Existence and Attributes*, 1:504; John Howe, *Works*, 2:1079.

[136] Thomas Boston, *Works*, 1:25. . .

[137] Ibid., 1:40; *Puritan Sermons: 1659-1689*, 5:69, 78.   Jacombe exhorted, "In all inquiries into the truths of the mind of God, consult those sacred oracles.   Here are mines of truth; O dig here, make them the rule of faith and life.   While a Papist makes the church his rule, and the enthusiast pretends to make the Spirit of God his rule, do you live by scripture."

[138] Stephen Charnock, *Works*, 5:502.   He illustrated this point saying, "Some were willing to rejoice in John's light, which gave a luster to their minds, not in his heat, which would have given warmth to their affections; for John was a burning and a shining light, and they would rejoice in his light, but not in his heat, and in that too but for a season."   Thomas Watson exhorted his readers: "Read the Scripture, not only as a history, but as a love letter sent you from God, which may affect your hearts." *A Body of Divinity*, 35.   Bates stated, "Other knowledge swells the mind, and increases the esteem of ourselves, this gives us a sincere view of our state.   It discovers our misery in its causes, and the almighty mercy that saves us.   Other knowledge enlightens the understanding, without changing the heart, but this inspires us with the love of God, with the hatred of sin, and makes us truly better.   In seeking after other knowledge, the mind is perplexed by endless inquiries: here it is at rest, as the wavering needle is fixed when turned to its beloved star." *Works*, 1:269; John Howe, *Works*, 2:1081.

wisdom."[139] He claimed their elevation of reason above scripture made human wisdom equal with God.[140] He also contradicted the Quakers, claiming the scriptures were absolutely necessary for humans to be able to fulfill their eternal purpose:

> We can have no delight in meditation on him unless we know him, and we cannot know him but by the means of his own revelation. When the revelation is despised, the revealer will be of little esteem. Men do not throw off God from being their rule, till they throw off Scripture from being their guide; and God must needs be cast off from being an end, when the Scripture is rejected from being a rule.[141]

He summed up his position on the superiority of scripture over the reason of the rationalist, the immediate revelations of the Quakers and the traditions of the Catholics by stating, "All truth must be drawn from Scripture."[142] In contradistinction to all of the above groups and in line with the original reformers he elaborated:

> The Scripture is the source of divine knowledge; not the traditions of men, nor reason separate from Scripture. Whosoever brings another doctrine, coins another Christ; nothing is to be added to what is written, nothing detracted from it. He doth not send us for truth, to the puddles of human inventions, to the enthusiasms of our brain; not to the See of Rome, no nor to the instructions of angels; but the writings of the prophets, as they clear up the declarations of the apostles. The church of Rome is not made here the standard of truth: but the Scriptures of the prophets are to be the touch-stone to the Romans, for the trial of the truth of the gospel.[143]

The puritans' understanding of the supremacy of scripture over other means of revelation was based on two auxiliary points: The perfection of God and his word, and the gross imperfection of humankind. Firstly, they believed the scriptures to be faultless. Richard Baxter stated, "The word of God is infallible."[144] He based this belief on the "infallible veracity of God."[145] Because of the weakness of humanity, God, in his mercy, inspired the writers of scripture to record that which was "universally necessary for all his subjects to know, in order to Divine belief, obedience, and salvation."[146] For Thomas Boston this infallibility and authority was specifically in reference to its

---

[139] Stephen Charnock, *Existence and Attributes*, 1:590.

[140] Ibid., 1:591. "It is to affect a wisdom equal with God, and an ambition to be of his cabinet council."

[141] Stephen Charnock, *Works*, 1:256.

[142] Stephen Charnock, *Existence and Attributes*, 1:504.

[143] Ibid.

[144] Richard Baxter, *The Protestant Religion Truely Stated and Justified*, 8.

[145] Ibid., 7.

[146] Ibid., 20.

purpose: "The Scriptures principally teach what man is to believe concerning God, and what duty God requires of man."[147]  Baxter was in agreement stating: "We hold that God's written Word and Law, is perfect in its kind, Psal. 19. and sufficient to its proper use and end."[148]  The puritans believed that the chief purpose of humankind was to glorify and enjoy God and the scriptures were "the only rule to direct us how we may glorify and enjoy him."[149]  They were willing to engage in minor textual criticism,[150] but because they believed the Bible was "that book which God himself hath written," they were not willing to doubt its content.[151]  Howe discussed the minor alterations in some of the texts, but concluded, "The books which we now have among us, in our time and in our hands, are the self-same books, in substance, (without any material corruption or alteration,) that those were, which went for the holy Scriptures, of divine authority at that time."[152]  In speaking of the writers of the Bible Boston surmised, "All of them were infallibly guided, so as they were put beyond all possibility of erring."[153]

Secondly, the puritans maintained a high view of scripture because they had such a low view of humanity due to the corruption brought about by Adam's fall.  Bates explained how the depravity of humankind brought about the necessity of a divine revelation:

> The fall of man was so wounding and deadly, that only an infinite understanding could find out the means for his recovery.  And if that mercy which moved the Lord to ordain the remedy, had not discovered it, a thick cloud of despair had covered mankind, being for ever unable to conceive the way of our redemption.[154]

If the fall had only slightly affected humanity in an adverse way, people could possibly discover a cure for their sinfulness with God's help.  But since the fall was so pervasive, humanity could not resort to its own means for aid.  The degeneracy of humanity necessitated a written revelation from God.  Both the Quakers and virtuosi who downplayed the need for the scriptures also minimized the doctrine of depravity.  The puritans maintained the early

---

[147] Thomas Boston, *Works*, 1:42.

[148] Richard Baxter, *The Protestant Religion*, 21.

[149] Thomas Watson, *A Body of Divinity*, 26.  Thomas Boston stated, "The next head which falls to be touched is the holy scripture, the rule which God has given to direct us how we may glorify and enjoy him." *Works*, 1:19.

[150] For example Boston entertained the idea that Moses may not have written all of the Pentateuch. *Works*, 1:21.

[151] *Puritan Sermons: 1659-1689*, 5:67.

[152] John Howe, *Works*, 2:1072.

[153] Thomas Boston, *Works*, 1:22.  He went on to say, "The penmen of the scriptures were infallible in their writing, so that they were not mistaken in any thing, even of the least moment: far less is there any real contradiction among them, being all guided by the same Spirit, who inspired the very words, and kept them from all error, 2 Pet. I. 20,21." Ibid., 33.

[154] William Bates, *Works*, 1:257; John Howe, *Works*, 2:1192-1233.

reformers' belief in the inherited depravity of humankind due to Adam's fall.[155] In describing this view they recognized they were disagreeing with the popular position of their day. Peter Vincke rejected the rationalists who had embraced a Pelagian view of depravity stating, "To think that it is *rasa tabula*, like 'white paper' without any thing good or bad written in it, is but a philosophical fiction, which scripture nowhere owns, and Christianity every where explodes."[156] This depravity was so all-encompassing it affected every aspect of the soul including the mind. John Wells queried, "How come our understandings to be prisons of darkness, our wills stages of rebellion, our affections heaps of dung or dross?" and answered by "Adam's sin...inherent in us."[157] Therefore not only because of the perfect nature of scripture, but also because of the gross imperfection of humanity, scripture was seen as the supreme rule "which he hath given us to direct us both as to faith and practice."[158]

Concerning the question of the superiority of scripture over other means of revelation the virtuosi and rationalists denied its supremacy over natural revelation and many of the radicals, at least in practice, subjugated it to the immediate revelation of the Spirit. The Anglicans upheld the preeminence of scripture, but in practice departed from the reformers view, elevating reason to a place of near equality partially due to their softening of the doctrine of depravity. The latitude puritans maintained the reformers high view of scripture, even though they gave general revelation a more substantial place in their theology, because they retained the reformers strong view of depravity.

*b. What the Scriptures Reveal About God*

The second question concerning the significance given to scripture in the various groups in seventeenth century England is, "What does the scriptures reveal about God and how does this revelation affect the hearer?" Whereas Spinoza believed that "the aim and object of Scripture is only to teach obedience,"[159] the Anglicans, puritans and radicals saw a wider goal in that the scriptures were also designed to reveal God and his attributes. Charnock's most influential work was *The Existence and Attributes of God* in which he expounded the scriptures teaching about God. He believed "the word is a glass

---

[155] Howe wrote, "The nature of man is now become universally depraved and sinful." *Puritan Sermons: 1659-1689*, 5:86.

[156] Ibid., 5:121.

[157] Ibid., 5:111. Thomas Watson elaborated on the pervasiveness of sin, "It has, as poison, diffused itself into all the parts and powers of the soul. 'The whole head is sick, and the whole heart is faint.' Isa I 5. Like a sick patient, that has no part sound, his liver is swelled, his feet are gangrened, his lungs are perished; such infected, gangrened souls have we, till Christ, who has made a medicine of his blood, cures us.... As there is salt in every drop of the sea, bitterness in every branch of wormwood, so there is sin in every faculty." *A Body of Divinity*, 144.

[158] Thomas Boston, *Works*, 1:37.

[159] Spinoza, *A Theologico-Political Treatise*, 183.

wherein we behold the reflections of God.... It discovers as much of the nature and amiableness of God as can be drawn in lines and letters, and presents the soul with such attractives in him as turns it fully to him."[160]    He said that because the works of nature are inferior to special revelation they divulge far less about God, whereas through the Bible "we shall behold the greatness, majesty, loveliness, and love of God, more than any rational discoveries can present to us."[161]    The Anglicans and radicals were in agreement with the puritans that the Bible is a source for discovering more fully the attributes of God, but their understanding of God derived from the scriptures determined their experience of him differently.   It appears that their predisposition toward mind or heart partially determined their understanding of God and experience of him.   The Anglican leaning toward the mind lent to a more cerebral contact with God.   The radical bent toward the heart tended to neglect a rational encounter and in acute cases moved toward altered states of consciousness. The latitude puritan balance of mind and heart helped them undergo communion with God without overt mysticism.    The way each group interpreted Enoch's walk with God brings to light these differences of what it means to know God through the discovery of his attributes found in the Bible.

William Clagett included a sermon on Enoch in his *Seventeen Sermons*.  In this work he defines Enoch's walk with God in ethical terms alone: "In short, to walk with God, is to be universally good and righteous."[162]    Enoch was translated by God simply because he had "arrived to a great perfection."[163]   In this sermon there is no description of an experiential relationship, communion or use of "enthusiastic" language.  Clagett is typical of the seventeenth century Anglicans who downplayed the affections in their attempt to emphasize morality and the mind.   Cragg described this temper as a reaction to the puritans: "The recent excesses of certain of the Puritan sects had left all sober men with an ingrained horror of 'fanaticism'.   They reacted against the 'enthusiast' and all his ways."[164]    Whether the Anglican disposition was a reaction to puritanism or simply due to their interpretation of scripture can be debated, but the idea that they were more cerebral and less affectionate in their language is demonstrated by Claggett's interpretation of Enoch's walk with God, especially when compared with the puritans and radicals.

The radical William Freke understood the experience of Enoch in a much different way from the Anglicans.   Like the Anglicans he believed Enoch obtained a kind of perfection, but drew very different conclusions from this premise.  He compared Enoch, Elijah and Christ, believing they all had similar experiences due to their attaining the kingdom of God.  From his observation of Enoch, Elijah and Jesus he extrapolated two major insights.  Firstly, he believed

---

[160] Charnock, *Works*, 4:104.

[161] Ibid.

[162] William Clagett, *Seventeen Sermons*, 393.

[163] Ibid., 386.

[164] G.R. Cragg, *From Puritanism to the Age of Reason*, 64.   He also said of the Latitudinarians, "They emphasize reason and exalt morality." Ibid., 63.

since Enoch did not know Christ and yet was translated to glory and was a medium for prophecy, all religions are acceptable in God's eyes as long as they are righteous and sincere.[165]   Secondly, he taught that the power that these major religious figures attained in the kingdom of God was available to everyone and included prophecy, miracles and translations.[166]   So whereas the Anglicans believed that the fullness of God's blessing would only be available after the parousia, the radicals were open to supernatural and abnormal phenomena as part of present experience.   The Quaker Jane Lead also perceived Enoch's walk with God to include a mystical element.   In her book *The Enochian Walks With God* she described outer body experiences where a person can meet angels and even meet God himself in heaven.[167]   Like Freke she held to the possibility of the miraculous when an individual enters the kingdom and is "baptized with the Holy-Ghost."[168]   But she went into far more detail on the "translated state" that is possible to experience just as Enoch did. She described this outer body manifestation: "Another evidence of the Spirit, is, internal gusts, and breaths of divine air by which the soul is often mounted up upon the wing of this word, or breath of the Spirit, and so gets up to the heavens, entering into the Celestial Globe of Eternity, while its outward body remains in time."[169]   She illustrated these experiences with mystical and metaphorical language far more elaborately than the puritan might depict communion with God.  For instance she detailed several steps on this mystical journey that included "Sharon's walks, adorned with the Spicy-beds, that gives forth their ravishing odors."[170]   From these examples of the radicals' interpretations of Enoch's walk with God we see that their starting point of the supremacy of the heart partially determined their conclusion of mystical experiences.  Not all radicals embraced mysticism, but to varying degrees their emphasis on the heart encouraged an emotional rather than cognitive treatment of the Bible, where the Bible was used more as a springboard to experience rather than the rule of life.

Thomas Jacombe, who ministered in the latitude puritan circles, preached a sermon at Richard Vines funeral on Enoch's walk with God.  He brought out both a historical exegetical understanding of the passage as well as practical applications.  He mentioned how God revealed himself to Enoch, describing

---

[165] He stated, "This tract…is not intended to exclude its self from the use and encouragement even of Jews, Mahumetans, and all other professions also: The author endeavors to open wide to all the common way to God, and tis one end of his writing to demonstrate that the righteous of all religions are accepted, and while they are sincere, have equally right to be the heirs of the kingdom."  William Freke, *A Full Enquiry into the Power of Faith, the Nature of Prophecy, the Translation of Enoch and Elias, and the Resurrection of Christ* (London: s.n., 1693), preface.

[166] Ibid., 2-3.

[167] Jane Lead, *The Enochian Walks With God* (London: D. Edwards, 1694), 10-11.

[168] Ibid., 2, 6.

[169] Ibid., 6.

[170] Ibid., 10.

general revelation in a positive light.[171]   He also pointed out Enoch's relationship with God using emotional terminology.[172]   Seeking a balance of heart and mind the puritans attempted to exegete the Bible in such a way that the mind, affections and will were challenged without neglecting any particular aspect of the soul and without going into esoteric altered states of consciousness.

## 2. The Place of the Spirit in the Comprehension of Scripture

During the seventeenth century there was a variety of ways in which groups explained the role of the Spirit within their understanding of scripture.  Once again the predisposition toward the head or the heart partially determined the importance placed on the need for the Spirit in correctly comprehending the Bible.  The reformers saw the necessity of the Spirit and the word working together to bring salvation and sanctification.  Typical of the reformers, Bullinger wrote of how the Spirit quickened in our hearts "the seed of God's word."[173]   He believed that both the mind and heart needed to be moved and this was only possible by the Spirit instilling faith into the believer.[174]   When the Holy Spirit opened up the word to the mind and heart of the believer, "it driveth away the misty darkness of errors, it openeth our eyes, it converteth and enlighteneth our minds, and instructeth us most fully and absolutely in truth and godliness."[175]   In other words, the Spirit and the word worked hand in hand to conform the mind and heart of the person with the result of the salvation of the person and the glory of God.[176]   This balanced emphasis of both word and Spirit working together changed in differing ways by the seventeenth century as can be seen in how they understood the illumination of scripture and their interpretation of what it meant to worship in Spirit and truth.

The rationalists did not see a need for the Spirit's help in the comprehension of the Bible.  Hobbes seemed to deny the Spirit as a separate person from the Father and the Son, explaining the passages that refer to the Holy Spirit as

---

[171] Thomas Jacombe, *Enochs Walk and Change* (London: T.R. and E.M., 1656), 12-13.

[172] Ibid., 5-9.  He spoke of "soul-ravishing communion" which is "better felt then exprest."

[173] Henry Bullinger, *Decades*, 1:66.

[174] Ibid., "For what will it avail to hear the word of God without faith, and without the Holy Spirit of God to work or stir inwardly in our hearts?"  He went on to say, "If therefore that the word of God do sound in our ears, and therewithal the Spirit of God do shew forth his power in our hearts, and that we in faith do truly receive the word of God, then hath the word of God a mighty force and wonderful effect in us." Ibid., 67.

[175] Ibid., 67.

[176] He concluded, "Let us therefore beseech our Lord God to pour into our minds his holy Spirit, by whose virtue the seed of God's word may be quickened in our hearts, to the bringing forth of much fruit to the salvation of our souls, and the glory of God our Father." Ibid., 70.

simply referring to God's actions.[177]   He said, "*Jesus full of the Holy Ghost*...may be understood, for *zeal* to doe the work for which he was sent by God the Father: but to interpret it of a ghost, is to say, that God himselfe (for so our Saviour was,) was filled with God; which is very unproper, and unsignificant (sic)."[178]  Spinoza rejected the idea that any supernatural means was necessary to interpret scripture, claiming those who held to that idea show nothing supernatural in their interpretations.[179]  He said that everyone had the ability to interpret scripture and therefore "the rule for such interpretation should be nothing but the natural light of reason which is common to all – not any supernatural light nor any external authority."[180]

Many of the Anglicans also rejected a need for the Spirit to interpret the Bible, but for differing reasons than the rationalists.  They believed that the Spirit inspired the biblical authors to write in such a way that the Bible was kept from error.  Tillotson spoke of the Spirit's inspiration saying, "that he [the Spirit] did superintend them [the writers of scripture] in the writing of them so far as to secure them from any material error or mistake in what they have delivered."[181]  Because the believer possessed an infallible assurance of the divine revelation he or she would not require further help from the Spirit in interpretation.[182]  He remained agnostic as to the specifics of the nature of inspiration, whether it was dictation or not and whether or not it guaranteed infallibility concerning "any history or matter of fact."[183]  His sin qua non of inspiration was that it accomplished God's purpose:

> I shall only say this in general, that considering the end of this inspiration, which was to inform the world certainly of the mind and will of God, it is necessary for every man to believe that the inspired pen-men of scripture were so far assisted as was necessary to this end; and he that thinks upon good grounds, that this end cannot be secured, unless every word and syllable were immediately dictated, he hath reason to believe, it was so; but if any man upon good grounds thinks the [...?] of writing the scripture may be sufficiently secured without that, he hath no reason to conclude, that God, who is not wanting in what is necessary, is guilty of doing what is superfluous.[184]

He did not see the testimony of the Spirit as an inner persuasion of secret understanding that the unbeliever did not have.  He explained that the witness

---

[177] Hobbes, *Leviathan*, 205-215.  He also denied either good or evil spirits entering into people.
[178] Ibid., 210.
[179] Spinoza, *A Theologico-Political Treatise*, 114.
[180] Ibid., 119.
[181] John Tillotson, *Sermons on Several Subjects and Occasions* (London: printed for J. and R. Tonson and S. Draper, etc., 1748), 11:186.
[182] Ibid., 11:188.
[183] Ibid., 11:184.
[184] Ibid., 11:184-185.  He seemed to be open to the writers writing in their "own style and manner of expression."  Ibid., 11:184.

of the Spirit referred to the miracles performed by the Apostles and prophets that verified the supernatural nature of the writings.[185]  God did not need to strengthen the faculty of the mind by "raising and enabling our understanding to yield assent to the gospel," because "our understandings are naturally endowed with a sufficient power to assent to any truth that is sufficiently propounded to them."[186]  God does not make us more capable of believing or understanding because we are already fully capable of doing so already.  Here we see that due to the milder view of depravity held by the Anglicans, they believed people were already capable of understanding God's word without the further need of illumination by the Spirit.[187]  Reedy suggests two other reasons for the Anglican view that all could interpret scripture apart from a supernatural illumination of the Spirit: the disruption in the political arena caused by the "Spirit-oriented interpretation," and the "larger orientation toward rational scriptural interpretation."[188]  They were certainly leery of what they saw as the abuse of the Spirit during the civil war, which explains their reaction against those who claimed that only those with the Spirit could properly interpret scripture.  Their emphasis on the mind also led them to see its potential to comprehend at least the parts of scripture necessary for salvation.  To admit one's inability to understand the Bible apart from spiritual enlightenment would have minimized the place of reason for them.

     The radicals were diametrically opposite to the Anglicans and rationalists. Evidence of their dissemblance can be seen in their interpretation of *the candle of the Lord*.  Each group believed the candle of the Lord came from God but disagreed on what faculty it came in.  The typical Anglican understanding of the concept found in Proverbs 20:27 following that of the Cambridge Platonists was that the candle referred to the rational faculty and was lit by God.[189] Culverwell's Latin translation was *Mens hominis lucerna Domini*, which did not follow the Vulgate (*lucerna domini spiraculum hominus*).[190]  His translation of נִשְׁמָה as *mens* rather than breath or spirit revealed his preoccupation with reason.  The rationalists also followed suit calling the light of reason the candle

---

[185] Ibid., 11:193-198.

[186] Ibid., 11:197-198.  He went on to state, "There can be no necessity to assert, that the Spirit of God doth, in the work of faith, raise and elevate our understanding above their natural pitch."

[187] William Clagett wrote his book *A Discourse Concerning the Operations of the Holy Spirit* (London: Printed for Ch. Brome, 1690) in order to refute John Owen's suggestion that the Spirit was necessary for a person to understand the Bible, believing that all had a natural ability to comprehend it.

[188] Gerard Reedy, *The Bible and Reason*, 59.  He said, "In their larger orientation toward rational scriptural interpretation, they intended to be inclusive rather than exclusive to put the ability to interpret Scripture on a broad basis, and to rise above the possibility of using Scripture for narrow political ends."

[189] Nathaniel Culverwell, *An Elegant and Learned Discourse of the Light of Nature*, 13; *A System of Divinity and Morality*, 5:90.

[190] Ibid.

of the Lord.[191]  George Fox disagreed, seeing the candle as the spirit rather than reason.[192]  He taught that everyone has this candle, but natural humans put it out by turning away from the Lord.[193]  He also taught that "there is a Light in all People," referring to Christ enlightening every human by "pouring out his Spirit on all flesh."[194]  This universal reception of the Spirit went contrary to the views of both the Anglicans and puritans, but revealed the radical emphasis on the Spirit rather than the word and the heart rather than the head.

The radicals were much further away from the Anglicans than they were from the puritans concerning the necessity of the Spirit in understanding scripture, but they engaged in more polemics with the puritans than the Anglicans regarding this issue.  In 1639 John Goodwin and Samuel How disagreed on the issue of whether or not a person could preach without human learning.  Goodwin sent the passage of 2 Peter 3:16 to How, challenging the uneducated cobbler and pastor to preach.  He in turn preached on that passage in front of Goodwin, entitling his message *The Sufficiency of the Spirit's Teaching Without Human Learning*.  Goodwin suppressed the printing of this sermon in London, but it was sent to Holland where it was printed and brought back to London.[195]  This incident and the content of this sermon reveal the intense disagreement between the puritans and radicals on the issue of the necessity of the Spirit in the proper interpretation of scripture.  Both groups believed in the requirement of the Spirit's illumination of the scriptures for a right understanding of the Bible, but the radicals also rejected any need of human learning.  By human learning How meant any knowledge of the arts, sciences or languages other than one's own mother tongue.[196]  He believed that God's Spirit teaches spiritual things and so the Spirit was the only prerequisite for correct hermeneutics.[197]  He claimed passages like 1 John 2:26-27, Luke 10:21-24; Colossians 2:8, Acts 4:13-14 and 1 Corinthians 1:17 teach that unlearned men can preach and understand scripture better than the educated and that human learning actually hindered preaching.[198]  William Dell explained that the Spirit leads the believer "into the truth" and therefore also keeps the believer from error.[199]  The cause of all divisions in the church came from people being led by other people rather than the Spirit.[200]  The word of God can only be preached by the power of the Spirit, otherwise it is simply the word of

---

[191] John Locke, *The Reasonableness of Christianity*, 55.

[192] George Fox, *Gospel-Truth Demonstrated in a Collection of Doctrinal Books* (London: Printed and sold by T. Sowle, 1706), 627.

[193] Ibid., 638.

[194] Ibid., 640-641.

[195] Samuel How, *The Sufficiency of the Spirit's Teaching Without Human Learning* (Aberdeen: J. Strachan, 1780), preface by William Kiffen.

[196] Ibid., 12.

[197] Ibid., 14.

[198] Ibid., 12-22.

[199] William Dell, *Select Works of William Dell*, 19.

[200] Ibid., 20, 27.

humans and is "cold" without "heat."[201]  Dell did not reject an educated
ministry like How, but he did believe that if there was no minister available a
person could preach God's word if he is anointed with the Spirit.[202]  To varying
degrees the radicals rejected the use of natural wisdom in understanding God's
word, seeing the Spirit as the only real prerequisite for proper interpretation.

The latitude puritans declared the absolute necessity of the Spirit for a true
understanding of scripture, without rejecting the need for human learning.
Bates said, "The mind convinces the mind, and the heart persuades the heart,"
and went on to describe the necessity of both Spirit and word.[203]  Baxter
categorically stated against the radicals, "God hath made Reason essential to
our nature.... They that wrangle against us, for giving reason for our religion,
seem to tell us, that they have none for their own; or else reprehend us for being
men."[204]  He believed that reason was a part of our being made in the image of
God and so any rejection of reason and human wisdom, in favor of the Spirit
alone was not appropriate.  He also believed in the necessity of the Spirit's help
before one "can savingly understand and apply the Scripture."[205]  His "infallible
rule for understanding the holy scripture" was: "The evidence of its own
meaning is inherent in its self, discernible or intelligible by men prepared and
instructed, by competent teaching and study, and the necessary help of Gods
grace and Spirit."[206]  Here we see that Baxter upheld the need for human
learning as well as the guidance of the Spirit for correct hermeneutics.
Charnock also saw the need for both education and the Spirit for understanding
spiritual truth, and so appealed to the practice of prayer.[207]

This balance of word and Spirit, reflecting an equal emphasis on the mind as
well as the heart can be seen in the puritan reflection on what it means to
worship in Spirit and in truth.  Charnock wrote extensively on spiritual
worship.  He believed that the requirement of spiritual worship could be
detected in both general and special revelation.  The light of nature reveals the
necessity of spiritual worship in that by nature humans should realize that there
is a God and he desires to be worshipped with their best faculties.[208]  He argued

---

[201] Ibid., 29-30.  He said, "Without this Spirit, a man's ministry is cold, it warms the
hearts of none, it inflames the spirit of none; but leaves men still frozen in their sins."
[202] Ibid., 45.
[203] William Bates, *Works*, 2:493-495.
[204] Richard Baxter, *Practical Works*, 2:94.
[205] Richard Baxter, *The Protestant Religion Truely Stated and Justified*, 30-31.  Richard
Vines agreed saying, "It is not possible for a naturall man to see spirituall things with a
naturall light, natural light cannot bring him to salvation...this spirituall light (which is a
beam of the spirit) though it be never so small, yet falling into the heart, it's a changing,
a healing, an humbling light." *Christ a Christians Onely Gain: or The Excellency and
desireableness of the Knowledge of Jesus Christ, above all other things whatsoever*
(London: Printed for Thomas Johnson, 1660), 16 also 68; John Howe, *Works*, 2:1071.
[206] Richard Baxter, *The Protestant Religion Truely Stated and Justified*, 2.
[207] Stephen Charnock, *Works*, 4:101-103.
[208] Ibid., 1:285-290.

that nature teaches that true worship must be from both the mind and the heart and include the affections otherwise "it is else a mocking God with a feather."[209]   His description of this natural worship is revealing: "Such a worship wherein the mind thinks of God, feels a sense of God, has the spirit consecrated to God, the heart glowing with affections to God."[210]   Charnock admitted that though everyone should know that worship must be holistic, they do not know how to worship God in such a way that glorifies God unless he reveals what kind of worship pleases him; this brings the necessity of worshiping in truth and therefore the special revelation of the Bible.[211] Charnock's understanding of the balance of mind and heart is revealed in his reflection on priorities in evangelical worship.   He believed the rational faculties were the most important, but the faculties of the will and affections were also essential.   Unlike many of the radicals, he did not elevate the affections above the rational powers.  He declared:

> All spiritual acts must be acts of reason, otherwise they are not human acts, because they want that principle which is constitutive of man, and doth difference him from other creatures.  Acts done only by sense are the acts of a brute; acts done by reason are the acts of a man; that which is only an act of sense cannot be an act of religion.  The sense without the conduct of reason is not the subject of religious acts, for then beasts were capable of religion as well as men.  There cannot be religion where there is not reason; and there cannot be the exercise of religion, where there is not an exercise of the rational faculties.[212]

But unlike the Anglicans and rationalists he did not see the affections as optional in evangelical worship; a contribution of both mind and heart was necessary:

> Worship is an act of the understanding, applying itself to the knowledge of the excellency of God, and actual thoughts of his majesty, recognizing him as the supreme Lord and governor of the world, which is natural knowledge; beholding the glory of his attributes in the Redeemer, which is evangelical knowledge; this is the sole act of the spirit of man.... It is also an act of the will, whereby the soul adores and reverenceth his majesty, is ravished with his amiableness, embraceth his goodness, enters itself into an intimate communion with this most lovely object, and pitcheth all his affections upon him.[213]

He demanded that a holistic approach to worship was the only acceptable worship to God.

When we compare the latitude puritan understanding of spiritual worship with that of the Anglicans and radicals we discover the different priorities in

---

[209] Ibid., 1:289.
[210] Ibid.
[211] Ibid., 1:285-286.
[212] Ibid., 1:298.
[213] Ibid.

these different expressions of Christianity. Unlike the puritan descriptions of a spiritual encounter with God in worship that moved the affections, the Anglicans spoke of experiences with the Spirit as unnoticeable. Isaac Barrow's depiction of the Spirit's influence on the Christian reveals this contrast:

> Now although the natural and ordinary manner of this divine Spirit's operation…is not by violent and sensible impressions, but rather in way of imperceptible penetration, or gentle insinuating of itself into the subject upon which it worketh, hardly discovering itself otherwise than by the notable effects resulting from it.[214]

Stillingfleet's sermon "On the Nature and Spiritual Worship of God" gives his understanding of what it means to worship in Spirit and truth. In his treatment he used some of the same terminology as the puritans, but always with the emphasis on duty rather than enjoyment.[215] This is in stark contrast with the Quakers who not only brought out the affections like the puritans, but also included the supernatural gifts of the Spirit such as prophecy and excluded the ordinances of baptism and the Lord's Supper.[216]

A debate between the puritans and Anglicans took place at the end of the seventeenth century over the meaning of spiritual worship. The Anglican Edward Oliver published a sermon on John 4:24 as a polemic against the "will worship" of the "Romanists" and the "enthusiasm" of the "Dissenters."[217] When he described spiritual worship, he primarily focused on duty as the main idea of what it means to worship in Spirit.[218] He advocated outward acts of ceremony in worship and rejected "heat and passion" as signs of spiritual worship.[219] An anonymous puritan had a sermon by Matthew Poole reprinted in response to Oliver, which was originally published for similar reasons in

---

[214] Isaac Barrow, *The Works of the Learned Isaac Barrow* (London: F.R., 1700), 3:451.

[215] Edward Stillingfleet, *Sermons on Some of the Principle Doctrines of the Christian Religion, with Practical Inferences and Improvements* (York: G. Peacock, 1794), 26-47. Like the puritans he warned, "He will never rest in a mere formal attendance on outward ordinances," but his application only focused on duty, calling the people to "walk circumspectly," "submit to him," "act agreeably" toward God, and "perform what is required on our part."

[216] Thomas Taylor, *A Testimony to the True and Spiritual Worship* (London: s.n., 1670), 3-11.

[217] Edward Oliver, *A Sermon Preach'd in St. Paul's Cathedral, Before the Lord-Mayor* (London: Printed for Edward Castle, 1698), 1-22.

[218] He said, "And all this with humility and reverence, decency and order, with obedience to authority, and respect to those whom he has set over us: These being most certain and spiritual duties, nay the only things wherein we are capable of testifying that we really do worship him in Spirit." Ibid., 10; William Clagett wrote similar views on the same passage in *A System of Divinity and Morality*, 3:1-13.

[219] Edward Oliver, *A Sermon Preach'd*, 13-15.

1660.[220] Poole was mainly writing against the use of ceremonies and outward acts in worship, seeing them as a distraction in spiritual worship. He admitted that not all who embraced ceremonies neglected communion with Christ in worship, but he believed most substituted outward acts for inner experience.[221] Poole did not use elaborate emotional terminology in discussing what it means to worship in Spirit, but rather attempted to balance the dual focus of worshiping in Spirit and in truth.[222] Oliver and Poole came up with opposite conclusions while arguing from the same text of scripture at least partially due to their differing priorities concerning head and heart.[223] In seeking to interpret scripture concerning worship and the place of the Spirit in this endeavor, Anglicans promoted the mind in what they saw as spiritual worship, the radicals endorsed the emotions and prophecy, and the latitude puritans advocated both mind and heart.

*3. The Appreciation of Mystery in Knowing God While Attempting to Interpret Scripture*

The element of mystery in theology was something of a watershed among Christians in seventeenth century England. At that time the more a theologian concentrated on the mind the less likely he or she would be open to the concept of mystery as an explanation of the difficult doctrines in the Bible. This dividing wall put rationalists and Anglicans on one side and puritans and radicals on the other. Could paradoxical, if not ostensibly irreconcilable, truths be held if they were both to be found in the Bible? In his analysis of the Amyraut controversy, Armstrong noticed that the more scholastically minded were not willing to embrace the concept of paradox and so condemned Amyraut's views that God both predestines the elect and wills the salvation of all men at the same time.[224] His statement of the Amyraut position fits well that of the latitude puritans, but not that of the Anglicans or rationalists: "It is not necessary for everything in theology to be perfectly reconciled and perfectly coherent, since man is at all times incapable of comprehending God and his actions."[225] Although Amyraut was contested by the scholastics, the arguments of Anglicans and scholastic reformers were similar. A brief look at the

---

[220] Matthew Poole, *A Reverse to Mr. Oliver's Sermon of Spiritual Worship, A Sermon on the Same Subject Preached before the Lord Mayer, at St. Paul's Church* (London: Printed for A. Baldwin, 1698), Advertisement.

[221] Ibid., 20-21.

[222] His arguments were also very polemical concerning the use of adiaphora, stating that each should worship according to their conscience without forcing "things indifferent" on those of a different persuasion. Ibid., 14-15, 19.

[223] Poole said, "It is one of the first steps and works of God's grace to direct a man's thoughts and enquiries to these things [religious concernments]. This is that which most fills head and heart." Ibid., 2.

[224] Brian Armstrong, *Calvinism and the Amyraut Heresy*, 169-170.

[225] Ibid., 170.

Anglican view of mystery in contrast to the puritan perspective shows that even though scholasticism and rationalism were two separate systems, they came to the same conclusions because they were both based heavily on the mind rather than the heart.  A method that neglected the heart usually rejected the concept of mystery, at least in practice.

The rationalists rebuffed the concept of mystery as being nonsensical and therefore worthless.  Westfall quotes Newton's view on the Trinity, "What cannot be understood is no object of belief."[226]  He explains the situation at that time, "Religious mysteries could not survive the drive for complete intelligibility."[227]  Due to the scientific and philosophical revolutions, coherent thought was at a premium, and so suggestions of mystery were not acceptable. Spinoza said the appeal to mystery was a characteristic of the ignorant, a diversion from what is important and a trademark of speculation.[228]  Newton claimed people embrace mystery due to temperament: "It is the temper of the hot and superstitious part of mankind, in matters of religion, ever to be fond of misteries, and for that reason, to like best, what they understand least."[229]  He pleaded for those who veered toward enthusiasm to use good sense rather than feeling.  By the end of the seventeenth century Toland had set the stage for the complete abandonment of mystery in his work *Christianity Not Mysterious*.

There were Anglican reactions to Toland's *Christianity Not Mysterious*, but even in these reactions a rationalizing of the faith can be observed.[230]  They were adamant about the need to retain the doctrine of the Trinity, but they were equivocal toward other reformation doctrines.  Reedy commented on the Anglican "commitment to the affinity of revelation and the human mind," stating, "They tried in various ways, to rationalize the mysteries of scriptural Christianity."[231]  He revealed Tillotson and Stillingfleet's "commitment to the integrity of scripture," but admits the influence their debates with the Socinians had on them where they upheld the maxim: "One must be reluctant to admit the

---

[226] Richard Westfall, *Science and Religion*, 213.
[227] Ibid.
[228] Benedict de Spinoza, *A Theologico-Political Treatise*, 81, 99, 175-176.
[229] Isaac Newton, *Two Letters of Sir Isaac Newton to Mr. Leclerc* (London: Printed for J. Payne, 1754), 77. He wrote these letters as means of biblical criticism, rejecting 1 John 5:7 as original and therefore not proof of the Trinity.
[230] Samuel Bold, *The Christian Belief: Wherein is asserted and Proved, That as there is nothing in the Gospel Contrary to Reason, yet there are some Doctrines in it Above Reason; and these being necessarily enjoyn'd us to Believe, are properly call'd, Mysteries; in Answer to a Book, Intituled* (sic)*, Christianity not Mysterious* (London: W. Onley, 1697), passim; John Norris, *An Account of Reason and Faith in Relation to the Mysteries of Christianity* (London: Printed for S. Manship, 1697), passim; *A System of Divinity and Morality*, 1:217-230; Peter Browne, *A Letter in Answer to a Book Entituled* (sic)*, Christianity not Mysterious* (London: W. Sayes, 1703), passim.
[231] Gerard Reedy, *The Bible and Reason*, 18.

category 'mystery' into Christian theology."[232]   Bishop Atterbury revealed this hesitancy to embrace mystery except when absolutely necessary:

> Hence then it appears evident, that those truths ought to be most readily embraced, which are clearest and plainest to our reason; and that, that religion is the best, not which fills our minds with curious speculations, or clogs our belief with the most unaccountable mysteries; but that which informs the judgment with the most weighty truths, such as have a direct influence upon practice, and most clearly discovers the will and mind of God to us, and lays down the most encouraging motives to engage the performance of it.[233]

Sherlock castigated Jacombe for using the concept of mystery in describing the Christian's union with Christ arguing that the mysterious nature of the Old Testament was done away with in Christ's arrival.[234]   They still maintained the authority of scripture over reason: "If the scriptural data resist understanding, no matter what the genius of the age toward rationalization, Scripture must be put before the complaints of aggrieved intellect,"[235] but their list of mysteries was much shorter than that of the puritans and their toleration of ambiguity was miniscule.

In his dispute with Toland, Peter Browne, Church of Ireland Bishop of Cork and Ross, defined mystery as: "something which relates to another life, which it was impossible for us to know, without divine revelation; and now that it is reveal'd we know it but in part, and cannot fully comprehend it."[236]   He goes on to describe the two parts to this definition in that mystery is a truth that is so foreign to humanity it could not be known apart from divine revelation and that once revealed it remains a mystery in that it is above or beyond the human capacity to fully comprehend.   He confronted Toland's objection to the possibility of some truth being above reason.   John Norris also wrote to this objection introducing the idea of the incomprehensible nature of God.[237]   These men were careful to distinguish between that which is contrary to reason and that which is above reason.   They did not believe God or his ways could be considered illogical, but they did say that due to his infinite nature there would be areas that went beyond the ability of finite humanity to fully understand. Browne suggested that Toland's goal was "to set up natural religion in opposition to all revelation."[238]   In all of these discussions we see philosophical

---

[232] Ibid., 127-131.

[233] *A System of Divinity and Morality*, 5:88.

[234] William Sherlock, *A Discourse Concerning the Knowledge of Jesus Christ, and Our Union and Communion with him* (London: J.M., 1674), 196-197.  He also said, "And thus the gospel of our Saviour is defaced and obscured by affected mysteries, and paradoxes, and senseless propositions." Ibid., 2.

[235] Ibid., 131.

[236] Peter Browne, *A Letter*, 11.

[237] John Norris, *An Account of Reason and Faith*, 100-136; Matthew Hale, *A Discourse of the Knowledge of God, and of our Selves*, 119-122.

[238] Peter Browne, *A Letter*, 9.

attempts to provide a rationale for the mysteries of Christianity from a Cartesian perspective. The language of "clear and distinct" ideas is found throughout these treatises.[239] Though Norris and the others attempted to show that they kept the scriptures as the "measure and standard of all truth,"[240] claiming that the rationalists put reason as the final arbitrator of reality, their reckoning allowed reason to slip in as the ultimate rule of truth. Littleton attempted to prove the Bible as true through the use of reason and then admitted to its subservience:

> Revelation is indeed another help, but then is no more than a help to reason: It discovers to us many secrets of nature, many great designs of providence, many engaging motives to the practice of our duty, which would otherwise have been concealed from us. But revelation itself can have no credit and authority, till it has received the approbation of our reason. For whatever articles of faith are revealed to us, in holy writ, are founded on no further evidence, than that the scriptures are the word of God; and that they are so, we can only discover by our reason. So that whatever degree of certainty those articles may be supposed to have, it can be no greater than our reason gives.[241]

If scripture's trustworthiness is dependent on a rational underpinning of its divine authority, then the Bible acquiesces to reason. This form of argumentation was at variance with the original reformers who refused to place reason above revelation in any way. The reformers would have agreed that the rationalists' placing of reason above revelation put the finite above the infinite, but they would have said that the Anglicans in turn did the same thing by demanding that scripture had to be proven rationally before accepting it as being God's word.

The latitude puritans made room for a much wider expression of mystery in their theology. Because of their understanding of the limitations of human nature, they were not ashamed of mystery, but rather exulted in the concept. By embracing mystery they did not encourage the mystical elements so prominent in the radicals, but instead promoted a fully experiential understanding of the God they could not fathom. The latitude puritan endorsement of mystery can be seen in that they presented a much more thorough use of the concept of "incomprehensible" as it pertained to God and in their promoting the reformers' idea of accommodation due to the impenetrable nature of God.

---

[239] John Norris, *An Account of Reason and Faith*, 62-69; *A System of Divinity and Morality*, 5:88.

[240] Ibid., 9-11. He also spoke of how placing reason and therefore humans as the deciders of truth was to rest on fallible ground, whereas making God "the very ground and pillar of truth" was to rest "upon the most sure grounds, and cannot possibly err in his assent." Ibid., 61-62.

[241] *A System of Divinity and Morality*, 1:225; Matthew Hale, *A Discourse of the Knowledge of God, and of our Selves*, 99.

Charnock used the word *incomprehensible* forty four times in his *Existence and Attributes of God* and another thirty seven times the words *mystery* or *mysterious*. In his use of the notions of mystery and the inexplicable nature of God he sought to exalt God without rejecting a place for reason. He avowed:

> It is folly to deny or doubt of a Sovereign Being, incomprehensible in his nature, infinite in his essence and perfections, independent in his operations, who hath given being to the whole frame of sensible and intelligible creatures, and governs them according to their several natures, by an unconceivable wisdom; who fills the heavens with the glory of his majesty, and the earth with the influences of his goodness.[242]

The idea that God's unfathomable nature is actually rational goes back to the reformers. Bullinger taught that if God could be comprehended by the mind then the mind would be greater than God because it was able to fully conceive how great God is; even one's speech is seriously limited in being able to express his majesty.[243] Like Charnock after him, he praised God by describing the limitations of human speech and knowledge: "For to the thinking upon and uttering out of his majesty all eloquence is mute and dumb, and the whole mind is too too little."[244] The reformers along with the latitude puritans believed that it made sense that God was beyond understanding due to his infinite nature. Charnock declared, "Incomprehensibility ariseth from an infinite perfection, which cannot be fathomed by the short line of man's understanding."[245] They believed that "God is only comprehended by God" because only God is infinite.[246] This is why certain doctrines appear to be mysterious. They do not contradict reason, but they are above reason due to the finite nature of humankind. God gave sufficient testimonies to the veracity of scripture, therefore it is rational to accept its teachings that go beyond reason.[247]

The Anglicans accepted the idea of God's incomprehensibility, but the puritans increased the categories of belief that were included as mysteries. John Tillotson wrote a treatise called *The Incomprehensibleness of God* expressing a view which would have been acceptable by most puritans,[248] but

---

[242] Charnock, *Existence and Attributes*, 1:29. He includes a footnote on this page rejecting the idea that something could be true in philosophy and not in theology saying, "Truth, in what appearance soever, doth never contradict itself."

[243] Henry Bullinger, *Decades*, 2:127-128.

[244] Ibid., 2:127. Just before this he quoted Tertullian, "Concerning God and those things that are of him and in him, neither is the mind of man able to conceive what they be, how great they be, and of what fashion they be; neither doth the eloquence of man's mouth utter in speech words in any point answerable unto this majesty."

[245] Charnock, *Existence and Attributes*, 1:290. T.H.L. Parker confirms Calvin's beliefs stating, "The idea of *Deus absconditus* is as native to Calvin's theology as to Luther's, with whom it is generally associated." *The Doctrine of the Knowledge of God*, 11.

[246] Charnock, *Existence and Attributes*, 1:512.

[247] Ibid., 2:280-281; John Howe, *Works*, 2:1072-1076.

[248] John Tillotson, *The Remaining Discourses on the Attributes of God*, 377-401.

for the Anglicans the only named doctrines that fell under the category of mystery were the Trinity and the incarnation.[249] Along with the reformers the puritans also included the doctrine of election in the category of unfathomable doctrines.[250] Although the Calvinism of the latitude puritans was markedly softer, they still believed that God elected only a few to salvation. This election was not based on anything foreseen in the people, but rather simply in accordance to God's good pleasure. Charnock especially emphasized the mystery involved in this doctrine.[251]

Firstly Charnock upheld the complete foreknowledge of God without rejecting the liberty of the human will. He stated, "That God doth foreknow everything, and yet that there is liberty in the rational creature, are both certain; but how fully to reconcile them, may surmount the understanding of man."[252] He recognized the difficulty involved in this paradox and challenged his readers to be content with a duality because "his designs are so mysterious, and the ways of his conduct so profound, that it is not possible to dive into them."[253] Even in election God does not supersede the human will but rather conquers it. "God forces no man against his nature; he doth not force the will in conversion, but graciously and powerfully inclines it."[254] He maintained the sovereignty of God and the freewill of humanity because he believed both ideas to be biblical

---

[249] *A System of Divinity and Morality*, 1:229; 5:88; John Norris, *An Account of Reason and Faith*, 7, 16; Matthew Hale, *A Discourse of the Knowledge of God, and of our Selves*, 122; Seth Ward, *An Apology for the Mysteries of the Gospel* (London: Andrew Clark, 1673), 26-27. Charnock was in full agreement that the Trinity and the incarnation are examples of the incomprehensible nature of God. *Existence and Attributes*, 1:451, 561, 565 and 599. But he also included God's power, goodness, presence, eternity and knowledge as well as the doctrines of faith, redemption, election and the crucifixion as being above the confines of reason. Ibid., 1: 294-295, 395, 411, 512-513, 552-553, 599; 2:10, 261, 280-281. He said, "The counsels of a boundless being are not to be scanned by the brain of a silly worm, that hath breathed but a few minutes in the world." Ibid., 1:295.

[250] John Calvin, *Institutes*, III. 21,7; Martin Bucer, *Common Places*, 95-118. Bucer stated, "We must accordingly reject the judgment of reason in this area, and confess that the judgments of God are 'a great abyss' and inscrutable, yet righteous. For God is just in all his ways, even when to our reason he seems otherwise." Ibid., 98. McAdoo notes that the Anglicans rejected the doctrine of absolute reprobation because it contradicted God's justice and therefore was contrary to reason, citing Jeremy Taylor as an example. Henry McAdoo, *The Spirit of Anglicanism*, 62; Taylor rejected any doctrine containing "great mysteries" as being a fundamental article of belief. Jeremy Taylor, *Treatises* (London: printed for R. Royston, 1648), 59-60.

[251] Stephen Charnock, *Existence and Attributes*, 2:394-413.

[252] Ibid., 1:450.

[253] Ibid. He went on to say, "The force of our understandings is below his infinite wisdom, and therefore we should adore him with an humble astonishment." Ibid., 1:450-451.

[254] Stephen Charnock, *Works*, 1:27. He went on to say, "He doth never force nor incline the will to sin, but leaves it to the corrupt habits it hath settled in itself."

and therefore did not attempt to reconcile the mystery. A person's affective response was really his or her own, but God remained in complete control; Charnock held these two ideas in dialectical tension, not willing to discard either because he believed both were taught in the Bible.

After lecturing on God's knowledge, Charnock appealed to God's wisdom in election stating, "He is only wise incomprehensibly."[255] He argued that though God's wisdom in election "lies in the secret places" and is therefore "incomprehensible," people should not question this important truth, but rather "should adore it instead of disputing against it; and take it for granted, that God would not order anything, were it not agreeable to the sovereignty of his wisdom, as well as that of his will."[256] He went on to illustrate what he saw as the foolishness of challenging God simply because we do not understand all things about him or his ways:

> Though the reason of man proceed from the wisdom of God, yet there is more difference between the reason of man, and the wisdom of God, than between the light of the sun, and the feeble shining of the glow-worm; yet we presume to censure the ways of God, as if our purblind reason had a reach above him.[257]

In considering the doctrine of election we see the latitude puritan willingness to embrace tension without needing to solve the apparent difficulties, much like the humanist Huguenots. The scholastic post-reformers attempted to solve all logical difficulties with elaborate schemes including charts, lapsarian views and limited atonement, and the Anglicans, both those with scholastic leanings and Cartesian tendencies, solved the perplexity by abandoning the Reformed view of election. The latitude puritans relished in the idea of mystery, accepting the basic Reformed understanding of election and praising God for his impenetrable ways.[258]

---

[255] Stephen Charnock, *Existence and Attributes*, 1:512.

[256] Ibid., 1:513. In his section on God's dominion he reiterated, "There was no cause in the creature, but all in God; it must be resolved into his own will: yet not into a will without wisdom. God did not choose hand over head, and act by mere will, without reason and understanding; an Infinite Wisdom is far from such a kind of procedure; but the reason of God is inscrutable to us, unless we could understand God as well as he understands himself.... The rays of his infinite wisdom are too bright and dazzling for our weakness." Ibid., 2:398.

[257] Ibid.

[258] Matthew Poole commented on Deuteronomy 29:29: "The ways and judgments of God, though never unjust, are ofttimes secret and hidden from us, and unsearchable by our shallow capacities, and are a matter for our admiration, not for our inquiry." *A Commentary on the Whole Bible* (The Encyclopedia Puritanica Project, 2006), Deuteronomy 29:29. John Calvin talked of "God's incomprehensible plans" and concluded, "Yet his wonderful method of governing the universe is rightly called an abyss, because while it is hidden from us, we ought reverently to adore it." *Institutes*, I. 17.2.

   The latitude puritan application of mystery in describing God and his ways can also be seen in their use of the concept of accommodation in regard to God's self-revelation. They borrowed this idea from the humanist reformers. Both Calvin and Bullinger heavily depended on accommodation to describe how the infinite could be understood by the finite.[259] The humanist French reformers also taught that God accommodated his revelation of himself to the capacity of finite and sinful humanity. Armstrong observes that accommodation was "the key concept in Amyraut's doctrine of the knowledge of God," but notes, "This teaching practically disappeared in orthodox Calvinism."[260] This insight bolsters the idea that the more one focused on the mind the less one emphasized mystery in the knowledge of God. The scholastics and rationalists shied away from accommodation by either intricately explaining the mysteries of God or by pronouncing the paradoxical teachings in scripture as being in error.[261]

   Dowey defines accommodation: "The term accommodation refers to the process by which God reduces or adjusts to human capacities what he wills to reveal of the infinite mysteries of his being, which by their very nature are beyond the powers of the mind of man to grasp."[262] He notes that Calvin believed God used accommodation in order to reveal himself in such a way that humans would glorify him.[263] Charnock was in full agreement with Calvin stating:

> God accommodates himself in the Scripture to our weak capacity.... When we cannot fully comprehend him as he is, he clothes himself with our nature in his expressions, that we may apprehend him as we are able, and, by an inspection into ourselves, learn something of the nature of God.[264]

He goes on to warn that this is no excuse for people thinking God has a body or passions like humans, but rather these "ought to be understood in a manner agreeable to the infinite excellency and majesty of God."[265] Calvin cautioned against excessive speculation into the nature of the being of God and encouraged his readers to be content with mystery concerning the nature of God and his ways.[266] He described God's revelation as a type of baby talk and then concluded, "Thus such forms of speaking do not so much express clearly

---

[259] Edward Dowey, Jr., *The Knowledge of God in Calvin's Theology*, 3-17; John Calvin, *Institutes*, I. 13,1; Henry Bullinger, *Decades*, 2:127-130.

[260] Brian Armstrong, *Calvinism and the Amyraut Heresy*, 173. He also commented that he had not found a single example of the use of accommodation in reference to God's self-revelation in seventeenth century orthodox writers.

[261] Francis Turretin, *Institutes of Elenctic Theology*, 1:311-430; Spinoza, *A Theologico-Political Treatise*, 175-181.

[262] Edward Dowey, Jr., *The Knowledge of God in Calvin's Theology*, 3.

[263] Ibid., 8.

[264] Stephen Charnock, *Works*, 1:401.

[265] Ibid.

[266] John Calvin, *Institutes*, I. 13,1.

what God is like as accommodate the knowledge of him to our slight capacity. To do this he must descend far beneath his loftiness."[267]  Those who practiced speculation did not appear to take into consideration this accommodation factor.  Speculation was seen as a product of over-rationalizing the knowledge of God often accompanied by the neglect of enjoying the wonder of the incomprehensible nature of God, and was therefore repudiated by the humanist reformers and latitude puritans.[268]

*Conclusion*

The radicals, puritans, Anglicans, virtuosi and rationalists held different views on the doctrines of general and special revelation.  In varying ways they either elevated or depreciated both types of revelation, partially due to their emphasis of heart and head and their beliefs concerning the doctrine of depravity.  Those who focused more on the cognitive elements of the soul (rationalists, virtuosi and Anglicans) tended to heighten the importance of general revelation, lessen the ultimate authority of scripture, minimize the negative effects of the fall, reduce the place of the Spirit in understanding the Bible and diminish the place of mystery in knowing God and his ways.  Those who were more attentive to the heart (radicals and Quakers) were more inclined to negate the usefulness of general revelation, question the absolute authority of scripture, advocate the supreme necessity of the Spirit for knowledge of God and his ways and reject reason as a valid source for the doctrine of the knowledge of God.  The latitude puritans attempted to balance the mind and heart in a similar way to the original reformers, especially those of the humanist persuasion, and the humanist French reformers.  They saw value in general revelation without placing it above special revelation, upheld the ultimate authority of scripture over all other means of knowledge, maintained a strong view of depravity, believed in the necessity of the Spirit for proper interpretation of the Bible, holding up the dual emphasis of Spirit and Word, and delighted in the mysteries of the faith without needing to solve all the problems of theology through reason.

---

[267]  Ibid.  Bullinger also spoke in this manner describing the word of God as "attempering itself to our imbecility." *Decades*, 2:129.  Charnock used similar analogies saying, "God therefore frames his language to our *dullness*…as nurses talk broken language to young children." *Works*, 1:401.

[268]  Wolfgang Musculus, *Common Places*, 2, 7-8; Henry Bullinger, *Decades*, 2:130, 142, 181, 185, 172; Richard Vines, *Christ A Christians Onely Gain*, 51-52, 66-67; Thomas Manton, *Works*, 10:152, 158.

# CHAPTER FIVE

# KNOWLEDGE OF GOD: UNITY AND TRUTH

The seventeenth century witnessed several events that caused many to question the precise correlation between religion and politics. At the beginning of the century continental Europe experienced the ravages of the Thirty Year War (1618-1648) where the population of the Hapsburg empire dropped from 21 million to 13.5 million due to war and "the disease and starvation that came in its wake."[1] People began to question, "On what grounds did theologians dare to affirm that they were correct, and that others were mistaken? Could any doctrine be true that produced the atrocities of the Thirty Years' War?"[2] In England the civil war and regicide caused many to question the importance of doctrine and call for toleration concerning religious differences. A variety of alternatives were proposed in the latter half of seventeenth century England pertaining to religious unity. The Anglicans were divided between the latitudinarians' call for a more comprehensive church and the Laudian view of uniformity. The puritans were divided between moderates seeking comprehension and Independents and radicals looking for toleration.

The balance of head and heart considerably influenced the answers to the questions of unity and how to deal with the nonconformists after the restoration. The importance placed on both doctrine and unity directly affected the outcome. If the mind was emphasized, a premium was placed either on doctrine (the way of the scholastic) or philosophy (the way of the rationalist), which lent toward either division or indifference in doctrinal matters. If the heart was emphasized to the neglect of the mind, doctrinal concerns were also neglected and toleration of various religious practices was advocated. In his doctrine of the knowledge of God, Charnock attempted to balance the head and heart and therefore advocated the importance of both doctrine and unity. Three areas must be investigated to reveal the impact the head/heart issue had on restoration England: i. Unity in the Church of England; ii. The importance of truth; iii. The idea of fundamental articles.

*1. Unity in the Church of England*

There had been a measure of disunity in the Protestant Church of England that brought persecution upon those not in power up to the Act of Toleration in 1689. This discrimination began with John Hooper's brief stint in Fleet prison

---

[1] Jonathan Hill, *Faith in the Age of Reason*, 23.

[2] Justo Gonzalez, *The Story of Christianity* (Peabody, MA: Prince Press, 2001), 2:140-141.

due to his challenge concerning vestments in *The Regulative Principle and Things Indifferent.*[3]   A. Harold Wood describes the attempts to enforce uniformity from Elizabeth's reign to William III's including the Laudian aggression toward the puritans, Presbyterian forced uniformity (1645-1649) and the Anglican backlash at the restoration.[4]  Within the seventeenth century the Anglicans and puritans acted with equal harshness toward one another with some from both sides calling for either comprehension or toleration.  Wood also recounts the endeavors for comprehension that were terminated for various reasons.[5]

Most of the attempts at comprehension entailed some form of 'reduction of episcopacy' as proposed by Archbishop James Ussher.[6]  Ussher's suggestion would have maintained bishops, but would have given them a reduced role in order to negate some of the more objectionable aspects of prelatism.  This view was rejected by the Westminster Assembly of Divines not, initially, because of any inherent objection to considering the principle, but because of Charles I's antipathy to the assembly itself. Although invited to attend, Ussher and other moderate Episcopalians declined out of deference to the king; this tipped the assembly to favor a complete abolition of episcopacy.[7]  Baxter would continue to bring up a moderate form of episcopacy as a compromise between the Presbyterians and Anglicans in the hope of a more comprehensive church, but without success.

The failure of unity after the restoration can be attributed to two significant factors: The unpopularity of the puritans and their disunity.  Both the cavalier parliament and a substantial amount of the common people disliked the puritans.   The Anglican House of Commons passed The Corporation Act (1661), The Act of Uniformity (1662), The Five Mile Act (1664) and The Conventicle Acts (1664 and 1670) collectively known as the Clarendon Code.[8]  These measures were taken partially out of fear and revenge.  Cragg explains the motives of the House of Commons:

> Their policy was partly dictated by revenge: the squires who had suffered during
> the Interregnum were eager to repay their enemies in kind.   In part it was

---

[3] Iain Murray, *The Reformation of the Church: A Collection of Reformed and Puritan Documents on Church Issues* (London: The Banner of Truth Trust, 1965), 51-58.

[4] A. Harold Wood, *Church Unity Without Uniformity: A Study of Seventeenth-century English Church Movements and of Richard Baxter's Proposals for a Comprehensive Church* (London: Epworth Press, 1963), 54-96, 225-240.

[5] Ibid., 97-224, 241-262.

[6] Ibid., 127-137, 217-222; James Spalding and Maynard Brass, "Reduction of Episcopacy as a Means to Unity in England, 1640-1662" in *Church History*, 30 (December, 1961), 414-432.

[7] James Spalding and Maynard Brass, "Reduction of Episcopacy as a Means to Unity in England, 1640-1662," 420.

[8] Henry Bettenson (ed.), *Documents of the Christian Church* (Oxford University Press, 1947), 401-407.

prompted by fear. The Puritans had been overthrown, but no one knew when they might again give evidence of the prowess which had so recently proved irresistible.[9]

The puritans had also become unpopular among "the general body of Englishmen" because of their over-strictness.[10] The legalism in much of puritanism left its mark on the common people.

The breakdown of union can also be attributed in part to the disunity among puritans.[11] The king called the Savoy Conference so that the bishops and Presbyterians could try to work out a plan where 'tender consciences' would be respected. The Independents, however, were not included at this conference, neither could the Presbyterians agree among themselves. Most were unwilling to make any concessions at all and very few "reconcilers among the ministers themselves" were present.[12] The puritans were still divided into three major groups (Independents, Presbyterians and those who favored a reduced episcopacy) with little feeling for a compromise that would help them face a common foe. The Independents had no desire to join a national church and most of the Presbyterians thought reconciliation was impossible. Baxter led the movement toward comprehension through concessions, presenting a form of Ussher's reduced episcopacy, but to no avail.

It is patent that one reason for the failure of conciliation was the scholastic tendency toward disputation. Between the time of Laud to William III, there was a marked unwillingness to concede a thing, whereas a measure of compromise was essential were ecclesiastical unity to be achieved. No one was completely unaffected by the scholastic method, but those who downplayed unnecessary speculation and elitism tended to be more conciliatory than the rest.

For the most part the early reformers were as one as long as the doctrines of justification by faith alone and the bondage of the will were maintained.[13] This irenic spirit and accord can also be seen among the Huguenots, Cambridge Platonists, latitudinarians and latitude puritans. All of these groups were seemingly influenced to varying degrees by northern humanism's chief tenants: i. *Ad fontes*: the principle of returning to the original biblical text in order to discover true doctrine and correct ethics. ii. The use of rhetoric: Illustration and persuasion was preferred over hypercritical dogmatism. iii. Spiritual experience: This was truer of northern humanism than southern humanism[14]

---

[9] Gerald Cragg, *The Church and the Age of Reason: 1648-1789* (Grand Rapids: Eerdmans, 1960), 53; A. Harold Wood, *Church Unity Without Uniformity*, 210-211.

[10] A. Harold Wood, *Church Unity Without Uniformity*, 213.

[11] Ibid., 211.

[12] Ibid., 212.

[13] Lutherans may have been less likely to compromise because they were less affected by humanism. Pedobaptism was also deemed essential by the early reformers.

[14] William Bouwsma, *The Culture of Renaissance Humanism* (Washington D.C.: American Historical Association, 1973), 31-40.

(though the latitudinarians de-emphasized this). iv. Opposition to the negative effects of scholasticism: Everyone questioned over-speculation, but these groups seemed to speculate less than their more scholastic counterparts. A comparison of prolegomena and actions will substantiate the hypothesis that the more scholastic a group became the more prone toward speculation and disunity it became.[15] When scholasticism was brought into the Reformed branch of the reformation, tests for conformity increased.[16] It is not the case that scholasticism necessitated disunity and separation, but this was an inherent danger with this method. Muller correctly states that the original reformers maintained continuity with the post-reformers in their "drive toward true or correct doctrine,"[17] but this statement needs to be nuanced. The reformers' drive toward correct doctrine came alongside an experimental faith shared with others, a balance of head and heart. When correct doctrine became the driving force rather than a felt piety due in part to the tendency of the scholastic method, things became discontinuous. Muller notes, "Ideally, the sermon will reflect at the level of piety and personal need the objective teaching of confession and system, while confession and system will not become insensitive to piety."[18] He suggests that a study of the post reformers' prolegomena and *principia* will exonerate them from Gerhard Eberling's accusation of driving a "destructive wedge" between objective and subjective faith.[19] Eberling describes the affects of scholasticism as resulting in "a hypertrophy of doctrine, a multiplication of theological problems, the tendency to a degree toward an intellectual and theological imperialism."[20] Muller makes his case for the post reformers, revealing Eberling's analysis to be too simplistic, but scholasticism does seem to have had a negative affect on unity in seventeenth century England and Eberling's thesis has some justification, as we will see in the next section.

When the scholastic method was de-emphasized two attitudes, influenced by the Cambridge Platonists and exemplified to varying degrees by the latitudinarians and the latitude puritans, became prominent. Firstly, there was a

---

[15] cf. Francis Turretin, *Institutes of Elenctic Theology*, 1-54 for a highly scholastic presentation, advocating speculation; Thomas Watson, *A Body of Divinity*, 1-26 for a much more practical presentation of prolegomena with a high regard for the affections; William Ames, *The Marrow of Theology*, 77-80 for a Ramian arrangement that seeks the practical and rejects speculation, "It is self-evident that theology is not a speculative discipline but a practical one – not only in the common respect that all disciplines have ευπραξια, good practice, as their end, but in a special and peculiar manner compared with all others."

[16] Cf. the comparatively detailed *Westminster Confession, Canons of Dort*, and especially the *Formula Consensus Helvetica*.

[17] Richard Muller, *Post-Reformation Reformed Dogmatics*, 1:47.

[18] Ibid., 1:49.

[19] Ibid., 1:48.

[20] Gerhard Eberling, *The Study of Theology* (Philadelphia: Fortress Press, 1978), 134.

broader acceptance of those with differing beliefs and liturgy.[21]   The Anglican
and puritan latitudes sought a more comprehensive church because they were
able to get along with each other and saw unnecessary division as harmful to
the church.   The latitude Anglicans embodied this approach partially due to
their relative disregard for doctrine, but both groups typified this stance because
they divided doctrine into two categories.   The latitudinarians separated
doctrine into essential and non-essential types and ignored the non-essential
doctrines.  The latitude puritans maintained the two classes of essential and
important doctrines, refusing to ignore anything taught in the Bible, but also
refusing to countenance division unless it was a fundamental of the faith.

Secondly, the latitude Anglicans and puritans manifested a gentler manor of
persuasion.  The harsh combative nature of both the Laudian Anglicans and
more scholastic puritans can be contrasted with the latitudes.  The Anglican
Calvinist John Edwards and the latitudes were both similarly opposed to the
Socinians, but their approach differed markedly.    Alan Sell reveals the
belligerent attitude of John Edwards, who used the common practice of the day
of exaggerating the mistakes of one's opponent.[22]   Edwards attacked his foe,
whereas Howe, Manton, Bates and Charnock simply let the Bible persuade.[23]

Richard Baxter is a unique case among the latitude puritans.   Nuttall
describes the complexity of Baxter's thought: "Baxter's desire for clarity in
things of the mind, which led him constantly to categorize and subdivide, was
accompanied, as we have seen, by an equally eager desire for unity in Christian
faith and practice."[24]   He put in more effort at bringing unity between the
Anglicans and puritans than any other individual, but he also inadvertently
hindered his attempts by his tactless and at times harsh manner.[25]   Baxter's
"incorrigible disputatiousness" does not come from the influence of the
Cambridge Platonists and the French school of Saumur, but rather from a
scholastic affect.  Baxter wrote numerous practical works, but he also wrote
highly scholastic treatises such as *Methodus Theologiae*.  Carl Trueman has
shown the scholastic influence on Baxter, including the metaphysics of
Tommaso Campanella.[26]  Although all the blame for Baxter's temper cannot be
laid to his scholastic readings, it did have some impact.  Because of these
inconsistencies, Baxter should not be considered the best example of the

---

[21] Gerald Cragg, *The Church and the Age of Reason*, 68-77.

[22] Alan Sell, *John Locke*, 186-199.

[23] John Howe, *Works*, 457-484; Thomas Manton, *Works*, 1:413-426; William Bates,
*Works*, 1:415-417; Stephen Charnock, *Works*, 5:254-261.  Charnock presents his beliefs
in contradistinction of the Arminians but does it with his usual politeness.

[24] Geoffrey Nuttall, *Richard Baxter* (London: Nelson, 1966), 64.

[25] A. Harold Wood, *Church Unity Without Uniformity*, 106, 126, 201, 212; Gerald
Cragg, *The Church and the Age of Reason*, 51.

[26] Carl Trueman and R.S. Clark, editors, *Protestant Scholasticism*, 184-195.  Trueman
reveals that Baxter received his view that even the doctrine of the Trinity can be proven
by nature from Campanella's metaphysics.

latitude puritan, who both highly valued unity as well as doctrine, without inheriting the argumentative nature prevalent in seventeenth century England.

## 2. The Importance of Truth

The way in which truth was understood and how it cohered with the concept of church unity is illustrated by the use of polemics. The place given truth was partially influenced by the presence or absence of scholastic leanings. Quirinus Breen wrote a helpful discussion on the influence of Aristotle on Melanchthon that bears light on this subject.[27] He discusses how Aristotle wrote on rhetoric and dialectic as well as analytics (logic) though he was drawn to logic due to its precise nature.[28] By taking the latter more seriously, Aristotle revealed that people could find fulfillment in the contemplation of truth itself, seeing truth as the end rather than a means to a further end. His contemporary Isocrates did not agree. He believed that "knowledge is not an end in itself or an object of enjoyment through contemplation; it is an instrument to use socially. Man is not primarily a rational being; he is primarily a social being. Man achieves his highest development in the orator."[29]   Here we see two major differences concerning the place of truth; it is either the end or a means to an end. Breen then describes how a misunderstanding of Aristotle led Cicero to focus on rhetoric and dialectic, holding more to Isocrates' ideal. The scholastics later discovered other aspects of Aristotle's thought and emphasized logic, valuing truth for its own sake. Breen states, "[The scholastics'] quarrels became over-refined, and in the opinion of many the schoolmen had largely lost touch with realities."[30]   The humanists such as Agricola and Erasmus turned to the classical literature, and without discarding Aristotelian logic, displayed a more practical aim of education. The original reformers were the beneficiaries of this approach. They highly valued knowledge, but for the purpose of relationship with God. Like Isocrates they saw humans primarily as relational beings, especially in association with God. Knowledge was seen as a necessary means to the end being reconciliation with God. Breen concludes with Melanchthon's use of Aristotle in the classroom. Melanchthon brought back Aristotle who had been discarded by the humanists, but primarily for his rhetoric.[31]   Melanchthon

---

[27] Quirinus Breen, *Christianity and Humanism* (Grand Rapids: Eerdmans, 1968), 93-105.

[28] Breen differentiates dialectics and analytics stating, "In dialectical propositions exact truth can only be approximated, often only distantly;" whereas "Analytics (particularly Posterior) pertain to certain knowledge." Ibid., 94-95.

[29] Ibid., 96.

[30] Ibid., 98. He does warn, "Generalizations about the Renaissance era should be made with great caution."

[31] Ibid., 101-103. Breen states that Melanchthon's use of Aristotle "is thoroughly Ciceronian" concerning his use of the loci method. "It is not the 'point of view' which Aristotle intended the *locus* to mean. But especially un-Aristotelian is equating logic with *topica* and both under dialectics." Ibid., 102.

also appreciated Aristotle's point of absolute truth in logic, but always from a pastoral standpoint without the extended speculation that often accompanied a more scholastic approach. Melanchthon brought in Aristotle primarily for the classical author's rhetorical help to pastors.

> But just as sometimes a pagan classic was saved under the veil of allegory, so Aristotle was, in the present case, saved under the veil of eloquence and the arts that belong to it. Once in theology, Aristotle may give forth, to a generation that knows him better, things that may alter the Melanchthonian concept of theology. It may have its uses that Melanchthon had not too carefully examined his Trojan horse.[32]

This survey of Breen's thought reveals that scholasticism could be used affectively in varying degrees by the reformers so long as they kept the priority of the heart in focus, even in the classroom. But when the mind began to take precedence over the heart, speculative doctrines became essential doctrines worth dividing over. The place given to truth had a major impact on unity; this was true in the early stages of the reformation as well as in the seventeenth century Church of England, whether a scholastic or rationalist method was used.

The relative importance of truth can also be seen in the polemics of the day. During the reformation and post-reformation the church was willing to debate and even divide over several issues, revealing that truth was imperative to them. The battle lines shifted over the centuries but the idea that certain truths were essential and of utmost significance was not debated, but that there were differences over which truths were crucial to the faith. At different times between 1517 and 1717, those in the Reformed camp saw seven major groups as their enemy: Catholics, Anabaptists, Arminians, Socinians, Quakers, antinomians and deists. As a general rule, the more the scholastic method was used the more enemies the church had because it was willing to divide over additional issues. A case in point is the doctrine of predestination. Calvin held a strong view of double predestination, but was willing to labor, correspond and associate with Bullinger who held to single predestination and Melanchthon who embraced a synergistic view of salvation similar to what would become known later as Arminianism. The original reformers were relatively more flexible concerning doctrinal differences. The next generation of reformers, leaning more heavily on the scholastic method, was not as conciliatory, fighting over supralapsarianism and even having some of the Remonstrants killed over the monergism/synergism debate. How much doctrinal deviation was acceptable was the question, which doctrines were worth dividing over and which ones were simply worth discussing academically? The way in which the English Protestants answered these questions reveal whether they focused on either the heart or the head.

---

[32] Ibid., 105.

Most Protestants of the sixteenth and seventeenth century saw Roman Catholicism as a deviant religion in both doctrine and practice. Many considered the papal office to be the antichrist.[33] The early reformers were especially opposed to the Catholic understanding of justification, transubstantiation and spiritual authority. Martin Luther wrote three treatises in 1520 attacking these doctrines, setting the stage for the Protestant confrontation with Rome.[34]

The doctrine of justification by faith alone was a critical doctrine for the original reformers. Calvin called justification "the main hinge on which religion turns."[35] The original reformers believed that justification was the sin qua non of the gospel where the righteousness of Christ was imputed to the believer: "Therefore, we explain justification simply as the acceptance with which God receives us into his favor as righteous men. And we say that it consists in the remission of sins and the imputation of Christ's righteousness."[36] They did not repudiate works as essential to life, but they saw them as the fruit of justification, whereas faith was the root.[37] The Roman Catholic church responded in the canons of the Council of Trent stating, "If any one saith, that the justice received is not preserved and also increased before God through good works; but that the said works are merely the fruits and signs of justification obtained, but not a cause of the increase thereof: let him be anathema."[38] Because the reformers valued certain truths as indispensable, such as justification through faith alone, they believed they had a responsibility to separate from the Roman Church.

---

[33] Luther said, "The papacy is truly the kingdom of Babylon and of the very Antichrist." Martin Luther, *Luther's Works* (Philadelphia: Fortress Press, 1959), 36:72. He also said, "The Pope is the true, genuine, final Antichrist." Ibid., 36:219; Martin Bucer, *Common Places*, 247, 391-392; John Calvin, *Institutes*, IV. 2,12.

[34] Martin Luther, *Three Treatises* (Philadelphia: Fortress Press, 1970), including "To the Christian Nobility of the German Nation," "The Babylonian Captivity of the Church," and "The Freedom of a Christian."

[35] John Calvin, *Institutes*, III. 11,1.

[36] Ibid., III. 11,2; Cranmer said, "This faith God imputes for righteousness in his sight." Thomas Cranmer, *The Work of Thomas Cranmer* (Appleford, England: The Courtenay Press, 1965), 3-4; Bucer said, "The heart of our salvation, that is, our justification, is our free acceptance before God, whereby he pardons our sins, imputes righteousness to us, and bestows on us eternal life." Martin Bucer, *Common Places*, 167; Henry Bullinger, *Decades*, 2:46-47; 1:104-121.

[37] Cranmer explained, "For good works are necessary to salvation, not because they make an ungodly man righteous, nor because they are a price for sins or a cause of justification; but because it is necessary that he who is already justified by faith and reconciled to God through Christ should have a care to do the will of God.... He who has no care to do these works...has no true faith." *Work*, 4; Henry Bullinger, *Decades*, 1:118, 120; Martin Bucer, *Common Places*, 166.

[38] Philip Schaff, *Creeds of Christendom*, 2:115.

Roman Catholicism continued to be considered apostate by most Protestants, but not always for the same reasons. John Daille, representing the Reformed church in France, wrote *An Apologie for the Reformed Churches, Wherein is shew'd The necessitie of their separation from the Church of Rome* describing why the Protestant separation from Rome should not be considered schism. He listed two major doctrines that were considered of serious enough nature to validate division: making other beliefs not found in scripture to be equal to scripture and worshiping the host in communion.[39] Daille focused on "the adoration of the Eucharist" saying it overthrew "the foundation of pietie and salvation" and should be considered idolatry.[40] Baxter agreed: "Popery is idolatry teaching men to worship the creature with divine worship, as the consecrated host or bread in their mass," also declaring, "The Papists are the greatest schismaticks on earth, most desperately rending the Church, and separating themselves from the main body thereof."[41] Justification was also still considered by many to be a doctrine worth dividing over.[42] So far the post-reformers were in agreement with the reformers.

Divergence from the original reformers took place over the understanding of the place of works in justification. Some whom their opponents called antinomians taught that the elect were not only predestined, but also justified from all eternity. Others also taught that "God takes no notice of the sins of the justified."[43] Baxter spoke out against the antinomians who seemed to have no place for works in their system, calling them libertines.[44] He followed the opposite tendency of English Protestantism in what Cooper describes as a shift "from grace to moralism."[45] Some Anglicans and puritans began to question the belief of imputed righteousness.[46] Nicholas Tyacke recounts a group of Anglican divines embracing moralism and some even rejecting the doctrine of justification by faith alone, including Richard Allestree, John Fell, Gilbert

---

[39] John Daille, *An Apologie for the Reformed Churches, Wherein is shew'd The necessitie of their separation from the Church of Rome*, 10-11, 26-27.

[40] Ibid., 26-72.

[41] Richard Baxter, *Select Arguments and Reasons Against Popery* (London: s.n., 1675), 2-3.

[42] John Howe, *Works*, 1:465; William Bates, *Works*, 1:390-402; Thomas Watson, *A Body of Divinity*, 226-231; Matthew Poole, *A Dialogue Between a Popish Priest and an English Protestant* (London: E. Cotes, 1667), 30, 99, 208-213; Ezekiel Hopkins called the doctrine of justification "the very sum and pith of the whole Gospel, and the only end of the Covenant of Grace." *Works*, 2:205.

[43] J.I. Packer, *A Quest For Godliness*, 155.

[44] Tim Cooper, *Fear and Polemic in Seventeenth-Century England* (Aldershot: Ashgate, 2001), 9. Cooper exonerates John Eaton, Tobias Crisp, John Saltmarsh, William Dell and John Traske from the extreme accusations of libertinism. Ibid. 22-25, 33.

[45] Ibid., 29; Dewey Wallace, Jr., *Puritans and Predestination*, 160.

[46] William Sherlock attacked the doctrine of imputed righteousness as unscriptural and a new false doctrine. *A Discourse Concerning the Knowledge of Jesus Christ*, 244-279.

Sheldon and especially George Bull in his treatise *Harmonia Apostolica*.[47]
Baxter did not abandon the doctrine of imputation wholesale, but rather
rejected what he called "their invented sense of imputation."[48]   But in his
response to the antinomians he goes beyond the original reformers' view that
works were necessary fruits of justification and called them "necessary
condition[s] of our continued justification."[49]

    The move toward moralism was often accompanied with an aversion to
enthusiasm.   It would appear that a skepticism concerning the emotional
aspects of the heart, moved one to a heightened concern for the will and the
mind with moralism and rationalism as the natural outgrowth.[50]   Even in the
fear of Catholicism, the concern was more political than doctrinal for many by
the end of the seventeenth century.   Jonathan Scott exposes the recent attempts
to interpret the popish plot crisis of 1678-1683 as a tale of widespread mass
hysteria and provides evidence that there was a very real danger threatening at
that time.[51]   The plot was not conjured up for political reasons, but the fear
concerned the tyranny Rome would bring, more so than the doctrinal changes.[52]
Scott describes how the 'Irish massacre' of 1641 and the 'fear of popery'
helped usher in the English civil war,[53] which resulted in a revival of Calvinism
with doctrine held at a premium.   The popish plot brought the same degree of
fear, but did not result in any renaissance of Reformed theology; this was partly
due to the deep mistrust of puritanism brought on by the aftermath of the civil
war, but also that doctrine in general was not seen as significant as it had been
viewed in the past.   The more rationalistic Protestants of the latter part of
seventeenth century England were opposed to Catholicism because of the

---

[47] Nicholas Tyacke, *Aspects of English Protestantism*, 284, 296-298.   Bishop Gilbert
Burnet upheld justification by faith alone, but explained Paul's exclusion of works as
referring only to the works of the Mosaic law and concluded, "In the strictness of words,
we are not justified till the final sentence is pronounced: Till upon our death, we are
solemnly acquitted of our sins, and admitted into the presence of God."   Gilbert Burnet,
*An Exposition of the Thirty-Nine Articles of the Church of England*, 122-127.

[48] Richard *Baxter, Of the Imputation of Christ's Righteousness to Believers: In what
sence sound Protestants hold it; And, of the false devised sence, by which Libertines
subvert the Gospel* (London: Printed for Nevil Simons, 1675), preface.

[49] Ibid.; Tim Cooper, *Fear and Polemic*, 75-78.   Cooper reveals that Baxter was close to
Arminianism in his soteriology and even had "secret sympathies" toward Roman
Catholic theology.   Ibid., 66, 196.

[50] Cragg says, "The appeal to reason was strengthened by the force of the reaction
against the 'enthusiasm'... of the Puritans."   Gerald Cragg, *The Church and the Age of
Reason*, 70.

[51] Tim Harris, Paul Seaward and Mark Goldie, editors, *The Politics of Religion in
Restoration England*, 107-131.

[52] Scott states, "The fear, in short, was of an 'imminent' invasion, led by France, and
involving Ireland, resulting in the 'extirpation' of protestantism 'root and branch', by
'fire and sword' in the manner understood to have occurred in Germany, France, Ireland
and Piedmont."   Ibid., 119.

[53] Ibid., 123.

danger it presented, rather than its doctrinal deviancy. This does not imply that Anglicans were completely unconcerned about doctrine; any caricature like that would be inappropriate.[54]   But it does appear that doctrinal concerns were becoming less important.   The restoration Anglicans were more focused on ecclesiology than doctrine.   The list of essential doctrines shrank, with justification by faith alone being one of the casualties;[55] this tendency is especially seen in the polemic against the Socinians.

Both Anglicans and puritans wrote against the Socinians, but in a different manner and with diverse argumentation. *Socinian* was a name given to a broad group of opponents, who either rejected/downplayed the doctrine of the Trinity or held questionable views of the satisfaction of Christ.   Faustus Socinus attacked the doctrine of the deity of Christ and the satisfaction theory of the atonement primarily on rational grounds.   He held to the peculiar position that Christ was not God but should be paid divine honors.[56]   He also believed that Christ died "to make a new moral impression upon mankind," rather than providing a legal satisfaction.[57]   His views became popular in Poland, especially in Rakow where the *Racovian Catechism* was printed in 1605.   The catechism and Socinus' book *De Jesu Christo Servatore* were brought into England, causing a fury among Anglicans and nonconformists alike.

Most who wrote against Socinianism advocated the necessity of the doctrine of the Trinity.   Socinians and Arians rejected the doctrine of the Trinity primarily for rational reasons, so the rebuttals attempted to reveal that the doctrine was above reason, but not contrary to it.   Anglican Isaac Barrow wrote *A Brief State of the Socinian Controversy Concerning a Trinity in Unity* with

---

[54] Edward Stillingfleet wrote an extensive treaty examining the Council of Trent finding it wanting in several areas: Their view of scripture, merit, the sacraments and auricular confession.   He presented a Protestant view of merit, but even here never mentions justification by faith alone. *The Council of Trent Examin'd and Disprov'd by Catholick Tradition in the Main Points of Controversie Between Us and the Church of Rome With a Particular Account of the Times and Occasions of Introducing Them* (London: Printed for H. Mortlock, 1688), passim (59-74 on the subject of merit).

[55] Matthew Hale wrote on the nature of true religion, speaking out against those who held doctrines or philosophies that brought unnecessary division in the church.   He rejected justification as an essential doctrine, calling it a disputation of "lower allay," without saying whether he believed justification was by faith alone or not.   Matthew Hale, *The Judgment of the Late Lord Chief Justice Sir Matthew Hale, of the Nature of True Religion, the Causes of its Corruption, and the Churches Calamity by Mens Additions and Violences With the Desired Cure: In Three Discourses* (London: Printed for B. Simmons, 1684), 7; John Cosin wrote *The Differences in the Chief Points of Religion Between the Roman Catholics and Us of the Church of England; Together With the Agreements* (Preston: T. Walker, 1799), without mentioning any differences in salvation or justification.

[56] This was known as the doctrine of the invocation of Christ.   H. John McLachlan, *Socinianism in Seventeenth-Century England* (Oxford University Press, 1951), 14.

[57] Ibid., 15.

the premise that humans were "the lowest rank of intelligent creatures" and so their intellectual capacity made it impossible for them to comprehend the doctrine of the Trinity; with this in mind he stated:

> These [truths of the Trinity] are the notions which may well puzzle our reason, in conceiving how they agree, but should not stagger our faith, in assenting that they are true. Upon which we should meditate, not with hope to comprehend, but with disposition to admire, veiling our faces in the presence, and prostrating our reason at the feet of wisdom so far transcending us.[58]

Barrow also gave thorough scriptural evidence for the Trinity in his *Exposition On the Creed* revealing that there is only one God, the Father, Son and Holy Spirit, each have the attributes of God and are called God, and each relate to one another as separate persons.[59]

The other doctrine the majority of anti-Socinians touched on was the satisfaction of Christ. Stillingfleet wrote *A Discourse Concerning the Doctrine of Christ's Satisfaction; or The True Reasons of his Sufferings; with an Answer to the Socinian Objections* in response to the Socinian Crellius. Typical of the cordial manner of the Latitudinarians he presented the case that Christ's death for the world included the ideas of "redemption, propitiation, reconciliation by his blood, of his bearing our iniquities, and being made sin and a curse for us," and that to deny these obvious truths would compel one to deny everything else the scriptures taught.[60] John Edwards praised this book for its thoroughness.[61] Charnock also wrote extensively on the atonement, but not so much from a polemic stance, but rather a positive and biblical perspective. In several discourses he promoted a multifaceted understanding of Christ's work on the cross that included the exemplarist theory of the Socinians, the satisfaction theory of Anselm, penal substitution of Calvin, the ransom theory of the early medieval church and his own unique insights.

First, in agreement with Abelard before him, he declared the death of Christ was given as an example for his disciples to follow. This did not mean the exemplary theory was the final statement on the matter, and he was careful to reject Crellius' statement that Christ's death was only *like* a sacrifice, but he was not afraid to promote the idea that Christ died as an example for believers.[62]

---

[58] Isaac Barrow, *A Brief State of the Socinian Controversy Concerning a Trinity in Unity* (London: Printed for Brabazon Aylmer, 1698), 8-11.
[59] Isaac Barrow, *The Works of the Learned Isaac Barrow* (London: Printed for James Round, 1716), 1:413-415, 462-464.
[60] Edward Stillingfleet, *A Discourse Concerning the Doctrine of Christ's Satisfaction; or The True Reasons of his Sufferings; with an Answer to the Socinian Objections* (London: F. Heptinstall, 1697), 5.
[61] John Edwards, *The Socinian Creed* (London: Printed for J. Robinson, 1697), 6, 15.
[62] Stephen Charnock, *Works*, 4:502-503, 540-541. The Laudian Henry Hammond made this the primary point of the cross, completely neglecting any substitutionary aspect.

He also discussed the concept of Christ's death bringing about the honor that was due God, but that sinners were not able to perform, including the legal element of punishment for dishonoring God. Christ was punished by God as our substitute, completely satisfying his honor and justice.[63] He explained that a finite creature's sin was infinitely heinous because of the infinite nature of the one sinned against. Only an infinitely valuable satisfaction could rectify an infinite evil; this was the beauty of the sacrifice of Christ: "As therefore an infinite sin deserves an infinite punishment, because it is committed against an infinite God, so the sacrifice of Christ deserves an infinite acceptation, because it is offered by an infinite person."[64]

A third valid understanding of the atonement for Charnock was that the death of Christ brought about a defeat of Satan, what Gustaf Aulen calls the classic theory held by the Fathers.[65] The serpents head was bruised in such a way that he was no longer able to accuse the brethren, his tempting force was broken and his weapons disarmed.[66] Charnock did not get into the details of who the price was paid to or the specifics of how the enemy is disarmed, but rather made declarations such as, "The blood of Christ…reduceth Satan to so impotent a condition, that all his strength and all his stratagems cannot render him master of that soul that is once freed from his chains."[67]

Finally, Charnock added his own contribution to the affects of the blood of Christ in what he called the "expiatory reconciling sacrifice."[68] Christ's blood sacrifice was pleasing to the Father because of the person offering it and the cleansing virtue it had on sinful humans. He stated, "God smelled a greater fragrancy in his death than stench from our sins; the sweetness of the one did drown the noisomeness of the other: his death was more satisfying to God than our sins were displeasing."[69] Christ's blood cheered God in such a way that everyone who came to God through Christ was also accepted, reconciled to him. God's acceptance of Christ and his death "redounds to every believer. Grace and glory depend upon this; take away God's approbation, and the whole chain of privileges, linked together by it, falls in pieces."[70] Few had such a rich and comprehensive theology of the cross as Charnock in England at that time,

---

Henry Hammond, *Of Fundamentals in a Notion Referring to Practice* (London: J. Flesher, 1654), 36-37.

[63] Stephen Charnock, *Works*, 4:522-537, 569-574.

[64] Ibid., 4:570; see also 3:514; *Puritan Sermons: 1659-1689*, 5:267.

[65] Gustaf Aulen, *Christus Victor* (New York: The MacMillan Company, 1966), 6.

[66] Stephen Charnock, *Works*, 4:501-502.

[67] Ibid., 4:514. Ezekiel Hopkins expounds on this view, answering the questions the Socinians brought up. *Works*, 2:610-620.

[68] Stephen Charnock, *Works*, 3:425.

[69] Ibid., 3:430.

[70] Ibid., 3:432.

especially compared with the one-sided perspective of the Socinians, which Anglicans and puritans saw as heretical.[71]

Most English Protestants confronted the Socinians on the doctrines of the Trinity and the atonement, but the Calvinist believers, both conformists and nonconformists, added other doctrines and insights to the controversy. John Edwards discussed the Socinians "notions concerning the Scriptures."[72] Edwards advocated the infallibility of scripture, claiming this view as "owned by all Christian Churches." He revealed how Socinus, Crellus and their followers claimed the Bible had errors, even saying most of the precepts of the Old Testament were not worthy of God.[73] Charnock also found their doctrine of scripture wanting because they placed reason over revelation:

> The contempt of Divine wisdom, in making reason the supreme judge of Divine revelation, was the fruitful mother of the heresies in all ages springing up in the church, and especially of that Socinianism, that daily insinuates itself into the minds of men.[74]

He explained that this was the heresy that birthed all other heresies because it placed the human above God in wisdom, with the "ambition to be his cabinet council."[75] He believed that there were things in the Bible that no one could fully comprehend simply because of the greatness of God, but that did not give the person the right to censure these things and it did not mean these things were not important. Hopkins agreed and also pointed out that the Bible was full of profound mysteries that were necessary nonetheless and should be diligently searched to gain as much understanding as possible. He challenged:

> That many of these things are abstruse and difficult, I cannot deny; but, that any of them are vain and frivolous, I do.... Many of the great and precious truths of

---

[71] Another multifaceted description of the atonement directed against the Socinians can be found in fellow latitude puritan Thomas Manton's treatise *Christ's Eternal Existence and The Dignity of His Person Asserted and Proved, In Opposition to the Doctrine of the Socinians* in *Works*, 1:413-426.

[72] John Edwards, *The Socinian Creed*, 3-22.

[73] Ibid., 4-6. It should be stated that *The Racovian Catechisme* declared the dependability of scripture. Valentin Smalcius, *The Racovian Catechisme* (Amsterdam: Printed for Brooer Janz, 1652), 1-10.

[74] Stephen Charnock, *Existence and Attributes*, 1:591. Matthew Poole similarly stated, "If once a truth be evident from plain scriptures, we ought not to be moved with the cavils of wanton wits, or the difficulty of comprehending those great mysteries by our reason. When the Socinians can solve all the phenomena of nature, which are the proper object of man's reason, then, and not till then, we will hearken to their rational objections." *Puritan Sermons: 1659-1689*, 5:267; John Edwards, *The Socinian Creed*, 138-144.

[75] Stephen Charnock, *Existence and Attributes*, 1:591. He also said, "He that censures the words or actions of another, implies that he is, in his censure, wiser than the person censured by him."

the Gospel are delivered obscurely; not to excuse us from, but on purpose to engage us a diligent search and study of them. If these things were not expedient to be known, why should the Holy Scripture so abound with them? The Epistles of St. Paul are full of these profound mysteries, which he wrote to the Churches in common, and every member of them: these were read in public assemblies; and it concerned all the people to hearken to them, and consider of them: and, if the pressing only of practical duties of Christianity had been sufficient, most part of the Apostle's writings had been needless and superfluous.[76]

Hopkins revealed a major difference between the Anglicans and Reformed believers. He believed the scriptures were full of mysteries, rather than simply one or two, and these were by God's design for the believers' good. At least in this regard the Anglicans had more affinity with the Socinians and rationalists than with the original reformers.[77]

A fourth doctrine Reformed theologians advocated while claiming the Socinian view as heretical was the doctrine of original sin and human depravity. John Gibbon gave a puritan perspective on Socinian belief regarding original sin:

> The Socinians here, and others, will have us believe that we all are born as innocent as Adam in Paradise; that is, say they, in an *equilibrium* and perfect indifferency to good and evil; assigning no other cause of the general corruption of men's lives and manners, but the infection of example, and evil custom: which is, methinks, as wise a guess as to affirm the wolf and vulture to be bred and hatched with as sweet and harmless a nature as the innocent lamb or loving turtle, but only the naughty behaviour and ill example of their ancestors and companions have debauched them into ravenousness and ill manners.[78]

Edwards attacked the Socinians extensively on this matter. He condemned their belief that Adam was not originally created immortal and their conviction that after Adam sinned his progeny was not born depraved.[79] He also exposed their view that people do not need any help from God other than the Bible to be saved, calling it the old heresy of Pelagianism.[80] He believed that it was essential to the doctrine of grace to believe that the assistance of the Spirit was

---

[76] Ezekiel Hopkins, *Works*, 2:172.

[77] Cragg describes the latitudinarians as standing "halfway between the unquestioning reliance on authority which was characteristic of the early seventeenth century and the rationalism of the early eighteenth" holding "that essential beliefs were few and simple." *The Church and the Age of Reason*, 72. Compare the latitudinarian idea of the scriptures as simple and clear concerning what is important to the Socinians. Valentin Smalcius, *The Racovian Catechisme*, 9-10; John Tillotson, *The Indispensable Necessity of the Knowledge of Holy Scripture in Order to Man's Eternal Salvation and Ignorance Therein, the Mother of Idolatry and Superstition Asserted in a Sermon* (London: Printed for Wil. Norris, 1687), 6.

[78] *Puritan Sermons: 1659-1689*, 1:108.

[79] John Edwards, *The Socinian Creed*, 73-79.

[80] Ibid., 79-84.

necessary for "beginning, continuing, and perfecting good actions in us."[81] Edwards and other puritans saw the doctrine of depravity and original sin as essential to the faith, but many Anglicans shied away from this perspective. Jeremy Taylor disagreed with the Augustinian view of original sin, but did not see that as a reason for division nor that it should be considered an essential doctrine.[82] Henry Hammond advocated a moralism that rejected *sola Fide* and embraced works as necessary for justification in part because he did not see the effects of the sinful nature as completely debilitating.[83]

The two major antagonists of English Protestantism were Roman Catholicism and Socinianism. The Anglicans and puritans alike gave sustained attacks on their doctrines and practices. But a general pattern appears revealing the differences between the Anglicans and puritans. The more the mind was revered above the heart in the rational perspective of the Anglicans, the less importance was given to doctrine. This was seen in the Anglican polemics concerning Catholicism and Socinianism where it tended to leave out doctrines such as justification by faith alone and human depravity. But it is also generally true that the more scholastic the puritans were, the more they were inclined toward divisiveness over less essential doctrines, at least in comparison to the original reformers. The great question of the day was, "What are the fundamental articles of the faith?"

*3. The Idea of Fundamental Articles*

Since the beginning of the reformation most Protestants believed that not all doctrines were essential to salvation. Fundamental articles (*Articuli fundamentales*) were the basic doctrines necessary to the Christian faith, or as Richard Muller defines them, "those doctrines without which Christianity cannot exist and the integrity of which is necessary to the preservation of the faith."[84] Muller is correct in insisting that identifying "certain fundamental truths of the faith" was "at the very heart of the Reformation."[85] Calvin diligently sought a "pan-protestant union," because he believed in a catholic or universal church.[86] His test for a true church was whether it had the pure preaching of the gospel and the right administration of the sacraments.[87] He said that when these two marks are in place, no matter how deficient in other

---

[81] Ibid., 82. Edwards also attacked the Socinians' views on the future state and the last judgment as heretical. Ibid., 85-119. He then, unfairly, put Locke in the same category as the Socinians. Ibid., 119-143; for the unfairness of this accusation see Alan Sell, *John Locke*, 185-267.

[82] Henry McAdoo, *The Spirit of Anglicanism*, 76-80.

[83] Henry Hammond, *Of Fundamentals*, 8.

[84] Richard Muller, *Dictionary of Latin and Greek Theological Terms*, 45.

[85] Richard Muller, *Post-Reformation Reformed Dogmatics*, 1:408.

[86] Martin Klauber, "Short Study – Calvin on Fundamental Articles and Ecclesiastical Union" in *Westminster Theological Journal* 54:2 (Fall, 1992), 343.

[87] Richard Stauffer, *The Quest for Church Unity*, 3-4; John Calvin, *Institutes*, IV. 1,9.

areas, a church should not be neglected and "no one is permitted to spurn its authority, flout its warnings, resist its counsels, or make light of its chastisements – much less to desert it and break its unity."[88]  He divided doctrine into articles necessary to be known and disputable articles, basing his distinction on Philippians 3:15.[89]  He argued that it is important for Christians to "agree on all points," but recognized due to ignorance and depravity this is not possible, therefore as long as people agree on "the sum of religion" they can still be saved.[90]  It is important to notice three things concerning Calvin's understanding of the fundamental articles: Firstly, he recognized some doctrines as essential to the faith as well as two marks essential for a true church.[91]  Secondly, his emphasis was on maintaining unity, rather than separation, seeing who is in more than seeing who is outside the faith.  Calvin's efforts to unite with Zwinglians, Lutherans and Anglicans bears this point out.[92]  Thirdly, all doctrine is important.  He did not countenance any idea that some doctrines should be ignored simply because they were not fundamental.[93]  It was Calvin's belief that the Church of Rome did not have the two marks of the church and diverted from essential doctrines of the faith and therefore was not a true church.[94]  He squarely put the blame of schism on the Roman Church.[95]  Calvin did not present a list of the fundamental articles other than summarizing them, including "God is one; Christ is God and the Son of God; our salvation

---

[88] John Calvin, *Institutes*, IV. 1,10.  He later reiterated that unity was necessary "even if it otherwise swarms with many faults." Ibid., IV. 1,12.

[89] Ibid.  He later stated, "We have, moreover, shown that the errors which ought to be pardoned are those which do not harm the chief doctrine of religion, which do not destroy the articles of religion on which all believers ought to agree." IV. 2,1.

[90] Ibid., IV. 1,12.

[91] Bullinger similarly saw two types of doctrine.  The "firm and immutable" include the Apostles Creed as well as the principles, "That all men are sinners, conceived and born in sin; That none but those that are regenerate can enter into the kingdom of God; That men, not by their own deserts, but through the grace of God, by the only merits of Christ, are justified by faith; That Christ once sacrificed for sin is no more sacrificed, that he is the only perpetual priest; That good works are done of those that are justified…and if there be any more of the same sort." Henry Bullinger, *Decades*, 2:55-56.

[92] Richard Stauffer, *The Quest for Church Unity*, 13, 15.  In 1564 the humanist Jacob Acontius warned that the devil's strategy was to bring in dissention through the use of differences of belief in non-fundamental doctrines to identify heresy.  *Darkness Discovered. Or the Devils Secret Stratagems Laid Open* (London: F.M., 1651), 75-76; R. Rouse and S.C. Neill (eds.), *A History of the Ecumenical Movement* (Philadelphia: The Westminster Press, 1967), 75.

[93] John Calvin, *Institutes*, IV. 1,12; *Selected Works of John Calvin Vol.3 Tracts Part 3*, 222-223.

[94] Ibid., IV. 2,5 and 9.  He did agree that there is a "remnant of his people" still in the Roman Catholic Church. Ibid., IV. 2,12.

[95] Ibid., IV. 2,5; Richard Stauffer, *The Quest for Church Unity*, 5.

rests in God's mercy; and the like."[96] Elsewhere he pointed out the doctrine of "the son of God manifested in the flesh" as "the chief and fundamental point of all heavenly doctrine,"[97] the doctrine of the resurrection of the flesh as a "fundamental article of the faith,"[98] the gospel including "the manner in which justification is obtained" as "a fundamental article of the Christian faith."[99] The doctrines of the Trinity, deity of Christ, resurrection of the dead and justification by faith alone were all considered fundamental articles by Calvin.

The post-reformation Reformed church did not go so far as the Roman Catholics and Lutherans in their lists of fundamentals, but they did in practice depart from the simplicity of the original reformers. Herman Witsius described three distinctions of fundamentals:

> We observe that doctrines may be said to be necessary, - to Salvation, - or to Religion, - or to the Church. A doctrine, without the knowledge and faith of which, God does not save grown-up persons, is necessary to Salvation; that, without the profession and practice of which, no one can be considered religious, is necessary to Religion; and that, without which none is admitted to the communion of the visible church, is necessary to the Church.[100]

He does not elaborate on the second two types of fundamentals, but they were a common feature in the sectarianism of scholastic Reformed churches. The first major division took place over the Arminian debate at the Synod of Dort. By 1619 there was far less room for variation in the doctrine of predestination than at Calvin's time. The rift was started when Arminius was asked to write refutations of the humanist Coornhert and sublapsarian Delft ministers (1591) on the issue of supralapsarian and infralapsarian views of the decrees.[101] Though the Reformed church managed to embrace both supralapsarianism and infralapsarianism, there was not enough room for the Arminian position and

[96] John Calvin, *Institutes*, IV. 1,12.

[97] John Calvin, *Commentary on the First Epistle to Timothy* (Albany, OR: Ages Software, 1998), 9.

[98] John Calvin, *Commentary on the Second Epistle to Timothy* (Albany, OR: Ages Software, 1998), 44.

[99] John Calvin, *Commentary on the Epistle to The Galatians* (Albany, OR: Ages Software, 1998), 7. He also indicted the Roman Catholics saying, "Thus, in our own times, the Papists, choosing to have a divided and mangled Christ, have none, and are therefore removed from Christ." He went on to say, "When the glow of justification is ascribed to another, and a snare is laid for the consciences of men, the Savior no longer occupies his place, and the doctrine of the gospel is utterly ruined." Ibid., 20-21; he also mentioned justification by faith alone "in the merit of Christ's passion" including the idea that Christ's sacrifice is a propitiation for sins as a fundamental article in *Selected Works of John Calvin Vol.3 Tracts Part 3*, 104.

[100] Herman Witsius, *The Apostles Creed*, 16-17.

[101] Carl Bangs, *Arminius: A Study in the Dutch Reformation* (Grand Rapids: Francis Asbury Press, 1985), 141. Bangs reveals that Arminius was probably never in agreement with Beza concerning the decrees.

predestination became a fundamental article at least in Witsius' category of *necessary for the church*.

Francis Turretin observed that some had too few fundamentals such as the Socinians and Arminians and others had too many like the Roman Church and the Lutherans, and therefore opted for a "mean between both."[102] After a lengthy discussion on the concept of fundamental articles he listed several, but claimed no one can give an exact list.[103] He asserted that all the orthodox agreed on the following articles as fundamental:

> The doctrines concerning the sacred Scriptures as inspired (*theopneusto*), being the only and perfect rule of faith; concerning the unity of God and the Trinity; concerning Christ, the Redeemer, and his most perfect satisfaction; concerning sin and its penalty – death; concerning the law and its inability to save; concerning justification by faith; concerning the necessity of grace and of good works, sanctification and the worship of God, the church, the resurrection of the dead, the final judgment and eternal life and such as are connected with these.[104]

In his explanation of not knowing an exact number he revealed his focus, stating, "it is also useless and unnecessary [the question concerning the number of fundamental articles] because there is no need of our knowing particularly the number of such articles, if we can prove that they err fundamentally in one or more."[105] Here we see a shift in application from Calvin, in that Turretin used the fundamentals primarily to determine who was outside the camp of Christianity rather than who was inside. His *Institutes of Elenctic Theology* is an extensive case in point, where this systematic theology is written as a polemic against the numerous groups he opposed. Besides the list that would fit into Witsius' category of fundamentals of salvation, Turretin introduced other fundamentals which he believed were necessary for the health of the church. One example is his opposition toward the school of Saumur. He led the attempt to procure a statement of faith called *The Formula Consensus Helvetica* that would exclude candidates for pastor in the cantons of Switzerland if they came from the school of Saumur. This measure was not passed in Geneva until 1679 and was rescinded by Turretin's son, Jean-Alphonse Turretin, in 1706. The *Formula* brought division between the Swiss cantons and Saumurians over three issues: the originality of the vowel points in the Hebrew text, the extent of the atonement and the question of whether Adam's sin imputed guilt or simply a sinful nature upon his progeny. Martin Klauber describes the scholastic nature of the *Formula*:

---

[102] Francis Turretin, *Institutes of Elenctic Theology*, 1:48.

[103] Ibid., 1:48-54.

[104] Ibid., 1:53. The last statement, "such as are connected with these," seems to open the door for a lot of interpretation.

[105] Ibid., 1:54. He goes on to indict "the papists, Socinians, Anabaptists and similar heretics."

The Helvetic Formula Consensus represents a reformed scholasticism characterized by a thorough definition of orthodoxy along credal lines. Its minute detail was intended to defend reformed theology against any tint of remonstrant thought. Theologians such as Turrettini refused to countenance any possibility of a repeat in Geneva or in Switzerland of the theological diversity in the Low Countries, where Arminianism held its stronghold. They saw any compromise, such as in the doctrines of Saumur, as the first step toward the dissolution of the heritage of Calvin.[106]

Klauber alleges the *Formula* to be an attempt to maintain the heritage of Calvin, but it was actually a departure from his irenic program and thoughts concerning fundamental articles. Turretin and the scholastic reformers diverted from two of the three points of Calvin concerning the necessary truths of Christianity; they added non-salvific doctrines as necessary for unity and they shifted toward polemic rather than irenic tendencies.[107] The scholastic method, with too much attention on the mind and not enough on the heart contributed to this departure and the disunity of Protestantism.

In seventeenth century England the concept of fundamental articles remained, but the principles changed as well as what was considered fundamental; a variety of positions developed. The rationalists maintained Calvin's emphasis of using the fundamental articles primarily to determine who was a Christian rather than who was not. However, they seriously limited the number of fundamental articles, because of their disdain for doctrine. Locke reduced the articles to the belief that Jesus was the Messiah "together with those concomitant articles of his resurrection, rule and coming again to judge the world, be all the faith required, as necessary to justification."[108] He went on to discuss how the epistles were written to those who were already Christians and so could not be used to determine what the fundamental articles were; the gospels were all that were needed for understanding what was essential for justification.[109] Blount, in agreement with Lord Herbert of Cherbury, listed five fundamental articles:

> I. That there is one onely (sic) Supreme God.
> II. That He chiefly is to be worshipped.
> III. That virtue, goodness, and piety, accompanied with faith in, and love to God, are the best ways of worshipping Him.
> IV. That we should repent of our sins from the bottom of our hearts, and turn to the right way.

---

[106] Martin Klauber, "The Helvetic Formula Consensus (1675): An Introduction and Translation," *Trinity Journal* 11:1 (Spring 1990), 113.
[107] They maintained Calvin's third idea that non-fundamental articles are still important and worthy of discussion, but not important enough to divide over. We will see that some in the Church of England abandon this point as well.
[108] John Locke, *The Reasonableness of Christianity*, 71.
[109] Ibid., 71-72.

V. And lastly, that there is a reward and punishment after this life.[110]

Spinoza declared that the fundamentals could only deal with that which is clearly understandable. Anything that we "cannot grasp…with our reason and understanding" "we need not be much troubled about."[111] He argued for a few basic truths, discarding all other truths in scripture as "more curious than profitable."[112] He lists the "fundamental dogmas" similarly to Blount, stating that one must simply believe that God exists, that he is one, omnipresent and sovereign, that "the worship of God consists only in justice and charity, or love towards one's neighbour," that all who obey God are saved, and that God forgives those who repent.[113] By and large the rationalists rejected many of the articles seen as fundamental to the original reformers, such as the doctrines of the Trinity, the deity of Christ, the satisfaction of Christ and justification by faith alone. By elevating the mind to the neglect of the heart, science and philosophy became more important to them, rather than detailed doctrine. They still needed a deity and a moral code for their philosophical system, but the god and theology of their "Christianity" barely resembled that of Calvin.

The Anglicans should be divided into two groups in regards to the fundamental articles, the latitudinarians and the cavaliers. Both groups narrowed the list of fundamentals, at least when specific articles were mentioned, to the Apostles Creed. The departure from Calvin and the original reformers is evident in that many Anglicans began to believe that Roman Catholics held to all the necessary fundamental articles because they embraced the Apostles Creed.[114] The doctrines of the satisfaction of Christ and justification by faith alone are noticeably absent from their discussions on the fundamental articles. They did not reject Roman Catholicism for its doctrine, but rather due to its worship, which they believed was idolatrous.[115] The cavaliers diverged from the latitudinarians in their view of fundamentals in the area of worship. Both groups believed division was necessary with the Roman Church due to its worship, but the cavaliers also believed separation was

---

[110] Charles Blount, *Religio Laici*, 49-50.

[111] Benedict de Spinoza, *A Theologico-Political Treatise*, 113.

[112] Ibid.

[113] Ibid., 187.

[114] Edward Stillingfleet, *A Discourse Concerning the Idolatry Practiced in the Church of Rome, and the Hazard of salvation in the Communion of it* (London: Printed for Henry and George Mortlock, 1709), 7-8; John Tillotson, *Sermons on Several Subjects and Occasions* (London: Printed for C. Hitch and L. Hawes, etc., 1757), 6-8; William Sherlock, *An Answer to a Discourse Intitled* (sic) *Papists Protecting Against protestant Popery* (London: Printed for John Amery, 1686), 28; William Chillingworth, *Religion of Protestants: A Safe Way to Salvation* (Oxford: Leonard Lichfield, 1638), 129-130, 193-235.

[115] Stillingfleet argued that the Roman Church was a true church, but that it was not safe due to its idolatry. *A Discourse Concerning the Idolatry Practiced in the Church of Rome*, 8.

compulsory from the puritans because of their refusal to use the Book of Common Prayer; this was not a doctrinal, but rather a liturgical reason for disunity.[116] The latitudinarians attempted to make room for the puritans by seeking a more comprehensive liturgy, but were stifled in their efforts. Many of the Anglicans reduced the fundamental articles as far as doctrine was concerned, but increased them as far their practice of exclusion due to liturgy was concerned.[117] They also tended to ignore other doctrines that were not directly connected with the fundamental articles, diverting from Calvin's understanding that all doctrine was important.

The Reformed bishops seem to have been an exception to the rule concerning the Church of England. Ezekiel Hopkins held to the satisfaction of Christ, the doctrine of the fall and justification by faith alone, as well as the doctrines of the Trinity, the two natures of Christ, the resurrection and judgment to come as "fundamental articles…of absolute necessity to be believed."[118] He also taught that all doctrine was important, holding to Calvin's two categories of doctrine.[119] Finally Hopkins departed from the typical Anglican position concerning the discussion of the fundamental articles, by seeing a holistic response as necessary rather than a simple intellectual assent to the articles.[120]

---

[116] Herbert Croft wrote a controversial treatise called *The Naked Truth* where he agreed that the Apostles Creed contained the only necessary articles; but that the church must have the same form of worship otherwise chaos would reign. Herbert Croft, *The Naked Truth or, the True State of the Primitive Church* (London s.n., 1675), 1-2, 23, 64-65; Gilbert Sheldon, *The Act of Parliament Against Religious Meetings* (London: s.n., 1670), 1-8.

[117] Henry Hammond reduced the fundamentals to two doctrines – belief in the death and resurrection of Christ (along with the subsidiaries to these doctrines), but advocated enforcing adiaphora. *Of Fundamentals*, 24-56; *Of Will Worship* (Oxford: Henry Hall, 1644), 1-26. The puritans accused Roman Catholics of "will worship," referring to human-inspired worship not found in the Bible, but Hammond exonerated the slanderous term, justifying it as referring to the voluntary worship of a free-will offering.
. He also used Colossians 2:23, which contains the word ἐθελοθρησκία puritans translated as *will-worship*, as justifying the enforcement of religious practices not commanded in the Bible (adiaphora). He used the same passage to prove the exact opposite of how the puritans understood it. Cf. Richard Sibbes, *Works*, 2:387; John Flavel, *Works*, 4:522-523. Flavel defines *will-worship*: "Those services that are performed to him for immediate worship, when as they were not prescribed and commanded by him for that end; because this, as it is expressed Psal. Cvi. 59, 'is to go a whoring with their own inventions.'"

[118] Ezekiel Hopkins, *Works*, 2:611, 3:452-457.

[119] Ibid., 2:172.

[120] He said the evidence of Christianity consists of "(i.) certain principles of faith in the understanding; (ii.), certain gracious impressions upon the heart and will; and (iii.), a certain regular obedience in the whole course of a man's life and conversation." Ibid., 3:452.

Many of the radical Quakers acted similarly to the rationalists in that they did not see doctrine as significant as the reformers and puritans did; they used the Bible, but doctrine was not as essential for salvation to them, at least to the same degree as it was seen by the original reformers. George Fox focused on the experience of being born again and worshiping in the Spirit rather than doctrinal beliefs.[121] The one "article" necessary is whether one has the Spirit or not. He said the test of whether a professor of Christianity actually has unity and conformity with other Christians and with the Father and Son is if that person believes in and walks in the light, which transforms them into the image of Christ.[122] William Penn rejected the idea of fundamental articles, arguing that living a righteous life is all that matters.[123] In his controversial work *The Sandy Foundation Shaken* he discarded all doctrinal tests and then denied the doctrine of the Trinity, the satisfaction of Christ and the doctrine of imputed righteousness.[124] He was thrown into jail for this work. He wrote *Innocency With Her Open Face* to explain himself where he confessed the deity of Christ, seemingly embracing a form of modalism,[125] though he rejected this idea in *The Sandy Foundation Shaken*.[126] By focusing on the heart to the neglect of the mind, the extreme radicals abandoned the fundamental articles as a means of unity, solely relying on an experience to verify true Christianity.

The post-restoration puritans can be divided into two groups as far as their beliefs in the fundamental articles are concerned. Those who wanted toleration rather than comprehension held as fundamental the same basic doctrines as Calvin and the original reformers. John Owen disputed the idea that the church should enforce certain forms of worship on those opposed for conscience sake, even though they held to the fundamentals of the Christian religion.[127] He believed that as long as a church acknowledged the fundamentals they should be allowed to operate, without interference by the state. This view was different from the comprehensive church model in that there was no mechanism for cooperation. The toleration model held to diversity without unity. Often

---

[121] George Fox, *Gospel-Truth Demonstrated*, 898-899.

[122] Ibid., 853.

[123] William Penn, *Innocency with Her Open Face Presented by Way of Apology for the Book Entitled The Sandy Foundation Shaken, To all Serious and Enquiring Persons, Particularly the Inhabitants of the City of London* (London: s.n., 1669), 3. Laudian Henry Hammond referred to a man who was made bishop before he knew about the resurrection of the dead, advocating this due to his godly life. The point he was making was similar to Penn in that a person living out Christian practice and obedience could be saved before understanding the fundamentals of the faith, works rather than doctrine brought salvation. *Of Fundamentals*, 21-23.

[124] William Penn, *The Sandy Foundation Shaken* (London: Andrew Sowle, 1684 originally 1668), preface to the unprejudiced reader and 9-28.

[125] William Penn, *Innocency with Her Open Face*, 5-12.

[126] William Penn, *The Sandy Foundation Shaken*, 12. He presented the idea of modalism without using the term and described it as absurd.

[127] John Owen, "Indulgence and Toleration Considered" in *Works*, 13:656-681.

these churches saw most doctrine as extremely important, including the minute points scholastically extrapolated from basic doctrines.[128]

The latitude and moderate puritans were the closest examples of Calvin and the original reformers concerning the fundamental articles. Baxter, Bates, Howe and others sought a comprehensive church because they believed unity was as essential as doctrine. Uniformity on the essentials without demanding consistency on the nonessentials maintained both fellowship and doctrine so long as nonessential doctrine was still seen as important. Manton declared, "There is nothing superfluous in the canon. The Spirit of God is wise, and would not burden us with things unnecessary;"[129] this position was very different from that of the Anglicans and rationalists who held, at least as seen in their actions, that doctrine was unimportant.[130] The latitude puritans were zealous for truth, while conscious of the danger of being divisive.[131] Manton believed all doctrine was important, but not all doctrine was a reason for division: "The most weight should be pitched upon the fundamentals and essentials of religion; and when there is an agreement there, private differences in smaller matters should not make us break off from one another."[132] The latitude puritans were especially opposed to speculation. They believed that there was mystery involved even in the fundamentals, but curiosity over what is not revealed was prohibited. Bates warned:

> We are obliged to believe supernatural doctrines no farther than they are revealed. God does not require our assent to an object beyond the merit of it: that is, the degrees of its revelation. We cannot see an object more fully than it is visible. The truth of evangelical mysteries is clearly revealed, the manner of them is not discovered. To attempt the comprehensive knowledge of them, is perfectly vain: for it is impossible, impertinent, and of dangerous consequence.[133]

Manton also believed that truth had to be received by both the mind and heart to be affective: "It is not enough to receive the truth in the light of it, but we must also receive it in the love of it, or it will do us no good.... There is a *notitia per visum, et notitia per gustum* – a knowledge by sight, and a

---

[128] Cf. John Owen, *The Death of Death*, passim.

[129] Thomas Manton, *Works*, 5:117.

[130] Benedict de Spinoza, *A Theologico-Political Treatise*, 175-181 chapter eight entitled "It Is Shown That Scripture Teaches Only Very Simple Doctrines, Such As Suffice For Right Conduct." Joseph Glanville, *The Vanity of Dogmatizing* (London: E.C., 1661), passim.

[131] In his commentary on Jude Manton stated, "We live in a frozen age, and cursed indifferency hath done a great deal of mischief. Christians! Is error grown less dangerous, or the truth of religion more doubtful? Is there nothing certain and worth contention, or are we afraid to meddle with such as shroud themselves under the glorious name of saints?" Thomas Manton, *Works*, 5:116.

[132] Ibid., 5:118.

[133] William Bates, *Works*, 2:369. He suggested that the previous debates over the nature of the decrees fall into the category of dangerous. Ibid., 371; *Puritan Sermons*, 2:13-14.

knowledge by taste."[134]    While listing the fundamental articles, Edward Veal similarly noted, "It must be an effectual, lively faith; (James ii. 17;) not only an assent of their minds to the truth of the scripture, but the consent of their hearts to the terms of the covenant."[135]

In discussing the doctrine of the knowledge of God Charnock explained the concept of necessary doctrine in detail and should be considered a wonderful representative of latitude puritanism for his thoroughness.    There are three important points in considering Charnock's contribution to the question of fundamental articles.  Firstly, he saw three overarching doctrinal concepts as fundamental with specific doctrines falling under each concept: the doctrine of God, the doctrine of salvation and the doctrine of humanity.  It was essential to have the right God; otherwise one's faith was in vain.   Without a proper understanding of God that can only come from the scriptures, a person cannot properly worship God, obey him, receive his grace or experience union and communion with him.[136]    One also had to have the right gospel.   Without justification by faith alone in the satisfaction of Christ a person had a false gospel devoid of saving effect.[137]    Finally it was essential to have a proper knowledge of humanity and its depravity in order to be saved: "To know God without knowing ourselves, is a fruitless speculation."[138]

Charnock's second point concerning fundamental articles is that knowledge must increase.[139]   One cannot be satisfied with the least amount of knowledge necessary for salvation.[140]   He contended for a detailed knowledge of God as necessary because the less we know the worse off we are;[141] the more we know the better off we are.[142]

Finally, Charnock believed that the Holy Spirit was necessary for a person to understand the fundamentals from the heart.  This encompasses two thoughts: i.

---

[134] Thomas Manton, *Works*, 3:80.

[135] *Puritan Sermons*, 7; William Bates noted, "Light opens the mind by clear conviction, but love opens the heart by persuasive insinuation, and makes an easy entrance into the soul." *Works*, 2:296.

[136] Stephen Charnock, *Works*, 4:25-30, 161. He said, "The holiness, power, and eternity of God, are the fundamental articles of all religion, upon which the whole body of it leans: his holiness for conformity to him, his power and eternity for the support of faith and hope." Ibid., 1:372.

[137] Ibid., 4:25; 3:240, 310-313.

[138] Ibid., 4:52-56.

[139] He said, "If the first beams of spiritual light give life, the further increase more abundantly increaseth that life; it being eternal life, we are nearest to life when we rise highest in knowledge." Ibid., 4:87.

[140] Quality was more important than quantity; he stated, "A great heat with a little light is better than a clear light with an hard frost and benumbed limbs;" but that could not be an excuse for laziness. Ibid., 4:82.

[141] Ibid., 4:27, 62, 88.

[142] He said, "The more distinct and savoury our notions of God and his goodness are, the more ardent flame will be in our wills." Ibid., 4:32, 35, 59, 89.

"God only can open the mind,"[143] and ii. knowledge must affect the whole soul
to be profitable.  He believed it was possible for an unbeliever to understand
the Bible at an intellectual level without comprehending it spiritually; this
answered the objections of Spinoza, who claimed the Spirit was not necessary
for interpreting the Bible because the human mind could grasp the simple truths
of scripture.[144]  Charnock responded to this critique by saying, "We may indeed
by study find a proposition so clear as to engage our assent, but not without
supernatural influence have such a knowledge of God as to change our
souls."[145]  He deemed the Spirit necessary because true or full knowledge
(ἐπίγνωσιζ) was only capable of being perceived by the whole person, but each
faculty of the soul was equally corrupted by sin so a person was hopelessly lost
unless the Spirit illumined his or her heart and mind.[146]  True knowledge "Is an
active and expressive knowledge; it expresseth in the life what is in the head
and heart;" it affects the will.[147]  It also ultimately touches the affections,
bringing an enjoyment of God which is the chief end of human existence:
"Knowledge gives us a sight, and love gives us a possession; we find him by
knowledge, but we enjoy him by love.  Let us improve our knowledge of him
for inflaming our affections to him, that we may be prepared for the glory of
our eternal life."[148]  The puritans were not afraid of the affective or an
emotional experience in their encounter of God, so they brought in the
affections as necessary to fully comprehend the fundamental articles in the way
they believed God meant for them to be perceived; this was especially true of
Stephen Charnock.

The rationalists and Anglicans truncated the original view of the reformers
in their understanding of the fundamental articles.  They neglected some of the
doctrines seen as essential by Calvin such as the doctrine of justification by
faith alone, going so far as to say that the Roman Church held to the
fundamentals simply because it embraced the Apostles Creed.  They also
strayed from the original Protestant understanding by not connecting the heart
with the mind in their descriptions of the fundamental articles.  This divergence
was partially due to their overemphasis of the mind, to the neglect of the heart.
Many of the Quakers abandoned the entire concept of fundamental articles and
with it discarded key biblical doctrines deemed essential by the reformers; this
deviation was partially owing to their disregard for the mind, only pursuing the

---

[143] Ibid., 4:101.
[144] Benedict de Spinoza, *A Theologico-Political Treatise*, 114-119.
[145] Stephen Charnock, *Works*, 4:102.
[146] Ibid., 4:102-105, 108.  Concerning the mind he stated, "Since our understanding is
corrupted by sin, and filled with error, it is not sufficient to understand the things of God
without an internal illumination, as well as an external revelation."
[147] Ibid., 4:49.  He went on to say, "A change in the heart engenders affection, and
affection will break out in action; love will lay a constraint upon the heart."
[148] Ibid., 4:86.  He also said, "God stands not so much upon our knowledge of him, as
our delight in him; and it is no sign of our union with God, unless affection to him be
joined with it."

heart.  The puritans at various levels sought to maintain a balance of head and heart in regard to the fundamentals of the faith and therefore authentically represented the original reformers.  The latitude puritans remained faithful to Calvin in their pursuance of unity without discarding the fundamentals of the faith.

# CONCLUSION

The seventeenth century was a century of turmoil and change. Politically England witnessed two monarchial depositions; philosophically scholasticism gave way to rationalism; religiously Calvinism was supplanted by Arminianism within the Church of England with a some exceptions; there were a few bishops that remained Calvinist but the vast majority embraced Arminianism. The scientific and philosophical revolutions ushered the age into the modern era, but not without a struggle. The educated elites' worldview began to shift from a God-centered awe to a human-centered wonder. God was not forgotten, but he was no longer the starting point for many philosophically or theologically. Whether these events were caused by or resulted from an overemphasis on the mind to the relative neglect of the heart, they certainly coincided with this phenomenon for many. This emphasis had a major impact on the Church of England. The Anglicans, virtuosi and Rationalists moved in the direction of elevating the cognitive side of religion and shied away from the emotional sphere for fear of enthusiasm. In reaction to this course the radical puritans and Quakers exalted heart religion while rejecting reason's place in theology. The latitude puritans attempted to balance head and heart, seeking to learn from both perspectives by valuing all three faculties of the soul: mind, affections and will.

By looking at Stephen Charnock's doctrine of the knowledge of God we have been able to note the repercussions of the various emphases made by twelve different parties in England by comparing them to the original reformers.[1] Kendall, Hall and others questioned the faithfulness of the puritans to Calvin, but we attempted to judge all of the various groups in England on whether they continued either to reflect or to distort the thought of the original reformers. We also considered the possible causes and consequences of any departure from their views.

Like Calvin and the humanist reformers, Charnock embraced a holistic definition of the doctrine of the knowledge of God. The puritans in general were not afraid of the affective and advocated an experiential faith where real knowledge of God included deep affections and emotions where the Christian had contact with God in communion with him. This may have been heightened in the puritan experience due to their unique situation but it was not a departure from Calvin or the early reformers. Some of the radical puritans, mystics and Quakers made significant modifications to the original reformers by downplaying the part the mind plays in the process of knowing God, while the Anglicans, virtuosi and rationalists, because of their phobia toward enthusiasm, diverged from the reformers by elevating the mind to the detriment and neglect of experiential religion. Of course these observations run the risk of overgeneralization, with a myriad of nuances being recognized, but as a whole three interpretations of what it means to know God became current in

---

[1] See appendix A.

seventeenth century England: either a neglect of the mind, a neglect of the heart or a balance between the two. Charnock suitably mirrored Calvin and the other humanist reformers in his holistic understanding of the doctrine of the knowledge of God.

In discussing how we come to know God, Charnock included the concept of natural theology. Like the reformers he saw serious limitations to natural theology, but he was not afraid of using it if kept under proper check. He went beyond Calvin in his discussion of the proofs for the existence of God, but like Calvin maintained that the proofs were useless apart from the Spirit's work of effectual calling. Once again the more radical groups moved away from the reformers by completely rejecting natural theology while the more rational parties traveled in the opposite direction by seeing little if any limitations to natural theology and subsequently devalued special revelation.

Charnock believed the primary source for a proper knowledge of God was the Bible. With little variation from the reformers he advocated the supreme authority of the scriptures over all other sources of knowledge. His deep appreciation for the Bible is evident in his voluminous use of the Bible in his theology. Like the reformers he held to the presupposition that the Bible was God's word and therefore did not seek to prove the veracity of the Bible before accepting its authority. Those who elevated the mind also tended to promote the intellect above scripture, sometimes subtly by seeking to prove it rationally before accepting it, and other times not so subtly by lessening its necessity for theology. Those who advanced the heart over the head also tended to downplay the scriptures in preference to the immediate revelation of the Spirit. Some from the extremes on both ends, Quakers and rationalists, ended up denying the Bible's trustworthiness and their questioning of the accuracy of the Bible gave rise to the advent of biblical criticism.[2] Both Calvin and Charnock advocated a doctrine of word and Spirit seeing the necessity of the absolute authority of the Bible and the essential place of the Spirit in interpreting the Bible.

Finally in discussing the doctrine of the knowledge of God, Charnock recognized the balance of doctrinal integrity and unity. The original reformers fought for what they believed to be the essential doctrines of the faith, but also maintained an irenic spirit concerning doctrines that were not crucial to the faith. The post-reformation scholastics did not preserve this unity and began to divide over more minute differences. Those who bandied around reason as the supreme source of truth began to downplay doctrine, clearly departing from the reformers. The various uses of the concept of fundamental articles reveals the consequences of the differing groups' emphasis on either heart or head. Like the reformers, Charnock upheld the important Protestant doctrines of justification by faith alone, the substitutionary atonement of Christ, the deity of Christ and the depravity of humanity. The Anglicans limited the fundamentals to the Trinity and the atonement, though many were loyal to the *Articles*,

---

[2] Samuel Fisher, *The Rustic's Alarm to the Rabbies*, esp. "Additionall Appendix;" Spinoza, Benedict de. *A Theologico-Political Treatise and a Political Treatise*, passim.

revealing a diminished view of doctrine, and the rationalists and the Quakers rejected doctrine as a guide for unity. Even within the puritan camp differing nuances can be seen in their emphases and additional doctrines recognized as fundamental to the church. Those more scholastically oriented were willing to separate from one another rather than seek comprehension within the one church, partially because of the additions of essential doctrines such as limited atonement; this was a clear departure from the early reformers.

In this study we have attempted to evaluate the claim that scholasticism necessitated deviancy from Calvin. The scholastic method cannot be blamed for the churches' digression from Calvin, but owing to its preponderant focus toward the mind it lent to alteration concerning the original focus of the reformers. Rationalism alone cannot be blamed for the doctrinal changes that took place in the Reformed churches of Europe. When rationalism or scholasticism was coupled with an experiential faith, aberration was not necessitated, but often, because of the emphasis on the mind, the heart was neglected which led to a truncated faith. Calvin, Bullinger, Bucer, Musculus and other humanist reformers encouraged a deep spiritual communion with Christ while promoting the Reformed doctrines of the faith; they sought a balance of mind and heart once freed from the shackles of scholasticism. They understood the scholastics as disrupters of true Christianity, rejecting their speculation and elitism as destructive to the faith. The puritans were more scholastic than the humanist reformers, embracing a Ramian version of scholasticism, but the latitude puritans moved more toward the humanist method by the use of a tempered Cartesianism. The potential pitfalls of the scholastic method were avoided for the most part because of the latitude balance of head and heart. Alan Sell, in *Theology in Turmoil*, quotes John "Rabbi" Duncan, whose statement could be considered a good summary of the latitude puritan attempt at striking the correct scriptural balance:

> Some persons preach only doctrine; that makes people all head, which is a monster. Some preach only experience; that makes people all heart, which is a monster too. Others preach only practice; that makes people all hands and feet, which is likewise a monster. But if you preach doctrine and experience and practice, by the blessing of God, you will have head, and heart, and hands, and feet – a perfect man in Christ Jesus.[3]

Charnock appreciated Calvin's emphasis on union and communion with Christ in an experiential relationship that affected the whole person, mind, affections and will. He also esteemed his Reformed theology that exalted the sovereignty of God and took seriously the depravity of humanity. He was a serious thinker concerning God and his ways, as well as a passionate lover of God, just like Calvin.

Just as theology has emphasized God's transcendence and then his immanence at different junctures throughout Christian history, the same can be

---

[3] Alan Sell, *Theology in Turmoil* (Grand Rapids: Baker Book, 1986), 145.

said of the balance between head and heart. Further studies should be made of eighteenth century thought, comparing the more rationalistic theology of the likes of Charles Chauncy and the more affectionate theology of Jonathan Edwards and Joseph Bellamy. What effect did the emphasis of the heart to the possible neglect of the head of the pietists have on Schleiermacher and modern liberalism in the nineteenth century? The contemporary debate between charismatics and evangelicals might also bring further light on the subject. Patristic scholars may find stimulation and recompense by comparing Origin and Tertullian as well as considering Augustine and his contemporaries. But we shall give the final word to the latitude puritan Stephen Charnock, the subject of this study:

> By meditation we enter within the veil and behold his glory. He meets those that humbly aspire to him; frequent ascents of the mind to God is the way to attain the manifestations of him, Exod. xix. 3.... But let our affections keep an equal pace with our meditations, that the heart may be inflamed with a divine love. Endeavour to have a savour of Christ's ointments. Cant. i. 3; we shall then profit more in the knowledge of God in a week, than, without blowing up our affections, we shall do in many years; for then God will communicate himself to us with a more cordial affection than we can embrace him.[4]

---

[4] Stephen Charnock, *Works*, 4:108.

# APPENDIX

This is a chart for the seventeenth century English theological perspectives comparing them to the humanist reformers; these are generalities rather than absolute definition:

1. Rationalists[1]: Thomas Hobbes, John Locke, Charles Blount, Benedict de Spinoza, Rene Descartes, John Toland.
2. Virtuosi: Francis Bacon, Robert Boyle, John Ray, Walter Charleton, Nehemiah Grew, John Wilkins, Isaac Newton.
3. Laudian Anglicans: William Chillingworth, Henry Hammond, Peter Heylyn, Lancelot Andrewes, Meric Casaubon, William Clagett, George Hicks, Samuel Parker, Jeremy Taylor, Gilbert Sheldon, George Bull, William Sherlock.
4. Latitudinarian Anglicans: Edward Stillingfleet, Isaac Barrow, Gilbert Burnet, Robert South, John Tillotson.
5. Cambridge Platonists: Ralph Cudworth, Nathaniel Culverwell, Henry More, Benjamin Whichcote.
6. Calvinist Bishops: John Davenant, Ezekiel Hopkins, Edward Reynolds, Edward Leigh, James Ussher.
7. Latitude puritans: William Bates, Richard Baxter, Stephen Charnock, John Howe, Thomas Jacombe, Thomas Manton.
8. Moderate puritans: Hugh Binning, Thomas Boston, David Clarkson, William Fenner, John Flavel, Matthew Poole, Thomas Vincent, Richard Vines, Thomas Watson.
9. Independents: John Owen, John Eaton, Thomas Goodwin.
10. Radical puritans: Thomas Beard, Walter Craddock, Thomas Collier, William Dell, Samuel How, Francis Rous, John Saltmarsh, Gerrard Winstanley (Digger).
11. Mystics: Jane Lead, William Freke
12. Quakers: George Fox, Robert Barclay, Samuel Fisher, George Keith, William Penn.
13. Humanist reformers: John Calvin, Martin Bucer, Henry Bullinger, Wolfgang Musculus.

---

[1] We are using the term "rationalist" in a very broad sense to refer to those who were predominately philosophers. John Locke would better be labeled an empiricist concerning his epistemology.

Theological Perspectives Chart

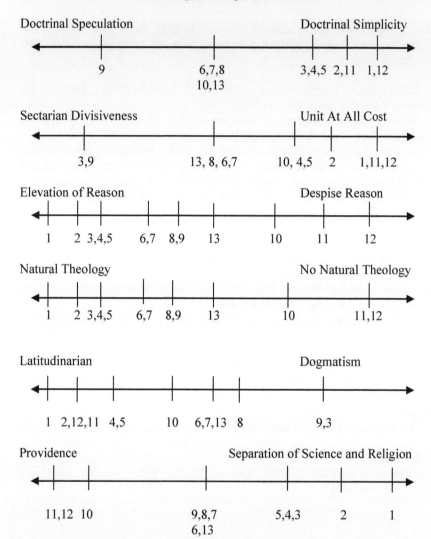

These are generalizations and approximations.

# BIBLIOGRAPHY

**Primary Sources:**

Abused Quaker. *The Holy Scripture Owned, and the Athenians Injustice Detected, by the Abused Quaker*. London: s.n., 1692.

Acontius, Jacob. *Darkness Discovered. Or the Devils Secret Stratagems Laid Open*. London: F.M., 1651.

Ames, William. *The Marrow of Theology*. Grand Rapids: Baker Books, 1997.

Amyraut, Moise. *A Treatise Concerning Religions*. London: M. Simmons, 1660.

Amyraut, Moise and Richard Lum. *Brief Treatise on Predestination and its Dependent Principles*. United States: R. Lum, 1985.

Andrewes, Lancelot. *The Pattern of Catechistical Doctrine at Large*. London: Printed for M.G., 1675.

Anon. *A Most Notable Example of an Ungracious Son, Who in the Pride of His Heart Denyed His Owne Father, and How God for His Offence, Turned His Meat into Loathsome Toades*. London: Printed by M. Parsons, 1638.

----- *A True Relation of an Apparition in the likeness of a Bird with a white brest, that appeared hovering over the Death-Beds of some of the children of Mr. James Oxenhame of Sale Monachorum, Devon. Gent.* London: I.O., 1641.

Aquinas, Thomas. *Summa Theologica*. Albany, OR: Ages Software, 1997.

Arrowsmith, John. *Armilla Catechetica*. Cambridge: John Field, 1659.

Astry, Thomas. *A True Relation of A Yong Man About Seventeen Years of Age, who was struck Dumb for the space of Twenty Four Hours, Because he would not believe what was said unto him*. London: Printed for the Author, 1671.

Atkinson, Peter. *The Spirits Voice Concerning Himselfe: or, A Faithful and Clear Discovery Of the Operations of the Spirit in The Hearts of the Saints*. London: Thomas Lock, 1659.

Bacon, Francis. *A Confession of Faith*. London: Printed for William Hope, 1641.

----- *Essays*. Hertfordshire: Wordsworth Editions, 1997.

Barclay, Robert. *Theses Theologicae: or The Theological Propositions, which are Defended by Robert Barclay, in his Apology for the True Christian Divinity as the Same is Held Forth and Preached, by the People Called Quakers.* London: s.n., 1675.

Barrow, Isaac. *A Brief State of the Socinian Controversy Concerning a Trinity in Unity.* London: Printed for Brabazon Aylmer, 1698.

----- *The Works of the Learned Isaac Barrow.* London: F.R., 1700.

----- *The Works of the Learned Isaac Barrow.* London: Printed for James Round, 1716.

Bates, William. *The Complete Works of William Bates.* Harrisonburg, VA: Sprinkle Publication, 1990.

Baxter, Richard. *Catholick Theologie.* London: Robert White, 1675.

----- *Of the Imputation of Christ's Righteousness to Believers: In what sence sound Protestants hold it; And, of the false devised sence, by which Libertines subvert the Gospel.* London: Printed for Nevil Simons, 1675.

----- *Select Arguments and Reasons Against Popery.* London: s.n., 1675.

----- *The Autobiography of Richard Baxter being the Reliquiae Baxterianae Abridged from the Folio 1696.* Mobile, AL: R.E. Publications, n.d.

----- *The Practical Works of Richard Baxter: Vol. 4.* Morgan, PA: Soli Deo Gloria Publications, 2000.

----- *The Practical Works of the Late Reverend and Pious Mr. Richard Baxter: Vol. 1-2.* London: Printed for Thomas Parkhurst, 1707.

----- *The Protestant Religion Truly Stated and Justified.* London: John Salisbury, 1692.

----- *The Reasons of the Christian Religion.* London: R. White, 1667.

----- *Universal Redemption of Mankind.* London: John Salisbury, 1694.

Beard, Thomas. *The Theatre of Gods Judgements.* London: Adam Islip, 1631.

Beheme, Jacob. *A Brief Explanation of the Knowledge of God and of All Things.* London: M.S., 1661.

----- *The Way to Christ Discovered.* London: M.S., 1648.

Bellamy, Joseph. *True Religion Delineated; or, Experimental Religion, as Distinguished from Formality on the One Hand, and Enthusiasm on the Other.* Ames, IA: International Outreach, 1997.

Beza, Theodore. *A Briefe Declaration of the Chiefe Points of Christian Religion Set Forth in a Table.* London: Tho: Man., 1613.

----- *A Little Book of Christian Questions and Responses.* Allison Park, PA: Pickwick Publications, 1986.

----- *Propositions and Principles of Divinitie.* Edinburge: Robert Waldegrave, 1591.

----- *The Christian Faith.* East Sussex, England: Focus Christian Ministries Trust, 1992.

Binning, Hugh. *The Works of Reverend Hugh Binning.* Ligonier, PA: Soli Deo Gloria Publications, 1992.

Blount, Charles. *Miracles No Violation of the Laws of Nature.* London: Printed for Robert Sollers, 1683.

----- *Religio Laici.* London: Printed for R. Bentley, 1683.

Bold, Samuel. *The Christian Belief: Wherein is asserted and Proved, That as there is nothing in the Gospel Contrary to Reason, yet there are some Doctrines in it Above Reason; and these being necessarily enjoyn'd us to Believe, are properly call'd, Mysteries; in Answer to a Book, Intituled* (sic)*, Christianity not Mysterious.* London: W. Onley, 1697.

Bolton, Samuel. *The Truebounds of Christian Freedome.* London: P.S., 1656.

Boston, Thomas. *Human Nature in its Fourfold State.* Carlisle, Penn: Banner of Truth Trust, 1964.

----- *The Works of Thomas Boston.* London: William Tegg and Co., 1853.

Boyle, Robert. *The Theological Works of the Honourable Robert Boyle.* London: W. Tatlor, 1715.

Bradford, John. *The Writings of John Bradford.* Carlisle, PA: The Banner of Truth Trust, 1979.

Browne, Peter. *A Letter in Answer to a Book Entituled* (sic), *Christianity not Mysterious*. London: W. Sayes, 1703.

Bucanus, William. *Body of Divinity*. London: Printed for Daniel Pakeman, 1659.

Bucer, Martin. *Common Places of Martin Bucer*. Appleford, England: Sutton Courtenay Press, 1972.

Bullinger, Henry. *Common Places of Christian Religion*. London: Tho. East and H. Middleton, 1572.

----- *The Decades of Henry Bullinger*. Grand Rapids: Reformation Heritage Books, 2004.

Burnet, Gilbert. *An Exposition of the Thirty-nine Articles*. London: R. Roberts, 1700.

Calvin, John. *Calvin's Ecclesiastical Advice* translated by Mary Beaty and Benjamin W. Farley. Louisville: Westminster; John Knox Press, 1991.

----- *Commentary on Genesis*. Albany, OR: Ages Software, 1998.

----- *Commentary on the Epistle of James*. Albany, OR: Ages Software, 1998.

----- *Commentary on the Epistle to the Colossians*. Albany OR: Ages Software, 1998.

----- *Commentary on the Epistle to the Ephesians*. Albany, OR: Ages Software, 1998.

----- *Commentary on the Epistle to The Galatians*. Albany, OR: Ages Software, 1998.

----- *Commentary on the Epistle to the Philippians*. Albany, OR: Ages Software, 1998.

----- *Commentary on the Epistle to the Romans*. Albany, OR: Ages Software, 1998.

----- *Commentary on the First Epistle of John*. Albany, OR: Ages Software, 1998.

----- *Commentary on the First Epistle to Timothy*. Albany, OR: Ages Software, 1998.

----- *Commentary on the Gospel According to John.* Albany, OR: Ages Software, 1998.

----- *Commentary on the Prophet Ezekiel.* Albany, OR: Ages Software, 1998.

----- *Commentary on the Psalms Vol. 1.* Albany, OR: Ages Software, 1998.

----- *Commentary on the Second Epistle to Timothy.* Albany, OR: Ages Software, 1998.

----- *Institutes of the Christian Religion,* edited by John T. McNeill. Philadelphia: Westminster Press, 1960.

----- *Institutes of the Christian Religion 1536 Edition.* Grand Rapids: Eerdmans, 1995.

----- *Letters.* Albany, OR: Ages Software, 1998.

----- *Secret Providence.* Albany, OR: Ages Software, 1998.

----- *Selected Works of John Calvin Vol. Two, Tracts Part Two.* Albany, OR: Ages Software, 1998.

----- *Selected Works of John Calvin Vol. Three, Tracts part three.* Albany, OR: Ages Software, 1998.

----- *Sermons on Job.* Carlisle, PA: Banner of Truth Trust facsimile of 1574 edition, 1993.

Cappel, Louis. *The Hinge of Faith and Religion; or, A Proof of the Deity against Atheists and Profane Persons, by Reason, and the Testimony of Holy Scripture.* London: for Thomas Dring, 1660.

Casaubon, Meric. *A Treatise Concerning Enthusiasme.* London: R.D., 1655.

Charleton, Walter. *The Darkness of Atheism Dispelled by the Light of Nature: A Physico-Theologicall Treatise.* London: J.P., 1652.

Charnock, Stephen. *Discourses Upon the Existence and Attributes of God.* New York: Robert Carter and Brothers, 1853; reprint Grand Rapids: Baker Book House, 1979.

----- *The Complete Works of Stephen Charnock* Vol. 1 and Vol. 5. Edinburgh: James Nichol in 1866; reprint Lafayette, IN: Sovereign Grace Publishers, 2001.

----- *The Works of Stephen Charnock* Vol. 3 and Vol. 4. Edinburgh: James Nichol in 1865; reprint Carlisle, PA: The Banner of Truth Trust, 1986.

Chillingworth, William. *Religion of Protestants: A Safe Way to Salvation.* Oxford: Leonard Lichfield, 1638.

Clagett, William. *A Discourse Concerning the Operations of the Holy Spirit.* London: Printed for Ch. Brome, 1690.

----- *Seventeen Sermons.* London: Printed for W. Rogers, 1704.

Clarkson, David. *The Works of David Clarkson.* Carlisle, PA: Banner of Truth Trust, 1988.

Collier, Thomas. *The Marrow of Christianity.* London: Printed for Giles Calvert, 1646.

Cosin, John. *The Differences in the Chief Points of Religion Between the Roman Catholics and Us of the Church of England; Together With the Agreements.* Preston: T. Walker, 1799.

Cradock, Walter. *The Saints Fulnesse of Joy.* London: Matthew Simmons, 1646.

Craigie, Sir William. *A Dictionary of the Older Scottish Tongue: From the Twelfth Century to the End of the Seventeenth.* The University of Chicago Press, 1931.

Cranmer, Thomas. *The Work of Thomas Cranmer.* Appleford, England: The Courtenay Press, 1965.

Croft, Herbert. *The Naked Truth or, the True State of the Primitive Church.* London s.n., 1675.

Cudworth, Ralph. *The True Intellectual System of the Universe.* London: Printed for J. Walthoe, D. Midwinter, etc., 1743.

Culverwell, Nathaniel. *An Elegant and Learned Discourse of the Light of Nature.* University of Toronto Press, 1971.

Daille, John. *An Apologie for the Reformed Churches.* University of Cambridge: Th. Buck, 1653.

Danson, Thomas. *The Quakers Folly Made Manifest to all Men.* London: J.H., 1659.

Davenant, John. *A Dissertation on the Death of Christ, as to Its Extent and Special Benefits.* Springfield, IL: Good Books, 1995.

----- *An Exhortation to the restoring of Brotherly Communion betwixt the Protestant Churches.* London: R.B., 1641.

----- *An Exposition of the Epistle of St. Paul to the Colossians with a Dissertation on the Death of Christ.* London: Hamilton, Adams, and Co., 1832.

Dell, William. *Select Works of William Dell.* London: Printed for John Kendall, 1773.

Descartes, Rene. *Discourse on Methods and Meditations.* Indianapolis: The Bobbs-Merrill Co., 1960.

Dyche, Thomas and Pardon, William. *A New General English Dictionary (1740).* New York: George Olms Verlag, 1972.

Eaton, John. *Honey-Combe of Free Justification by Christ alone.* London: R.B., 1642.

Edwards, John. *The Socinian Creed.* London: Printed for J. Robinson, 1697.

Edwards, Jonathan. *The Works of Jonathan Edwards.* Carlisle, Penn: The Banner of Truth Trust, 1974.

Evans, Theophilus. *The History of Modern Enthusiasm, From the Reformation to the Present Times.* London: W. Owens, 1752.

Faithfully Communicated by a Person of Quality. *Wonderful and Strange NEWS from Scotland, being A true and full Relation of a Person lately Deceased at the Town of Dumfreez, whose Corps could by no Art of Man, or Strength of Cattle, be Removed from the Place where it Lay. And when the House wherein it was, was wholly Burnt down to the Ground, the Body, Coffin, and Table whereon it stood, remained Whole and Untoucht, and so Continues to the great Astonishment of all Spectators.* London: Printed for B.H., 1673.

Fenner, William. *A Treatise of the Affections.* London: E. Tyler, 1657.

Fisher, Edward with Notes by Thomas Boston. *The Marrow of Modern Divinity.* Edmonton: Stillwater Revival Books, 1991.

Fisher, Samuel. *The Rustic's Alarm to the Rabbies.* London: Printed for Robert Wilson, 1660.

Flavel, John. *The Mystery of Providence*. Carlisle, PA: The Banner of Truth Trust, 1963.

----- *The Works of John Flavel*. Carlisle, PA: The Banner of Truth Trust, 1968.

Fox, George. *Gospel-Truth Demonstrated in a Collection of Doctrinal Books*. London: Printed and sold by T. Sowle, 1706.

Freke, William. *A Full Enquiry into the Power of Faith, the Nature of Prophecy, the Translation of Enoch and Elias, and the Resurrection of Christ*. London: s.n., 1693.

Gadbury, John. *Natura Prodigiorum: or, a Discourse Touching the Nature of Prodigies*. London: Printed for Fr. Cossinet, 1665.

Gastrell, Francis. *The Certainty of the Christian Revelation, and the Necessity of Believing it, Established*. London: Printed for Thomas Bennet, 1699.

Gillespie, George. *The Works of Mr. George Gillespie*. Edinburgh: Robert Ogle and Olives and Boyd, 1846.

Glanville, Joseph. *Reason in the Affairs of Religion*. London: E.C. and A.C., 1670.

----- *The Vanity of Dogmatizing*. London: E.C., 1661.

Goodwin, Thomas. *The Works of Thomas Goodwin*. London: James Nichol/Ballantyne, 1861.

Grew, Nehemiah. *Cosmologia Sacra: or a Discourse of the Universe as it is the Creature and Kingdom of God*. London: W. Rogers, S. Smith, and B. Walford, 1701.

Grotius, Hugo. *The Truth of the Christian Religion*. Edinburgh: Thomas Turnbull, 1819.

Hale, Matthew. *A Discourse of the Knowledge of God, and of our Selves, I. By the Light of Nature. II. By the Sacred Scriptures*. London: Printed for William Shrowsbery, 1688.

----- *The Judgment of the Late Lord Chief Justice Sir Matthew Hale, of the Nature of True Religion, the Causes of its Corruption, and the Churches Calamity by Mens Additions and Violences With the Desired Cure: In Three Discourses*. London: Printed for B. Simmons, 1684.

Hammond, Henry. *A Practical Catechism: whereunto is added The Reasonableness of Christian Religion.* London: Printed for J. Nicholson, 1715.

----- *Of Fundamentals in a Notion Referring to Practice.* London: J. Flesher, 1654.

----- *Of Will Worship.* Oxford: Henry Hall, 1644.

Heylyn, Peter. *Theologia Veterum, or, The Summe of Christian Theologie, Positive, Polemical, and Philological, contained in the Apostles Creed, or Reducible to it according to the tendries of the antients both Greeks and Latines.* London: E. Cotes, 1654.

Hickes, George. *The Spirit of Enthusiasm Exorcised.* London: Printed for Walter Kettiiby, 1680.

Hobbes, Thomas. *Leviathan: Parts One and Two.* Indianapolis: Bobbs-Merrill Educational Publishing, 1958.

----- *Leviathan, or The Matter, Forme, and Power of a Common-Wealth Ecclesiasticall and Civill.* London: Printed for Andrew Crooke, 1651.

Hole, Matthew. *The True Reformation of Manners, or the Nature and Qualifications of True Zeal: in a Sermon.* Oxford: L. Lichfield, 1699.

Hooper, John. *The Writings of John Hooper.* London: Religious Tract Society, n.d.

Hopkins, Ezekiel. *The Works of Ezekiel Hopkins.* Philadelphia: The Leighton Publications, 1874.

How, Samuel. *The Sufficiency of the Spirit's Teaching Without Human Learning.* Aberdeen: J. Strachan, 1780.

Howe, John. *The Works of John Howe.* New York: John Haven and Son, 1857.

Jacombe, Thomas. *Several Sermons Preach'd on the whole Eighth Chapter of the Epistle to the Romans.* London: W. Godbid, 1672.

----- *Enochs Walk and Change.* London: T.R. and E.M., 1656.

Johnson, John. *Eklampsis ton Dikaion.* London: Thomas Parkhurst, 1680.

Keith, George. *Divine Immediate Revelation and Inspiration, Continued in the True Church.* London: s.n., 1685.

Lead, Jane. *The Enochian Walks With God.* London: D. Edwards, 1694.

Leigh, Edward. *A Treatise of Divinity.* London: E. Griffin, 1647.

Locke, John. *An Abridgment of Mr. Locke's Essay Concerning Human Understanding.* London: Printed for J. and J. Knapton, 1731.

----- *The Reasonableness of Christianity.* Stanford University Press, 1958.

Luther, Martin. *Luther's Works.* Philadelphia: Fortress Press, 1959.

----- *Three Treatises.* Philadelphia: Fortress Press, 1970.

Manton, Thomas. *Works of Thomas Manton.* London: William Brown, 1845.

Matthews, A.G. *Calamy Revised.* Oxford: Clarendon Press, 1934.

Mestrezat, John. *The Divine Portrait.* London: A.M., 1631.

More, Henry. *A Collection of Several Philosophical Writings.* London: James Flesher, 1662.

Musculus, Wolfgang. *Common Places of Christian Religion.* London: Henry Bynneman, 1578.

Newton, Isaac. *Four Letters from Sir Isaac Newton to Doctor Bentley containing some Arguments in Proof of a Deity.* London: Printed for R. and J. Dodsley, 1756.

----- *Two Letters of Sir Isaac Newton to Mr. Leclerc.* London: Printed for J. Payne, 1754.

Nichols, James, notes and translations. *Puritan Sermons: 1659-1689.* Wheaton: Richard Owen Roberts Publishers, 1981.

Norris, John. *An Account of Reason and Faith in Relation to the Mysteries of Christianity.* London: Printed for S. Manship, 1697.

----- *The Grossness of the Quaker's Principle of the Light Within, with Their Inconsistency in Explaining it. Discours'd in a Letter to a Friend.* London: Printed for Sam. Manship, 1692.

Olevianus, Casper. *An Exposition of the Symbole.* London: H. Middleton, 1581.

Oliver, Edward. *A Sermon Preach'd in St. Paul's Cathedral, Before the Lord-Mayor*. London: Printed for Edward Castle, 1698.

Owen, John. *The Death of Death in the Death of Christ*. Carlisle, PA: Banner of Truth Trust, 1959.

----- *The Works of John Owen*. Rio, Wisconsin: Ages Software, 2000.

Parker, Samuel. *Bishop Parker's History of His Own Time*. London: Charles Rivington, 1727.

Pascal, Blaise. *Pensees*. New York: E.P. Dutton, 1958.

Penn, William. *Innocency with Her Open Face Presented by Way of Apology for the Book Entitled The Sandy Foundation Shaken, To all Serious and Enquiring Persons, Particularly the Inhabitants of the City of London*. London: s.n., 1669.

----- *The Sandy Foundation Shaken*. London: Andrew Sowle, 1684.

Perkins, William. *The Work of William Perkins*. Appleford, England: The Sutton Courtenay Press, 1970.

----- *The Workes of William Perkins*. Cambridge: John Legate, 1608.

----- *The Works of That Famous and Worthy Minister of Christ in the Universitie of Cambridge, M. William Perkins*. London: John Legatt, 1631.

Pictet, Benedict. *Christian Theology*. Philadelphia: Presbyterian Board of Publication, n.d.

----- *True and False Religion Examined*. Edinburgh: J. Ogle, 1797.

Polanus, Amandus. *The Substance of Christian Religion*. London: R.F., 1597.

Poole, Matthew. *A Commentary on the Holy Bible*. Carlisle, PA: Banner of Truth Trust, 1962.

----- *A Commentary on the Whole Bible*. The Encyclopedia Puritanica Project, 2006.

----- *A Dialogue Between a Popish Priest and an English Protestant*. London: E. Cotes, 1667.

----- *A Reverse to Mr. Oliver's Sermon of Spiritual Worship, A Sermon on the Same Subject Preached before the Lord Mayer, at St. Paul's Church.* London: Printed for A. Baldwin, 1698.

Powel, Gabriel. *De Adiaphoris. Theological and Scholastical Positions, Concerning the Nature and Use of Things Indifferent.* London: Felix Kyngston, 1607.

Ramus, Peter. *The Art of Logick.* London: I.D., 1626.

Ray, John. *The Wisdom of God Manifested in the Works of the Creation.* London: Printed for D. Williams, 1762.

Robinson, Ralph. *Christ All in All.* Ligonier, PA: Soli Deo Gloria Publications, 1992.

Rous, Francis. *Oile of Scorpions.* London: W. Stansby, 1623.

----- *The Arte of Happines.* London: W. Stansby, 1619.

----- *The Great Oracle: Or, the Main Frame and Body of the Scriptures, Resolving the Question, Whether in Man's Free-will and Common Grace, or in God's Special and Effectual Grace, stands the Safety of Man, and the Glory of God by Man's Safety?* London: S. Palmer, 1718.

----- *The Heavenly Academie.* London: Robert Young, 1638.

----- *The Mysticall Marriage.* London: William Jones, 1631.

----- *Treatises and Meditations.* London: Robert White, 1657.

S.W. *A Short and plain Explication of the Shorter Catechism.* London: 1667.

Saltmarsh, John. *Sparkles of Glory.* London: Printed for Giles Calvert, 1648.

Sheldon, Gilbert. *The Act of Parliament Against Religious Meetings.* London: s.n., 1670.

Shepherd, Thomas. *The Works of Thomas Shepherd.* New York: AMS Press, 1967.

Sherlock, William. *A Discourse Concerning the Knowledge of Jesus Christ, and Our Union and Communion with him.* London: J.M., 1674.

----- *An Answer to a Discourse Intitled* (sic) *Papists Protecting Against protestant Popery.* London: Printed for John Amery, 1686.

Sibbes, Richard. *Works of Richard Sibbes*. Carlisle, Pennsylvania: Banner of Truth Trust, 1983.

Smalcius, Valentin. *The Racovian Catechisme*. Amsterdam: Printed for Brooer Janz, 1652.

South, Robert. Robert *Sermons Preached on Several Occasions*. London: Printed for H. Lintot, 1737.

Spinoza, Benedict de. *A Theologico-Political Treatise and a Political Treatise*. New York: Dover Publications, 1951.

Stillingfleet, Edward. *A Discourse Concerning the Doctrine of Christ's Satisfaction; or The True Reasons of his Sufferings; with an Answer to the Socinian Objections*. London: F. Heptinstall, 1697.

----- *A Discourse Concerning the Idolatry Practiced in the Church of Rome, and the Hazard of salvation in the Communion of it*. London: Printed for Henry and George Mortlock, 1709.

----- *Irenicum*. Philadelphia: M. Sorin, 1842.

----- *Origines Sacrae: Or a Rational Account of the Grounds of Natural and Revealed Religion*. Oxford: At the Clarendon Press, 1797.

----- *Sermons on Some of the Principle Doctrines of the Christian Religion, with Practical Inferences and Improvements*. York: G. Peacock, 1794.

----- *The Council of Trent Examin'd and Disprov'd by Catholick Tradition in the Main Points of Controversie Between Us and the Church of Rome With a Particular Account of the Times and Occasions of Introducing Them*. London: Printed for H. Mortlock, 1688.

Swinnock, George. *The Works of George Swinnock*. Edinburgh: James Nichol, 1868.

Taylor, Jeremy. *A Moral Demonstration of the Truth of the Christian Religion*. London: Printed for T. Cadell, 1775.

----- *The Golden Grove*. London: J. Leake, 1713.

----- *The Rules and exercises of Holy Living*. London: J. Heptinstall, 1703.

----- *Treatises*. London: Printed for R. Royston, 1648.

Taylor, Thomas. *A Testimony to the True and Spiritual Worship*. London: s.n., 1670.

Tillotson, John. *Sermons on Several Subjects and Occasions*. London: printed for J. and R. Tonson and S. Draper, etc., 1748.

----- *Sermons on Several Subjects and Occasions*. London: Printed for C. Hitch and L. Hawes, etc., 1757.

----- *Several Discourses upon the Attributes of God*. London: Ralph Barker, 1699.

----- *The Indispensable Necessity of the Knowledge of Holy Scripture in Order to Man's Eternal Salvation and Ignorance Therein, the Mother of Idolatry and Superstition Asserted in a Sermon*. London: Printed for Wil. Norris, 1687.

----- *The Remaining Discourses on the Attributes of God*. London: Ralph Barker, 1700.

----- *The Works of the Most Reverend Dr. John Tillotson*. London: Printed for R. Ware, etc., 1743.

Toland, John. *Christianity Not Mysterious*. London: Printed for Sam. Buckley, 1696.

Tuckney, Anthony. *Forty Sermons*. London: J.M., 1676.

Turretin, Francis. *Institutes of Elenctic Theology*. Phillipsburg, NJ: P and R Publishing, 1992.

----- *The Atonement of Christ*. Grand Rapid: Baker Book, 1978.

Turretin, Jean-Alphonse. *Dissertations on Natural Theology*. Belfast: James Magee, 1777.

Tyndale, William. *The Work of William Tindale*. London: Blackie and Son Limited, 1938.

Ussher, James. *A Body of Divinitie*. London: R.J., 1702.

Vermigli, Peter Martyr. *Early Writings*. Kirksville, MO: Sixteenth Century Journal Publishers, 1994.

----- *Philosophical Works*. Kirksville, MO: Sixteenth Century Essays and Studies, 1996.

----- *The Common Places*. London: Anthony Marten, 1583.

Vincent, Thomas. *An Explanation of the Assembly's Shorter Catechism*. Escondido, CA: Ephesians Four Group, 1998.

----- *The True Christian's Love to the Unseen Christ*. Morgan, PA: Soli Deo Gloria, 1993.

Vines, Richard. *Christ a Christians Onely Gain: or The Excellency and desireableness of the Knowledge of Jesus Christ, above all other things whatsoever*. London: Printed for Thomas Johnson, 1660.

Viret, Peter. *A Christian Instruction, conteyning the law and the Gospell, Also a Summarie of the Pricipall Poyntes of the Christian Fayth and Religion*. London: Abraham Veale, 1573.

Voetius, Gisbertus and Hoornbeeck, Johannes. *Spiritual Desertion*. Grand Rapids: Baker, 2003.

Walker, Henry. *The Protestants Grammar*. London: Robert Ibbitson and John Clowes, 1648.

Ward, Seth. *An Apology for the Mysteries of the Gospel*. London: Andrew Clark, 1673.

Warner, Ferdinando (ed.). *A System of Divinity and Morality*. London: Printed for R. Griffiths, 1750.

Watson, Thomas. *A Body of Divinity*. Carlisle, PA: The Banner of Truth Trust, 1965.

Whichcote, Benjamin. *Moral and Religious Aphorisms*. London: Printed for J. Payne, 1753.

Wilkins, John. *Of the Principles and Duties of Natural Religion: Two Books*. London: Printed for R. Bonwicke, W. Freeman, etc., 1715.

Winstanley, Gerrard. *Fire in the Bush*. London: Printed for Giles Calvert, 1650.

----- *The Mystery of God Concerning the Whole Creation, Mankinde*. London: I.C., 1649.

----- *Truth Lifting up its head above Scandals*. London: s.n., 1649.

Witsius, Herman. *The Apostles Creed*. Phillipsburg, NJ: Presbyterian and Reformed Publishing, 1993.

Wollebius, Johannes. *The Abridgement of Christian Divinity*. London: T. Mabb, 1660.

Zanchius, Girolamo. *The Whole Body of Christian Religion*. London: John Redmayne, 1659.

Zwingli, Ulrich. *On Providence and Other Essays*. Eugene, OR: Wipf and Stock Publishers, 1999.

**Secondary Sources:**

Armstrong, Brian. *Calvinism and the Amyraut Heresy*. The University of Wisconsin Press, 1969.

Aulen, Gustaf. *Christus Victor*. New York: The MacMillan Company, 1966.

Baker, Herschel. *The Wars of Truth*. Gloucester, MA: Peter Smith, 1969.

Baker, J. Wayne. *Heinrich Bullinger and the Covenant*. Ohio University Press, 1980.

Bangs, Carl. *Arminius: A Study in the Dutch Reformation*. Grand Rapids: Francis Asbury Press, 1985.

Barth, Karl. *The Gottingen Dogmatics*. Grand Rapids: Eerdmans, 1991.

Beardslee, John (ed.). *Reformed Dogmatics*. New York: Oxford University Press, 1965.

Beeke, Joel. *The Quest for Full Assurance*. Carlisle, PA: Banner of Truth Trust, 1999.

Benedict, Philip. *Christ's Churches Purely Reformed*. New Haven: Yale University Press, 2002.

Bettenson, Henry (ed.). *Documents of the Christian Church*. Oxford University Press, 1947.

Bierma, Lyle. *German Calvinism in the Confessional Age: The Covenant Theology of Caspar Olevianus*. Grand Rapids: Baker Books, 1996.

Bonar, Horatio. *Catechisms of the Scottish Reformation*. London: James Nisbet and Co., 1866.

Bouwsma, William. *John Calvin*. Oxford University Press, 1988.

----- *The Culture of Renaissance Humanism*. Washington D.C.: American Historical Association, 1973.

Brauer, J.C. *Francis Rous: Puritan Mystic 1579-1659: An Introduction to the Mystical Element in Puritanism*. Ph.D. dissertation for the University of Chicago Divinity School, December, 1948.

Breen, Quirinus. *Christianity and Humanism*. Grand Rapids: Eerdmans, 1968.

Bromiley, G.W. (ed), *Zwingli and Bullinger*. Philadelphia: Westminster Press, 1953.

Brown, John. *The English Puritans*. Ross-shire, Great Britain: Christian Focus Publications, 1998.

Burns, William. *An Age of Wonders*. Manchester University Press, 2002.

Cairns, Earle. *Christianity Through the Centuries*. Grand Rapids: Zondervan, 1981.

Collie, Rosalie. *Light and Enlightenment: A Study of the Cambridge Platonists and the Dutch Arminians*. Cambridge at the University Press, 1957.

Collinson, Patrick. *English Puritanism*. London: The Historical Association, 1983.

----- *The Birthpangs of Protestant England*. New York: St. Martin's Press, 1988.

----- *The Elizabethan Puritan Movement*. Oxford: Clarendon Press, 1967.

Cooper, Tim. *Fear and Polemic in Seventeenth-Century England*. Aldershot: Ashgate, 2001.

Cragg, G.R. *From Puritanism to the Age of Reason*. Cambridge University Press, 1966.

----- *The Church and the Age of Reason: 1648-1789*. Grand Rapids: Eerdmans, 1960.

Cragg, G.R. (ed.). *The Cambridge Platonists*. New York: Oxford University Press, 1968.

Cross, F.L. and Livingston, E.A. (eds.), *Oxford Dictionary of the Christian Church*. Oxford University Press, 1971.

Dowey Jr., Edward. *The Knowledge of God in Calvin's Theology*. New York: Columbia University Press, 1952.

Duffield, G.E., (ed). *John Calvin*. Grand Rapids: Eerdmans, 1963.

Eberling, Gerhard. *The Study of Theology*. Philadelphia: Fortress Press, 1978.

Elwell, Walter (ed). *Evangelical Dictionary of Theology*. Grand Rapids: Baker Books, 1984.

Ferguson, Sinclair, Wright, David and Packer, J.I., (eds). *New Dictionary of Theology*. Downers Grove: Inter Varsity Press, 1988.

Force, James and Popkin, Richard (eds). *The Books of Nature and Scripture: Recent Essays on Natural Philosophy, Theology, and Biblical Criticism in the Netherlands of Spinoza's Time and the British Isles of Newton's Time*. Dordrecht, The Netherlands: Kluwer Academic Publishers, 1994.

Gerson, Noel. *The Edict of Nantes*. New York: Grossett and Dunlap, 1969.

Goldman, Lawrence (ed.). *Oxford Dictionary of National Biography*. Oxford University Press, 2004.

Gonzalez, Justo. *The Story of Christianity*. Peabody, MA: Prince Press, 2001.

Graham, W. Fred, editor. *Later Calvinism*. Kirksville, MO: Sixteenth Century Journal Publishers, 1994.

Greaves, Richard. *God's Other Children*. Stanford University Press, 1997.

Greengrass, Mark. *The French Reformation*. Oxford: Basil Blackwell, 1987.

Harris, Tim, Seaward, Paul and Goldie, Mark. *The Politics of Religion in Restoration England*. Oxford: Basil Blackwell, 1990.

Helm, Paul. *Calvin and the Calvinists*. Carlisle, PA: Banner of Truth Trust, 1982.

Hesselink, I. John. *Calvin's First Catechism*. Louisville: Westminster John Knox Press, 1997.

Heyd, Michael. *Be Sober and Reasonable*. Leiden: E.J. Brill, 1995.

----- *Between Orthodoxy and the Enlightenment*. Jerusalem: The Magnus Press, The Hebrew University, 1982.

Hill, Christopher. *The World Turned Upside Down*. London: Penguin Books, 1991.

Hill, Jonathan. *Faith in the Age of Reason*. Downers Grove: Inter Varsity Press, 2004.

Hinson, Edward (ed.), *Introduction to Puritan Theology: A Reader*. Grand Rapids: Baker Book House, 1976.

Holt, Mack. *The French Wars of Religion, 1562-1629*. Cambridge University Press, 1995.

Keeble, N.H. and Nuttall, Geoffrey. *Calendar of the Correspondence of Richard Baxter*. Oxford: Clarendon Press, 1991.

Kendall, R.T. *Calvin and English Calvinism to 1649*. Carlisle, Cumbria: Paternoster Press, 1997.

Knappen, M.M. *Tudor Puritanism*. University of Chicago Press, 1939.

Knox, R. Buick, (ed.), *Reformation Conformity and Dissent*. London: Epworth Press, 1977.

Kristeller, Paul. *Renaissance Thought*. Harper Torchbooks, 1961.

Lake, Peter. *Anglicans and Puritans?* London: Unwin Hyman, 1988.

-----*Moderate Puritans and the Elizabethan Church.* Cambridge University Press, 1982.

Lamont, William. *Puritanism and Historical Controversy*. Montreal: McGill-Queen's University Press, 1996.

LaVallee, Armand Aime. *Calvin's Criticism of Scholastic Theology*. unpublished Ph.D. thesis, Harvard University, 1967.

Lindberg, Carter. *The European Reformations*. Oxford: Blackwell, 1996.

Loach, Jennifer. *Edward VI*. Yale University Press, 1999.

Margolin, Jean-Claude. *Humanism in Europe at the Time of the Renaissance*. Durham, NC: The Labyrinth Press, 1989.

McAdoo, Henry. *The Spirit of Anglicanism: A Survey of Anglican Theological Method in the Seventeenth Century*. New York: Charles Scribner's Sons, 1965.

McGrath, Alister. *Reformation Thought*. Oxford: Blackwell Publishers, 1999.

McKim, Donald (ed.). *Readings in Calvin's Theology*. Grand Rapids: Baker Book House, 1984.

McLachlan, H. John. *Socinianism in Seventeenth-Century England*. Oxford University Press, 1951.

McNeill, John. *The History and Character of Calvinism*. Oxford University Press, 1954.

Montgomery, John Warwick (ed.). *God's Inerrant Word*. Minneapolis: Bethany Fellowship, 1974.

Muller, Richard. *After Calvin*. Oxford University Press, 2003.

----- *Dictionary of Latin and Greek Theological Terms*. Grand Rapids: Baker Books, 1985.

----- *Post-Reformation Reformed Dogmatics*. Grand Rapids: Baker Academic, 2003.

-----*The Unaccommodated Calvin*. Oxford University Press, 2000.

Murray, Iain. *The Reformation of the Church: A Collection of Reformed and Puritan Documents on Church Issues*. London: The Banner of Truth Trust, 1965.

Nicole, Roger. *Moyse Amyraut and the Controversy on Universal Grace*. Unpublished thesis for the degree of Doctor of Philosophy at Harvard University, April 1966.

Nuttall, Geoffrey. *Richard Baxter*. London: Nelson, 1966.

----- *The Holy Spirit in Puritan Faith and Experience* 2nd ed. University of Chicago Press, 1992.

Ong, Walter. *Ramus: Method and the Decay of Dialogue*. Harvard University Press, 1983.

Packer, J.I. *A Quest for Godliness*. Wheaton: Crossway Books, 1990.

Parker, T.H.L. *The Doctrine of the Knowledge of God: A Study in the Theology of John Calvin.* Edinburgh: Oliver and Boyd, 1952.

Plum, Harry Grant. *Restoration Puritanism.* Port Washington, NY: Kennikat Press, 1972.

Reedy, Gerard. *The Bible and Reason: Anglicans and Scripture in Late Seventeenth-Century England.* Philadelphia: University of Pennsylvania Press, 1985.

Rogers, Jack and McKim, Donald. *The Authority and Interpretation of the Bible: An Historical Approach.* San Francisco: Harper and Row, 1979.

Rouse, R. and Neill, S.C. (eds.). *A History of the Ecumenical Movement.* Philadelphia: The Westminster Press, 1967.

Schaff, Philip. *Creeds of Christendom.* Grand Rapids: Baker Book, 1977.

Sell, Alan P. F. *John Locke and the Eighteenth-Century Divines.* Eugene, OR: Wipf and Stock Publishers, 1997.

----- *The Great Debate: Calvinism, Arminianism, and Salvation.* Grand Rapids: Baker Book, 1983.

----- *Theology in Turmoil.* Grand Rapids: Baker Book, 1986.

Sheldon, Henry. *History of the Christian Church.* New York: Hendrickson Publishers, 1988.

Simpson, Alan. *Puritans in Old and New England.* Chicago: University of Chicago Press, 1955.

Sproul, R.C. *Essential Truths of the Christian Faith.* Wheaton: Tyndale, 1992.

Stauffer, Richard. *The Quest for Church Unity.* Allison Park, PA: Pickwick Publications, 1986.

Stiles, Samuel. *Huguenots in England and Ireland.* London: John Murray, 1876.

Thomas, G. Michael. *The Extent of the Atonement.* Carlisle, UK: Paternoster, 1997.

Toon, Peter. *Puritans and Calvinism.* Swengel, PA: Reiner Publications, 1973.

Torrance, T.F. *Calvin's Doctrine of Man.* Grand Rapids: Eerdmans, 1957.

Trinterud, Leonard, (ed.), *Elizabethan Puritanism*. New York: Oxford University Press, 1971.

Trueman, Carl R. and Clark, R.S., (eds). *Protestant Scholasticism*. Carlisle, Cumbria: Paternoster Press, 1999.

Tyacke, Nicholas. *Anti-Calvinists*. Oxford: Clarendon Press, 1987.

----- *Aspects of English Protestantism*. Manchester University Press, 2001.

Wakefield, Gordon. *Puritan Devotion*. London: Epworth Press, 1957.

Wallace Jr., Dewey. *Puritans and Predestination*. University of North Carolina Press, 1982.

Walsham, Alexandra. *Providence in Early Modern England*. Oxford University Press, 1999.

Warfield, Benjamin. *The Works of Benjamin Warfield*. Grand Rapids: Baker Books, 2003.

Weathers, Willie. *Edward Taylor and the Cambridge Platonists*. EBSCO Publishing, 2003.

Wendel, Francois. *Calvin*. London: William Collins Sons, 1963.

Westfall, Richard. *Science and Religion in Seventeenth Century England*. University of Michigan Press, 1973.

Wood, A. Harold. *Church Unity Without Uniformity: A Study of Seventeenth-century English Church Movements and of Richard Baxter's Proposals for a Comprehensive Church*. London: Epworth Press, 1963.

**Articles:**

Becker, George. "Pietism's Confrontation With Enlightenment Rationalism: An Examination of the Relation Between Ascetic Protestantism and Science." *Journal for the Scientific Study of Religion*, 30 (1991).

Calvin, John. "A Warning Against Judiciary Astrology and Other Prevalent Curiosities" translated by Mary Potter. *Calvin Theological Journal* ( 1983).

Deibler, Edwin. "The Chief Characteristic of Early English Puritanism." *Bibliotheca Sacra*, 129 (1972).

Gamble, Richard. "Brevitas et Facilitas: Toward an Understanding of Calvin's Hermeneutic." *Westminster Theological Journal*, 47 (1985).

Klauber, Martin. "Short Study – Calvin on Fundamental Articles and Ecclesiastical Union." *Westminster Theological Journal*, 54 (1992).

----- "The Helvetic Formula Consensus (1675): An Introduction and Translation." *Trinity Journal*, 11:1 (1990).

----- "Theological Transition in Geneva from Jean-Alphonse Turretin to Jacob Vernet." Portland: Theological Research Exchange Network, n.d.

Muller, Richard. "*Fides* and *Cognitio* in Relation to the Problem of Intellect and Will in the Theology of John Calvin." *Calvin Theological Journal*, 25 (1990).

Spalding, James and Brass, Maynard. "Reduction of Episcopacy as a Means to Unity in England, 1640-1662." *Church History*, 30 (1961).

Thorson, Stephen. "Tensions in Calvin's View of Faith: Unexamined Assumptions in R.T. Kendall's *Calvin and English Calvinism to 1649.*" *Journal of Evangelical Theological Society*, 37/3 (1994).

VanderMolen, Ronald. "Providence as Mystery, Providence as Revelation: Puritan and Anglican Modifications of John Calvin's Doctrine of Providence." *Church History*, 47 (1978).

Wallace, Dewey Jr., 'Natural Theology Among the Dissenters: Richard Baxter and His Circle' presented at the Annual Meeting of the American Society of Church History December 27-30, 1992.

ND - #0083 - 090625 - C0 - 229/152/14 - PB - 9781842276709 - Gloss Lamination